Staring at the
Nyanza Sun

A Kenyan-American Memoir

Staring at the Nyanza Sun

A Kenyan-American Memoir

Dr. Amos Otieno Odenyo
and Odera Odenyo

Spear & Shield
Publishing

Staring at the Nyanza Sun
A Kenyan-American Memoir
All Rights Reserved.
Copyright © 2010 Dr. Amos Otieno Odenyo and Odera Odenyo
V5.0

Spear & Shield Publishing

PB ISBN: 978-0-9828065-0-0
HB ISBN: 978-0-9828065-1-7

Library of Congress Control Number: 2010933187

PRINTED IN THE UNITED STATES OF AMERICA

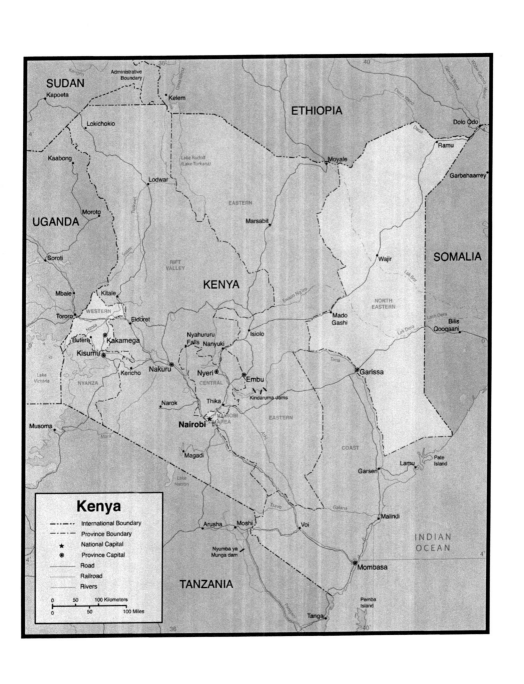

SUDAN

Kapoeta

Administrative
Boundary

Kelem

ETHIOPIA

Dolo Odo

Lokichokio

Ramu

Kaabong

Moyale

Garbahaarrey

Lodwar

Lake Rudolf
(Lake Turkana)

UGANDA

Moroto

EASTERN

Soroti

Marsabit

RIFT
VALLEY

Wajir

SOMALIA

Mbale

Kitale

KENYA

NORTH
EASTERN

Tororo

Eldoret

Mado
Gashi

Bilis
Qooqaani

WESTERN

Butere

Nyahururu
Falls

Nanyuki

Isiolo

Kakamega

Ewaso Ng'iro

Kisumu

Tana

NYANZA

Kericho

Nakuru

Nyeri

Embu

Garissa

Lake
Victoria

Narok

CENTRAL

Thika

Kindaruma dams

Musoma

Nairobi

NAIROBI
AREA

EASTERN

Magadi

COAST

Lamu

Pate
Island

Garsen

Lake
Natron

Malindi

INDIAN
OCEAN

Kenya

—·—·—· International Boundary
—··—··— Province Boundary
★ National Capital
◉ Province Capital
——— Road
——— Railroad
——— Rivers

Arusha

Moshi

Voi

Nyumba ya
Munga dam

TANZANIA

Mombasa

Pemba
Island

| 0 | 50 | 100 Kilometers |
| 0 | 50 | 100 Miles |

Tanga

Table of Contents

Acknowledgements

Many thanks are due to a number of people for their assistance in preparing this book.

First and foremost, I am indebted to my sister Dina Atieno, who gave guidance based upon our many shared experiences on two continents. I am grateful to my mother, who believed in Dad in 1967 and encouraged me to finish this family memoir. I am also thankful for my children, who served as a daily reminder why I needed to preserve our history. *Erokamano* Mama Ayiera, for becoming a valuable part of Got Regea.

I am appreciative of my father's life-long friends, Martin Miruka Nyiendo and Dr. Laban Otieno, for their detailed reviews of my draft manuscripts. My father's close friends Shem Arungu Olende and Winston Ochoro Ayoki gave suggestions regarding Kisii High School. Joanne Nyiendo, Linda Ayoki, Sheryl Eaton, and Jeanne Branciforte gave their thoughts on chapters nine through sixteen. Dr. William H. Hodge solicited much of the information in chapters one through four from my father in 1965 and 1966. Uncle Victor Odenyo and Uncle Booker Odenyo elaborated on historical events in our home in Nyanza, Kenya.

This historical book would not have been possible without the foresight and leadership of the late Tom Mboya, the architect of the "Kennedy Airlift" that brought my father from Kenya to America in September 1961.

I give my deepest thanks to the United States of America for opening its doors to my father and allowing me, a son of Nyanza, to become a citizen and patriot of the noblest of nations.

Odera Odenyo

Introduction

In the late 1970s, my father, Dr. Amos Otieno Odenyo, sent a letter from New York City to my brother in Kenya, East Africa. The letter included the following message:

> My father, Zablon Sangoro Odenyo, gave me essentially two things in life—respect for education, and inspiration. After my father's death, my inheritance was a small piece of land in my village that I cannot sell, even if I wanted to.

Three decades later, as I reflect upon my father's words in that letter, I realize how blessed I am that my own inheritance consists of essentially the same two things, as well as the same plot of African land that I cannot sell, even if I wanted to. For thirty-six years of my life, I had the honor of referring to my father not as Dr. Odenyo, but as Dad. He was single-handedly the greatest role model and inspiration in my life. His life story spoke for itself.

Amos Otieno Odenyo was born in 1935 in a rural village of western Kenyan during the height of British colonialism. He was born in a grass-roofed "hut." By the age of nine he was a house servant for strange people in distant places. When he returned to his village he endured the painful adult initiation rites required by the elders. As a result, he was required to move out of his parents' house and build his own. At night he shared the darkened footpaths with ghosts and leopards. During the day he ran barefoot to school.

Despite humble origins, my father managed to become the first Kenyan to obtain a University of Minnesota doctorate degree (in 1970). He become the chairman of Social Sciences at York College (City University of New York), and served on the Board of Trustees for World Education in Boston.

I know much of Dr. Odenyo's story because he was not only a teacher in the classroom, but an oral historian in his own family. In August 2005, I sat down with my father, turned on the video cassette recorder, and asked him questions about his family history and personal life, from approximately 1800 until 1976. The interviews were conducted over the course of a week, resulting in approximately twenty hours of priceless history. These videos supplemented existing interviews of my father recorded during trips to Kenya in 1998, 2001, and 2005.

When my father passed away in 2007, I discovered in his office an unpublished autobiography which he wrote around 1975. He also left behind transcripts of interviews he granted to Professor William H. Hodge (an American anthropologist) between 1965 and 1966. In these transcripts, my father provided a detailed account of his personal experiences growing up in his village of Got Regea, and of the culture of the Luo, his ethnic group. Much of this information was already familiar to me based upon my own interviews of him, but the transcripts from the 1960s provided a richness of detail and corroboration for stories he would share with me forty years later. My father also kept a scrapbook of photographs, letters, and documents (including a pocket-diary from 1961), which revealed critical information about dates, places, and events.

The above material forms the basis of the first eight chapters (1815–1970) of this family memoir, which is organized much like the orchestral arrangements of the Congolese "Lingala" songs my father played for me as a child in New York City. These African songs start with a slow and steady background rhythm, but suddenly a split-second pause—followed by a multitude of progressively faster rhythms in alternating succession as if starting a new song. The beats drum faster and faster until you are now dancing along to not only the main singer, but the introduction of new voices and instruments. Yet, it is unquestionably one song.

The first three chapters are those slow and steady African rhythms that provide the historical and cultural background of my father. As a child, he grew up learning the old Luo traditions from the elders and musical storytellers of his village. These *nyatiti* (harp) storytellers have long ago stopped singing their songs in Got Regea, and many of the youth have no recollection of their past. Therefore, it can be argued from a cultural and historical perspective that chapters one, two, and three are the most valuable sections of this book.

My father's personal story begins in chapter four. In his own words he narrates his life's journey from barefoot child in Nyanza Province to Ph.D. graduate in America (1935–1970). Chapters nine through sixteen tell the remainder of his story (1970–2007), but woven through my own experiences and perceptions. I was raised in racially-charged New York City by a traditional African father and a white mother from rural Minnesota. This memoir is rich with lessons about multiculturalism, family and community relationships, gender and age roles, economic development, African history, tradition versus modernity, and moral values. These lessons are applicable not only to persons of Kenyan heritage, but to a variety of readers, including the various students of sociology, anthropology, political science, and history who sat through Dr. Odenyo's lectures at York College.

I must admit, however, that I co-wrote this book with only one particular audience in mind. This audience is Dr. Odenyo's descendants, both his grandchildren whom I know, and their grandchildren whom I will never know. For them, this book is a gateway to their past, as well as a road map for their future. I am providing them with their inheritance, handed down from the great Zablon Sangoro Odenyo, which consists primarily of education, inspiration, as well as directions to a piece of land in Nyanza Province that they will never be able to sell, even if they wanted to. If there is one single theme that Dr. Odenyo's descendants should pick up from this book, hopefully it is the realization that the biggest determining factor in their success is personal character. Compassion, self-determination, respect for education, and inspiration were the key elements that defined my father. They were the guiding principles throughout his life, which were instrumental in making him such a successful, decent, and respected man. These principles do not cost anything. They are free. My hope is that all of Dr. Odenyo's descendents, as well as children throughout the world, will embrace these values, incorporate them into every aspect of their lives, and create a better life for themselves, their family, and for their community.

On the morning of my father's final day in his earthly life, with his last breath he asked that his family never forget his home village of Got Regea. This book is the first step in fulfilling my father's last wish. It is also hoped that with this book, Got Regea will never forget one of its steadfast supporters and faithful sons, just as I can never forget my father.

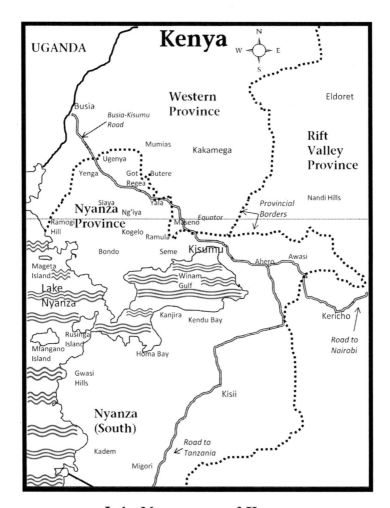

Lake Nyanza area of Kenya.

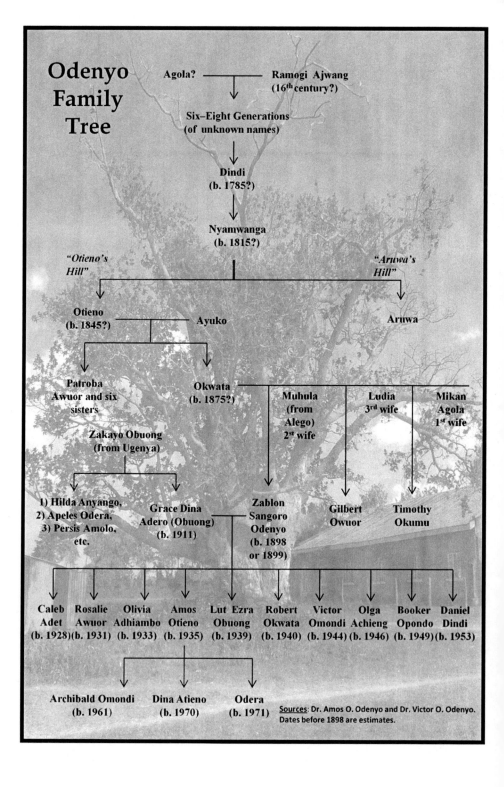

Odenyo Family Tree

Agola? —————— Ramogi Ajwang
(16th century?)

Six–Eight Generations
(of unknown names)

Dindi
(b. 1785?)

Nyamwanga
(b. 1815?)

"Otieno's Hill"

"Aruwa's Hill"

Otieno
(b. 1845?)   Ayuko

Aruwa

Patroba
Awuor and six
sisters

Okwata
(b. 1875?)

Muhula
(from
Alego)
2st wife

Ludia
3rd wife

Mikan
Agola
1st wife

Zakayo Obuong
(from Ugenya)

1) Hilda Anyango,
2) Apeles Odera,
3) Persis Amolo,
etc.

Grace Dina
Adero (Obuong)
(b. 1911)

Zablon
Sangoro
Odenyo
(b. 1898
or 1899)

Gilbert
Owuor

Timothy
Okumu

Caleb
Adet
(b. 1928)

Rosalie
Awuor
(b. 1931)

Olivia
Adhiambo
(b. 1933)

Amos
Otieno
(b. 1935)

Lut Ezra
Obuong
(b. 1939)

Robert
Okwata
(b. 1940)

Victor
Omondi
(b. 1944)

Olga
Achieng
(b. 1946)

Booker
Opondo
(b. 1949)

Daniel
Dindi
(b. 1953)

Archibald Omondi
(b. 1961)

Dina Atieno
(b. 1970)

Odera
(b. 1971)

Sources: Dr. Amos O. Odenyo and Dr. Victor O. Odenyo.
Dates before 1898 are estimates.

1
Origins (1815–1935)

Chien kiyany' (The past is never despised).

—Luo Proverb

My name is Amos Otieno Odenyo, and I was born in Kenya, East Africa, in April 1935. I am from Siaya District, in Nyanza Province, located in the western part of Kenya.[1] Siaya District is sub-divided into "locations," and my location is called North Gem. Within North Gem is my home village of Got Regea (Hills of Regea). If you are unfamiliar with the area, look at a map to identify the largest lake on the African continent. This lake is commonly referred to as Lake Victoria or Lake Nyanza, although my people originally called it Lolwe. On the eastern side of that lake you will find Kisumu, the third largest city in Kenya. From Kisumu there is a road heading north-west toward Busia, a town located on the Kenyan-Ugandan border. As you travel from Kisumu towards Busia you will pass through small towns such as Maseno, Luanda, and Yala, until you eventually find a market called Dudi—approximately thirty miles from Kisumu. From Dudi, branch right for approximately three miles along a narrow dirt road which is often impassable for cars during rainy season. This is my village, the place of my birth, the land of my ancestors.

I am of the Luo tribe of Kenya, which is ranked as either the second or third largest tribe in Kenya. Anthropologists generally agree that our people migrated to Kenya from the Bahr el Ghazal region of Sudan. However, there are a few among us who say our people originated even further north in a place called Misiri (Egypt). There is speculation about an ancient Luo-Egyptian link based upon our proximity to the Nile River, and cultural emphasis on the sun, the moon, and our ancestors.

What is confirmed, however, is that by the sixteenth century, our ancestors began migrating south from Sudan along the banks of the Nile River, acquiring new lands by conquest and intermarriage. This migration was probably the result of population growth made possible by the successful political consolidation of a variety of fragmented tribes. The migration of the Luo people from Sudan, through Uganda, and towards the Lake Nyanza region is a central theme of our identity and oral history. The name of our tribe is a derivative of the verb *luwo*, which means "to follow," as in to follow the Nile to its source. When I was a young boy I heard stories about Ramogi Ajwang', a quasi-mythical leader who led our people from Uganda into an area in Nyanza now called Ramogi Hill. Ramogi is revered by the Luo of Kenya as a Biblical "Abraham."

Due to our origins along the Nile, anthropologists refer to us as "Nilotes," thus distinguishing us from the many "Bantu" tribes in Kenya. A Luo might be able to understand many of the languages spoken near the Nile River far outside of Kenya, but might not understand any of the Bantu languages spoken nearby within Kenya. For example, when I was a boy, if I walked just twenty minutes north or east of my village, I would have left Luo-land and would not have been able to communicate with our neighboring tribe, the Abaluhya (or Luhya people), without a translator.

I was born within an era in Kenyan history that witnessed many cultural and political changes among my people. These changes started in the middle of the nineteenth century, when British explorers came across Luo people fishing in Lolwe, and renamed it Lake Victoria after the Queen of England. By the turn of the century (around the time my father was born) all Africans in the area found themselves to be colonial residents of the British Empire. Asians brought in from India by the British as contract laborers to build a railroad from Mombasa to Kisumu were allowed to stay in Kenya once their work obligations had been fulfilled. Asians soon developed and directed the bulk of commercial activities in the country. By the 1920s, Africans found themselves in economically, politically, and socially inferior positions to Indian businessmen and British government officials.

My ancestors settled in the village of Got Regea more than a century before I was born, prior to the arrival of the Europeans. The furthest back that I can accurately trace our lineage in Got Regea is four generations to my great-great-grandfather, Nyamwanga, who moved into Got Regea from a place called *bar* Malanga. Counting backward four generations from my birth in 1935, and using thirty years as an estimate for one generational cycle, Nyamwanga would have been born around 1815. Nyamwanga had two sons, Otieno and Aruwa, and also a daughter Nyangula. It was during this time that our family claimed the two hills of Got Regea, most likely using force against the Abaluhya people who are said to have inhabited the area prior to the Luo migrations. Nyamwanga's oldest son, Otieno (my great-grandfather) claimed one hill (Got ka Otieno), and the other son Aruwa, claimed the other hill (Got ka Aruwa). Otieno married Ayuko, and had one son, Okwata (my grandfather), and seven daughters, Abongo, Nyamwanga, Atieno, (Patroba) Awuor, Otina, Nyariro, and Ogoye.

I learned a lot about my grandfather Okwata from his sister Patroba Awuor, who lived adjacent to us in Got Regea. She told me stories about him late at night when she visited our home. She said that Okwata was a very wealthy man due to him being the only son and therefore the beneficiary of the bride price provided for his seven sisters. Okwata had many heads of cattle and was an enterprising young man. He had exceptional physical strength and was "quick with a stick," meaning he did not hesitate to fight when his path was crossed. Okwata was also a *jathum* (musician) who played the *nyatiti*, a traditional eight-string instrument unique to the Luo. Due to his wealth, Okwata was able to marry three wives, the first being Mikan Agola, with whom he had a son (Timothy) Okumu. Okwata's second wife was Muhula (from the Sege clan in Ndere, Alego), with whom he had a son named Odenyo, my father. Okwata's third wife was Ludia, with whom he had a son (Gilbert) Owuor. During the years preceding his death my grandfather Okwata lived in an area within Got Regea called *gunda* Nyangwira. *Gunda* in Dholuo refers to a deserted homestead due to the death of its owner. Okwata may have been forced to relocate to this *gunda* due to being forced out of Got ka Otieno, or alternatively his place of death was named *gunda* after Okwata died. Okwata died relatively young, perhaps in his early forties. He died in land-battles within Got Regea, most likely trying to protect Got ka Otieno from warriors of neighboring clans. Okwata's death likely occurred between 1915 and 1920, and had disastrous consequences for his children, especially his three sons, Okumu, Odenyo (my father), and Owuor. Okwata's sons were too young to forcibly claim their inheritance of land around Got ka Otieno. Due to the violent land disputes at the time, and the fact that Okwata had no male siblings, Okwata's children were at the mercy of other villagers who assisted in their upbringing, but at the same time exploited their land and property. Okwata's second wife (Muhula) is said to have died soon after the death of her husband, making my father, Odenyo, born around 1899, an orphan by his teenage years.

When my father was a teenager, Gem (currently divided into south and north) was ruled by a famous Luo chief named Odera Akang'o. I used to hear stories about Odera Akang'o, and his impact on Gem is still evident today. During the early years of British rule, Chief Odera Akang'o visited Kampala in Uganda, and was very impressed with the impact of education and Christianity on the advancement of the Baganda people. When Odera Akang'o returned from his visit to Uganda (around 1915), he imposed on us the same development policies that had been imposed on the Ugandans by the British. Chief Odera Akang'o forced my grandparents' generation to send their children to school, directed that roads be built, and ordered trees planted alongside the roads. These are the same trees that you may still see today in Gem. Chief Odera Akang'o was often harsh in his methods, for he literally caned those who did not fully abide by his edicts. But through the development measures imposed by Chief Odera Akang'o, Gem became a modernizing force not only in Nyanza, but within the entire country. Gem produced Kenya's first lawyer (Argwings Kodhek), one of the first medical doctors in Kenya (Wellington Aruwa), and the first African government minister in the colonial government (Benaiah Apolo Ohanga[2]). Mr. Ohanga and Mr.

Aruwa were immediate neighbors to our home in Got Regea, and were good friends of my father. While growing up, I viewed them as uncles. There is a secondary school named after Ohanga in my village.

Around the time of my grandfather's death, European missionaries had built centers for religious and literacy training in Kenya. One of these centers was located at Maseno, south of Got Regea. This institution was established (around 1906) by the Christian Missionary Society of England, and it became known as C.M.S. Maseno. Soon afterwards, an order arrived from the Chief's camp (perhaps directly from Chief Odera Akang'o) that every village in Gem had to provide a certain number of young men to the missionaries for training. This order must have caused much anxiety and apprehension since the Europeans were only recent arrivals in Kenya and brought with them strange ways and practices. More importantly, their intentions were not trusted. Chiefs were hesitant to volunteer their own sons or nephews to be taught strange religious beliefs and customs. Very few elders viewed the literacy training of the missionary schools as a useful skill within the village. In order to test the waters and relieve themselves of the burden of caring for parentless children, many villages offered up their young orphans to the missionaries. It is likely this was the reason my father, Odenyo, was selected for missionary school training in Maseno. However, there are some elders of my family who have separately heard that Okwata himself, in the year prior to his death, encouraged the two oldest boys (Okumu and Odenyo) to join the missionary school, and that Odenyo actually attended for one year prior to Okwata's death. In this version of the story, Okumu (as well as his uncle Musa Oludhe), refused to attend the missionary school, but Odenyo was actually interested in attending. It is unlikely that the full circumstances surrounding Odenyo's selection for missionary school training will ever be known. However, what is important to remember is that this training had a profound effect not only on Odenyo's life, but on the lives of Odenyo's children.

Odenyo's training at C.M.S. Maseno influenced every aspect of his future. Anglican missionaries provided Odenyo and his classmates with religious training, as well as reading, writing and arithmetic skills.

Odenyo qualified as an elementary school teacher, learned how to operate a printing press, and taught printing at Maseno. Odenyo was thus a pioneer among his peers, acquiring both education and a marketable skill during the infancy stages of a modern economy. Odenyo embraced the religious training provided by the missionaries and became a Christian. Odenyo became immersed not only in Biblical teachings, but in European traditions, which were often incompatible with traditional African practices. Throughout Nyanza, Luo converts to Christianity were required to be baptized under Biblical names as a sign of their true rebirth into the Christian faith. It is likely that in the early years these baptismal names were assigned to converts by the European missionaries. Perhaps a few Luo converts randomly selected their new names out of the Bible. My father either chose or was given the baptismal name of Zablon. Therefore he was no longer known as "Odenyo *wuod* (son of) Okwata," but Zablon Odenyo. Odenyo became his last name and henceforth the family name in future generations.

Zablon eventually became known as Zablon Sangoro Odenyo. The origin of the name Sangoro is uncertain. Most people say he was named after a famous football (soccer) player. However, many years after my father's death my mother gave a different explanation. She told me that Sangoro was a nickname that the Luo or Abaluhya used to refer to a European surveyor who was the first white person to visit Got Regea. If this is accurate, I suspect this surveyor's interest in the area was linked to the high altitude of the Regea Hills. In particular, Aruwa's peak is one of the highest land points in the area. From the top of Got ka Aruwa, one can get a clear view of the surrounding areas up to the Ugandan border. The Luo word for draw, or map, is *goro*, although its connection to the name Sangoro is speculative. I have also heard that Sangoro was a reference to the way the European was using his eyes, either to see far distances (perhaps using binoculars), or otherwise using his eyes in an unusual manner (perhaps by staring at people or objects). Many children born during this European's visit were named Sangoro, including some as far away as Butere, which is in the land of the Abaluhya.

Before I was born, Got Regea may have actually been considered by the missionaries, or their converts, as a post. Missionaries usually selected high-altitude areas (such as Maseno) as their posts because these places provide cooler weather. My elders have told me that missionaries made such an impact on Got Regea that around 1920 we had religious dormitories where Luo people lived together as if they were in a commune. Their living quarters were lined up in straight rows of rectangular shaped houses, which was contrary to the Luo custom of building round houses. The Christian converts ate together, prayed together, and followed strict religious rules that prohibited polygamy and many Luo rituals.

However, many early converts became disillusioned with the faith and began to fuse traditional practices (such as polygamy) with Christianity. A few went even further by totally abandoning Christianity and European customs. Those in this third group eventually found themselves in a growing minority that neither remembered the old ways nor embraced the educational opportunities associated with missionary and colonial institutions. They found themselves without a firm anchor in either the traditional or modern worlds.

By 1923 Zablon Odenyo completed basic religious training at C.M.S. Maseno. He was sent into the Luo countryside as part of an internship to provide biblical instruction to new Christian converts. It was during one of these rural visits that my father met my mother, Adero, daughter of Zakayo Obuong. Like my paternal grandfather (Okwata), Obuong was the only male son among many sisters, and as a result, was the beneficiary of many heads of cattle provided by in-laws as dowry. Obuong had five wives. The wives, in order of seniority, were Doris Wambasi, Bethseba Adera (my grandmother), Penina Agina, Nora Okumu, and Asin. Obuong fathered twenty-five children, but only seventeen survived past childhood. Obuong and Bethseba's children are Adero (my mother), Charles Aduwa, Apeles Akong'o, Alice Otolo, Hilda Anyango, Persis Awuor, and Jasper Okoth. Obuong and his family lived in Kagonya of northern Ugenya, which is a location in Siaya District between Got Regea and the Ugandan border. Obuong was from the Umrembo clan.

Zablon Sangoro Odenyo, circa 1920.
The first photograph known to exist in the Odenyo family.

While Zablon provided religious training in Ugenya, he stayed in Obuong's homestead. Zablon took an interest in Adero and eventually asked Obuong for permission to marry his daughter.[3] Obuong consented, but stipulated that Zablon must wait two years until Adero was approximately fourteen years of age. Zablon's interest in Adero was proven genuine since he waited the two full years to marry her in 1925 (making her year of birth approximately 1911). Their wedding, at the Anglican Church in Ng'iya, was one of the first Christian ceremonies among the Luo people and was talked about by their peers for several decades. The main reason for this was that Adero wore shoes on her wedding day. Apparently the villagers had never seen a woman wearing shoes and therefore nicknamed my mother *"rawuoche"*—the one who wears shoes. It was around 1925 that my mother was baptized as a Christian, and thereafter officially named Grace Dina Adero.

The afternoon of their wedding, Grace Dina Adero walked the long distance with Zablon Sangoro Odenyo from Ng'iya to Got Regea, and joined a Kagola household. This sub-clan is very well known in the Gem area, and many of the persons mentioned in this book are JoKagola.[4] As a youth I was told by my elders that long before the arrival of Europeans, the JoKagola were influential due to their ability to make rain. If we moved to a new place with dry land, we would create rain for the local people, thus increasing our wealth and stature in the community. Since these early times, the JoKagola have continued to be the "rainmakers," for we have often been in the forefront of political, economic, and educational events in Gem. I estimate that perhaps 10 percent of the persons living in Got Regea trace their lineage to Kagola, and many, like me, are the descendents of the group that conquered Got Regea in my great-great grandfather's generation. The remaining 90 percent of people in Got Regea have a loose affiliation with Kagola or have been assimilated from outside groups into the Got Regea community. Those who have been assimilated from outside groups are referred to as *jodak*.

2
Home and Community (1935–1954)

This is my village. I am of it and it is of me.

—Amos Otieno Odenyo, 1975 autobiography.

Buildings and Landscape

During my youth, Got Regea consisted of approximately one-hundred homesteads. A typical homestead (*dala*) is encircled by euphorbia trees, which are fireproof and give the occupants privacy. There is one major gate (*rangach*) and one minor gate (*roth*) in every homestead. All visitors enter through the main gate, which leads directly to the house of the senior wife. If there are additional wives, the house of the second in seniority will appear on the left, and the third in seniority will appear on right, as you face them from the gate. If the head of the homestead has grown sons, the *simba* or small dwelling of the eldest son is located to the left, close to the main gate. The second son's *simba* is also close to the gate, but on the right. These *simbas* are built close to the gate to protect the home. It is said that before the coming of the white man, *simbas* served as barracks for our warriors when they traveled.

At night, cattle are kept in a pen located in the center of the homestead. Crops are stored in granaries, which are scattered along the inner circumference. The homesteads are linked by narrow, winding paths. The most traveled paths lead to the approximately five water wells in the village. Two small rivers, the Dienya and the Siga, provide water for cattle and bathing and mark the northern and southern boundaries of Got Regea.

Our home was similar to many Luo homes, except we had no houses for co-wives, and our fence and main house were square, not round. It is likely that my father built a square house because he was influenced by European architecture at C.M.S. Maseno. Our house was larger than most houses in Got Regea. The frame was constructed with long straight pieces of wood, to which was added a network of support poles. The walls and floor were made of unburned bricks. The interior walls were painted with whitewash referred to as *chokaa*, made from a soil called *atoya*, obtained from the banks of the river Siga. In homes with cattle, floors were surfaced with a mixture of cow dung and soil. This dries after about two months and has to be redone. The roofs of all our buildings were made of *olenge* grass. We chose *olenge* over *lum* grass because *olenge* can last six years, while *lum* can only last six months before needing repair. We placed corrugated iron on a small section of the top of the roof where it is most susceptible to a water leak. Our furniture was constructed of wood and cowhide. We slept on cotton mattresses, although many people in Got Regea preferred to stuff their mattress with dry grass. We had basic household items, but no luxuries. Like many Luo homes, ours held a spear. My father kept it close to his bed, where it was easily in reach.

We had a separate building for cooking. The kitchen had three fireplaces, each consisting of three stones to provide support for the cooking pot. The kitchen had a few low stools, but it was considered impolite to sit on these stools when not cooking. Doing so implied you are greedy and have come to wait for food to be prepared to eat. When I was very small the fuel we used was dry wood gathered from the hills. As I grew older we switched to charcoal, which was bought from the market in bags weighing up to two-hundred pounds. We cooked with pots made of clay, aluminum, or copper. The women cooked certain food in clay pots, and other food in copper pots, believing that the type of pot influenced the taste of the foods and beverages. Only the insides of the pots and pans were cleaned since the women believed that cleaning the outsides would wear them out. As a result, the outsides of all of our pots and pans had a very thick coat of black soot.

Traditionally, the kitchen is supposed to be for the women and their daughters. Boys would only enter if they are thirsty and want some water which we kept in large clay pots. Girls were supposed to bring water from the well, however, in my home, despite all the arguments, the boys also had to haul water. The only other source of drinking water was rain water which we collected as it poured off of the roof.

On the other side of the wall in the cooking structure was a private bedroom called *siwindhe*. This is where my two older sisters and their girlfriends slept. There were four beds and three wooden chairs in this room, but no table. There were ropes along the walls used to hang clothes and blankets. My sisters' friends often slept there because their own homes were too crowded. On any one night there might be three to six other girls from the village sleeping there that did not belong to my family. The girls did not eat in the *siwindhe*; they just needed a place to sleep.

Teenage boys similarly slept in one of the *simbas* close to the gate. They call it *lawo nindo* or "looking for a place to sleep." The *simba* is usually a two-room house built by a boy in his middle-teens to show his father that he is a man. The *simba* is a place where he can entertain his girlfriends. At puberty it is considered improper for a girl or boy to sleep in the same house as the parents.

We had what some people refer to as an "outhouse." A person bathed from a bucket on one side of the wall, and the excess water flowed through a gap in the wall and into the latrine section. The outhouses were constructed to last for only six months as the latrines often become unsafe. There were very few families in Got Regea that had such a modern structure. Most families only had a latrine and bathed in the secluded sections of the river near trees and rocks. Women and men had their own separate sections of the river.

I was told that the older generation grew up washing themselves with a certain fruit. However, my generation washed with a locally made black and white soap made by the Asians called *radier*. We did not have toothbrushes or toothpaste, but cleaned our teeth by chewing on a special stick. I have forgotten the name of this stick, but it had a unique and pleasant taste.

Got Regea, Kenya.

Food and Agriculture

We had six granaries, each consisting of a wooden frame structure set on top of a large foundation of four large stones. The granaries were set about two feet off the ground to help protect the crops from soil moisture, insects, and rodents. The walls of the granaries were made of wood with spaces between them large enough to keep air circulating but small enough to prevent the maize, cassava, millet or other crops from spilling outside.

Sweet potatoes were not stored in the granaries but eaten right away when harvested from the gardens. We had multiple potato gardens on different harvesting cycles. Planting season is between February and March. The man clears the land, and the wife and children plant the crops. If a man does his own planting, it is often on a piece of land separate from the land farmed by his wife and children. He will also keep a separate granary to store his own crops. The father's granary is not used to feed the family, but to buy more cattle and function as a reserve in case of a bad harvest.

During my early years I remember a water-powered grinding mill operating on the banks of the Siga River. Customers paid the miller forty cents to grind a basket of grain, which can feed a household for two weeks. This mill closed down when a more refined mill, operated by a generator, was opened near the Dudi market in the early 1950s.

People frequently ate potatoes mixed with blood. The blood was obtained from a living cow shot in the neck with an arrow. We preferred oxen blood over bull blood (an ox is a castrated bull). We took two to three pints of oxen blood and either dried it in the sun or in a pot over the fire. We then ground the dried blood into a fine reddish powder. Water and oil were slowly added and the mixture was boiled in a pot. The result was thick gravy which we spread over the boiled potatoes.

On a few occasions, a swarm of grasshoppers or locusts invaded Got Regea. This was not a good event as they ate our crops. We chased the grasshoppers with empty sacks, trapping many of them. We killed the insects, removed their legs and wings, fried them in oil, and ate them. They became a tasty and nutritious meal, so when they infested our area we made the most out of the opportunity. When I first heard the story about Moses and the ten plagues in Egypt, I wondered why the Egyptians did not catch and eat the locust during the time of famine that followed.

Our compound had many orange, papaya, mango, and guava fruit trees. If we wanted a snack, we simply climbed a tree, plucked a fruit, and ate it. Fruit was so plentiful that you could not find a person willing to purchase them, and they often fell to the ground uncollected. I used those oranges to play football (soccer) with my friends. We lost one orange tree when my brother Adet cleared an area to build his *simba*.

Societal Relationships

I remember a set of relationships and obligations among family members. Sons are always required to obey and be subordinate to the father. This is not unquestioned obedience; a good son really wants to abide by the wishes of the father. A boy is taught to always protect his mother's honor, and he is duty-bound to fight anyone, including his best friends, if they are disrespectful. In general, mothers are accommodating to their sons' friends. A son helps his mother and sisters with the clearing of land. Before a son can build a *simba*, the father must chop down the first tree which the son will use as building material. The father is required to pay the first dowry in the form of a cow to his son's new in-laws. Even if the son is rich, his father has to pay the cow as a demonstration of fatherhood.

From an early age, daughters have a close relationship with their mothers, who teach them home care duties such as cooking, collecting firewood, and fetching water. If you meet a young lady who cannot perform these duties, it suggests a lack of proper instruction in her home. When a daughter shows an interest in boys, it is the mother's responsibility to instruct and guide the daughter about relationships. The daughter usually obeys her mother. A daughter is required to ask her parents for permission to marry, and must not run away with her suitor before her parents have received dowry. A person marries with the expectation the spouse is capable of producing children, and when children are born it is the wife who is responsible for most aspects of child-rearing. Wives are responsible for the home, and fathers are responsible for economic support.

It used to be that if a marriage fails to produce children, the husband or wife would be permitted to leave the marriage for "experimental" purposes. Whoever produces a child during separation would likely stay with that new partner as a permanent spouse. However, the person who does not produce a child in a temporary marriage will have little chance of finding a permanent spouse. A man who cannot produce a child is called *bwoch*, and the female equivalent is *lur* (or more formally, *migumba*). The two are likely to marry each other, but people will look down on them and may even tell false stories about their reason for not being able to produce offspring, usually related to their alleged promiscuity. Before the emergence of modern land rights in Kenya it was very difficult for a *bwoch* and *lur* couple to claim any land in Got Regea. The community would say, "For whom are you claiming land? You don't have a son to pass it on to!"

The head of the home is the father, or husband. To ensure that his large household is running properly, he maintains some social distance as a necessity of management. Thus, there is not a lot of room to cultivate or maintain romantic relationships with his wives. Romantic love is not openly displayed, and if it exists, it takes a back seat to priorities such as social-economic security and raising children. The individualistic emotional needs that appear to exist in Western culture between husband and wife are in Africa diffused and satisfied through the multiplicity of adult relationships within the home, which includes extended family members. A spouse's "emotional eggs" are not placed in one basket, and once the "honeymoon" exuberance has waned, the marriage holds enough value for the relationship to be maintained.

In a way, the father is more of a supervisor than a parent. His children learn to look up to him as a symbol of authority in the home, and will not act inappropriately in his presence. Each person in the home knows his or her particular role based upon gender, age, and seniority. In almost all instances, a woman is supposed to be obedient to her husband. If she starts bossing people around in the home she is referred to as *wange tek,* which literally means "strong-eyed," but is generally used to refer to a female whose behavior is masculine. However, in a polygamous household, the most senior wife has a bit more room to administer the home, especially when it comes to daily tasks. In this way she acts somewhat like a foreman, but she must not do her job in an overbearing manner. She must be a relatively strong woman, capable of straightening out quarrels among the co-wives. Her position in the home is elevated since without her strong presence, the husband would not be able to sort out the various concerns among the extended family. The senior wife should be consulted by the husband if he wants to add a wife, for her approval is critical for maintenance of family harmony.

There is a strong recognition of age between siblings. The elder brother can direct the younger brother and act like a junior father. However, he must not do it in a heavy-handed way that would cause the younger brother to become resentful and request intervention from the father. Younger brothers and sisters are not supposed to marry before their older brother or sister. If a son marries while his older brother is not married, it is an affront to the older brother. It appears by his actions he is saying he is older and wiser than his elders, and this creates shame for the older brother.

All persons are expected to eventually marry, or else they are considered somewhat strange. An unmarried person is a threat to the kinship and inheritance system upon which Luo culture is based. To choose not to marry is interpreted as a sign of disrespect for the community. Since everyone in the village is considered a distant relative, youths are encouraged to seek spouses from other villages, such as the Jokalanyo from across the Dienya River in Huluwinu village, or even beyond. Elders of the bride and groom's families conduct discrete background checks to ensure there is no common ancestry for at least four generations. If a man and woman marry without consulting with their families, and later it is found they are related by blood, they will be ostracized by the entire village. The community will demand that the couple display their shame by placing a pot on the roof of their house. This was very rare to see in Got Regea, but I remember on the way to the town of Yala there was a man with such a pot on his roof. Perhaps the owner of the house was not so popular with women so he decided he must resort to marrying a distant relative.

A Luo son does not inherit land until he is married. Although he inherits the land, it is symbolically given by his mother to his bride, who is often from another village. For example, if the bride is from Seme, her husband's land in Got Regea will be referred to as belonging to *Nyar* Seme (daughter of Seme). It is referred to as her land because she is actually the one who will be cultivating it. However, if she and her husband divorce, she cannot take the land from her husband. It is she who will have to return to Seme. By the time the matriarch of the family is nearing old age she will have likely parceled out most of her land to her new "daughters." This works out because she is no longer physically able to farm large pieces of land, her married sons are required to build their new home within the family compound, and these new families need land to cultivate. By the 1940s it was very common for sons to live in the cities, yet they could always return even after twenty years and claim a part of their father's land. The brother at home may be cultivating it for his brothers in the city, but knows that all the brothers have equal land rights. Alternatively, a husband would work in the city but leave his wife behind in the village to farm the land and further legitimize his land rights and community status. The death of the land owners results in the temporary abandonment of the homestead, which is now referred to as *gunda*. It is not cultivated for several years for fear of disturbing the ghosts who linger near the graves.

It is expected that your spouse be a Luo, and not a *jamwa* (someone who does not speak your language). However, marrying a *jamwa* is still preferable to marrying a relative. Perhaps a close but not perfect example of this could be the marriage between my grandfather's sister Patroba Awuor and Ojwanga. Although Ojwanga spoke Dholuo, he was of Abaluhya heritage, a descendent of the previous land owners of Got Regea. It was on Ojwanga's land that we lived during my father's exile (–1959) from his birthplace near the valley between Got ka Otieno and Got ka Aruwa.

If a young man is looking for a wife he may ask his female cousin, one who lives in another village, to scout around for potential brides. The cousin will introduce the bachelor to her friends, and the bachelor may invite one of them to his village to engage in casual conversation and have a meal in his *simba*. If this meeting goes well she may visit again and stay a little longer in the family compound. She will be expected to mingle with the bachelor's sisters and join them in their household chores. The mother of the bachelor will closely observe the visiting girl, and make sure she is energetic, focused, and properly trained in household affairs. The girl is trying to impress the mother of the home, and if the mother approves, she actually becomes the girl's best advocate to be married into the home. Should the mother not approve, her son will likely reject the girl and try again. It is very important for the mother to approve of her daughter-in-law, for the two of them will be living in the same home and working together for many years. The daughter-in-law must not only be a good manager of the home, but well-mannered.

A very different relationship exists between a husband and his mother-in-law. Instead of being close, they have a relationship built on avoidance. You are never supposed to show you are too relaxed around your wife's mother. For example, if you visit your mother-in-law's house, you are not supposed to walk around the house, lest you happen to catch a glimpse of her sleeping quarters. Instead, you must sit in a specific area reserved for guests. A man would not even shake hands with his mother-in-law, for if he tried, she would say, "you can't shake the hands of my daughter and shake mine too."

Children regard their uncles and aunts with the same respect as parents. In fact, we simply referred to an aunt as "mother" or an uncle as "father." My father's brother had a right and obligation to discipline me in the same manner as did my biological father. A similar closeness exists among cousins. We did not call each other cousins, but referred to each other as brothers and sisters. We could visit each other uninvited and be treated like part of the family. We would not have any strong obligations to cousins but were expected to help in times of trouble or participate in ceremonies such as delivering dowry.

Grandparents are often surrogate parents. Grandparents can discipline you, but more often would provide guidance on matters that the parents overlook. For example, fathers sometimes avoid advising their sons on how to approach and talk to girls. However, if your *kwara* (grandfather) sees that among your age mates you alone cannot talk to girls he might approach you directly and say, "Now Odhiambo, what are you doing? Why don't you act like your agemates? Why don't you try this or try that." In other words, if he sees you are not going through the proper life cycles he will not hesitate to interject, and if he sees you doing the right thing he will not hesitate to praise you. Old men are supposed to be wise and above scandal. They are not supposed to be seen drunk and must counsel young men who drink too much. The old men are sometimes called on to resolve family quarrels and other issues such as land boundaries.

Grandmothers have a similar instructional role to play with regard to their granddaughters. This instruction is often conducted in strict privacy within the *siwindhe*, which functions like a girl's dormitory. A grandmother may assign herself to a particular group of teenage girls and give them basic knowledge of what to expect as housewives. Basic sex education may be taught here, with special emphasis on maintaining virginity until marriage. This is a very important topic because the matron's reputation is at stake with regard to the number of girls from her *siwindhe* who are found to be virgins on their wedding night.

When a girl marries and moves to another village, it is often expressed as "she has gone elsewhere to cook." She may occasionally return to visit her old home and stay overnight in her former *siwindhe*. She will share with the younger girls her experiences as a woman. She may even act like a scout for her husband's younger brothers by recruiting her sisters or cousins to marry into her new family. If she is particularly fond of a sister, she may make special effort to encourage that sister to become her co-wife in her new home. She may assume her husband may take a second wife, and therefore it might as well be someone she already knows.

In traditional Luo culture there is really no need for a man to have a mistress. If he really liked another woman other than his wife, he would simply legitimize the relationship by making her a second wife.

Grandchildren must always be willing to assist their grandparents. For example, your *dana* (grandmother) may no longer be able to walk the long distance to the market, so she might summon you to run the distance and bring her back some sugar or salt for her cooking. Your *dana* may want to sleep near a fireplace at night for extra warmth so you should know this and split some wood for her. I never had a *dana* in Got Regea but I split wood for my grandfather's sister, Patroba Awuor, who lived directly across the road.

Young people used to have a strong awareness and appreciation for their family, community, and clan. During my youth there was really no escape from one's birthplace, so social deviance was controlled through the threat of exile from the community. The threat of exile no longer holds the same weight. Today, banishment from the village may be a relief to a young person, for it absolves him of having to share his or her income with the extended family. Youths no longer have the same sense of social obligation to stay out of trouble.

Commerce and Trade

There was once a flourishing market close to our home, near the Dienya River. Had you accompanied me to the Regea market when I was growing up, you would have seen a large open field filled by a crowd numbering in the hundreds. Along the circumference are ten shops. The corner building is a butchery, run by five proprietors who take turns using the premises to slaughter and sell meat. Gideon Obuolo is the head of this group. He has a reputation for stinginess with his meat although his companions consider him to be a good business-man. He has earned that reputation by sticking to the standard weights and measurements for selling meat. Since this is a village market, all relatives, friends, and other village companions expect Obuolo to give them special privileges, such as a little meat beyond the weight price. However, Obuolo refuses to show favoritism and treats all customers equally. His business partners, on the other hand, occasionally give in to the demands of relatives and friends. They sometimes experi-ence financial loss, but Obuolo always makes a profit. Inside the shop, the meat is hung on hooks. The customers make their selections, and Obuolo cuts the carcass, weighs it, and wraps it in clean banana leaves. His customers often grumble about the small cuts of meat and his stinginess. A partner is allowed two business days to sell the remaining meat if Obuolo does not sell it all on the first market day.

Blasio Osiro manages the adjacent animal hides and skins shop. He buys many of the skins from the five meat dealers, who regard him as a junior partner. All villagers who slaughter cows sell the skins to Osiro, giving him a virtual monopoly on Got Regea skins and hides. Osiro prepares the hides and skins and many are shipped to a whole-sale dealer in the city.

Next is the shoe repairman's shop. The cobbler repairs and sells imported shoes, but he also makes his own local brand referred to as *akala*, a type of sandal made of used automobile tires. By deal-ing in both imported and local shoes, he hopes to attract customers of a wider variety, but the strategy does not work well. Those who can afford imported shoes prefer to travel to the town of Yala, where the storekeepers, mostly Indians, sell new shoes made in the cities.

However, local people who look after cattle find *akala* more durable and comfortable.

The rest of the buildings in the Regea market are retail shops for all types of imported items. These include kerosene for lamps, bars of soap, cigarettes, and cheap rolls of cloth to be tailored into shirts and dresses on Singer sewing machines. The tailors are men. Outside, a crowd of people mill around bargaining for this and that, without any set order. Those who have bananas to sell simply walk into the compound, choose a place, sit down, and display their bananas. Those selling pottery, baskets, maize, millets, potatoes, and sugar cane do the same. Bicycle owners transport fish all the way from Lake Nyanza to sell in the Regea market.

The art of bargaining in these markets is an elaborate skill. For an article worth one shilling, the seller may begin by asking for two shillings while the buyer offers half a shilling. The bargaining continues until the buyer walks away protesting the price. The seller then announces that he has reduced the price. The buyer returns and the bargaining process resumes. Completing one sale may take ten or more minutes of bargaining, punctuated with heated protestation. However, there is always a well-understood standard of market value. Three bananas would be about one shilling, and a sack of potatoes would be five shillings. Sugar cane is measured by the number of nodes contained within the stalk. A big traditional pot would be approximately fifty cents. This may now seem cheap, but in the 1950s it was not easy for a person in Got Regea to come up with fifty cents. We used to buy many pots from the Abaluhya women who came to Got Regea from across the river Siga. Their soil is very good for making pots but not as good for growing millet, maize, and potatoes, which they bought from us.

Business is not a full-time occupation for most of those who set up shop in the Regea market. Most people go to the market around ten in the morning after working at least four to six hours in their fields. Buying and selling takes second place to horticulture and livestock. However, the market has other significant functions in the lives of all of the residents. More than other local institutions, it is a place where the outside world impinges upon local and economic habits of the people. It is also an arena of intertribal exchange and good will between the Abaluhya and the Luo. The Regea market is situated on the boundary of the Luo and Abaluhya tribes where bilingualism is common. The two groups get along quite amicably in most spheres of life in Kenya. The Regea market is a significant source of outside news, gossip, and rumor. In a land where few rural people read newspapers, the news from the cities is carried by word of mouth by the bus drivers and passengers from the cities. People greet one another and immediately relate every piece of gossip they have come across along the way, ranging from important political happenings to unfounded rumors. People in local markets often discuss matters which are guarded secrets in the bureaucracies in the capitol. Government employees freely discuss with their relatives matters they encounter when performing their duties. The word spreads quickly. What is finally printed in the newspaper is already quite familiar to many. The Regea market is also a place for social happenings. Young men and women dress up to go to the market to see and be seen by potential future mates.

I remember a lending and transportation company that was formed by Simeon Nyende, B.A. Ohanga, and other prominent families in Got Regea. Families pooled thousands of shillings to form a corporation known as *karadha*. The corporation bought a surplus World War II truck, and Okoyo, a war veteran, transported items for a fee. Most people at the time were only accustomed to transporting their large items by hiring a *japunda* (a man who owns a lot of donkeys). The hired *japunda* and his team of donkeys hauled construction materials long distances, perhaps up to five miles. Therefore, the hired-truck driven by Okoyo was a revolutionary concept and service for us in Got Regea. The corporation also loaned small amounts of money with the agreement that it would be repaid with interest. Within five years this business died out completely. The problem was that people in Got Regea who borrowed money or commissioned the truck never paid back the money. They simply looked upon the loan as a gift from a family member. The business owners were not willing to go around saying "you must pay" to relatives and friends. So eventually the loans dried up, the corporation died, and the truck also became old and it soon died too.

Bank accounts were rarely used since they were only available in major towns such as Kisumu. Seven miles away in Yala, one could deposit money into a savings account at the post office. Unfortunately, most people in Got Regea did not earn enough disposable income to merit establishing any type of savings account. If we had an extra ten or twenty shillings, we simply kept it at home, under the mattress. However, once money became common in Got Regea, thieves learned to look under mattresses for money. People had to come up with ingenious methods of safekeeping money, such as placing it on top of doorways. The thieves were typically between the ages of eighteen and thirty-five, never went to school, had no skills, and spent their time idling away in the village bars. They were often envious of wealthy families and caused mischief by burning crops and damaging buildings. I remember we had about five families with children like this. Their problems usually start with the oldest siblings who either decide not to go to school or cannot pass their examinations. The younger siblings have no role models, and are not encouraged to work hard towards acquiring education. So, an entire family settles for the lowest possible standard of achievement. Education had the biggest impact on the success of most families in Got Regea. Those who embraced it tended to prosper. Those who ignored education tended to fill the lower ranks of society.

Communication and Transportation

A radio was one of the most important possessions to have in Got Regea. It was often the first item a family would request of a relative who had managed to find work in the city. Battery powered radios provided speeches by politicians and news of the world beyond Nyanza. Women listened to the informational programs that taught how to wash or wean babies. Young people listened to modern African music played by guitars. The entire village regarded the radio as a form of political and social awakening.

To make a telephone call or receive a telegram, a person walked seven miles to the post office in Yala. This was very time-consuming, so the people of Got Regea eventually organized themselves and provided a bicycle to my father's uncle, Musa Oludhe, to ride to Yala every Tuesday and Friday to pick up letters. When Musa returned to Got Regea, he handed over the mail to a community leader who distributed it under a large fig tree.

The nearest railroad station was located in Yala. However, the train was not frequently used because buses that stopped at the Dudi market were more convenient. Vehicles were frequently seen on the Kisumu-Busia road, but they were almost always owned and operated by Europeans and Indians. Cars were a novelty and were kept primarily as a status symbol and not as a daily means of transportation. I remember that our neighbors B.A. Ohanga and Simeon Odera were one of the first vehicle owners in the area. Ohanga drove a Peugeot 203, and Simeon a Ford Anglia. It was an amazing sight to see these vehicles moving on narrow and bumpy footpaths where cars are really not meant to travel. I still remember the day Mr. Ohanga drove my father and me all the way to Alego to visit the brothers of my grandmother Muhula. It was one of the few opportunities to ride in a car during my youth.

Virtually all people in Got Regea commuted by the oldest form of transportation—walking. It was not unheard of for a young person to depart Got Regea at sunrise, walk three miles to the Dudi market, and continue walking another thirty miles to Kisumu. If he was strong enough he would make it before sunset. A "middle-class" family owned one bicycle, and "upper-middle" class families owed more than one bicycle. Our family owned three bicycles, so we were part of the upper economic class in Got Regea, comparatively speaking.

Governance

Community development and planning policies were formed during group meetings called *baraza*. The *baraza* was similar to a town hall meeting. A *baraza* could be held to decide where to build a school, a well, or a church. When it was a *baraza* to address a religious matter, it was Reverend Simeon Nyende who officiated (often at his house on a Sunday morning before church). If it was a civic meeting, it was his brother Alfayo Kodhe who officiated. Kodhe's position was *mlango* (village headman). The *mlango* officiated meetings every other Wednesday and he dispensed orders from his superiors. For example, he might say that every Monday men of the village have to terrace land in the village that was prone to flooding or erosion. The *mlango* also collected annual taxes, which people had to pay by selling their crops or cattle. Villagers were often mad at the *mlango*, but most of the time they cooperated, and even supported his authority. They knew that if they had any petty complaints such as "that man's cattle ate in my garden" or "that person is rumor-mongering," that they could approach the *mlango*, who might adjudicate the dispute by issuing small fines of perhaps ten shillings. The *mlango* is not paid regularly, but takes a commission on the fines he issues. To command respect, it was important that the *mlango* be born from the dominant clan or lineage (*dhoot*) in the village.[5] My father often attended the *baraza* and wrote down all the important statements and decisions. The men gathered under the large fig tree next to Saint Peter's Church. In Luo we call this tree *ngowo*. When a man told someone "*adhi ngowo* (I am going to the tree)," it was understood this man was heading to a *baraza*. When I was a boy, this fig tree had many branches and leaves and provided shade for up to fifty men. Here these men would shout and argue why they should not have to give up the rights to this land, why the well should be built on that land, or why the road should travel this way instead of that way. It was under that fig tree that the village decided where to build the adjacent Got Regea Primary School. Until the 1940s the current school grounds were occupied by five families, including Daniel Dindi and Musa Oludhe. After the community decided to build the school on their land, these families had little choice but to vacate their homes. The community allocated other land where they could rebuild.

The *baraza* was used to settle community disputes without involving the police or court system. The *baraza* worked on a system of peer pressure and respect for the community. A man who had done wrong could be persuaded to remedy his actions by the elders directing unfavorable community opinion on him. The *baraza* was a function that only men could attend, and it was expected that all honorable men of Got Regea participate from time to time. To not do so would demonstrate that you are not part of the community. This *baraza* was a very efficient and effective self-governance system in Got Regea, but over time it became less frequent and more ineffective.

The *mlango's* boss is called *miruka* (sub-chief). The *miruka* oversees not just one village, but perhaps five to seven villages. The position of *miruka* started around the time I was born, so you will find that many of my generation have been given the name *miruka*. One day in the early 1940s the *miruka* arrived in Got Regea and ordered everyone to line up their best looking oxen. Then he had his men herd the animals out of the village while the owners grieved. Later we learned our oxen had been sold to support soldiers fighting in World War II.

The *miruka's* boss is the chief, and he administers an entire area called a "location." Community disputes that could not be settled by the *baraza* were adjudicated at the chief's level. However, by the 1940s the powers of the chief had been seriously eroded, and he found he could not even officiate over serious legal matters like theft over 300 shillings, assault, or murder. Allegations of this nature would be handled by the chief's supervisors, who did not have a daily influence on the village. They are the "district commissioner" (who governs a district), the "provincial commissioners" (who governs from cities like Kisumu) and the "governor" (who governs from Nairobi).

Clothing

Many non-Africans have asked me whether I wore clothes in Kenya. The answer is yes. Men wore business suits to church, but wore shorts and heavy-duty *akala* sandals when working. Women covered their heads with scarves and wore loose cotton dresses that reached below the knee. Some people wore a *kanzu*, a one-piece cotton garment used by both sexes that covered the shoulders down to the ankles. Some of the older people in Got Regea were more comfortable in these garments even if they had modern clothing at home. Some people wore the *kanzu* because it had a traditional appeal. Visiting African politicians were aware of this fact and wore the *kanzu* when they came to the villages to solicit support. While I wore clothes, I did not have shoes. Shoes were an unnecessary expense for a child, and all children walked barefoot. It was not until I entered high school that I owned my first pair of second-hand shoes.

Many people in Got Regea bought their clothes from Daniel Dindi, the village tailor (and descendant of Aruwa). He was very skilled at his craft and provided many generations of my own family with various European and local style clothing. His shop was in the Regea market, but he acquired his raw materials from Yala. He was a memorable figure within the community. My youngest brother, Daniel Dindi Odenyo, was named after him.

Before my father's generation, clothing may have consisted of pieces of animal hides and imported cloth material from the coast of Kenya. However, I only observed this attire during traditional ceremonies such as funerals, dances, and weddings. A man's outfit is made of two pieces of soft animal skin, such as a well-tanned ox hide decorated with beads or shells. The more beads the better, as it signifies wealth and prestige. This big skin covers the body from the shoulders to the knees. There may be a soft goat skin wrapped around the waist. The person may have his face painted from red soil, and is clad in many different types of ornaments. Animal teeth are used to make a head-dress with feathers attached. They call this the *sidho*—it is worn during the *olo buru*. *Olo* means "to pour." *Buru* means "ashes." Together, the two words refer to a funeral. A young person would not wear this traditional clothing since he holds no stature among his peers, and for him it would only be a meaningless costume. You have to be an older person or have some kind of connection to the old ways for this traditional attire to hold any meaning. I remember old men wearing small rings of copper or aluminum on the outside of their ears, but I do not know if this was associated with rank or simply traditional Luo fashion.

Music, Dance, and Entertainment

When I was very young I observed many traditional dances. They were accompanied by drums and traditional Luo instruments, such as the *orutu* (fiddle), and the *nyatiti*. The *nyatiti* was the main instrument and it functioned much like a guitar. There are eight strings attached to one stick approximately two to three feet long. At the other end of the stick is a hollow box of wood covered in goat skin that acts as a resonator. The box vibrates and produces sound when the instrument is played. The tension of the string, which is controlled by twisting a small peg connected to the string's end, controls the pitch. When a man plays the *nyatiti*, he sits down, crosses his legs, and places the instrument in front of him. He wears a bracelet on one leg, and he bangs this leg against the wooden part of the *nyatiti* to accent parts of the music while he sings.

The *nyatiti* players sing traditional songs that are expressions of Luo entertainment and story-telling. In the old days before the coming of the Europeans to Kenya, the *nyatiti* player was the chief entertainer in the village. The stories are very intriguing and can range from a love affair to an important person or incident. You can find a moral to most of the stories. For example, the *nyatiti* player would tell a story of a very generous man, and then finish with another story of a stingy man. However, he says it in a humorous way to ridicule the stingy man and entertain the audience. The audience would often suggest what story the player should recite. This is significant because it meant the *nyatiti* player had to be a relatively sharp man. A good *nyatiti* player might sit at a funeral and learn for the first time the life of a deceased man, and within ten minutes come up with a decent song about him.

There are special dances attended by the *nyatiti* player. In one of these dances, called the *mboko*, girls dance alone, showing their dancing skills. As they dance they clap their hands. The *nyatiti* player may also perform for dances between men and women; however, there are always interruptions by audience members. We call this *pakruok*, which literally translated means "praising oneself." *Pakruok* is a way for the audience to become involved in the storytelling and have some influence on the direction of the story. A man in the audience will stop the music and tell a short story—usually a boastful story with lots of humorous exaggerations. This lasts just a minute or two, and the interrupter has to pay the musician perhaps five cents for the interruption. This earns him the right to request the musician sing a song based on his short story. Alternatively, he can dictate to the audience the pace of the dancing or which gender can dance.

Girls used to select an open field near someone's home and sing Luo songs using small drums and other local instruments. The most talented singer would start the song, and then the other girls would sing after her in chorus. It was very similar to the *nyatiti* entertainment in that the girls would sing about a beautiful girl or an important person. These gatherings had a master of ceremonies, referred to as "captain." When someone in the crowd wanted to perform *pakruok*, he or she would approach the captain who would blow a whistle and instruct the audience to keep quiet and listen. These gatherings were strictly for the young and unmarried people in the village, but at times a few married people would watch from a distance. These types of gatherings occurred in the weeks leading to Christmas, which is when families return home from school or the cities. They were common events in the 1930s and 1940s.

By the mid-1940s the *Nya*-Abongo era had emerged. The *Nya*-Abongo crowd was named after the followers of a very good *nyatiti* player named Abongo, who was originally from Sakwa. I was too young to join the *Nya*-Abongo crowd—I was mostly an observer.

During the late 1940s Agande Omolo played the accordion, which he learned during his tour in the army. By the time I had come of dancing age (around 1950), the *Nya*-Abongo crowd and Agande followers had been overtaken by the guitar crowd, led by Isaac Nyariro. He had learned to play the guitar in Mombasa and formed a band that played in Got Regea. The introduction of the guitar caused a big cleavage between the younger teenagers and the more conservative older generation, which preferred the *nyatiti*. The younger guitar enthusiasts laughed at the older people and the older people looked down on the youth and told them that they were "lost." It was within the guitar era that I first learned how to dance. This was my main form of entertainment in Got Regea.

Music parties were held at dusk and lasted well into the evening. Somehow the pitch-black darkness never posed a problem for us—we always managed to navigate the small, windy pathways leading from home to home. It was amazing that we never got lost. Through our constant walking throughout the day, we memorized the various roads and shortcuts, even to the point of anticipating each rock and hole.

I do not remember my parents enforcing any curfew. Instead, I had a self-regulating curfew. I knew that I had to get home at a reasonable hour because in the morning the rooster would crow and there would be chores in the house and fields. I was not permitted to sleep late while my mother and siblings were preparing breakfast or digging in the fields.

Beer drinking was a social event among many adults in the village, especially after the harvest season. These events occurred on Saturdays or during special events such as weddings. When a daughter is married, the mother invites her in-laws and friends to drink *kong'o* (home made beer). This is nothing like the commercial beer that you see in the towns. It is warm and looks like porridge. It is passed to the men and women in large calabashes. The men use long rods (*oseke*) up to seven feet long to drink out of one large pot. The beer is relatively harmless because you can drink it all day long and become only mildly drunk. No one really gets drunk at these parties because it is more of a social event and drunkenness would be frowned upon. A beer party will last one day at one home and then the next time it will occur in someone else's home. It is a reciprocal thing. You cannot drink beer at a man's house too often without inviting him to drink beer in your home. If you hop around from home to home drinking beer without making beer yourself the people will not like it and eventually tell you so.

There were two deviant families in Got Regea that made high potency alcohol (*chang'aa*) that could incapacitate or cause death. They hid their production stills deep in the forest, and at night they made their brew. It was sold in milk bottles at a cost of three shillings. Most people in Got Regea could not afford the commercial beer and liquor from Yala, so if they wanted to get drunk they bought this illicit alcohol. Those who overindulged were easily identified because the illicit alcohol wrecked havoc on the body, permanently interfering with speech and motor skills.

A few families discretely planted and harvested a narcotic called *njaga* (marijuana). They grew seven or eight *njaga* plants in the middle of their tobacco fields. The leaves of this plant were smoked in a *poko*, which is a gourd with a long thin stem. When smoked, the gourd makes a bubbling sound like dripping water. A few rogue boys in Got Regea smoked *njaga* before they went dancing. They then jumped around, talked crazy, and started fights. This plant distorts your senses, relaxes your inhibitions, or makes you brave. It will eventually send you off to sleep. In the old days Luo warriors may have used this plant before they went off to fight. Most people in our village did not approve of *njaga*. If the government caught you with it, you would be punished.

At one time, people all over Gem came to Got Regea to participate in church-based games. Various groups sang and a panel of judges issued prizes to the best singers. We had field and track, football, and running competitions. Women held contests such as placing small jars of water on their heads and walking fifty yards. The winner was the woman who reached the finish line quickest without spilling any water. Girls incorporated threading skills into a running game. They lined up in a row, each holding a thread. They raced to the other side of the field where they found a needle and had to thread the needle before running back to the starting line. This is very hard to do quickly since the girls would all be shaking so hard from the running and all the excitement. These community activities were very prevalent during my young days, but these events became less common over time.

We held wrestling competitions during periods of good weather (usually during the harvesting season). Men and boys from different sections of Got Regea wrestled with their peers from neighboring villages. The first match usually started with the best wrestler from each village. We did not wrestle to hurt one another, but we wrestled aggressively. The winners from each village were lifted onto shoulders and paraded around with much yelling and cheering.

Wrestling was an important indicator of strength and manhood. We practiced wrestling as young boys, often while herding cattle. Sometimes tempers flared. If you really wanted to wrestle someone but he did not want to wrestle you, all you had to do was to throw some grass on his head and say something insulting about his mother, such as, "Your mother's teeth are no good," "Your mother does not know how to walk properly," or "Your mother does not know how to cook." If someone says any of these things to you, you have no choice but to fight, because all boys must protect their mother's honor under any circumstances. The minute your mother's name is mentioned in a derogatory fashion, the fight begins, and it is often a very brutal one. However, if you only have grass thrown on your head and there are no insults, then it is simply a challenge to wrestle, and no one gets seriously hurt.

Livestock and Hunting

Cattle used to be a source of wealth among the Luo. There were some people in Gem who were famous for having more than one hundred heads of cattle. I remember attending my grandfather Obuong's funeral in Ugenya. There appeared to be an endless sea of cattle in his compound. It was possible that not all the cattle belonged to my grandfather's home. Some friends or relatives may have temporarily brought their own cattle to my grandfather's funeral to elevate my grandfather's wealth and stature in the eyes of the community. During his life there was enough land to support such herds, but these days have long disappeared. Because of land shortages, every piece of land capable of supporting crops is devoted to crops instead of cattle. Money has surpassed cattle as a form of value, wealth, and prestige. Today, a typical Luo home has only a handful of cattle. Many people who need meat or cattle for brideprice simply purchase them from the local market. For the most part I think this is better than having one hundred cattle of poor quality. On the other hand, it is bad because the young boys in the village will have more idle time and less responsibility. Fathers used to know if their sons were good herders because the cattle would come home at the end of the day well fed and content. If the cattle came home and started wandering around, the old man would know that his sons did not graze them well but instead spent most of their time playing.

My father owned several cows, but we did not keep them in our home. Instead, they were kept at Uncle Okumu's home, located on the west side of Got ka Otieno. Okumu's family took care of our cows, and my father reciprocated in other ways. In Luo, this arrangement with cows is referred to as *moso dhok*. It was my job to look after the cows once or twice a week, and to lead them back and forth from our home to Okumu's home. Uncle Okumu gave names to each of his cows and trained some of them to respond individually when called. He had a lead cow that walked to him when he whistled, which made all the remaining cows follow.

Villagers had a way of tracking down cattle thieves. If a man awoke in the middle of the night to find his cattle missing, he cried loudly: "*Yore! Yore! Yore!* (Roads! Roads! Roads!)" This alerted the neighbors to similarly shout "*Yore! Yore! Yore!*" until the entire village is awake and shouting the same cry. All the men would go to the road with their weapons and confront any cattle herder. Cattle herding is never done at three in the morning, so prior to the 1940s a person herding cattle at this hour after the shouts of "*Yore!*" was simply speared to death. I heard a lot of stories about this when I was really small, but over time these cattle thieves were only beaten up.

Occasionally, a group of *jodwar* (hunters) went out with bows and arrows and hunted for antelopes. The *jodwar* were typically composed of eight people, and returned to the village with two or three wild game which they divided among themselves. Only a few families in Got Regea hunted on a regular basis. Although game was once plentiful, over time game became much harder to find.

Not all animals were for eating. There were animals that could eat you. In our area, only the leopard was capable of this. I occasionally saw the animal's eyes at night while I walked along the pitch-black pathways in Got Regea. I could also smell the unusual scent that the leopard left behind. I was taught at an early age the way to act during an encounter with such a predator. My elders told me: "Leave them alone if possible, but if you see one in front of you, do not run. Walk away slowly. Do not stoop as if you are picking up a stone. Above all, do not provoke the animal in any way!" Adults were taught: "If you are attacked by a leopard, grab its tail, swing around with it, and then it can't hurt you. Hang onto the tail until it is tired, and in the meantime, scream for help!" When I was living in Got Regea I cannot remember anyone being attacked by a leopard. This is indeed fortunate since leopards would probably resent being grabbed by the tail.

We were also taught to be respectful of male monkeys. The larger variety, such as the baboon, could be extremely aggressive and had the potential to kill a human or cause serious injury. The smaller monkeys were our worst antagonists, for as soon as the corn and potato crops were ready to harvest, the monkeys came down from the trees to feast. Keeping monkeys out of the fields has long been a special job for the boys out grazing cattle. Snakes were avoided, but we knew that there were traditional remedies for most snake bites. The remaining animals, such as the fox, the *muok* (ant digger), and various types of squirrels were often sighted but posed no known danger.

Speaking about monkeys reminds me of a very interesting story. During World War II, Africans from all over Kenya were conscripted into the British army, and served in places like Egypt, India and Burma. When these war veterans came back to the village they brought with them strange items and influences, including syphilis and gonorrhea. Many veterans were authorized to carry their rifles and uniforms back to the village. This would not have caused problems had they simply stored these items in their houses and resumed their normal lives. Instead, many of these soldiers came back with an inflated sense of importance. Perhaps it was difficult for them to readjust to farming and village life after they had been all over North Africa and Asia fighting in the King's Army. It was not unusual to encounter a veteran still dressed in his tattered uniform and talking about his foreign exploits. Some of these men were prone to violence, which was a dangerous situation considering they had guns.

There was one veteran in Got Regea whom I cannot forget. Zakayo Were was a decent man as he was a good friend of my father. But from my young perspective, he was a terrifying figure and a man to avoid. He was fond of gathering the young children of the village and acting like their drill instructor, marching the little children around the village while yelling orders such as "Left—Right, Left—Right, Left—Right!" The older people in the village thought this was quite strange and worried about the fate of the children, especially after hearing he had a lot of spare ammunition stored within his home. On several occasions I encountered Zakayo walking toward me on a narrow dirt path. Hoping he had not yet seen me, I would turn around and walk in the other direction, or fling myself far into the safety of the bush. Eventually, the parents of Got Regea came up with a solution. They approached Zakayo as he was drilling these children and asked him, "Zakayo, why are you drilling our children while these monkeys are constantly stealing our crops? Why don't you take your rifle and go scare away these monkeys so that we can harvest our crops?" Zakayo thought this was a brilliant idea, and immediately set himself upon a new mission of shooting all the monkeys out of the trees until there was hardly a monkey left in our side of Got Regea for some time.[6]

3
Traditional Luo Beliefs

During the time I grew up, people in the village were attempting to combine the remnants of the old ways with what little they knew of the outside world. Because of my earnest desire to understand the world beyond the horizon, I had an even greater challenge in bringing the old and new together.

—Amos Otieno Odenyo, 1975 autobiography.

I was raised in a Christian household, the son of a very prominent lay minister in Got Regea. I was taught very little about Luo spiritual beliefs. What I know of the old ways I learned from observing other families and listening to the elders' stories.

It appears that prior to the introduction of Christianity in Luoland, spiritual worship centered on the sun, the moon, and our ancestors. People considered the sun (*chieng*) a representation of supernatural power. The sun was a creation or symbol of God (Nyasaye). When somebody was in need of good luck, he awoke early to sit in a spot where he could watch the sun rise. He might bring a little offering, perhaps a piece of quality meat or some good food. When he sees the sun, he would talk to it and plead with it. If he was a *jadwar* (hunter) he might say, "I am going hunting today, so please bless my spear." A herdsman might say "let me find some good pasture for my cattle." In other words, for whatever he needs to do he will always ask the sun. Now, I do not know the importance of this, but the person believes that spitting is a sacred act. The man will take the piece of meat, spit on it, and throw it toward the sun. This to him is a form of communication—the best, most sincere, whole-hearted communication. Once he has done this he has successfully communicated with Nyasaye and good luck is supposed to come his way. Spitting is also used when an old man wants to bless his son.

When a Luo son is born, the parents must not remove him from the house until after the fourth day. When a Luo daughter is born, she is required to stay inside for a total of three days. Coinciding with these numbers, when a man dies and is buried, on the fourth day his mourners will conduct the throwing of the earth (or ash) ceremony.[7] The younger people come to the funeral with spears and gather around the grave of the deceased. Then they take a little earth and begin a trip which may go many miles depending on the man's importance. If he is an important man, they will travel until they have crossed a river. In my area they ran about seven miles from Got Regea to the Yala river with weapons and all the cattle of the deceased. This is a display of wealth, and if he was a wealthy man there will be a long line of cattle. Women are in front of the cattle and men are in the back, and they are all yelling. They appear to be in a celebratory mood, with singing and no crying or moaning. The men do some sort of war dance, but they do not really do anything destructive. It is a very long trip but they are not supposed to show that they are tired because if they do, bad luck will befall them. When they reach Yala river they take the earth that they have carried from the deceased's grave and throw it across the river. The throwing of the earth is supposed to be throwing the bad luck across the river where it will not bother anyone in Got Regea. At some point during this ritual, the spear of the deceased father is given to the oldest son, signifying that he is the new head of the house. This spear is thrust into the dirt over the deceased, and the son picks it up.

If all the above steps are not taken, the deceased will come back and cause trouble for those still alive, especially his close relatives. The ancestors are capable of hunting for bad people or bringing good luck. It often depends on the manner in which they died or were buried. Let us say that a woman did not die under favorable circumstances. Either she went mad or thought someone had bewitched her to death. It is believed that she will come back and haunt the person who caused her to die like this. On the other hand, if you have a respected man who died in peace and all the required burial rites were done, he is supposed to be capable of restoring or giving blessing to his people. One of these rites is that he be buried in a certain place in his homestead, usually in front of his eldest wife's house with his head facing the house.

The spirits of the dead who come back to haunt you are called *jachien*. They are supposedly wandering around the village between ten o'clock in the evening until five o'clock in the morning. People actually claim to have met "so and so" who died five years ago. They would say "he came to the gate of our home and was singing this," or "he was saying that." I especially remember a very talented *nyatiti* player who happened to be a thief. He was killed when he stole some cattle. He is supposedly wandering around every night because he thinks he was killed unjustly. I heard a few people say that they met him at night and he was singing the very same song he used to sing while playing the *nyatiti*. It is supposed to be a very frightening sight when you meet a *jachien*. Sometimes you do not see him. You are walking alone at night and you hear a voice, but when the voice comes closer to you, you do not see anybody. A few minutes later you hear the same voice behind you, but still you do not see him. But he is seeing you. When this happens, very soon you are going to die. The older people were wondering what to do with this *jachien* so that he does not kill people when he walks around. So they made a big celebration consisting of local beer and meat, and invited many of the deceased's closest relatives. They gathered around the large pot of beer, sipping it slowly from their long straws. They left one straw free for the *jachien*, since he is supposedly sitting there unseen sipping the beer alongside the living. They all pleaded with the dead man not to come back. They said things like, "Please enjoy yourself—don't harbor bad feelings against your people." A bull was slaughtered and the eldest son cooked the meat. He took the tender parts and reserved them for his deceased father. These parts he tossed into the sky toward the *jachien* while pleading with his father not to come back and destroy his people. A middle-aged son, a brother, or uncle of the deceased would fill this role, as long as that person was an older man, not a woman. Afterwards, if the *jachien* does not come back, it means he was pleased with the beer and meat.

Virtually the same thing occurred with an in-law of ours. She began to see dead people haunt her, and claimed that these people wanted to kill her. She used to walk naked five miles to the place that she
was born, and claimed that her hands were being held by someone the
entire way. While she walked, she described the person who was holding her hands, and the villagers claimed it was the same man killed by
her father. The people of Got Regea tried to cure her, so they brought
a ram and beer. While saying a prayer, an old man took some of the
meat, tossed it into the air while beseeching the dead man to be kind to
this woman, because it was not her, but her father, who had killed him.
Our afflicted in-law picked up the same piece of meat and repeated the
ritual, begging her tormenters to leave her alone. Her family conducted
the same rituals, while pouring beer on the ground. A narrow piece of
skin from the ram was attached to her left arm. This was to enable her
to peacefully communicate with the *jachien* during the next few weeks.
I cannot say whether it was this ritual that cured her, but within three
months she became well.

There are specific death rituals that apply to young women so that
they do not become *jachien*. If a teenage girl dies before she is married,
she is not supposed to be buried with her hymen intact. A very old
lady is hired to break it. The Luo believe that this is a very dirty job,
so it must be done by an old lady who cannot have any more children.
There is actually a term in Luo (that I cannot remember) for a lady who
performs this job. She may be paid a goat, given some food, and entertained. Some importance is attached to the hymen because it shows
good upbringing. In fact, when a girl gets married, the next day women
from the girl's home come to determine whether or not the girl was a
virgin. If she was, this is a matter of great pride. On the other hand, if
she dies with her hymen intact, she will come back as a *jachien* and take
her revenge on her age mates and do something bad to their hymens.
As a result, these young girls may become pregnant before marriage
or some other bad thing will happen. No one close to me ever saw a
jachien, and it was only the older people who heard or saw them. But
stories of the *jachien* used to frighten me when I was small, especially
since there were no lights at night and a lot of tall grass and trees.

A *jachien* (or an intermediary of the jachien), can also appear in animal form. A rare bird, such as an owl, is a common symbol of *jachien,* or the *jachien's* messenger. An old man in the village may happen to see a certain type of bird at a certain time of day and that is sufficient for him to know that something is wrong. This old man will go to a *jabilo* (diviner) who can predict the future. The *jabilo* will interpret the message from the bird—usually that the old man forgot to provide the deceased with some death ritual. There were many Christians in Got Regea who preached against the *jabilo,* stating that he did not tell the truth. However, it seems to me that the system worked for many people and they got a lot of comfort from following the advice of the *jabilo.*

I remember one instance when a bird visited the home of a close neighbor, and it was interpreted as a bad omen. This bird may be what is called a hawk or raven in English. It is a very powerful black bird that comes to eat chicken. This is quite common and bears no hidden significance. But if the bird sits on or flies through the *rangach* (gate) of the home it is a very bad sign. All traditional Luo homes have the same entrance, built with two vertical poles eight feet high connected on top by another vertical arched pole. So when this bird flew through my neighbor's gate, he assumed something bad was going to happen to him.

There is another type of bird that does not often come to people's houses, but when it comes, it sings. His song is very melancholy, and you can sit and actually enjoy his singing. However, if this bird sings while sitting on top of the home's gate, it is a very bad sign. If the bird does this repeatedly over a short period of time, the owner will become extremely worried.

In a village near Ndiru Intermediate School I once saw the equivalent of an insane asylum. Ten to sixteen insane people stayed at the home of one man and his four wives. I was always afraid to venture near this home, for I feared being beaten up by all the insane people. But the owner of the house and his wives were quite strong and could wrestle the patients and control them quite well. They managed to tie them up if they became unruly. The man used to administer a type of tobacco to the nostrils of the infirmed, which caused them to violently sneeze. He administered this treatment until he showed them a locust or larvae that supposedly came out of their nostrils. The larvae never came out of the patients, but to the sick person it demonstrated that the source of the mental sickness had now been removed. The patients believed it and a few actually became better as a result.

In Got Regea, most people believed in what we call the *jajuok* ("night-runner"). He is someone you may know as a normal man throughout the day, but late at night he is a totally different person. At night he runs around the village, scaring people. He prefers to run naked, hoping his fellow villagers will not recognize him by his clothes. He likes to knock on your windows when you are asleep, then run away. If you are walking home alone at night, he is running behind you, making noises, imitating you. He might hide in a tree and shake it violently as you walk by. The night-runner is supposed to keep a leopard in his house that joins him at night. He will either run around you with the leopard or instruct the leopard how to frighten you. Adjacent to our home lived one particular night-runner who liked to pour dust through the ventilation of our house and into our beds while we were asleep.

There is another type of strange person similar to the night-runner, but he is supposed to make people sick or kill them. A close term in English may be to "bewitch" someone. In our language this is called *kingo ngato*. For example, suppose you are in a dispute with your neighbor over land. Maybe you are more prosperous than him and he resents you for it. Well, he might hire someone to *kingo* you. This *kingo* means that he will bewitch you so that soon you will die. The witch may use a piece of clothing or piece of hair from his victim and turn it against him.

This bewitching activity was believed to have occurred in Got Regea because a lot of people died as a result of arguments over land. Around 1946 my father, Zablon Sangoro Odenyo, was very sick and close to dying. My mother's oldest (half) brother, John Apel, visited Zablon in the missionary hospital in Maseno and told the rest of us that someone had "*kingo-ed*" him. John was adamant that someone in the village was envious of Zablon's wealth and successful children. Even the rest of the village believed the same theory. They suspected one particular old man to have supposedly *kingo-ed* people he considered prosperous out of envy that his own were not successful. Most of his children were either thieves or people who never got married or people who never amounted to anything. John Apel wanted to bring an *ajuoga* (medicine-man) to cure my father. But no one from our family paid any attention to this belief and after two months at the hospital my father got well and returned home.

Cranky old women were said to have similar magical powers, but directed towards children. It was believed if a certain old lady visited your house while your children are eating, she could simply look at the food and implant a disease. She does this just with her eyes—there is no physical contact between her and the food. The children's stomachs may swell and unless the old woman is called back to undue her magic the children will die. Of course this sort of thing is impossible and my family did not subscribe to this belief, but all around us in Got Regea people thought such witchcraft was possible. I would often see some young mother running, running, running to the home of this witch and say to her, "Well, I was told that you came to my house at such and such a time and now my daughter is sick. You must have done something to her and you must come back to rescue her!" Sometimes the witch comes back and the child gets well. Other times the witch comes back and the child dies. If this happens several times people will complain to the *mlango* and the witch will be tried by the village elders. This is why the lady that is called a witch will do everything in her power to cure the children of her accuser. If she fails, the elders will see to it that she is kicked out of the village. If she has a husband, both of them will be removed.

Sometimes, instead of the witch being called back to reverse her curse, the family of the dying child might call in a healer to perform *chio*. This is the same practice used to cure chest infections. The child is cut on the stomach, and a hollowed-out antelope horn is placed on the cut and blood is sucked out of the area. It is supposed to have a healing effect. I personally think that those women who complained that their children were bewitched were actually careless in feeding their children. Perhaps the young children were left with inexperienced baby sitters and the children ate something from the floor. To my family this was all a game and a witch never called on us. As long as no one got hurt we used to be amused by the people running after the witch.

If you believe in all this superstition, you can call on the *ajuoga* to come to your home and place a particular kind of plant around the gate that will prevent the witchcraft from being effective. People do this before they build a house, and it must be kept secret where the new house is to be built. To test your luck first take a rooster and leave him tied overnight to the place where you will build your house. If something happens to it—say an animal eats it, you better select another place. If the rooster is still alive the next day, it is alright to build there.

I remember Uncle Gilbert Owuor's sister Penina (who lived in Huluwinu) advising him not to build a house on a certain piece of land. Penina told Gilbert Owuor that he had not properly completed certain cleansing or inheritance rituals before his father Okwata died. Penina argued that should he proceed with building his house, he would soon die and his offspring will be subjected to all kinds of misfortunes.

A person who does not engage in traditional Luo customs (*kweche*) is considered "lost." Our village used to refer to Ameda (Aunt Patroba Owuor's only son) as a lost man. Once Ameda became old enough he sought his fortunes outside of Got Regea. He became a laborer on the railroad, and later an *mpishi* (cook) for a European. He never married, and never came back home. He was completely disconnected to his heritage, they said. He did not take care of his health, and died.

Certain community disputes were not resolved at the level of the *baraza*, but were at the same time not suited for adjudication under the British legal system. For example, Africans did not traditionally claim ownership of land through title deeds. Divorce and accusations of theft were also not traditionally documented. Africans had rules and traditions that differed from those of Europeans. Among Luos, if someone steals your food, you cannot kill the thief. Instead, you are supposed to give him more food because he is hungry. However, if you catch someone stealing your cow, you could strike him or perhaps even kill him, and everyone would understand. This is why Luo cattle pens are located in the center of the homestead as a protective measure, but granaries are located along the perimeter—a location less protected from thieves or hungry kinsman.

The British were not interested in administering justice to a poor farmer whose cow was stolen, or to ensure equitable distribution of land. The British were in Kenya to tax the cow, and appropriate the land. The British therefore created the African Tribunal Courts, which enabled indigenous peoples to resolve disputes using a mixture of the British legal system and traditional African customs. Beginning in the late 1940s my father was a judge in the African Tribunal Courts, first as its vice-president and eventually as president. My father traveled as far as Ramula, Ahero, Bondo, and Sifuyo, where he settled disputes in which the British colonialists really did not want to get involved. Zablon understood how to administer justice by mixing a little bit of the British code with a little bit of common sense and Luo tradition. He did not actually render verdicts on his own. Zablon was part of a five-panel judiciary consisting of president, vice-president, and three Luo elders.

During breaks from high school I often sat all day in the courtroom and observed the proceedings. The five judges wore robes, and the court proceedings were administered in a semi-modern way. The plaintiff would stand up and allege that "Mr. Osewe exceeded his piece of land," or "Mr. Onyango did not repay a loan." The defendant would voice his counter-arguments. All of this was recorded in a big book. Eyewitnesses could provide testimony. My father and the other judges would leave the room and attempt to render a verdict. Often times they could not decipher the truth, so they resorted to administering oaths.

If the testifier was a Christian, my father provided a bible and had him recite a religious oath of truthfulness. In instances when the testimony of a non-Christian witness was difficult to evaluate, my father and the other Tribunal officials implemented a Luo oath ritual:

The Tribunal would escort the witness to the rear courtyard. There, amidst the open grass, was a hole dug two feet deep, five feet long, and three feet wide. It was supposed to symbolize the grave of a man. Next to the hole was a hoe representing the equipment used for digging graves. Bones representing the skeleton of a dead man were laid out before the witness. A pot symbolizing the making of funeral beer was present. All these items were symbols that the judges used for extracting the truth from witnesses suspected of lying. Zablon would first ask the witness to swear that he was to tell the truth. Zablon then gave the witness a pot to carry while stepping over the grave and providing testimony. This process was known as *tingo mbira*. The witness believed that if he lied, he would drop dead in the very near future, and placed in a grave just like the one behind the court. Dirt would be covered over him with a hoe just like the one at the court, and mourners would drink beer from a similar pot. This method was often effective in extracting the truth from the witness, for some broke down and recanted whatever they had previous stated.

I noticed there were two main instances when both the Christian and the traditional Luo oaths did not work. The first instance was when the witness was neither a Christian nor a staunch believer in Luo superstitions. The oath administered to such a person would have no psychological effect on him. The second instance was when the person was such a strong believer in Luo customs that he thought he could simply go to the village medicine-man (*ajuoga*) and buy a potion that would overcome the effects of the *mbira*. The medicine-men made a hefty profit until the African Tribunal Courts discovered this "witness tampering" business and put a stop to it through the threat of arrests.

My father's position as judge in the African Tribunal Courts defined my father as a man of two worlds. On the village level, he was subject to the orders of his cousin, the *mlango* (Alfayo Kodhe). Yet my father adjudicated legal cases three administrative levels beyond the authority of the *mlango*, and knew what orders the *mlango* would dispense before he even received them from the *miruka*.

My father's appointment to the African Tribunal Courts roughly coincided with the Colonial Government's 1954 Swynnerton Plan, which recommended land consolidation and registering of title deeds. Prior to this there was no private land ownership in a formal sense. Instead, families handed down scattered pieces of land to their male heirs. Perhaps prompted by the legal ramifications of the Swynnerton Plan, my father moved swiftly to re-establish his claim to his ancestral land. By 1959 he successfully exchanged our home near the Regea market for part of his ancestral land near the upper valley between Got ka Otieno and Got ka Aruwa. In this location Zablon built a smaller but permanent brick house, to the dissatisfaction of those families who claimed it after the premature death of my grandfather Okwata. In the 1960s my father hired a land surveyor and obtained a title deed from Siaya, in the hope that the land ownership issue would be settled once and for all.

Luo families tended to be large, consisting of at least five children. A polygamous or extended household might have over twenty children, and many aunts and uncles. An evening meal was therefore a social event. Mealtime was usually between five and six in the evening. Timing is important because if your neighbors know your family eats after the sun sets, they will think you are hiding. If it is dark and you are eating, it may be assumed you have purposely used the cover of darkness to conceal your food. To counter this impression, families often ate outside where they could be seen by neighbors. In Luo culture meals are shared. A Luo person should also not refuse to accept a meal. Sharing with others and not being greedy or aloof at mealtime are signs of being a good person. Songs are written about people's eating habits. If you have a meal prepared and a visitor stops by unexpectedly, you should share your meal with him. It is a mark of prestige to be known for your hospitality. It is a compliment to hear someone refer to your home as a place where food is readily available.

Evening meals served another purpose as well. It was a forum for the elders to interact with the young people, foster family solidarity, and perpetuate the intricate web of reciprocal obligations within the family. Old men narrated stories about past heroes, reviewed the history of the clan, and recited the names and origins of the ancestors. Central themes used to be war and expeditions, but the themes of bravery were balanced by stories involving respect, hospitality, and generosity. The nature of certain types of plants and animals were reviewed, as well as their usefulness to the community. Almost every story had a moral theme to it. Elders lavished praise on young people who were following in the footsteps of their ancestors, and young people who had lost their way were reprimanded. Evening meals were thus a very important part of the fabric of Luo society, and lack of attendance was generally not tolerated. Mealtime used to provide some of the same moral and educational lessons found in today's churches and schools, plus a little more. A central place for evening meals also served a practical purpose in that if one wife was sick, or died, her children would not go hungry.

Many nights after dinner, Aunt Patroba told me stories about legendary events in Luo history. She did not read these stories to me from a book, for she did not know how to read. Instead, she recalled stories that she had heard from her elders when she was a little girl. One of these stories is called Nyamgondho wuod Ombare: Nyamgondho (son of Ombare) was a Luo fisherman who lived near Gwasi Hills, in Southern Nyanza, near the lake. One day Nyamgondho was out fishing in the lake, and instead of catching a fish he caught an ugly lady who agreed to marry him. When the lady walked out from the lake, hundreds of cows, goats, and sheep followed her. The lady and all the animals followed Nyamgondho to his home and Nyamgondho instantly became rich. Time passed and eventually he began abusing his wife, especially after he came back home drunk. This lady decided to leave and return to the lake, but when she did she was followed by each and every cow, goat, and sheep from Nyamgondho's home. Nyamgondho and his friends chased after her trying to prevent her from leaving with all the cattle. When Nyamgondho and his friends reached the lake, they instantaneously became trees. From what I understand, there are currently trees at this spot at the lake that are bent, and when the wind blows through them they are said to make a noise as if they are weeping. When I heard this story from Aunt Patroba, I learned the moral of the story is to not hurt those who help you, not to abuse a wife, and not become so proud that you despise those around you.

Aunt Patroba also told me a story about a powerful Luo warrior named Luanda Magere. He proved himself in battle by conquering all the other tribes that he encountered. It was said that his body was impenetrable by all spears and arrows. When the enemy attacked him, their weapons bounced off his body as if it was made of iron or stone. One of the chiefs of another tribe said to Magere, "Instead of us becoming enemies, why don't we become in-laws? Why don't you take my daughter as your wife and let us live like relatives?" Magere agreed to this, and took the chief's daughter as his wife. Some time later, Magere fell sick, and his new wife witnessed Magere's doctor administering aid not to Magere's body, but to his shadow. It was then that the secret was revealed. Magere's strength and weakness lay not in his physical body, made of stone, but in his shadow. Magere's wife immediately passed this secret to her father and the next day there was war. Magere fought brilliantly. He repelled all advances by the enemy, until one warrior, informed of Magere's secret, plunged a spear directly into Magere's shadow, fatally wounding the great Luo warrior. Magere collapsed and his body settled into the earth as a stone. His body remains in Nyanza, and Luo hunters still sharpened their spears and weapons on Magere for good luck before they enter battle or go hunting. Now, what is the moral of the story? The moral of the story is not to marry outside the Luo tribe, and not to trust the intentions of neighboring tribes. They may appear as your friends but may actually be spies.[8]

4

My Earliest Memories (1935–1954)

*I have grown up so much on my own, and I have been so much alone,
that I think I can live wherever I am doing something that I like.*

—Amos Otieno Odenyo, interview in 1965.

Until my generation, dates of birth were neither recorded nor considered important. A person estimated his age by recalling specific events which occurred during childhood. Such events often influenced the names that parents gave their children.

The concept of time, and the position of the sun in the sky, is a large component of Luo culture. For example, a boy born during the day is called "Ochieng." *Chieng* is the Luo word for sun, and the letter "O" signifies a male. A girl is called "Achieng." The first character (O vs. A) denotes gender, but the rule is not always followed. Names may also be based upon memorable events at the time of birth. A girl born during rainy season is called "Akoth." The first born of twins is "Opiyo" (*piyo* means "quick"), or if it is a girl, "Apiyo." The last born twin is called "Odongo" or "Adongo" (*dong'* means "to remain behind"). If you were born with the umbilical cord (*wino*) wrapped around your head you are named "Owino" or "Awino."

My name is Otieno—indicating I was born at night. However, this is not the only name I remember being called as a boy. I was also called "Akoko." *Koko* refers to noise, trouble, or dispute. I was nicknamed Akoko because at the time of my birth (1935) there were violent quarrels over land in Got Regea. My father also called me "Kwara" (grandfather), since I share the same name as his grandfather—who claimed one of the two hills in Got Regea. I did not grow up on Otieno's Hill (Got ka Otieno). My father had been displaced from his childhood home near the hills after the death of his father (Okwata). Until 1959, our family lived less than one mile east of Otieno's Hill.

I had six brothers: Okwata (Caleb Adet), Obuong (Lut Ezra), Okwata (Robert), Omondi (Victor), Opondo (Booker), and Dindi (Daniel); I also had three sisters: Awuor (Rosalie), Adhiambo (Olivia), and Achieng (Olga). Two children born before me passed away. I cannot remember them, except that I was told my older sister was named Sande. A child born immediately after me also died as an infant. Of the ten surviving children, I was the fourth in line. The difference in age between my eldest and youngest sibling is twenty-five years.

I had a very close relationship with my younger brother Obuong. We played games together and shared the same bedroom. However, Adhiambo has always been my closest sibling. I remember she often ran to me after one of her many quarrels with our older sister Awuor. Adhiambo and I used to sit together and fantasize over our future. We talked about which schools we would attend, what jobs we would have, and what types of household items we would buy for ourselves and the family.

My first memory in life is waking up before dawn and joining my mother and three older siblings in the fields. We tended to our crops by moonlight. I must have been only four or five years old, but I was big enough to lift a hoe. My mother was an excellent farmer, and because of her hard work and instruction we never lacked a good crop. We returned to weed the crops two months after planting the seeds. My father was often working outside of the home, so he hired men to harvest the crops for him. They arrived early in the morning expecting to be fed. There was a belief, perhaps imposed on the land owner, that if you fed the worker a good meal, it would be a blessing for the land, and the owner would yield a bountiful harvest.

Once the sun had risen we returned to the house and drank *nyuka* (porridge) for breakfast. In the early years this *nyuka* was made of millet, but over time the community shifted to *nyuka* made from maize.

Lunch and dinner consisted of *kuon* (*ugali* in Kiswahili), which is a common dish throughout sub-Saharan Africa. It is usually made from maize flour and water, and can satisfy your hunger quickly, which is why we ate it daily. *Kuon* was accompanied by collard greens (*sukumawiki* in Kiswahili). We ate meat (beef or goat) no more than three times a week. Chicken was reserved for honored guests or special occasions. Pigs were considered unclean and never eaten.

My mother's younger sisters (Hilda, Persis, and Apeles) were frequent guests in our home in Got Regea. They stayed with us to receive religious and academic training from my father. Zablon Sangoro Odenyo was very progressive and believed education should be provided not only to boys, but to girls. He taught my mother and her sisters to read basic scripture from the Dholuo bible. Throughout her life, my mother Adero only spoke Dholuo and perhaps a few words of Kiswahili, but due to Zablon's influence her youngest sisters were exposed to education at an earlier age and many became tri-lingual and literate.

My aunt Hilda Anyango (born in 1922) is one of Adero's sisters that I remember fondly. During the late 1930s she stayed in our home for a short time as my babysitter while attending school in the area. There is a bond that often develops in the Luo community between the baby and his sitter. The child is always reminded of *japidi* ("the one who sat for you,") and is expected to defer to her as he does to his own mother. In fact, this became the relationship between me and Hilda. She was the first mother I knew.

After Hilda trained as a teacher in Ng'iya Girl's School (1936–1938), she began teaching grade school in Kagonya, and transferred to Yenga Primary School in 1941. Hilda wanted a small child to live with her to do various small errands. She asked Adero for me because of the bond that existed between the two of us. I joined Aunt Hilda in Yenga sometime around the age of six. This is the earliest that I can remember attending school. I do not know if I was formally enrolled in class, but I attended class with Aunt Hilda at Yenga Primary School half of the day and completed chores and errands the rest of the day. Hilda took special pride in me and worked me hard at night to learn to read, write, and do arithmetic. I remember well the exercise books we used in those days. On the last cover there was always a multiplication chart beginning with

2 x 2 = 4, all the way up to 12 x 12 = 144. Hilda made sure I studied this chart every night before I went to sleep and she unexpectedly tested me by throwing questions like "What is 4 x 7?" On the same cover of the book there were the twelve months of the year, the ounces that make a pound, the quarts that make a gallon, the inches that make a foot, the feet that make a yard, and the yards that make a mile. She drilled these lessons into me every night, often incorporating them into a song. For example, she would break the twelve months of the year into groups of three months and sing the months sequentially in a catchy little tune. I remember the pains she took to dress me in good clothes on Sunday morning and drill me on the Bible passage that I was to read in front of the congregation. Hilda was an exceptional teacher because I learned to read very well, a skill many children did not master. I practiced my arithmetic and spelling on my own by drawing numbers and letters into the dirt with a stick. I spent three years living and schooling with Aunt Hilda, and I am forever grateful to her for the experience. She made a strong impact on my appreciation for education and over the years has remained a strong influence in my life.

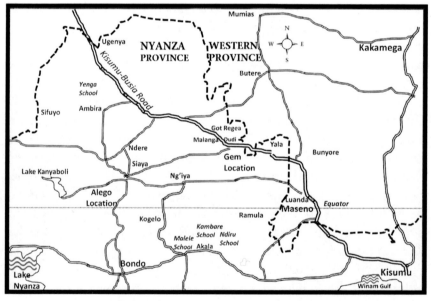

"Central Nyanza" in colonial Kenya.

My years in Yenga did not end as happily as they started. I remember once or twice a year a man visited the small house that Hilda and I occupied. He was always well-dressed and had a bicycle, a brand called Raleigh. I used to admire it and pestered him to teach me how to ride. I really did not know this gentleman, but I remember his name—Ibrahim Owuor Mango.[9] It must have been in the middle of a school year when Hilda agreed to be married to Ibrahim, who was employed as a station master by Kenya Railways near Mombasa. This meant that Hilda would relocate to the other side of the country where few of us had ever traveled. As a result, I was left in the hands of a family whose name I have now forgotten, but who did not care whether I ate or went to school. The year was 1944.

Hilda's replacement at Yenga was a poor untrained teacher who also worked as a commercial truck driver. I will refer to him only by his first name, Paulo. My memory of this bus driver is vivid, for he had one characteristic I have never been able to understand. Each week the teachers took turns as "Master on Duty." The MoD came early to school, made sure the bell rang at eight in the morning, gathered the students for a prayer and announcements, and then dispersed them to classrooms. The MoD disciplined students who violated school policy or did not learn their lessons. Paulo's way of disciplining tardy students was unique. At midday he gathered them, had them lie flat on their backs, and ordered them to open their eyes and stare straight at the sun without blinking. The students were staring at the Nyanza sun, which shines directly over the equator, at noon, the brightest time of the day.

I now lived with a family that kept me at home in the morning cleaning dishes when I should have been in school. It was inevitable that one day I would be late and subjected to Paulo's cruel punishments. When that day came, at noon, I found myself on the ground alongside a handful of other latecomers to school. Paulo barked out, "Open Your Eyes!" I was forced to obey. The pain was immense and immediate. The rays of the sun shone directly into my eyes, scorching them like a hot iron. I could hear Paulo walking up and down the row of students, barking out orders to reopen our eyes. When I sensed he was facing another direction, I quickly closed my eyes to block out the pain, but this would only provide token relief for the rays of the sun shone directly through my closed eyelids. The other students were similarly trying to avoid looking at the sun, but when Paulo caught us defying his orders, he took a thin long stick and struck us near the eyes. We individually had a terrifying choice to make—either risk being blinded by the sun, or risk the additional punishment of being struck on the eyes by our teacher. I cannot recall how long I lay there staring directly at the sun, but it may have been fifteen to twenty minutes. I do not know how many students Paulo managed to blind or damage, but his way of implementing discipline at the school in Yenga will forever live in my memory. I was subject to his cruel punishments on several occasions, and by the end of the school year I was having severe eye problems.

When I returned to Got Regea for the school holiday, my mother immediately called for my grandfather's sister, Patroba Awuor. Awuor had knowledge of traditional herbal remedies, and she came to our house every morning and evening to treat my eyes. She brought with her a strange plant that she had uprooted. After chewing the root, she blew into my eyes for ten or twenty minutes. She then took the remaining leaves, mashed them into powder with some stones, put them inside a clean handkerchief, dipped the handkerchief in water, and squeezed the liquid extract into my eyes. In time, my eyes fully recovered. I have always wondered which plant Awuor used to treat me. Unfortunately, she passed away before I learned this secret from her.

Awuor's traditional remedies were quite common when I was a young boy. A person in the village had a choice to walk many miles to a dispensary in Maseno, where if you had enough money you might be lucky to obtain some imported medicine that may or may not treat your medical ailment. Alternatively, you could go to a local herbalist who would dig around in the forest and come back with specific plants for you to drink, inhale, or apply to your skin. In our area of Gem we even had three local bone setters. They took fat made from milk, mixed it with a plant, and turned it into a liniment. They laid the broken limb on top of soft, clean banana leaves, and manipulated it very gently over an extended period of time. When the bone setter felt that the broken bones were properly aligned, he wrapped the entire limb with the banana leaves. Eventually, the bones healed. You showed your gratitude by giving the healer something of value, such as a goat or sheep. If he was a relative, you showed your gratitude in other ways, such as cooking a nice meal.

I suppose my bad experience staring at the sun at Yenga Primary School caught my parents' attention, because after having my eyes treated during school break, I did not return to Yenga. I wanted to stay in Got Regea and attend Luanda Primary School where my father was headmaster (since the 1930s). Instead, I was disappointed to learn that my father was sending me to Maseno Junior School. This school was a long walk from our house—perhaps twenty miles, which meant that I would not be staying at home except for holidays and the occasional weekend. Although I was disappointed to be leaving home once again, I believe my father thought he was helping me by providing me with higher quality education. Zablon himself had lived and studied in Maseno and was fond of the institutions in the area. Maseno Junior School had an excellent reputation because it was a unit attached to the famous Maseno High School which used the Junior School for teachers in training. My father was also convinced that his children should live with other people to learn to struggle and survive away from the easy surroundings of protective mothers, grandfathers, and other supporting kinsmen. My elder brother, Adet Okwata, had already spent several years living at Ambira School (in South Ugenya) with a rather cruel headmaster who treated Adet as a house slave. Yet my father insisted that since my brother received his meals regularly and was attending classes, hard work alone, no matter how difficult, was not a sufficient reason to complain. His belief was strengthened when my brother passed his competitive exams and was admitted to the prestigious Maseno High School. Zablon wanted me to have the same opportunity and responsibilities, so I was sent to Maseno around the age of ten (1945).

At Maseno I lived with my maternal uncle, Charles Aduwa, who was teaching carpentry at Maseno Veterinary School under Headmaster Oginga Odinga. Aduwa wanted a houseboy since his family stayed at home in Ugenya most of the season and only occasionally visited Maseno. This arrangement was fair because Aduwa was a relative and had a genuine interest in my welfare. I did not know how to cook, but he taught me. We got along well after I developed some proficiency in gathering firewood, making meals, cleaning the house, polishing his shoes, and washing and ironing his clothes on Saturdays. Once I had become a good servant, I was allowed to play Chinese checkers with his carpentry students.

It was while living with Charles Aduwa that I first had an opportunity to get a good look at white people. These Europeans came from other areas to Maseno to ride horses and play tennis. The closest that I came to them was at the tennis court, which I used to pass through on my way home from school. A number of African children were always there picking up the tennis balls that were hit outside the court. I learned that these kids were each tipped ten cents by the players after the game was over. I joined the group and picked up the balls for the Europeans, but all of this was done without any conversation. Over time, I noticed that of the many tennis balls that strayed outside the tennis court, very few were returned to the Europeans by the other boys. Whenever I ran after the balls and returned them to the players, the boys gave me dirty looks and talked among themselves. I could not understand them since they were from Bunyore and spoke Luhya whereas I only spoke Dholuo. However, I soon learned that the point was to hide the balls but pretend to keep searching for them. After the Europeans went home, the Luhya boys would retrieve the tennis balls and sell them to other kids who used them to play football. I quit before I became involved in this trickery because Charles Aduwa had noticed I was not coming home directly from school and his supper was not being made in time. The Luhya boys were also becoming unpleasant and I thought they would soon gang up on me and give me a good beating.

There was occasional tension between Africans and Indians. There were Indian shopkeepers in Yala and Kisumu but they wanted nothing to do with Africans unless we were customers. Indians were notorious for speeding past groups of Africans on the road without any apparent concern for our safety. The livelihood of the Indian shop owners depended almost entirely on African customers, yet it was not uncommon for them to run over goats being herded along the road or occasionally hit the young goat herders themselves. We began to resent this behavior. I was not a mischievous boy but can remember one day I positioned myself along the Busia road, standing as if waiting for a bus. On top of one of my toes I had placed a medium-sized stone. When a particular Asian driver notorious for speeding came barreling toward me, I launched the rock from my feet toward the vehicle much like a footballer would launch the ball into the goalkeeper's net. The stone went straight into the Asian's windshield and cracked it. I turned around and sped off into the fields. Of course I was wrong to have done this and I am somewhat embarrassed telling the story. However, it was a sign of the undercurrent of resentment we had for foreigners who called themselves Kenyans but did not treat us with respect.

I stayed with Charles Aduwa in Maseno for only one year because he was transferred elsewhere. My fortunes drastically worsened. Although my new master, Manoa, was Charles' friend, he was quite indifferent to the needs of his three sons and me. His household did not welcome me, and they often caned me for no good reason. I was unhappy, but found some consolation in the frequent trips that I made to Maseno High School to visit my brother Adet in his dormitory. If I had not eaten at Manoa's house, my brother and his friends shared their rationed dishes with me. The situation became so difficult that I was a regular absentee from school. Manoa was also transferred that year and I had to look for another person with whom to live.

This time it was a young man named Ahomo Owiti who had just finished grade ten at Maseno High School and started working on a new project called "Community Development." He lived and worked at the former army barracks called Maseno Depot some six miles from the junior school where I was enrolled. The main reason I went to live with him was that my elder brother who was also completing grade ten at Maseno was soon joining Ahomo Owiti as an assistant. Ahomo had four greedy and unpleasant sisters living with him. Their demands on the resources of a person hardly two years out of school were excessive since his wages were so little. My schooling suffered even more since I had to spend more hours cooking for an endless number of people who came to meetings at the community social hall and house guests who stopped by to see Ahomo. I became a virtual drop-out from school. My brother was not his assistant for long. Adet must have been there only two or three months and then enrolled at Kabete Jeanes School near Nairobi for his formal training as a community development officer. That second year (1946) at Maseno Junior School was wasted, and, needless to say, once more I was not chosen to try for the intermediate school entrance examination. With my brother at Kabete Jeanes School and Ahomo Owiti a perpetual bachelor and traveler who did not care whether there was food left in the house for his four sisters and me, life became intolerable. I became bitter and told my father that I did not want to stay in Maseno. At first my father insisted that I stay.

"Does Owiti feed you?" he asked.

"Yes, but not all of the time."

"Does he cane you or whip you?"

"Yes, he does."

"Does he allow you to go to school?"

"Yes, but once in a while when guests come he will have me go to school later."

My father did not seem concerned about my responses to the first two questions, but when he realized I had not attended school regularly, he began making alternative arrangements for my schooling.

I returned to Got Regea (around 1947) and for the first time attended Luanda Primary School where my father was still headmaster. I will never forget the years at this school because each day, rain or shine, I walked to school and my father headed the same direction on his bicycle without offering me a lift. My father and I departed from the same house, used the small dirt path, and reached the same destination on a daily basis. Yet, he never offered to carry me on the back of his bicycle, even if I was sick or running late. I resented this treatment at the time. However, when I look back I actually appreciate what he was doing for me. By allowing me to walk to school like the other children he was setting an example that there will be no favoritism. My father instilled in me the concept of self-reliance. I learned early in life that I would be judged solely upon my own efforts and determination.

Luanda Primary School had an excellent reputation. Zablon Sangoro Odenyo recruited the best teachers, including two brothers-in-law (Daniel Omolo and Simeon Odera) who also graduated from teacher-training at Maseno. Luanda was known for its relatively high success rate of preparing students for acceptance into intermediate schools (Nyanza's eminent scholar, Dr. Bethwell Ogot, attended Luanda under my father in the late 1930s). All my siblings attended Luanda, but not concurrently with me. It was a self-supporting school, which meant that in addition to studies, we had to work. The school had maize gardens that the students harvested. We were often hired out by residents to make construction bricks or to harvest crops. Our wages went directly to our books or uniforms.

At school I took turns as the bell ringer. I carried a clock with me, rang the bell at assembly, and then attended school. I got along well with my classmates. They respected me because I received no favoritism from my father. These five years (age twelve to sixteen), represent the only years of my childhood that I can recall actually living in Got Regea on a consistent basis. This short period of time is the basis for most of my memories of my parents and siblings.

My father was not only the headmaster of Luanda Primary School— he was also a lay minister in the Anglican Church. Zablon Sangoro actually participated in laying the foundation of Saint Peter's Church in Got Regea, where he performed all church functions except for communion, baptism, and burial. I remember that his sermons stressed love between family and community, and the importance of telling the truth. Saint Peter's Church functioned like a headquarters for five or six other churches in the region. Got Regea's sole ordained pastor was Simeon Nyende, who preached at the Got Regea church about once a month. Lazaro Okongo and later Blasio Osiro took *sadaka* (offerings) from the congregation. Before the current brick version of the church was built (in the 1960s) there was a large mud-walled and *olenge* grass thatched church in the same field. It was the best and most impressive church in the area, and it overflowed with congregants, especially when Simeon Odera arrived. Simeon Odera was not only a teacher at Luanda Primary School, but the church's choirmaster. I have never before or since witnessed such an inspirational scene in Got Regea. Odera arrived with a small organ which he operated by pushing pedals, much like a sewing machine. How he learned to play this musical machine

I do not know, but we all admired this new instrument and his ability to play it. His choir was well-trained and sang beautiful hymns in Dholuo. Odera taught his choir how to sing soprano, alto, tenor, and bass. After service, his choir packed up the organ and took it with them for use at another church service. It was a close-knit congregation of distant family members. For example, Reverend Simeon Nyende was a brother-in-law to Simeon Odera. Simeon Odera was my uncle, for he married my mother's sister Apeles Akong'o. Reverend Nyende was also a distant cousin to my father via Aruwa, the brother of my great-grandfather, Otieno.

My mother Adero was a very busy woman. Many of Saint Peter's parishioners came to our house after church for socialization and additional worship. Adero was always feeding people, and the work involved in entertaining all these guests trickled down to me and my siblings. My father constantly welcomed visiting teachers and pastors to stay with us. Reverend Festo H. Olang, who would later become the first African archbishop of the Anglican Church in Kenya, was one of many frequent guests at our house. During school breaks my brother Adet invited home school friends who lived across the gulf of the lake. I think they liked what they saw in Got Regea. Adet's friend Samson (from Kanjira) married my sister Olivia Adhiambo in 1954. The other friend, Japeth (from Kendu Bay), married my sister Rosalie in 1954.

It was my responsibility to cut the grass and clean the yard, especially in preparation for the weekends when we received many guests. I also washed and ironed my father's clothes and polished his shoes before we went to church. I think my father was one of the neatest men in Got Regea. I remember ironing one special suit that he bought in January 1952. My father was to travel with other leaders of the Anglican Church to Nairobi to meet Princess Elizabeth of England. She was already in Kenya with her husband and they were observing wildlife from "Treetops," a little hotel built on top of the trees near Mount Kenya. Unfortunately, my father came back home to Got Regea without greeting Princess Elizabeth. During her stay at Treetops, her father, King George VI of England, died. Princess Elizabeth immediately left Kenya for England to assume the throne and command over the British Empire, which at the time still included our little village of

Got Regea.

It was during my time living at home that my father retired from his position of headmaster at Luanda Primary School. Upon his retirement, Reverend Simeon Nyende presented him with a large warrior's shield, spear, and an elder's stool. This was a very prestigious honor, for these items are Luo symbols of seniority and leadership. Traditionally, the spear also had a superstitious function. In the event of fire in the village, you were supposed to throw the spear onto your roof, and it would ward off the fire from your house.

My father was leaving Luanda Primary School because he was appointed vice-president of the African Tribunal Courts in Ramula. This required that he administer cases far away from home, which resulted in me seeing less of my father, who returned to Got Regea only on weekends. My father retired as president from the Tribunal Courts around 1961.

When I look back at the situation, circumstances never allowed me to know my parents as intimately as did my siblings (who either spent more time at home or in Nyanza in general). However, I was fond of my parents, especially my father. My siblings tell me that of all Zablon's seven sons, I most closely resembled our father. I feel that my father tested me a lot in comparison to my siblings. However, perhaps my sisters and brothers would all say the same thing about themselves. I do know that my father went to great lengths to push me to the limits of my capabilities. Part of this may be that when my father left the house during the week, I was the oldest boy living at home. I was only around thirteen years old, but he put a lot of responsibility on me and wanted me to set an example for my younger brothers, Lut, Robert, and Victor. At this time my sister Olga was just a toddler, my brother Booker was just an infant, and my brother Daniel was not yet born.

My father was kind and generous, but a strict disciplinarian. He taught us to be content with what we had, and disliked being in debt to anyone. He was opposed to quarrelling and rumor-mongering. He was a determined man, and did not like excuses. My siblings who stayed home more than me say he executed punishments like caning without signs of anger. He made us repeat classes if we failed exams, and provided my sisters with the same educational opportunities as my brothers. He opened up our home to children of other villages so they too could obtain schooling and religious instruction. Father encouraged and recognized good performance, but was reserved with his compliments. He recited Luo proverbs such as *yie nimo ka dhi gowo* (a boat capsizes just when it is about to dock), to reinforce diligence and modesty. He showed he cared for us through his attention to our upbringing, and by his example. My father was fair and honest, distant yet approachable. During family meetings he made me feel like he valued my opinion. I looked up to him in the home like a student does to a teacher.

My mother Adero was very similar to my father. She was the hardest working person I have ever known. She literally kept our house together while father was working outside the home. She instilled in all of us a sense of responsibility, thrift, and a work-ethic—also by example. Mother was very obedient to her husband, and supported all his wishes. I think Zablon could not have been as successful a father and community leader without her. They were of the same mind, and never once did anyone in our family see them quarrel or fight. She was a woman of few words, but more likely to compliment us than Zablon. She fully embraced Christianity, but was more respectful of traditional Luo customs than my father.

When I was approximately fourteen years of age (1949), it was time for me to undertake the Luo adult initiation rite of *nak*. Most tribes in Kenya have some type of ritual that boys and girls have to go through to become adults. For example, Masaii boys may have to kill a lion, and Kikuyu boys are circumcised. Kamba people filed down their upper teeth. Luo boys must have their six lower teeth removed. This process has largely died out, but in the 1940s and 1950s *nak* was still a symbol of adulthood. I cannot say where this tradition originated, but I have heard there was a Luo warrior long ago who contracted "lockjaw" and could not be fed properly. Since that time all Luo teenagers of fighting age were instructed to have their six lower teeth removed so that if they contracted this disease they could still be fed. Apparently my parents saw no contradiction between *nak* and Christianity because not only did both of my parents undertake *nak*, my two elder sisters had undertaken *nak*. One day my mother came to me and told me it was my turn. My father was neutral and did not pressure me at all. However, my mother came from a more traditional upbringing and insisted.

I remember my older sister Olivia Adhiambo guiding me to an old man's home near the Regea market. In the courtyard, under a tree, I knelt down before this man. He took out a metal tool resembling a screwdriver. I knew it was going to be painful, but if I cried, I would never be considered a man. I opened my mouth, and the old man inserted the tool between my teeth. He began to maneuver the tool back and forth until he forcibly removed six of my lower teeth. It was very painful. There was no anesthetic or ice to numb my gums. It was just me, the old man, and his metal tool. It took several weeks for my gums to heal, but afterwards, my mother presented me with a very nicely cooked chicken. Following *nak*, it was time to build my own *simba*. I was now considered a man and it was expected that I no longer live in my parents' house.[10]

I was still attending Luanda Primary School, but with my father's retirement from the school, our new headmaster was now Daniel Omolo (future Bishop and husband to my maternal aunt Persis). Headmaster Omolo barred me from taking the entrance examination for intermediate school on the basis of my age. The two years cooking for people at Maseno and being a truant from school had worked against me. I was noticeably taller than my classmates in Luanda Primary School. Omolo told me that intermediate schools preferred younger pupils and that I was already too old. There was some truth to this since each primary school wanted to promote students who could not only pass the crucial intermediate school entrance examination but also find a seat available in class. When intermediate schools were faced with a choice of two qualified students for one seat, they chose the younger of the two. Headmaster Omolo therefore saw my age as a liability. However, during my first year at Luanda I had improved my standing in class, and Omolo was faced with a decision between age and class performance. This crisis was solved with the assistance of my elder brother Adet, who had finished studies in Kabete Jeanes School and had started work as a community development officer in Akala. Two miles from Akala was Malele Primary School, which was selecting their best students to sit for the intermediate school examination. Adet was friends with Malele Primary

School's headmaster, who agreed to list my name along with his pupils. I joined the students of Malele Primary School in taking the intermediate school entrance examinations (which were held at Kambare School). At least six of us passed and we were eventually admitted to various intermediate schools. I was one of three students selected to attend Ndiru Intermediate School at the end of January 1952.

Ndiru Intermediate School, located south of Got Regea (in Seme Location), had been a primary school for some time. In 1952 it had been granted intermediate status, meaning it would take its first grade five students. Some thirty-six of us from various primary schools in Central Nyanza formed the pioneering class of Ndiru Intermediate School. Although we were prepared for Ndiru, it was not prepared for us. It was supposed to be a boarding school, yet there were no dormitories. The construction of the first dormitory and classroom was in progress, and we were required to help. In our first year we had to live with nearby families while we labored on the construction of school buildings.

This time I lived with *Mzee* (Elder) Olenyo, an old cattleman and Sunday preacher who was quite influential in the Ndiru area. I attended his sermons at church, and received my Holy Communion admission card titled *"Ushiriki wa Meza ya Bwana."* One advantage of living in *Mzee* Olenyo's household was its nearness to school. I was joined by another young man from Kano location named Gerson Owiti. Several of Olenyo's own children were attending Ndiru Primary School. Olenyo was an understanding old man with a wife who made sure that we had breakfast before we went to school and supper when we returned. My only problem with the old man was that he expected Owiti and me to herd his cattle on Saturdays and Sundays. Owiti came from a cattle family and was familiar with milking and grazing cattle. Since my immediate family did not raise a lot of cattle, I knew little about them and did not care to learn. Instead, on most weekends I made a habit of going to visit my older brother Adet at his community center. Olenyo did not like my weekend absences and finally told me so in a heated fashion. His anger evaporated when I told him I was willing to do other chores, such as garden work, which I had done back in Got Regea.

Fortunately, the first dormitory was ready the second year. Most of the thirty-six students moved in with the exception of a few whose real homes were in the vicinity. Unfortunately, Ndiru still had no arrangements for cooks and maintenance support. This meant that four students were chosen every morning to go to the kitchen and make *nyuka* for breakfast, *kuon* for lunch, and more *kuon* for dinner. Headmaster Atudo and the prefect bought the food, but we, the students, cooked it. The prefect's job was to schedule some students to walk the two miles to fetch water from a local spring, some to gather firewood and others to work in the kitchen. This was done in rotation, and those who were assigned to cook often missed their classes. There were always four or five students missing from class and everyone knew that they were the day's cooks. Most of us did not know how to cook for thirty-six people, and so the food was often poorly prepared and tasted bad. After one semester, a cook was hired, although we still collected water and firewood for him and journeyed on weekends with sacks of maize on our heads to the local grinding mill located in Awach, approximately five miles away.

Living in the school compound was much better than living in private homes because student problems were shared and no one felt that he was laboring for someone else. We worked for our own welfare under a spirit of camaraderie. Eventually I became prefect and responsible for scheduling chores and handling the various complaints that arose from the student population. As we moved to grade seven and eight, a new group of students entered the school. They assumed more of the heavy, time-consuming work, and my class was tasked with lighter chores and allowed more time in the classroom. I should point out that while the students were only studying at the intermediate level, they were socially and emotionally mature young adults who had experienced many difficult trials. Our youngest student must have been sixteen and our oldest twenty-four. Many of these people started schooling late due to the distance between their villages and the few schools that were available.

It was at Ndiru that most of us received our first exposure to English and Kiswahili. Before Ndiru I only spoke Dholuo. I loved learning English, and was quite good at it, acquiring top grades in the subject among my classmates.

Our teachers were dedicated men. Many of them were trainees

at Siriba Teachers Training College, struggling for their teacher certification documents. Headmaster Atudo emphasized studies despite the fact that half of our time was spent in manual labor building the school. The students made strong and lasting friendships, and I often wonder what has become of their lives. At the end of 1954, we all faced the Kenya African Preliminary Examination, the gateway to high school. My final school transcripts, released in January 1955, showed a grade of A in English, and an average grade of B in most remaining subjects (Kiswahili, history, geography, civics, agriculture, handiwork, religion, and sports). I received an average grade of C in mathematics, which has always been my weakest area of study.

Although I did not obtain perfect grades in each subject, I felt I did quite well, considering that I spent much of my school time building dormitories, cooking, and collecting firewood instead of studying. Regrettably, the harsh demands of life had taken its toll on all of us and only two of thirty-six students were qualified to be admitted to high school. Their names were Nicholas Ajuoga Onunda, one of the youngest in class, and Amos Otieno Odenyo. In January 1955, Ajuoga entered Maseno High School, and I went to Kisii High School.

Odenyo family, circa 1940. (Back row, left to right)
Olivia, Zablon, Grace Dina, Hilda Obuong
(Front row) Amos Otieno, Rosalie, Lut, Adet.

Odenyo family, circa 1951.
(Back row) Amos Otieno, Victor, Robert, Lut, Olivia
(Front row) Adet, Zablon, Booker, Grace Dina, Olga, Rosalie.

Zablon Sangoro Odenyo, circa 1947. Retirement
ceremony at Luanda Primary School, where he received
a ceremonial spear, shield, and elder's stool.

5
Kisii High School, Mau Mau, & Nairobi (1955–1958)

I became a very ambitious person. Whatever I did I wanted to do it well and move onto the next step… the horizon beyond you. That is the biggest lesson [from Kisii High School] that stayed with me.

—Amos Otieno Odenyo, interview in August 2005.

To be merely selected to attend high school in Kenya was an accomplishment in the 1950s. At the time, the entire country had perhaps under twenty good high schools, and they could afford to be very selective in their acceptance of incoming students. When I learned I was going to Kisii High School (K.H.S.) I was quite happy. K.H.S. was an established Government African School (G.A.S.) with an excellent reputation. Although it was not as close to home as I would have liked, it was still in Nyanza Province. This meant I would be able to make three trips back home to Gem per year during school holidays.

In terms of distance, K.H.S. should have been only a three-hour drive from Got Regea, but if I did not plan my trip well it could take several days. Starting from the Dudi market I took a series of buses south to Kisumu, then continued south and west, below the gulf of Lake Nyanza. If I missed the connecting buses there were few travel alternatives. The roads and bridges near Ahero were often washed out by rivers, making land routes impassable. Therefore, many of us living north of the lake bypassed the flood-prone areas by taking a lake steamer from Kisumu to Kendu Bay. From there we continued the journey by local buses.

I arrived in Kisii in January 1955, at the age of nineteen. I found K.H.S. very different from the school I left in Ndiru. K.H.S. was modern and beautiful, complete with different buildings for various subjects. The school had running water and shower facilities. This alone was a privilege, but we also had a power generator that started at dusk, so we were able to study until ten at night without resorting to candles. K.H.S. was located on the slopes of a hill which exposed it to constant cool winds and frequent heavy rains. Instead of maize, the school gardens had coffee that we would cultivate in the mornings before attending class.

The dormitories did not have separate rooms for each student. Instead, they were large halls containing two rows of beds arranged in the style of army barracks. The dorms were named after hills in the South Nyanza region, such as "Manga," "Ruri," "Sameta," and "Wire." The dormitories were clean and quite comfortable, but since they each housed up to thirty students, they were never private. Our bed frames were elevated wood planks, and our mattresses were empty sacks which we stuffed with dry grass.

The teaching staff consisted of Europeans and Africans represented in nearly equal proportions. Most of these Europeans were dedicated teachers who were anxious to have their students pass college entrance examinations (such as the highly regarded Cambridge School Certificate Examination). Mr. Thomas Sharrad (the school principal and English teacher) soon left to take charge of Siriba Training College (now Maseno University). He was a fatherly gentleman and most of us liked and respected him.

Mr. Sharrad was replaced by Michael Grounds, a graduate of Oxford University, who also taught English. Grounds was a leader, instructor, and disciplinarian. Mr. Westwell, the Physics teacher, was a very dedicated instructor and gave much of his time to us in the laboratory, even outside school hours. The biology teacher, Mrs. Lynn Powes, a young Scottish mother of a six year old boy, was one of the best instructors I have ever known. The class highly respected her for her knowledge and teaching ability. We nicknamed her "*Okombe.*" In

Luo culture, it was common to give new lady acquaintances (especially the recently married) nicknames as a sign of camaraderie. During that period, nicknames reflected modern artifacts such as *ojiko* (spoon) *apoda* (powder) or *okombe* (porcelain tea cup). Modernity was a sign of respect. However, we resented Okombe's veterinarian husband who often walked into our classroom while she was lecturing and proceeded to sit on the teacher's platform to wait for her without paying attention to how he dressed. His pants were often unbuttoned, and his careless manner of sitting was an embarrassment to his wife. The students joked about how such a well-mannered, brilliant woman could marry such a man. However, our first experience with the British instructors (especially the English, physics, and biology instructors) was overwhelmingly positive. If they had the condescending attitudes that we heard existed in other schools, they seldom showed it.

At K.H.S. we met African teachers who had been educated abroad. Among them was Nicholas Otieno, a graduate of Makerere University (Uganda) and Durham University (Britain). Nicholas Otieno taught chemistry, and was so full of himself and overwhelmed by how civilized he thought he was that he constantly called us "bushmen." His ill-fitting blue Durham University blazer was worn perhaps seven days a week. The Durham University badge on the blazer was a fetish without which he could not exist. He was the archetype of the conceited, snobbish graduate that English education tended to produce at Makerere. He never inspired any of us, for he thought no one could match his academic accomplishments. However, I must say that he was a confident, capable, and conscientious instructor whom I managed to like before I graduated.

The most memorable history teachers were African. Mr. Julius Ger in particular was very knowledgeable and had vivid instructional methods. He literally acted through his narration of historical figures and events, giving the impression that he had been present at the scene during the time in question. It was fascinating to listen to stories of the world beyond Kenya's borders. Samuel Onyango Ayodo, who had just acquired a B.Sc. in Education from the United States, managed to instill in us a strong desire to see and experience the world. I was soon able to name every province in Australia, and identify every state in America. Ayodo was the complete opposite of Nicholas Otieno. Ayodo was the first instructor to introduce a test question that read "compare, contrast, and criticize..." Before him, our tests were mostly a re-gurgitation from a lesson book or lecture. He also taught a version of the American War of Independence that differed from our English text, *A Short History of British Expansion*, written by an English historian, J.A. Williamson. Ayodo later went into politics, becoming a cabinet minister in the KANU government. There was also Douglas Odhiambo, a quiet and knowledgeable scientist who taught mainly physics. Nathaniel Oluoch, best known for being very strict, taught us mathematics. Other African teachers at K.H.S. that I can recall were Arum (English), George King Omolo (English), Mtula (history), Omare (Kiswahili), and Shishia Shirao (geography). Most of these men had previously attended Makerere University.

In our third year, several new instructors to the school stained the respect that we held towards British teachers. For example, Loftus, an old retired army colonel, antagonized us by enforcing school rules to an extent that was sometimes unreasonable. One of the school's rules was lights out between ten o'clock in the evening and six o'clock in the morning. However, it was known and accepted that some juniors and seniors nearing their college entrance examinations often woke up around four o'clock in the morning, went to empty classrooms, and studied until everyone else woke up at six o'clock in the morning. Most instructors tolerated this as long as the seniors did not interfere with others who were still sleeping. Colonel Loftus, however, patrolled the school compound at four o'clock in the morning and punished those he found studying. Although I was caught several times, I kept waking up and finding alternative hiding places for studying early in the mornings.[11] I came to rely on the assistance of Shem Arungu Olende who slept two beds down from me in the Ruri dormitory. Shem was familiar with the school laboratory and with his access to that building we could covertly study at odd-hours of the night undetected by the Colonel.

There was tension at times between the European and African teachers. For example, there was an incident involving Mr. Wiesler, a new teacher from Germany. Mr. Wiesler was fluent in English, having obtained a degree on the subject at the prestigious Oxford University in England. The German always took the liberty of correcting the English pronunciation, not only of us students, but of his fellow African teachers. On one particular occasion he corrected the wrong person, the confident Nicholas Otieno. A brawl almost ensued. Otieno literally shouted at Mr. Wiesler within hearing distance of many students. Mr. Otieno affirmed that he was more qualified than the German, spoke better English, and warned him to never again correct his pronunciation (Mr. Otieno later obtained a Ph.D. in botany from Cornell University in Ithaca, U.S.A., taught at the University of Nairobi, and became a United Nations official). Incidents such as these tended to build resentment between a few African and European teachers at the school, but the exemplary attitude and dedication to teaching by the majority of European instructors made such conflicts infrequent.

There were discernable differences within the European teacher communities. Mr. Taylor, for example, was different from most of the other European instructors who voiced pro-British or pro-colonization sentiments in class. Mr. Taylor actually interjected a few anti-British comments in his lectures. Looking back, I think the reason for this was that Taylor was Irish, and the Irish have had their own struggles with British imperialism. Mr. Wiesler, however, did not share Taylor's sympathies towards us. This was somewhat strange because Mr. Wiesler was Jewish and had to flee Germany during WWII. He therefore should have had some anti-imperialist sympathies, but he did not. He was even more anti-African than some of the other teachers.

Instructor Huson came fresh from Scotland to teach history. He was convinced that Africans were inherently lazy and let his students know this opinion. He demonstrated this attitude in sports as well because he had previously excelled in long-distance running. He believed that a student who could not run long distances was lazy. He tactlessly exhorted us to greater physical efforts and soon alienated the entire student body. He was also the coach of the debating team, and I remember an incident when the topic of debate turned into the merits of having European teachers at K.H.S. One student, Akich Okola, told Mr. Huson that apparently the British government had taken to using our high schools as dumping grounds for Europeans who were unfit to teach at home, and that Huson was a typical example. Huson literally cried when he heard this. I think Huson's problem was that he was new to Kenya. He did not yet realize the African high school students, who were socially mature and keenly aware of the times, would not accept his patronizing attitude toward them.

Although K.H.S.'s staff was a mixture of Europeans and Africans, the student population was 100 percent African. Even the white instructors at K.H.S. did not dare send their own children to the school as that would imply blacks and whites were of equal intelligence. They sent their own children to exclusive institutions such as the Prince of Wales School (later renamed Nairobi School).

The African students at K.H.S. came from many parts of the country, but friendships were often made, at least on campus, without regard to tribal background. However, the strength of these friendships is hard to tell. I had several friends from other tribes, but they did not visit me in Got Regea nor did I visit them in their homes, primarily due to the distances involved.

I was one of perhaps six students at K.H.S. from Gem. Together we formed a Gem Student's Union. Akich Okola was our secretary. I had actually known of Akich and his family from Maseno Junior School in 1945. The Okola family was living in the Maseno school compound which I used as a shortcut to get from my living quarters to school. Akich's older brother did not like me and used to harass me in an attempt to deter me from using that shortcut. However, in 1955 Akich and I became good friends at Kisii. Achayo Ominde, who later went on to practice law in Kisii, was also from Gem. The Gem Student Union addressed various issues like academic standards, holiday events, and organized buses to take us back to Gem during school breaks.

K.H.S. was known for its liberal attitude compared to other high schools, especially those having missionary sponsorship (such as Maseno). If we could afford it, students were allowed to wear shoes, socks, jackets, and long pants during weekends. In other schools these minor and really meaningless privileges were reserved for the teachers. On Sundays students attended churches of their choice away from school if they desired, provided they returned to school on time (church attendance was deemed compulsory in other schools). On weekends we could venture into Kisii town and purchase non-cafeteria food. However, most of us did not have any money to buy anything.

I should point out that it was during my years at Kisii that I owned my first shoes. They were not new however. They were handed down to me by my brother-in-law, Japheth Odhiambo, who married my sister Rosalie in 1954. I was lucky that the shoes were too big rather than too small. I proudly wore them on weekends, and eventually managed to buy a pair of socks.

Amos Otieno Odenyo, circa 1955.
Wearing first pair of shoes at Kisii High School.

Saturday dances were frequent, although we were not allowed to invite women. This meant that boys at K.H.S. would partner with other boys as dancing partners, a scene which would easily be misinterpreted in some cultures as training for homosexuality. This, however, would be a cultural misinterpretation. As far as I know, the Nandi, Kipsigis, Kisii, Luo, and Abaluhya ethnic groups of the student population do not practice homosexuality. The idea of same gender sexual interest was not even a concept that I was aware of while living in Nyanza, but had such activity existed, the participants would have been banished from their communities. My dancing partners were Akich Okola and Martin Miruka Nyiendo, and together we won many dancing competitions. Although Martin was from Nyakach, not Gem, we became very good friends. He entered K.H.S. one year after me and I showed him how to adjust to school life and prepare for his exams.

Music was played from 78 RPM discs on a hand-cranked gramophone. The music was provided by the school as part of the policy of promoting fraternization among the students. The music was mostly Congolese and Cuban. We referred to Cuban music as G.V. based upon that being the record label of the production company. We danced to the famous soloists Tobias Oyugi, Othema, and George Sibanda from Rhodesia (Zimbabwe). There was music by Alango Obiye, and Mwenda Jean Bosco, a popular Congolese guitarist. The fact that K.H.S. allowed dancing at all was a testament to the school's liberal attitudes. Friends such as Laban Otieno, who attended Maseno High School, were strictly prohibited from organizing any dances on school grounds.[12]

I had two girlfriends from Gem during my years at K.H.S. The first was a Catholic girl from Yala. She was training as a primary school teacher in Southern Nyanza so we took the same bus and ferry most of the way to school, then parted ways. During holidays our dates consisted of walking around the Yala shops and sitting on the banks of the river. My other girlfriend was a dancing partner from Dudi. I did not spend much time with them as I was always studying.

K.H.S. was known for its performance in athletics. Its way of training athletes was to have yearly inter-dormitory competition in football, volleyball, swimming, hockey, and many other athletic activities. The fierce competition among dormitories produced the winners who then represented the school in varsity competition. Famous runners like Nyandika Maiyoro, the first Kenyan to win in an Olympic marathon, used to practice barefoot at the Kisii fields. Maiyoro was the coach to Stephen Machooka, who became the first Kenyan to compete and shatter athletic records in the U.S. collegiate system (Cornell University, 1960–1964).

I did not grow up near water suitable for swimming, so I was the worst swimmer in the Ruri dormitory. My friend Martin Nyiendo tried to teach me to swim, and eventually I was able to finish one lap without sinking. K.H.S. did not provide us with swimming costumes or towels. Our swimming competitions were held completely in the nude in front of male and female European spectators. After each race we shivered in the cold, trying to dry ourselves.

Although I was very poor in swimming, I was very accomplished in football, volleyball, field hockey, track, shot put, and discus throwing. I served as captain of the school's volleyball team, and remember Shem Olende as a very good player. I enjoyed playing field hockey more than any other game, and once won the school's championship medal. Akich Okola and I played the position of defense on the field hockey team, and when Winston Ochoro Ayoki joined the school he became one of our best goalkeepers. Together we won many games against our rivals from Kakamega, Kisumu, and Maseno.

For the last two years at K.H.S. I was elected "senior boy," and served as a member of the editorial board of the annual school magazine. I sang bass in the school choir. I was the soloist for the American song "Oh Shenandoah:"

> Oh Shenandoah, I long to hear you, Away you rolling river, Oh Shenandoah, I long to hear you, Away, I'm bound away, 'cross the wide Missouri.

We had entered high school during the height of a guerrilla war in Kenya, which the British refer to as the "Mau Mau rebellion." This rebellion was organized by Kikuyu fighters from the Mount Kenya area. They conducted military operations and acts of sabotage against the British to force them to leave Kenya. The Kikuyu took a military approach against the British because much of their land was stolen from them. The British imprisoned many Kikuyu leaders and tribesmen, including Jomo Kenyatta (who later became Kenya's first president). Most of the other tribes in Kenya were not active in the fighting but supported the Mau Mau politically. Achieng Oneko from Nyanza was one steadfast supporter. Oneko was the editor of the *Ramogi* newspaper that was distributed in Got Regea and all the other villages in Luo-land. The *Ramogi* was written in Dholuo and educated us on many things, including our struggle for freedom (*uhuru*) from the British. Oneko and Kenyatta were actually arrested by the British in 1952, and they spent nine years in a colonial jail along with four other leaders called the "Kapenguria Six." Kenya's first lawyer, Argwings Kodhek (from Gem) actually represented many Mau Mau leaders in court, doing so without pay. Later, when the British were negotiating independence terms, Luo politicians such as Oginga Odinga and Tom Mboya actually rallied around the imprisoned Kenyatta and told the British "No Kenyatta, No Uhuru." K.H.S. students of all tribes were similarly united in support of independence and the release of Jomo Kenyatta from prison. The European teachers were against this of course, and when one classmate placed a picture of Jomo Kenyatta on the wall of our dormitory, the colonial police were called to investigate.

Students gathered around the school's one radio receiver at seven o'clock every evening to hear the latest political events in the country. We listened to the colonial government's radio broadcasts and tried to decipher what was happening with the struggle for independence. Of course the British broadcasters said only negative things about the rebellion leaders, but we all secretly considered them heroes. These men included Waruhiu Itote (aka "General China"), a key leader in the Mau Mau rebellion who was captured by the British in 1954. Another freedom fighter, Field Marshall Dedan Kimanthi, was captured in 1956. He was called a "terrorist" by British newscasters and executed in 1957. We heard about his death by radio, but despite what was said about him, we considered him a martyr in our struggle for independence.

My only personal encounters with the Mau Mau struggle occurred on the few occasions I traveled to visit relatives in Nairobi during school breaks. I could not walk but a few blocks before being searched by the police, who wanted to see my *kipande* (identification card). I saw people being marched off to detention camps, and there were frequent early-morning raids by police. I saw Mau Mau supporters armed with *pangas* (machetes) hack two Indian brothers to death. They were owners of a butcher shop, and I was told that they failed to contribute food for the Mau Mau in the forest. Nairobi was a very tense place in the mid-1950s. There was unprecedented violence on both sides.

Nyanza Province did not have Mau Mau activity, but there were detention camps near Kisumu (e.g., Mageta Island) that held Mau Mau. One morning there were a lot of armed police in Land Rovers traveling through Got Regea, looking for seven escaped Mau Mau. The police even searched homes, for many people had sympathy for the Mau Mau detainees and would have sheltered them.

I graduated from K.H.S. in November of 1958, at the age of twenty-three. If one can summarize the mood of the fifty-eight students who took the Cambridge School Certificate Examination in 1958, one would say that they all left K.H.S. with a very strong determination to make successes of themselves in whatever they pursued. Many K.H.S. graduates have been educated abroad with several earning Ph.D. degrees. Other graduates from K.H.S. have become doctors, lawyers, and engineers. For example, Akich Okola became an accomplished attorney. Winston Ayoki became Principal of Ramogi Institute of Advanced Technology (RIAT) and a Member of Parliament. Shem Olende and Martin Nyiendo became Engineers. Frederick O. Ouka obtained a M.P.A. from Syracuse University in 1967 and held senior positions in the Kenyan government until 1994. Michael G. Okeyo became a Kenyan diplomat. Andronico O. Adede worked for the United Nations and in 1995 published a book (*The Quadrangle*) about our time at K.H.S.

Our group formed a strong relationship of comradeship and mutual respect. Although there was no organized alumni association to act as a means of maintaining contact, the relationship between many of the former students has continued through informal means. We were conscientious students, especially in our last year. It should be remembered that it was only the third year that Kisii had been a full high school, meaning that the class of 1956 was the first class to sit for their school certificate examinations, yet the entire school had a stake in the results.

School officials knew their reputations and our future depended on how well we performed in comparison with other high schools. Students themselves knew this and studied very hard, but the mediocre results of the 1956 and 1957 groups surprised everyone because the classes had some of the best students. While the students performed well in many subjects, their performance in English writing was poor, thus disqualifying many from admission to the prestigious Makerere College. Only one of the 1957 class was admitted to Makerere College. Most of us had watched our upper-classmates study through the night and expected them to do very well. When they did not, fear spread throughout the entire campus. This is why our 1958 group (the third high school class) studied even harder. Our results were better and K.H.S. for the first time sent three students to Makerere College and several were admitted to Royal Technical College (University of Nairobi). With the school certificate examination done in November 1958, our high school careers ended and we all went to different parts of Kenya to wait for the results which were released three months later.

It was the usual practice not to return home to wait for the results. Instead, students finishing high school left for the towns before the ink was dry on their last examination paper. The idea was to get a job in the city, especially Nairobi. This trend has continued up to now despite the efforts of the national government to promote a "back to the land" policy. Urban jobs for high school students have diminished considerably with the increase in college graduates. Every January, Nairobi welcomes an army of high school graduates joining one of the longest unemployment lists in Africa. During our time, however, with a diligent and persistent search, most of us found jobs by June. In fact, those who had not landed a job by June were often viewed by their peers, perhaps unfairly, as incompetents. I do remember three in our year who failed to get jobs, and I had a similar attitude toward them.

The job hunt itself was an art. It began by first finding someone to live with in Nairobi. The extended family was useful here and kin ties were often recognized and honored that had never been used before. It was common for a Nairobi resident to be confronted unexpectedly by an unknown job seeker claiming to be a relative and wanting a place to stay. The job seeker traced his genealogy to identify the relationship which, no matter how remote, must be recognized by the established resident. He could choose to ignore such a claim at his own peril since news of this lack of hospitality would reach those in his rural home village. Such people would resent his behavior. It would be said of him *ok en jawat*, meaning that he does not value family relationships. After obtaining accommodations through a relative or friend, the new resident began his search for employment.

I stayed with a maternal cousin, Paul Obara, who worked as a bookkeeper for the railways. We both woke up every day around six o'clock in the morning, made tea, and left. He took his bicycle to work, a thirty minute ride from his apartment in Ofafa Maringo (a newly built area for Africans). He wanted to be at work ten minutes before starting at eight o'clock in the morning in order to read the newspapers. I left the house soon after he did and walked the same distance to town. The strategy was that you allowed the office workers at least an hour to begin their routine before you knocked at the doors to ask for a job. By nine-thirty, job hunters had walked from their various temporary quarters to the offices. A job seeker had to work out his strategy each morning to cover one section of the town and then another, but became quite flexible depending on leads he received from friends, relatives, newspapers, and rumors. The job seeker had to present himself as well dressed as possible at the very time he could least afford it. Hence, he could not survive too long without a job. The cash resources of a job hunter were quickly exhausted. The fact that relatives at home expected him to send them money after working for three months added to his anxiety. For some it took a week to land a job, while for others it might have been a month or more depending upon their diligence, initiative, and luck.

I was very lucky. I was in Nairobi less than a week when I walked into a bookstore on Government Road to buy envelopes to write applications for jobs. I took the liberty of walking upstairs and asked the manager, Mr. Cutland, if there was a job. We chatted for a few minutes and then he gave me a slip of paper stating that I had an eleven o'clock appointment with him the next day. I went back and he showed me around the shop and finally told me they could use me as a shop assistant while I waited for the results of my exam. After the results came, I could stay if I liked them and they liked me, but he could not consider me a regular employee until I knew the results. I accepted the position and found myself an employee of the Education Suppliers Association (E.S.A.). The next day I was selling books, showing customers around the bookstore, packing the orders, and stealing a few minutes when possible to look inside some books. This was my first paid job.

I took the bus every morning to work, but to save money I walked home in the evening. I began to contribute to the buying of food where I lived, but Paul Obara was good to me in that he insisted I first buy other things I needed, such as an extra pair of shoes, or an extra shirt. Being shop assistant was interesting because many people whom I knew stopped by the shop to browse or buy books. When the results of the Cambridge School Certificate appeared in February 1959, I learned that I was one of eighteen students who had passed at the second level (Division II). I was given marks of distinction in history and English literature, but showed weakness in science and mathematics. Shem Olende was one of only eleven students to graduate in top honors within Division I. Twelve students graduated in Division III, and seventeen students failed.

On March 14, 1959, Michael Grounds, my former Headmaster at K.H.S., provided me with a professional recommendation:

> His result in English literature is the best this school has yet had. He is a conscientious and hard-working student, of lively intelligence and always ready to ask questions where he does not fully understand a point. His conduct and character during the three years I knew him were uniformly good. He was a capable and reliable senior boy, and on occasion deputized for prefects. He took an active interest in games and other house and school activities. He showed himself willing to listen to advice and correct any minor mistake.

With my satisfactory results, the manager at E.S.A. confirmed my job and increased my salary to 350 shillings a month. Unfortunately, it was still a low paying position compared to those who entered government service or private companies. Three of us Africans waiting for our high school exam results and several European girls were employed as shop assistants. In addition, a few older European women were working at the shop. There was a strategy in the mind of the manager. He wanted to train the three Africans for branch manager jobs in some of the smaller towns where E.S.A. was expanding. George, an African employee, was later transferred to Mombasa as branch manager, and I would soon be transferred to Kisumu to relieve a European branch manager going on vacation. However, we were soon dissatisfied. There was an obvious double standard in pay because the European girls who joined us as shop assistants were earning double our salary and doing less work. Their qualifications were the same as ours. Even when George was transferred as branch manager, his salary was not increased since the Nairobi manager argued that the cost of living in Mombasa would be lower. Finally, the job seemed to have no room for advancement since it was really a London-based firm and Nairobi was merely a branch. The only higher positions were the manager and his assistants, the accountant, and the shop supervisor. Hence we were actually looking for jobs while working at E.S.A.

I was the first to quit under circumstances unfavorable to the company. While I was working in the Nairobi shop I used my lunch breaks to attend interviews. I attended one in the police headquarters and I was waiting for results of that interview when I was transferred to the E.S.A. Kisumu branch. The European manager had shown me around the shop and was ready to start her vacation when I received a letter of acceptance to the Police Training College. This was a much superior opportunity and I could not turn it down. It paid approximately 450 shillings a month plus another 250 in housing, uniform, and travel allowances. When I told the old lady who was anxious to start her vacation that I was leaving, she almost collapsed and I felt embarrassed and guilty.

I had to take a medical examination and report to the Police Training College to begin training as an assistant inspector of police. George, who was at the Mombasa branch, later abruptly quit his job with the E.S.A. to join the Immigration Service. Another African employee left E.S.A. to join the American Information Service Library. I have since wondered whether our leaving under these circumstances was not unfair to the company, but, on the other hand, it was unfair of them to pay us so little.

I had no idea what police work involved except that I had seen policemen in the courtrooms, patrol cars and on traffic duty. However, I never had a personal desire to join the force. I knew that the police were both feared and respected by civilians, and it was one way for me to meet the challenges of the changing times. Independence was coming to Kenya, and greater opportunities for Africans were coming with it. The British had always imported their high school failures to the colonies to become police inspectors. Political pressure was on the British colonial government to open up the commissioned ranks for African high school graduates. Previously, there was always a resistance to such a course based on the assumption that Africans could not perform well at this level, and that they should join as constables but never be promoted above the non-commissioned ranks. Most Africans who had joined the police in the past were enlisted as constables since they were illiterate and could not hope to rise above the rank of sergeant. The police force provided one of the most prestigious and best paying jobs for Africans at that time. Hence it became a challenge for us who accepted the position of prospective officer to prove that Africans could go through the same training and become inspectors directly upon graduation.

Amos Otieno Odenyo, 1958.

6

Kiganjo Police Academy & Mombasa Station (1959–1961)

The rigidity of the course taught me one lesson—self help.

—Amos Otieno Odenyo, 1965 letter.

Kiganjo is located about one-hundred miles north of Nairobi to-wards Mount Kenya. It is a cold and rainy area. Kiganjo Police Academy trains all the police personnel in Kenya. The academy was divided into two sections. The "Junior Wing" trained constables, corporals, and ser-geants, and the "Senior Wing" trained inspectors and above. Our class of eight Africans, all from varied high schools, was known as course #2/59, under Chief Inspector Phillips. We were to train at the acad-emy for nine months.

Kiganjo Police Academy was similar in many ways to life at Kisii High School, except the police training was of a military nature and different subjects were taught. We woke up at six o'clock in the morn-ing to run three miles to downtown Kiganjo and three miles back to our training station. We showered, put on our uniforms (caps, boots, khaki shorts, and bush shirt), and ate breakfast in the mess hall. At eight o'clock we lined up in a squad formation. Each man alternated weekly as squad leader, and during that week the leader was respon-sible for making sure that the squad was at the right place at the right time, as well as properly saluting higher officials and returning salutes from the lower ranks. The squad leader of the week then marched us to the field for drilling. There we met our instructor, Phillips, who was an Irishman. Phillips taught us how to march with rifles, salute with rifles, and the rest of the manual of arms. After we learned to follow the drill commands we had to learn how to give them. Later he handed us over to the master drill sergeant of the whole college.

This sergeant was an African who commanded the whole evening parade consisting of more than seventy squads. I have never heard anyone who could shout louder than Sergeant Munyaū Kavindu from Ukambani. Sergeant Kavindu decided we did not know enough drills and said that before he would give us some of the recruit constables to practice on, he must make sure we knew the commands ourselves. I must say that despite his harshness, he knew his job well. Two elements of drilling ought to be mentioned. One is the constant harassment that the sergeant used. A slight mistake on our part brought a barrage of name calling. Sergeant Kavindu had a collection of dirty adjectives to describe a violator, most of them questioning our masculinity. We could not answer back or show facial disgust, for that would have been construed as disobedience. We had to learn to accept verbal abuse. If we could not adjust to this sort of treatment there was no point in our trying to become police officers because frustration formed a normal part of the work. An attitude of patience and calmness in the face of threats and tension was what Kavindu was attempting to develop. Sergeant Kavindu was also sensitive about his low rank and lack of education. He was basically illiterate, and had memorized the commands in English. Although he was a sergeant, it must have taken him some twenty years to reach that rank. Here we were, direct from high school, young and wearing inspector's uniforms. He was supposed to salute us at all times off the drill field. Any indication that we were looking down on him could have been disastrous. We respected him and actually admired his performance, especially in the evenings when all-college parades were held. Kavindu would prepare the whole parade and then hand it over to Superintendent Newman who would present us to the commandant of the college (an assistant commissioner of police).

At ten o'clock in the morning we marched from the drill field to the classroom, where we were taught the criminal code. This required a lot of reading. At noon we went for lunch. All the movement back and forth in the compound had to be done in squad formation. After lunch we resumed class from one to two o'clock in the afternoon. At two o'clock we learned about weapons. This centered on target practice with pistols, long range shooting with rifles, and weapons maintenance and safety. These skills were taught by a different instructor whose specialty was weapons. He was more like Sergeant Kavindu, although he was a European. He looked too old for his rank, compared to other Europeans.

Between three and five o'clock our most interesting class was held. Chief Inspector Brown specialized in crime investigation and was an excellent teacher. He taught us how to collect evidence without disturbing the scene of the crime. Brown demonstrated how to test a driver for sobriety, how one piece of hair can lead you to solve a rape crime, and how to spot various other clues. We learned how to make arrests, search for weapons, interrogate suspects, book prisoners into cells, and prepare a charge sheet. Mr. Brown was an excellent instructor in these things, bringing out many varieties of hypothetical situations and problems for us to solve.

In addition to teaching at the training college, Chief Inspector Phillips arranged some interesting tours to various government units that were relevant to our career as police officers. We visited a pathologist conducting post mortems in Nairobi Hospital. It was a traumatic experience watching human bodies being cut up like chickens. Some of us walked out, but most stayed. The pathologist explained every step he took and finally determined the cause of death of two victims. We visited the jails and the gallows used for execution of condemned prisoners. We visited courtrooms in session and watched how police officials presented evidence. I must say that we were exposed to experiences that others normally did not have.

Of the instructors that crossed my path at this college, Phillips and Brown were my favorites. I was completely absorbed in what they were teaching. However, the drill sergeant, weapons instructor, and the riot drill instructor were less inspiring. They were thoroughly action-oriented and did not care to explain the significance of what they taught.

By the time we finished in December 1959, three cadets had been discharged for reasons such as incompetence, conduct unbecoming of an officer (which usually meant consorting with females at unacceptable hours), and excessive difficulty with training. Five of us finished the course. We had a sense of satisfaction and accomplishment because we proved to the colonial government that Africans, when given the chance, can accomplish the same training that had previously only been provided to European cadets. At the start there was an attitude emanating from our instructors and their superiors that the entire Africans class would drop out of the academy due to laziness and ineptitude. Some of these instructors actually tried to place obstacles in our path that may not have previously been there for the British cadets. So the remaining five were filled with pride to stand up to the test and pave the way for future generations of African policemen in Kenya. In our class was Alfred Ouma, from Busia, who in later years became a Nairobi police station chief. A tall classmate from Nandi, Julius Kitur, was our best and brightest student. A student from Gem and another Kikuyu fellow were chosen for the Special Branch (Intelligence). I noticed that these two classmates had several things in common. First, they were very good talkers, and mingled well with the entire class and instructors. Secondly, they were very good drinkers. These two attributes probably caught the eye of the instructors who valued these skills for intelligence collection purposes. These two students, halfway through their training, no longer had to wear uniforms.

**Amos Otieno Odenyo (fifth from left).
Kiganjo Police Academy, 1959.**

On graduation day, Phillips had a party for our class. The commandant shook hands with us and gave his congratulations. We were then given our first assignments as police inspectors. I was assigned to the Central Police Station in Mombasa. The next morning I took the train to Nairobi where I had a one day layover. It was here that I became a frightened witness to a riot. Indian teenage drivers had killed a number of Africans by careless driving. In the courtrooms, most traffic judges were Indians. The practice of these judges was to fine Indian defendants a small sum which their parents could easily pay. Unfortunately, the families of the Africans maimed or killed in such accidents received no financial compensation. The practice became so widespread that it pushed the already strained relations between Indians and Africans to a crisis state. During my brief stay in Nairobi, Africans took matters into their own hands. I was standing on a median of an intersection when the news began circulating that an Indian driver had just run over two Africans and failed to stop his car. Africans began picking up rocks and sticks and watching every approaching car. If they saw an Indian driver, they stoned the car. Within thirty minutes the streets were full of wrecked Indian cars. The police attempted to restrain the Africans but were only partially successful. I saw a number of policemen injured by the mob. I thought to myself, "Is this what my job is going to be in Mombasa?" Since I was traveling to my first assignment and not wearing my uniform, I could observe the incident without getting involved. I continued on my journey and arrived in Mombasa the next day.

Mombasa is a major sea port for the entire east coast of Africa. The temperature is considerably warmer than that of Nairobi. It has an international flavor that is a result of the constant stream of sailors of all nationalities entering and leaving the port. In addition to Indian and various African tribal cultures, it has strong Arab and Persian influences. To the people in Luo country, Mombasa is where young men get "lost." They acquire strange ways and do not visit their homes frequently. The Luo blame it on the prostitutes of all races who inhabit the town for the purpose of vying for the sailors' entertainment money. Additionally, the distance between Mombasa and Luo-county is great enough to make most migrant workers feel that they are free from obligations to relatives and close friends at home. Few relatives see them often enough to gossip about their ways. There is an easier and slower tempo of life in Mombasa compared to Nairobi. The hot and humid temperature requires casual dressing most of the time. I noticed that a person who works in Mombasa is not as likely to bother buying decent clothes, while those living in Nairobi regard good clothing as a necessity. The hot temperature means that adequate housing is often considered an unnecessary expense. People can sleep in the open air as long as there is no rain. It may be called a leisure and pleasure city. Prostitution is more widespread than in other cities in East Africa, and for those who cannot afford the bottled beer, there is the cheap *mnazi* liquor, made from coconut palms. Needless to say, these and other aspects of the town have some correlation to the nature of police work in Mombasa.

I reported for duty at the Central Police Station the second day after my arrival in Mombasa, and was assigned quarters within the "Mbaraki" staff compound. Throughout Kenya, police officers were assigned brown khaki uniforms, but in Mombasa, due to the heat we were issued white uniforms. I spent a month in the front desk office booking in those arrested and learning how to keep the occurrence book records. Then I was assigned a patrol car. Prior to my arrival, car patrol had been the exclusive preserve of European inspectors. The patrol car, known as "999" after the emergency telephone number, had always been occupied by one European inspector, an African driver, and two African constables. Most African officers did the foot patrol. When I was assigned the car, the driver was amazed and told me, "You know, you are the first African inspector ever to be put in charge of a patrol car in this city," and he seemed very pleased. The two constables were equally happy. I did not know the procedures in patrol, but the driver and the constables were very willing to explain:

> Before you take the car out, inspect it because someone using it before you may have put a dent on it and failed to report it. Do not leave the station without

radioing to the control room to report your departure. Never unknowingly turn off your radio while on patrol. Report your whereabouts constantly. Do not leave the car without reporting.

The lighter moments of patrol included locating stolen cars and setting up surveillance to catch the thieves. I was thrown into unexpected situations such as assisting a mother giving birth on the side of the road. Our patrol often came across unemployed youths sleeping in football fields at three o'clock in the morning. We were required to enforce the vagrancy laws by detaining them and repatriating them back to their home villages throughout Kenya. However, this was a futile task. They simply came back to Mombasa the next day, looking for work.

We often encountered foreign sailors wandering around in the nude after midnight. We would offer them first aid blankets and attempt to learn what had happened. The frustrating part of this situation was that we knew that the prostitutes lured the sailors to their quarters only to have them robbed by their pimps. Yet the sailors, being new to the area, could not trace their previous whereabouts. The sailors could not name the prostitutes, for all the girls gave their names as "Maria." The cab drivers were often the pimps and the sailors would be robbed of everything of value before reaching their intended destination. The best we could do was to drive the sailors to their ships, although we were not supposed to provide such taxi service. However, periodic sweeps of the red light areas by the police decreased the practice for short periods of time.

The depressing moments of patrol were those involving death or injury. One terrible day I had to pick up from the road the body parts of school children who were hit by a truck. Another day I was the first to recover an abandoned infant found in a trash heap; along the way to the hospital I picked off the insects that were eating his flesh.

Police Inspector Amos Otieno Odenyo. Mombasa, 1960.

The closest I came to danger was the day my patrol car received a radio report of a madman wielding a machete in the middle of a major intersection. I received the call around quarter past eight in the morning, just fifteen minutes before the end of my shift. My unit was first to arrive at the scene and we observed a long line of vehicles at a standstill, drivers and passengers still in their cars. Ahead, there was a crazy man yelling at the drivers and pedestrians, threatening to kill them if they crossed his path. I slowly approached the man, accompanied by my constables. The man saw us and raised his machete toward me in an attempt to strike me. I had my fully-loaded Smith and Wesson gun in my right hand, ready to shoot him if needed, but my two constables grabbed his arms to subdue him. They did not quite succeed, so I holstered my weapon and assisted in arresting him. In the process, his machete cut my left forearm, creating a deep gash. The wound healed, but left a scar which is still noticeable today.

One afternoon while on patrol I recognized a European teacher from Kisii High School driving in the streets of Mombasa. It was my English teacher Wendy Spendlove, and her husband, District Officer Peter Roy Spendlove. I told my driver to follow their car and pull them over. When I approached their vehicle they were startled to see an African inspector, whom they assumed was trying to give them a ticket. Their initial shock was soon exchanged for recognition and amazement. Mrs. Spendlove, who only two years earlier was grading my exams in high school, was proud of me and congratulated me repeatedly. She must have taken my admittance into the police force as an indication of the quality of instruction in her classroom.

My all-African crew in the patrol car felt that we were continually in the midst of two opposing cultures. Many times we were called to European quarters, but when I knocked on the door I was met by a white person who said, "Goodness, I wanted to talk to a police officer!" On such occasions we ignored the rude welcome and inquired about the problem. We then went ahead and dealt with the situation as we saw fit. On the other hand, the calls from African quarters produced another kind of awkward situation. The 999 emergency patrol car had always been known in the African quarters for rough handling of the public. The European inspector gave the orders and the African constables did the beatings. To see an all-African crew in the car was something new for the African communities. They expected us to overlook some infraction of the law. We were often greeted by the Swahili code words *Uhuru, sisi kwa sisi*, meaning "Freedom, us for us." The implication was that we were one of them and that it was wrong for us to make arrests or enforce the colonial government's laws. One of my constables in the car, Corporal Penza, soon found a rebuttal phrase, *Uhuru na sheria*, meaning "Freedom and Law." We countered the initial slogan with our own and then went about the business of enforcing the law.

One particularly difficult situation occurred on a Sunday afternoon when we found five people, two men and three women, joined by a large crowd. The five people and the crowd were all youth members of the pre-independence political party—the Kenya African Democratic Union (KADU). The five had visited an office of the opposing party, the Kenya African National Union (KANU), and were given a severe beating. The crowd of KADU supporters was planning a counter-battle as the five victims huddled on the street suffering from their wounds. The crowd flagged our car down and I looked at the victims. I radioed for an ambulance and the three KADU members who were hurt more seriously were taken to the hospital. I asked the other two if they wanted to make a formal complaint and press charges. Not only did they want to do that, but their supporters wanted immediate revenge by going over to the KANU office with the victims to identify the assailants. The culprits were sitting inside an office, but the officials of the KANU party refused to let us in to talk to them or come out to the lobby to confer with us.

Meanwhile, outside in the street, the numbers of KADU supporters were growing and threats were being uttered. Stones were being picked up and made ready for the KANU culprits. This was a dangerous dilemma for me and my colleagues. It was dangerous to remove the culprits from their office because they might be killed before they entered our car. However, I still had to talk to them, or at least take their names. The KANU party officers flatly refused to cooperate with us. We were outnumbered since we were only three (plus the driver who was in the car outside) and on the verge of being attacked by the mob. We walked out of the office, got into the car, and I radioed to police headquarters. The superintendent in charge, Mr. Cook, picked up the radio at the other end and asked me to describe the situation in detail. He ordered me to return to the police station at once to pick up a senior European officer (a superintendent, and second in charge). I rushed to the station some six miles away and the senior officer rode back with me to the KANU branch office. The KANU officials now allowed us into the office, and the superintendent explained the situation in the same way I had done. The crowd outside was getting angry, and we wanted to take both suspects and victims to headquarters to give statements. In spite of the superintendent's urging, the KANU branch officers, especially Dennis Akumu (the Dockworkers' Union leader), were very unreasonable. At that moment the superintendent went back to the car and radioed for a riot squad. Within twenty minutes the first truck full of reinforcements was at the scene. Soon they were joined by four other trucks, and we handed the situation over to the riot squad inspector. The riot squad did not ask questions—it simply went to work with clubs and boots to break up the mob. That incident won us (the all-African patrol car) a bad name in the African quarters because we had not sided with our fellow Africans. But their judgment was unfair since we both wanted justice. Personally, I felt sorry for the innocent people who got clubbed along the way, but I felt that the KANU officers and their supporters were wrong and deserved the treatment.

It was difficult to make social contacts with my fellow policemen. There were four other African inspectors, but they had been on the job their entire adult lives and resented a newcomer just out of high school wearing the same uniform. The other Africans were old sergeants, corporals, or young constables who could not socially relate to someone higher up in the ranks, and I was not sure I wanted them as friends. It was almost impossible to make friendships among the European and Indian inspectors. They fraternized among themselves and my only contact with them was in the office. It appeared that African policemen of all ranks put down their uniforms after duty, donned civilian clothes, and went right back to town for beer or *mnazi* liquor. I knew there were a few schoolmates in town looking for work, but my irregular patrol hours made it difficult for us to meet. I was becoming dissatisfied with my job, the drudgery and monotony of living, and the fact that I did not seem to fit in anywhere except in my patrol car. I certainly did not enjoy drinking with the jealous, older African inspectors. I did not fit in with the Europeans with whom I had only the rank and uniform in common. Away from work, I did not fit into any group largely because of the reluctance of people to make friends with policemen unless they were calculated friendships.

I could not see myself spending the rest of my life patrolling the streets of Mombasa. Besides, the longer I stayed on the job, the more likely I would join the pattern of life of the older inspectors which I detested. I started to dislike the reality of police work as opposed to the ideal concept of police work that I was taught at the police college. In the academy, Instructor Phillips repeated so often to us the rules: "Do not use more force than necessary to make an arrest," and "after the arrest is made, you have no right to use more force." That became my ideal, but at the Mombasa Police Station that rule was violated many times by officers above me, so much so that I actually hated one particular European inspector because of his cruelty. Inspector "Cambrian"[13] had a particular joy of cracking the testicles of African prisoners whom he brought into the cells. At times he would almost castrate the prisoners. Inspector "Toole" was another notorious abuser who was very fond of caning the inmates. Cambrian and Toole repeatedly applied needles and electricity to handcuffed prisoners and relished in the sounds of the screams that followed. These British officers would find any reason to justify beatings, such as, "He didn't obey my orders quickly enough," or, "He looked at me in a disobedient way." I suspect these officers were partially motivated by the inevitability of Kenyan independence, and they were taking full advantage of their last years in power to remind Kenyans of their subservient status in society. However, I noticed that this culture of beatings was being absorbed by a few African colleagues who would inflict pain as an outlet for their frustrations with their jobs. Over time I realized that I was the odd-man out. Among those officers within the Mombasa Station who came in contact with arrested people, it may have only been me who never raised a hand to a prisoner.

I loathed the practice of using violence on prisoners so much that I began recording particular incidents in the occurrence book whenever I learned about them. I hoped some higher ranking officer would take up the matter since every entry made in the book concerning a problem was supposed to be resolved. One of my log entries was taken up by the superintendent, but not concerning the inspectors. Rather it concerned an older African lady whose husband had been a sergeant killed in the line of duty. The police compensated her by employing her as a guard. Her job was to search the arrested females, escort them to jail and trial, and finally to prison if they were sentenced. Every male officer who arrested a female handed the prisoner over to her. This guard had also taken to beating her prisoners. Since she was below me in rank, I warned her, but the second time I noted her misbehavior in the occurrence book. The superintendent promptly called her in for disciplinary action. This added to my problems, for the lady happened to be Luo, and I was the last person she expected this action from. She cried and blamed me for almost causing the loss of her job and reminded me that she was a widow. She spread rumors about the new inspector who was a troublemaker even to his own people.

I did not decide to become a law enforcement officer to abuse my countrymen. I joined the police force in the hope that if the British colonialists left Kenya, I could support a democratic African government. But it was evident to me that even if the British left the country tomorrow, there was a sub-culture of intolerance and oppression within the African ranks. I was standing alone against both European and African brutality. All these factors made me thoroughly dissatisfied with my job, and caused me to re-evaluate my future career options. I began to recall the advice of my history teacher at Kisii, Mr. Samuel Onyango Ayodo, who encouraged all his students to study abroad.

I started corresponding with specific colleges in the United States at the suggestion of a friend, James Orondo Opeyo, who had gone there a year earlier. He gave me the names of the colleges that he thought were good, and I began writing to them for applications. Two months later, in December 1960, I received my first set of application forms, from Augustana College in South Dakota. I pursued it immediately, and on February 22, 1961, I received a letter of admission. Although I received a full academic scholarship for the first academic year, I was told that the cost of the remaining three years of tuition, plus all incidental expenses (travel, housing, food, books, etc.), was my responsibility. I was excited to be accepted, but I realized that I did not have enough money to cover the incidentals. I wrote back to Augustana College with this explanation, but the school refused to increase its assistance. During this time I spent many afternoons at the library in Mombasa, researching and writing to other foreign universities. I eventually received a full four-year scholarship to the University of Negros Occidentals in Manila, Philippines. This was a fantastic opportunity. However, the scholarship was limited to business or economics, and math has always been my weakest area of study. I knew my academic strengths were English and history—areas of study available to me at Augustana College. I thought that I could do very well in journalism since my elder brother Adet had studied it and was a successful information officer with the Kenyan government. He was always on the radio or in the newspaper discussing government and community affairs. I thought that after four years in the United States I could return to Kenya and do the same type of work. I had also met several Africans who spent time in the United States, and they all recommended it highly. I did not know of any African who had ever traveled to the Philippines. Primarily for these reasons, I remained focused on preparing to meet the financial burdens of traveling to South Dakota.

At first I kept my change in career goals a secret from my police colleagues, but my disinterest in the job must have become evident because my superintendent called me into his office and asked me about it. I admitted I had been sending college applications all over the world. He expressed surprise and disappointment, citing how much time and effort the government had wasted training me. He added that the Europeans were soon leaving and African officers with education were going to eventually move up to positions of greater responsibility. This prospect held no appeal to me because I had already experienced too much of the harsh reality associated with police work in Kenya. In February 1961, I resigned from the Kenya Police.

I immediately traveled to Nairobi where I had secured arrangements to stay with my good friend Martin Nyiendo (from Kisii High School). I managed to obtain a temporary clerical position with the East African Posts and Telecommunications Administration (lasting from March 7 until August 31). On the first weekend of April, I traveled home to Got Regea to inform my parents of my educational plans. From then on, every free minute of my time I spent fundraising for my September departure. I contacted every organization, church, relative, friend, or politician (including Argwings Kodhek) whom I thought might spare a few shillings to support my travels to the United States. My relatives were very kind to me, contributing whatever East Africa Shillings (EAS) they could spare. I noted the contributions in my daily calendar: Nashon Ouma EAS 5, Musa Oludhe EAS 10, Paul

Obara EAS 100, Evan Okoth EAS 300, etc. Every little bit helped. I submitted an application for a Kenyan passport, which I received on May 16. I took medical exams required by the United States Embassy in Nairobi, which I passed on July 29.

My travel to the United States should not be discussed without explaining the role of a very notable Kenyan, the late Tom Mboya. Mboya was a prominent Kenyan statesman from my Luo tribe. He was only a few years older than me, yet he had accomplished so much for the Kenyan people. As a teenager, Mboya was the president of a student-union at Kabete Jeanes School. It is likely that Mboya and my brother Adet knew each other at this school in the late 1940s. In his early twenties Mboya was the secretary-general of the Kenyan Federation of Labor. Just a few years later Mboya became the president of the All-African People's Conference. He became a leading advocate for Kenyan independence and the release of Jomo Kenyatta from detention by the colonial government in Lodwar (a desolate location in northern Kenya). Mboya was a man of great foresight. Not only did he advocate a free and independent Kenya, but he tried to establish an educated African civil service that would be capable of governing the new Kenya. I had already been personally inspired by Mboya, because in 1958 he visited Kisii and encouraged the students in the area to pursue advanced educational courses and join the civil service to replace the British. He did not say these words openly, but expressed them in veiled parables. He used examples of other newly independent African states that were granted independence with an inadequate number of educated civil servants. It was Mboya's words that encouraged me to join the police force in 1959.

Mboya was a great pan-Africanist who traveled to the United States in the late 1950s to petition sympathetic educational organizations and wealthy individuals to provide scholarships and transport to Kenyan high school graduates. He was successful in this pursuit, which resulted in a number of my classmates from Kisii already departing Kenya for college education in far-off places like Ohio and Minnesota in 1959. In 1960, Mboya again used his influence to secure a large number of educational scholarships. However, the scholarships did not include airfare, which prevented many of the students from taking advantage of these educational opportunities. After the U.S. Department of State initially refused to provide travel assistance, Mboya turned to American Senator John F. Kennedy (JFK) for assistance. At the time, Kennedy was the chairman of the Senate Foreign Relations subcommittee on African Affairs. Mboya visited the senator's home in Massachusetts in 1960 and persuaded the Kennedy Foundation to contribute $100,000 to transport students from Kenya to the United States in September 1960. Not to be outdone by the success of the Kennedy family, the U.S. Government reversed its earlier decision and contributed funds for four flights in September 1961. In Kenya we called the transport planes the "Tom Mboya Airlifts," because it was Mboya who spearheaded this opportunity. In the United States they call it the "Kennedy Airlifts," because without the senator's last minute intervention, the airlifts of 1960 and 1961 may not have happened.

I had heard of the Tom Mboya Airlifts and was eager to join before my scholarship to Augustana College expired. It seemed that whenever there was a group of at least eighty students ready to travel, a plane would arrive at Embakasi airport and depart for the United States. I feared if I was among the remaining students who did not number eighty, I might find myself stranded without means to reach the United States. It was a relief to receive the news that I had been selected for one of the last airlifts leaving Kenya the first week in September 1961. The Institute of International Education had also agreed to supply funds for room and board during my first year at Augustana College. I received my travel visa on the fifth day of September, with literally no time to spare.

7
Mboya Airlift & Sioux Falls, U.S.A. (1961–1965)

My desire for higher education never escaped my mind.

—Amos Otieno Odenyo, 1965 letter.

The day finally arrived for me to leave Kenya. The date was September 7, 1961. I had already said farewell to my siblings and friends. During my last trip home to Got Regea I transferred my *simba* to my younger brothers. I knew I would not return to the village for four years and could not maintain the *olenge* grass roof and mud walls from America. My little house would be put to good use. I had five younger brothers and one of them, Victor, was seventeen years old and needed to move out of our parents' house. All my earthly belongings fit into two small suitcases, and I still had room to spare. In my luggage I carried two suits, four long-sleeve shirts, one pair of shoes, four pairs of socks, three neckties, and undergarments. I carried a separate briefcase with documents and an English-Swahili dictionary. As was customary during these days, I arrived at the airport that evening wearing a formal suit. My East African Airways ticket stated I had a seven o'clock flight.

I was accompanied to Embakasi airport by my parents, Uncle Gilbert Owuor, and my friend Martin Nyiendo. It was a great honor that my parents and uncle would travel all the way from Got Regea to Nairobi, a full day's journey, to bid me farewell. It was an historic event.

I would become the first in the family to travel in an airplane, the first to leave East Africa, and the first to attend college. I was heading into the unknown—away from my family, away from my culture, away from everything familiar to me. My father laid his hands on me, closed his eyes, and said a prayer and a blessing, asking that *Nyasaye* (God) protect and guide me during my travels. We said our goodbyes and I took my place in line to climb the steps to the airplane, flight 402. From the top of the steps I could catch a glimpse of my parents waving to me from the crowd. Little did I know this would be the last time I would ever see my father.

The plane was packed to the last seat with high school graduates from all over East Africa. We represented the best and the brightest of our generation and were dressed to look the part. There was a quiet feeling of excitement and fear. Most of us had never been in an airplane. Our plane (perhaps a DC3) could not travel directly from Nairobi to London as is done today. Instead, the plane landed to refuel in Khartoum and Rome. We camped out in the airport terminals instead of sleeping in hotels. From London our plane continued to Iceland, then Newfoundland, and ultimately to Idlewide airport (later renamed JFK airport).

We arrived in New York City at night, and my first impression of America was of amazement and intimidation. As we circled the airport preparing to land I saw an endless sea of lights. The entire city was glowing, and it was very beautiful. This was new to me since in Kenya there were very few lights at night except for the headlights of a small number of cars. We landed at eight o'clock on the 8th of September.

We were met at the airport by representatives of the Kennedy Foundation who drove us in buses from Idlewide airport to Manhattan. All of us were speechless as we looked out of the windows to take in our first glimpse of America. I remember tall buildings, fast cars, and again, endless lights. We spent two nights at the Great Northern Hotel, which was used on several previous occasions to house African students. On Saturday we were met by Kenyan students who were studying and living near New York. These students briefed us on their cross-cultural experiences to date. One of these students was David Onyango Ongiri, whom I had known in Kenya. Ongiri took us to the

Empire State Building (at the time the tallest building in the world) and gave us a walking tour around parts of Manhattan.

On Sunday, we were taken in groups to different transportation hubs. I was escorted to the Port Authority in Manhattan and placed on a Greyhound bus destined for Detroit, Michigan. I looked out of the window the entire trip, soaking in the scenery as we passed through Pennsylvania and Ohio. I remember being impressed with the road system which was entirely paved. From Detroit I took a small plane to Sioux Falls, South Dakota, located in the north-central part of the United States.

Augustana College is one of the numerous colleges under the auspices of the American Lutheran Church. It is a medium-sized liberal arts college with many pastors and former clergymen among its faculty. The campus offered a definite change from the distressing street patrol and oppressive warm weather of Mombasa. However, there were many adjustments that I had to make. My American classmates seemed very young and immature. In class, in the gym, and at the cafeteria, these students acted like adolescents. In Africa one is taught to defer to age, but I knew better than to expect them to show respect to me. I often wondered if these young Americans thought that I was stupid since I was beginning university training at the advanced age of twenty-six. However, I learned quickly enough that my classmates, and for that matter most white people, have a hard time telling the ages of other ethnic groups, especially blacks. I also learned there were students even older than me returning to college after pursuing other careers.

I initially found little to discuss with my classmates other than studies. Although my roommate, Robert Abraham, was a nice man, at first I could not confide in him since we were constantly judging each other's cultural habits very critically. Even Adolf (the school janitor and immigrant from Germany) had been following me around for weeks studying me. They both found it odd that I did not make use of the washer and dryer machines in the dormitory. I did not want to disclose to them that I had never even heard of such machines, so I insisted that my hands could do a better job. Finally I relented and was taught how to use the machines. After sniffing the clean clothes, I was convinced of the effectiveness of this new technology and henceforth found a new appreciation for the washer and dryer machines.

It was just a matter of a month or two before I was confronted with a change in season. Trees changed color then suddenly appeared to die and drop their leaves. Eventually, it snowed. I had heard about snow from textbooks in high school and knew that it snowed around Christmas. One morning the radio weatherman predicted snow, and I eagerly waited all day until I saw my first few flakes of snow gently falling from the sky. I watched this from inside the warm building until my classmates encouraged me to go outside and touch it, saying, "Don't worry, it won't hurt you." I waited until they left then walked outside alone and held the snow in my hands until it melted. It was exciting but too cold. After that I did not want to touch the snow, especially since I did not have any winter clothes. I also did not know how to walk in the snow without falling. Adolf the janitor eventually gave me some used winter boots. Some other students provided me with some of their spare winter clothing, which made it a little easier to adjust to the cold.

I felt extremely lonely my first and second year. In a way I felt "lost" or disconnected from my culture. I spent my first Christmas alone in room 213 of Solberg Hall at Augustana College. Most students, except for a handful of international students, left the campus for their homes during the holidays. I had nowhere to go and no money so I just stayed on campus. I think the college administrators recognized this since in subsequent years they encouraged American students to invite foreign students to go home with them. Professor Gerhard Schmutterer and his family invited me and a few African students for Christmas dinner in 1962. That year my new roommate and friend, Charles Chamberlin, invited me on several occasions to his home in Flandreau, South Dakota. His father, C. Bruce Chamberlin, was a Republican representative from Moody and Lake Counties and enjoyed questioning me about life in Kenya. My friend Wayne Weber invited me on several occasions to his home in Lesterville, South Dakota.

During these visits I often spoke to church congregations about life in Kenya. At first this was a difficult activity for me because I felt like I was on display. Most of the people I met had never talked to a black person. One old man shook my hand, but the only thing he wanted to talk about was why the palms of my hands were lighter than the other side of my hands. Many rural people assumed that I boarded a plane in Africa with a loin-cloth wrapped around my waist, spear and shield in hand, and monkey on my shoulder. They asked me very silly questions: "Did you wear clothes in Africa? Have you ever driven in a car before? How did you learn English so quickly?" At first I resented these questions and gave sarcastic responses: "We had no need for shoes because we preferred to swing from tree to tree. Yes, I bought my first shirt in America." I stopped saying these things when I realized that they actually believed me.

I found the church members very set in their ways. For example, the old ladies would question why I was attending a Lutheran School if I was not Lutheran. They wanted to criticize African culture more than understand it. They attributed everything good about me to missionaries. Although the church members were genuinely good people, I eventually stopped attending their services.

On the other hand I found high school students very receptive to learning about Africa. In particular, I enjoyed my visit to Washington High School in Sioux Falls. I talked to the Social Studies class about "Old and New Kenya," and we really had a frank and lively discussion.

Many conversations included a discussion about my teeth. I had my six lower teeth removed a decade earlier as part of my adult-initiation ceremony in Got Regea. Since then I had not discussed the incident because in Kenya it was an accepted part of Luo culture. In Kenya it was as common to see a Luo man missing six lower teeth as it was to see a European lady with painted nails, or an Indian wearing a turban. No one stopped to think about it much less discuss it. However, most Americans assumed I was in a car accident or lost a boxing match. Several people thought I was sick and malnourished as a boy and that my teeth fell out. When I explained the reason for my missing teeth, they either recoiled in horror or voiced pity for me. This was the ultimate paradox. What was a badge of honor in my culture was a badge of shame in another. I endured this until I found enough money to purchase a set of temporary false teeth.

I quickly picked up on several American customs. When Americans invite you to their homes they often give you a tour of the entire house, including their bedrooms. This greatly shocked and embarrassed me because in Kenya guests are not given tours of the bedrooms of people's homes. Visitors remain in the common area of the house, such as the living room or dining room. Even children past a certain age are not permitted to casually enter their parents' bedroom, so when my American friends and their parents invited me past their living rooms and into their bedrooms I was extremely embarrassed. To put it into perspective, imagine you are a guest in someone's house and your friend's mother walks out to greet you completely naked. Seeing the homeowner's bed provided me with a similar feeling of guilt and aversion.

I found Americans had the same love affair with their animals as did the British. They take their dogs along for rides in vehicles, and allow them to sit under the table during dinner. In Kenya the reaction to a dog under the table might be to give a gentle kick to the animal to remind it to go outside. However, I gave no such kicks to animals in South Dakota, for I remembered the story of Mr. Peter Poole in Kenya. Poole was an Englishman who in the late 1950s shot and killed his houseboy for defending himself against Poole's dogs. That incident made Kenyans realize that there are some white people who value their pets more than human beings.

It was not uncommon for an American host to ask me, "So, how did you like the food?" This was another unfamiliar custom. In Kenya, a guest would almost always appreciate the food, and if he did not like it he would not insult the host by revealing this. To be asked my opinion about my meal confused me. Did I do something that indicated the food was bad? Did I not eat enough? Does his question have any relation to the fact that his dog is sitting under our table and being handed the same food that I am eating? Even if I did not like the food, why would this American want me to insult him by telling him so? It was a very direct question. To make a rough analogy, it was like my host asked me, "So, do you think I am handsome or ugly?"

The same principle applied to gifts. In Kenya, if you received a shirt, you might wear it the next time you saw that person. Even if you could not use it, you could give it to someone else who would use it and appreciate it. The appreciation is generally understood. In

America, the person who gives you a gift expects a more formal response and actually waits for a pre-printed thank-you card in the mail. If you do not express your thanks formally, your host may actually be offended. At first it appeared to me that Americans could not give a gift for the sake of giving—it was the return ritual that was the goal. In Kenya, the return ritual may be that you eventually reciprocate by inviting that person to your home for dinner, or buying some sugar or roasted maize for them. The appreciation is more familiar, casual, long-term, and practical. In Kenya, if I had reciprocated by mailing a pre-printed thank-you card with no follow-up social contact, the person at the other end might stare at the card and not know what to do with it.

On the other hand I found some strange parallelisms between American and Luo culture. American country music told tales of family, tradition, love, and loss. I found the themes to be very Luo. I could not afford to buy my own radio in Sioux Falls, but whenever I had access to one I tuned into country music stations, and was reminded of home.

My first job in America was campus custodian at Augustana College. It was a simple job. Late at night I turned off the campus lights, secured the doors, and answered emergency calls from students who locked themselves out of their dormitory. Adolf the janitor would unlock the doors in the morning. It did not pay much but I was not yet allowed to work off-campus because of my immigration status. Once I obtained permission I looked for a better paying job. I had become friends with a senior student from Cameroon who worked from seven to eleven o'clock at night as a janitor in downtown Sioux Falls. He earned what appeared to me like a considerable amount of money and would soon graduate and look for work elsewhere. I asked that he introduce me as his replacement to his boss, Mr. Coakley. Mr. Coakley lived one block from campus, and was one of the first black Americans I had spoken to in my life. Mr. Coakley was very pleased with the work ethic of my Cameroonian friend and was anxious to test me out as a replacement. He had developed an impression of Africans as diligent workers. On my first day on the job, Mr. Coakley showed me around the building that I was to clean, which happened to be the editorial building for the local newspaper, the *Argus Leader*. Mr. Coakley left me with one of his sons who showed me how to clean the desks, mop the floors, polish the mirrors, and clean the toilets. I worked jointly with Mr. Coakley's son for one night, and from then on every evening after class I took the bus downtown and cleaned the entire building by myself.

Mr. Coakley and I came from two completely opposite worlds with little in common other than skin color. However, from the start, Mr. Coakley and I respected each other. There was one common interest that we shared that crossed all cultural lines—money. Mr. Coakley was a hard-working business owner with an established reputation in the city. I was a hard-working employee who shared the same work ethic and need for more money. My scholarship did not cover all expenses and I appreciated the opportunity to work for Mr. Coakley.

I must have cleaned the *Argus Leader's* building exceptionally well because the publisher of the newspaper, Mr. William H. Leopard, asked to be introduced to the new janitor. Mr. Coakley escorted me into Mr. Leopard's office suite where I was complimented for improving the cleanliness of the entire building. I was told that the editorial staff had noticed the improvements to the building and I should be congratulated for my diligent work. I was of course grateful for the compliment but at the same time wondered about the state of affairs with the cleaning staff before I arrived on the scene. For me, I was only performing my duties—to make things clean.

A foreign black student in Sioux Falls was easily recognized and in most cases welcomed. However, I may have been welcomed because I was considered a temporary guest who came to learn, not agitate. I recall that civil rights activist Louis Lomax was invited to Augustana College to participate in a series of lectures and debates on the issue of civil rights for American blacks. I enjoyed him thoroughly, as did many of the students. However, the parents of several students were upset as they felt such unorthodox subjects should not be discussed at a good Lutheran campus. A few influential benefactors actually withdrew their support from the school as a result.

My first personal encounter with the race issue occurred during my first summer in 1962, when I traveled by bus to a Lutheran conference at Stephens College, in Columbia, Missouri. After I arrived, I walked downtown to get a meal. Not knowing the town, I walked into the first restaurant I saw. A waitress told me, "We don't serve your kind." I walked to the next restaurant and got the same response. I tried to eat at every restaurant in the business district but was thrown out of all except one. The waitress sold me a glass of lemonade but told me to drink it outside. After I finished my drink I decided to see where the local black people ate. I walked with some black Americans until they pointed out an all-black barbeque restaurant. The patrons asked me if I had just arrived in town. I told them that this was so, but said nothing about my recent difficulty. The incident did not upset me too much since I had known there were restaurants in America which did not serve blacks.

The next incident angered me. After the conference I went to work as an assistant for the "International House" in Des Moines, Iowa, run by the Iowa Boards of International Education (IBIE). Mrs. Elinor Robson was my immediate supervisor. The IBIE linked foreign students with Iowans who provided housing and cultural assistance to foreign students. I rented a room in a black neighborhood and walked every morning to the International House. Each day I passed by a small lunch counter where the owner and his waitress served a steady clientele of construction workers. This became my daily place for breakfast. I often ordered two scrambled eggs, toast, and coffee. The waitress memorized this and usually gave it to me before I placed my order. However, the owner, a bulky looking ex-marine type who was always present as cook and dishwasher, decided that he did not want my business. One morning he offered to serve me. I gave my usual order and he went to the kitchen area to cook it. As I watched, he cracked two eggs into a frying pan. He placed the pan on the fire and began stirring the eggs. He then took a cup of salt and poured the entire contents on the two eggs. He let the eggs fry until they were burnt and dark like charcoal. They were clearly inedible. He put the charcoal eggs on a plate and tossed it to me saying, "Here is your food."

I was not the only one who observed this because the white customers were all staring at me. I asked, "How do you expect me to eat this?"

"Well, that's how we cook. If you don't like it, you can leave," was his sharp response.

"Do you expect me to pay for this?"

"I don't want your money," he shot back.

I looked at the other customers. Some were silent, while others were giggling, but they were all observing the situation unfold. I asked the cook, "Why did you not tell me that you do not want me to come here?" The man started to get visibly angry, so I placed some money on the counter and left.

Upon my arrival at the International House, Mrs. Robson noticed that I was upset. After I explained to her what had just happened, she picked up the phone, called the mayor's office, the Commission on Human Rights, the president of Iowa Restaurants Association, and a few pastors, one of whom was the chairman of her board. For half of that day I was on the phone explaining the details of the incident. I had created an international incident, and everyone wanted to capitalize on it in an attempt to improve race relations. The director of the Commission on Human Rights made me sign a formal complaint against the restaurant owner. Churches began sending in a stream of black Americans and African students from the International House to the restaurant hoping to be refused service, but the proprietor realized what was happening and served them. I was somewhat relieved as this meant the incident would soon be behind me.

However, the next morning I was visited by a high official of the Iowa Restaurants Association. He invited me to his office located on the second floor of an elaborate restaurant not too far from the International House. He had heard about my story from the mayor's office, the Commission on Human Rights, and other influential people. He wanted to apologize on behalf of the association. I went to his office, and from there we proceeded to the office of the president, who explained his non-discrimination policy. Finally, the president and the high official invited me downstairs to the restaurant. While we were served an exquisite meal they asked me about Kenya, by now a familiar topic of conversation for me with Americans. Before the meal was over, the president of the Iowa Restaurants Association apologized again and added, "You see, without the incident yesterday morning, you would not have had the opportunity to eat in this fine restaurant. We don't practice discrimination." I took his statement to mean that under normal occasions I would not be fit as a customer in this plush restaurant. His statement infuriated me to the point that I felt like dumping the remaining food on his head. Instead, I politely said, "Thanks, gentlemen," and left without saying more. I have since wondered how such a person could hold such a high position in that association if he could not even handle a small public relations job. Of all the racial incidents I have encountered in America, the scrambled egg-apology incident upset me the most, perhaps because of its indirect nature or perhaps because the association's president underestimated me and thought his plush breakfast was a satisfactory compensation for my debasement at the lunch counter. Besides, I had eaten in many restaurants better than that one. Even in colonial Kenya I had been subjected to racial discrimination, but this affected me differently. In any case, when I returned to Augustana College in the fall, I felt I had learned more than my African friends who had stayed on campus and attended regular summer sessions.

The following summer (1963) I remained in Sioux Falls and worked for Norlin Construction Company laying concrete on the sidewalks. I wore earplugs and operated a jackhammer to rip up old concrete on the streets. The labor was so intense that even during my days off my arms and hands felt the pulsing sensation of the jackhammer. Our five-member crew consisted of mostly white Korean War veterans. Their view of Africans was very interesting. They seemed to genuinely believe that I bought my first clothes in America—a belief I had already encountered with many Americans. These veterans had never touched a black person and were curious about my black skin and brown palms as I pushed wheelbarrows full of concrete mix. This was the summer I heard the statement from my co-workers, "I worked like a nigger today," when the pace had been particularly demanding. One crew member was fond of this statement whenever fifteen minute coffee breaks came and we left everything where it was and grabbed our thermos bottles. I finally asked, "Are they not supposed to be lazy?" My question started a short discussion during which he explained to me that while American blacks are lazy, I was African and therefore different. Since I had not been born in America, I could not be lazy even if I was black. I worked on this construction job for about two months. Before the end of summer, some of us were laid off. The company explained that it was raining too often to make more sidewalks.

I began sending money back to Kenya starting with my first pay-check in 1962. Whenever I had an extra twenty dollars I wired it to the post office in Yala. This is not a lot of money today, but it was a lot of money to me at the time. My father collected it and used it to pay school fees for my younger siblings. Zablon Sangoro retired from the African Tribunal Courts around 1961 and for several years only my elder brother Adet had steady income. Adet was supporting not only his own family, but the educational needs of our younger brothers and sisters. I also received letters from my father requesting money to pay for court fees. There were many envious neighbors who began to encroach on our land in Got Regea, but Zablon successfully held them at bay through legal proceedings. Helping my family from a distance strengthened my resolve during the depressing moments of cleaning the toilets of the *Argus Leader* building and operating a jackhammer under the blazing sun.

It was a tough life for many of the African students in America. Some could not adjust to the American lifestyle. Many had financial difficulties due to a lack of job prospects. Several of the African students were performing poorly in their academic studies and constantly talked about transferring out of Augustana College, falsely thinking that their academic performance would improve at another university. Most of the international students were just coping, and some students quit school altogether. Many of the Kenyan students who quit were those selected for the Tom Mboya Airlifts based on their political connections, rather than their educational abilities. You might find some of them today lost in the slums of America, by now adjusted to the American lifestyle, but too embarrassed to go back home. Life was tough for me too, but I was motivated by the fact that I seemed to be surviving better than most of my peers.

On November 22, 1963, around one o'clock in the afternoon, I heard on the radio that the president of the United States, John F. Kennedy, had been shot and killed. I was devastated and forgot about eating lunch. I felt a deep personal loss over Kennedy's death. Without his partnership with Tom Mboya in the 1960–61 airlifts, I might have never traveled to America.

There were lighter moments that I remember. Since there were few international students in Sioux Falls, I often took a bus to Minneapolis where there were a large number of African students. I was not the only one who made this journey. My friend James Orondo Opeyo, who was studying at Waldorf College in Iowa, traveled to Minneapolis for the same reasons. Whenever possible, I spent time with my high school friend Winston Ayoki, who was studying mathematics at the University of Northwestern in Ohio. I wrote letters to Frederick Ouka, who was studying at Shaw University in North Carolina. Ouka and I attended the same four years at Kisii High School, and we boarded the same plane to America on September 7, 1961.

I helped organize an Augustana College football team. I learned to call it soccer, as Americans used the term "football" to describe an entirely different sport in which you cannot touch the ball with your foot. I considered this very odd. To compile a team we pulled together the international students from Norway, Germany, and three or four African countries. We won a few soccer games against Sioux Falls College before our team disintegrated due to the graduation of several players.

In December 1963, Kenya became an independent nation. I had already clipped from the newspaper the lyrics to our new national anthem: "O God of all creation, bless this, our land and nation, justice be our shield and defender. May we dwell in unity, peace and liberty, plenty be found within our borders." Our flag looked very impressive. It had three horizontal stripes, with black representing the indigenous people, red representing our blood and struggle, and green representing our land and natural wealth. Each strip was separated by white, representing peace. A warrior's shield and two crossed spears were at the center of the flag, protecting the nation.

I was still working as a janitor at the *Argus Leader*, and the publisher remembered me and asked me for an interview about Kenya. Of course I was honored, and excerpts from the interview, as well as my photograph, were published in the newspaper. I was quoted as saying:

Kenya is physically exciting, with its snow-clad, 17,000-foot equatorial mountain; its great herds of wild animals ranging over wide plains and through thick forest and [Kenya also has] the broad streets of its modern capital, Nairobi. But Kenya's future is the most exciting of all. Its leaders have already plunged into the heady task, set by Prime Minister Jomo Kenyatta, of removing the blights of ignorance, poverty, and disease. It has an immense agricultural potential and its mixed African, Asian, Arab, and European population has the resources and know-how to realize this potential. This exciting prospect will loom large in the minds of Kenya's people during the three days of Independence celebration. The prime minister has said that if Kenya is to prosper, a spirit of national familyhood must be created—bringing all the communities together to work for a better future for all the people.

It was an exciting moment for me, and despite the distance from my homeland, I rejoiced for weeks and truly felt honored to be able to say I was a Kenyan.

My primary concern was the type of tests that we were given in class. I thought the material taught in class was fairly easy, but I could not score well on objective tests. All of our high school examinations in Kenya required written self-expression, but during my first two years of college I was subjected to sterile "objective" testing. However, the junior and senior years marked a great difference. Most of the advanced courses now required term papers and essay questions. At this stage I began to feel better adjusted. I found myself enjoying and performing well in subjects such as English, history, and sociology.

My sociology instructor, Mr. Orville Westby, was inspirational. His courses were fascinating and the heavy reading assignments were a challenge. I must have been the only student in class who did all the required reading. This often led to me getting the top scores in class. I was not necessarily smarter than anyone else; I think I simply devoted myself more to studying and being prepared for exams. There were several times when a few students failed exams while I received a perfect score. Professor Westby noticed this and congratulated me in front of the class as a way to motivate the other students to follow my example.

Professor Westby gave me a systematic introduction to the world of human behavior. I began to realize that my behavior and values as an African were only one of many possible human patterns of interaction. Such a conclusion came as a revelation to me. Like many foreign students, my interpretation of events was based exclusively on my African background. There were four African students on campus, and in our private conversations we used to denounce almost everything American. But with my change of attitude, I began to play the devil's advocate. For example, we all thought Americans deceive others with their quick smiles and greetings that are immediately withdrawn if you respond in kind. It is particularly embarrassing when it comes from a girl, for such a smile in Africa would mean an invitation to a conversation. I told my African friends at Augustana College that my high school history teacher in Kenya had acquired this habit. The students at Kisii High School could not understand how our history teacher, Samuel Onyango Ayodo, could smile and say "Hi," and then immediately go on his way without stopping to talk. I was unaccustomed to this informal greeting, because in Kenya we used a proper "Hello," and it was almost always followed by "How is your day?" or "What is your news?"

In my cultural anthropology class we read works by Bronisław Malinowski, as well as Ruth Benedict (*Patterns of Culture*). Their writings made me analyze my entire religious and cultural upbringing. Up until my junior year I whole-heartedly accepted my father's interpretation of Christianity which was based upon the teachings of the missionaries at C.M.S. Maseno. I now struggled with the missionary version of Christianity that essentially told us everything about our culture was wrong. I now asked why a polygamist who converts to Christianity must send his three extra wives away to suffer. Would this please God? Who has the spiritual authority to tell the old men in my village that their sacrifices and spitting was any less valid than bread and wine at communion? If Luos should not pray to the sun as a manifestation of

God, why do Christians kneel before the cross and wear it around their necks? In my junior year at Augustana College I began to interpret society, culture, and religion on a more functionalist basis. I also declared a double major in sociology and political science.

I greatly respected the personal qualities of the political science instructor, Professor Alfred J. Hotz, who had been a student of Hans Morgenthau, the famous professor of political science at the University of Chicago. We used Morgenthau's book, *Politics among Nations*, as a text. I do not remember any time I enjoyed learning more. I now think my delight stemmed from the fact that I began to see my own country in the context of the world and world politics. I had come from a colonial background where we did not know there was a distinctive area of study called political science. All that we knew were the repetitious speeches of African politicians asking for independence. We did not know that there was a difference between the terms "political scientist" and "politician." In fact, when I wrote to some of my friends in Kenya that I was enthusiastic about political science, their answer was "Why? There are already too many politicians in Kenya, and you did not have to go all the way to the United States to learn to play political games."

In any case, for the first time I was putting my country and my intense and parochial chauvinism in the context of the international scene. I came to realize that I should not be so offended when someone asked, "Is Kenya the British province of Australia?" I was intensely proud of Kenya and our struggle for independence. The realization that Kenya was a small internationally insignificant underdeveloped piece of real estate was painful. Professor Hotz opened up the world for me and actually corrected the emotional and narrow biases I had about Kenya. He instilled in his students a perception of what he called "the realities of how this world runs...power," which is the indispensible commodity which African countries lack. It was initially difficult for me to accept his statement that:

> African countries are like young babies in international
> politics. Instead of throwing tantrums and emotions in
> the United Nations, they ought to be concentrating on

building power resources they have. That is the only way the U.N. and others in the world will take them seriously.

Professor Hotz later complimented me at graduation and said he had taught many Africans and others from the developing world. His lectures had made most of them so angry that they had called him racist and other less than flattering names. Professor Hotz watched me struggle rather painfully with his ideas, but finally he was convinced that reflection had replaced uncritical emotional response. In 1965, Professor Hotz provided me with a recommendation (in part):

> Unlike some of our African students whose attitudes toward their native lands are either eulogistic or apologetic, and whose approach to the United States is either hypercritical or feigned enthusiastic, Mr. Odenyo has demonstrated forthright candor, objectivity, and maturity on both counts. Moreover, Mr. Odenyo is a valuable participant in our student International Relations Club, and has served on our Executive Committee for two years with distinction. His sound work with our student delegations to last spring's (April 1964) Model U.N. General Assembly Sessions, held at the University of Minnesota, was truly outstanding.

In the spring of 1965 I received another letter of recommendation, from Myles C. Stenshoel of Augusta College, stating (in part):

> I would rate Mr. Otieno [Odenyo] very highly in terms of character, integrity, and determination. His personality is reserved, for the most part, but by no means withdrawn. He is capable and correct in his social relationships; he is somewhat disdainful of the casual approach to education sometimes found among his American fellow students. He is an independent and self-assured person.

By my final semester I scraped together enough money to buy my first vehicle, a 1957 Chevy 150. After graduation I worked for two summer months in Mahopac Falls in upstate New York. I was employed as a counselor at Camp Henry for the underprivileged children from the Henry Street Settlement House on the lower-east side of New York City. From there I visited two friends from Kisii High School. The first friend was Akich Okola who was living in Harlem, New York. The second friend was Winston Ayoki, who would soon start postgraduate studies at Fordham University. I was happy to participate as Winston's "best man" in his wedding to his bride Linda, from Iowa. I also had an opportunity to further sightsee in the city. I headed west in September 1965, for I had been accepted for graduate school in the state of Wyoming.

Amos Otieno Odenyo, visited by Martin Miruka Nyiendo and Laban Otieno. Augustana College (Bergsaker Hall), December 1964.

Amos Otieno Odenyo with his two favorite professors,
Dr. Alfred J. Hotz (left), and Dr. Orville Westby (right).
Augustana College, 1965.

8
Graduate School & Return Home
(1965–1970)

*My desire is to become a public relations officer in my
government, and to this goal I will direct all my efforts.*

*If I hold public office, I hold office in the interest of Kenya. I wouldn't care
two bits whether someone is Jaluo, Kikuyu, or Mzungu. I will do what is
right. It is just a matter of principle to me that when I'm in a position to
decide something, I don't look at it from an ethnic bias at all.* [14]
—Amos Otieno Odenyo, 1964 and 1965.

The University of Wyoming is located in Laramie, some fifty miles
from Cheyenne, the state capitol. Its obvious difference from Sioux
Falls is the western influence, the cowboy hats, the guns in the cars,
and the jeans and boots. On my first day driving into Wyoming I felt
like I was entering dangerous and hostile territory, but this fear proved
to be unfounded. The outwardly tough-looking people were actually
returning from hunting trips, and the guns were not meant for me. The
campus was beautiful and the people friendly.

I moved into the graduate dormitory and reported to my department, headed by Mr. Edwin G. Flittie. My role as graduate assistant in
a combined sociology-anthropology department was outlined for me.
I was to proctor exams, grade papers, and conduct research for faculty
members. I would occasionally lecture about East Africa to students, and
become an informant on Luo culture to Professor William H. Hodge.[15]

I did not engage in a lot of extra curricular activities because I was focused on my master's thesis on the topic of educational and occupational aspirations of local junior high school students. This required a lot of field work, interviews and statistical analysis. During the 1966 school break I worked as a field researcher under Dr. Donald Pelz of the University of Michigan (Institute of Social Research). That same year I moved out of the dormitories in Laramie and into the basement of a German Studies teacher, Bob Lapoint, who was finishing his doctorate degree. I often ate meals with him and his wife, Gisela, and for the first time in many years, I became part of a family.

I did find time to join the Cosmopolitan Club. During "International Day" in April 1966, I was chosen to be the master of ceremonies. I took it upon myself to collect international music to play during the evening dinner. When the Arab members of the Cosmopolitan Club found out I included two Israeli songs on the playlist, they revolted, saying they would cancel the whole event if I played those two songs. I was among the few international students who argued the point that the Cosmopolitan Club should not be used by one group of countries to further their own prejudices against other countries. The Arab students argued back that they did not see eye to eye with Israel and the Cosmopolitan Club should honor their feelings. I fought back to the bitter end, countering that the Cosmopolitan Club should be a place where enemies could sit down together, talk, and have diplomatic relations. It was like a little United Nations squabble, and we even called for a vote to resolve the situation. I obtained 100 percent of the votes from the American members of the Cosmopolitan Club, and a minority of the international students' votes. However, my argument collected the most votes overall, and International Day turned out to be a very successful event, with no discrimination against any music or nation.

It was very difficult to communicate with my family back home in Kenya. Making a telephone call was impossible since no one had a telephone at home. I therefore communicated by mail, receiving updates of events well after they occurred. I learned that my brother Adet was still employed as an information officer. He was in charge of a radio broadcasting station in Mandera, which is in the dry northeastern part

**Amos Otieno Odenyo playing drums
on International Night, April 23, 1966.**

of Kenya, near the borders of Ethiopia and Somalia. My two eldest sisters, Rosalie and Olivia, were raising their families in South Nyanza. Following in our father's footsteps, my younger brother Lut was appointed headmaster of Luanda Primary School. My brother Robert found work as a salesman for a margarine company, but fell ill from tuberculosis and was recovering at home. My brother Victor found a job as a bank teller with National and Grindlays Bank in Nairobi (located in the future National Archives building). My sister Olga graduated from Alliance Girls High School near Nairobi. Booker was still in high school and Daniel was in intermediate school.

On January 17, 1966, I received a message from Kenya. My

immediate younger brother, Lut Ezra Obuong Odenyo, was dead. The news shocked me. He married on January 1, 1966, and there was a feast in our family compound involving many members of the community. Immediately after the feast, Lut's eyes turned yellow and he fell ill. He died on January 10. I could not make sense of this tragedy, and the events remain a dark cloud in our family history. There is speculation of murder through food poisoning. Several neighbors who volunteered as food servers during Lut's wedding not only declined to attend Lut's funeral, but held festive events in their compounds during his burial. A possible motive for murder could be jealousy of our family's perceived prominence in Got Regea society. A more likely motive would have been retaliation over Lut's outspoken advocacy and protection of our land rights. Lut consistently joined our father Zablon under the fig tree to argue with neighbors why the land we returned to in 1959 (where my grandfather Okwata is buried) belongs to the Odenyo family.

Land disputes have ranked among the most frequent causes of violent death in Kenya, even among friends and family. When you see old Luo men drinking *kong'o* (traditional beer) out of a single pot with the long *oseke* straws, the natural reaction is to admire their culture as peaceful and communal. But the hidden and mostly subconscious benefit of drinking from a communal pot is that if one of them wakes up dead the next morning, none of the surviving friends can be accused of murder. It is the same reason many Kenyans at a restaurant will not accept a soda or beer unless they witness the waiter opening the bottle.

After Lut's death, there was a lot of family discussion over what to do with Lut's new wife. In traditional Luo culture, when a husband dies, it is a younger brother of the deceased who "inherits" the widow. Anthropologists refer to this as the "levirate" system.[16] It does not matter if the younger brother already has a wife. He is expected to make the widow his second wife, either in real terms or symbolically. This tradition arose out of practical reasons. The basis for all societal relationships in Africa is the perpetuation of family and family relationships. Death threatens that foundation. Wife inheritance in a way restores it. There is no need to reverse the dowry process and relationship between in-laws. If children are involved, wife inheritance ensures the children are not destitute, and that they are raised by, identify with, and carry on the patrilineal name. Wife inheritance is consistent with the role of the extended family in Africa, where distant relatives are not so "distant." For example, the phrase for "uncle" in Kiswahili is *baba mdogo*, meaning "small father," reflecting that your uncles (and aunts) are all parental figures.

The wife inheritance tradition is so entrenched in Luo culture that my father, who was viewed by his peers as running a "un-Luo" household, was adamant that one of my younger brothers marry Lut's widow. The ideal candidate would have been Lut's immediate follower, Robert, but he was unemployed and recovering from tuberculosis. The next in line was Victor, who was in the process of making travel plans to Sweden, having recently received a prized scholarship to study soil science. However, Victor wanted nothing to do with our father's plans. From Wyoming I wrote Victor a letter of support, citing my own hardships as a student in the United States. Victor left for Sweden in 1966 without marrying Lut's widow, leaving Zablon Sangoro Odenyo feeling very angry that his parental authority was challenged. Eventually Zablon came to sympathize with Victor's position, even hosting a party for him when he returned to Kenya in 1968 for a visit.

Lut's passing was an incentive for me to return to Kenya after I graduated from the University of Wyoming in 1967. My brother Robert constantly wrote to me and encouraged me to return home and take up an administrative job in the new Kenyan government. He wrote that one of my maternal aunts was saying, "Where is Otieno? Everyone else from America is coming back home and buying *shambas* (plots of farmland)—why can't Otieno do the same?" There was a lot of concern in the family, voiced through Robert, that I was not coming home. I fully anticipated going back home, but the question was when.

Each year starting in 1963, representatives from the Kenyan government interviewed Kenyan students in America for government positions back home. I was interviewed in 1965 when I graduated from Augustana College. I was offered the position of district officer, which was an impressive job. However, I had already received a scholarship from the University of Wyoming in the field of sociology. I loved academia and thought that if I stayed in America two more years I could strengthen my credentials and return to Kenya at a higher professional level. I was forced to make this same decision in 1967. I had to choose between becoming a lecturer in Anthropology at Makerere University in Uganda, or accept a scholarship for a doctorate degree in sociology from the University of Minnesota. The decision was hard to make, but my love for learning and desire to reach the heights of my academic potential outweighed my desire to rush home. I accepted the scholarship in Minnesota and reminded myself that I could go home in three years having fully satisfied my educational goals.

While I was a student in South Dakota I visited the University of Minnesota on several occasions, so the campus was familiar to me when I enrolled there in 1967. I moved into Centennial Hall and quickly settled into the Minnesota routine. My job as a teaching assistant was similar to my duties at the University of Wyoming. There were many international students in Minnesota, and the university had an African students' union.

I was one of several editors of the *Law & Society Review*, and also served as the senior staff editor for the *African Image*, a monthly journal published by the Center for Advanced African Understanding (CAAU). The CAAU was a non-profit, non-partisan educational organization founded on June 21, 1968, by Daniel A. Okoronkwo (from Biafra), a fellow student at the University of Minnesota. Part of our goal was to help educate America on African culture, history, and political and economic developments. We wanted to erase negative stereotypes about Africa.

The mostly African membership of CAAU placed a huge wooden billboard outside our door at 1149 Aldrich Avenue North, inviting people with: "Inquire within for Lessons on African History, Geography, Politics, Economics, Language, Culture, by Competent Authorities; Demonstrations on African Food, Art, Patterns of Dress, Counseling on African Tours." We were African students living during the height of the American civil rights struggles and we wanted to do our part to break down cultural intolerance and replace it with multicultural appreciation. I also provided lectures on behalf of CAAU at Concordia College at Moorhead on the subjects of "African Social System" and

"African Religion." Okoronkwo lectured on "Pan-Africanism," and "African History." Joachim Banda, a biophysics student at the University of Minnesota, contributed articles for the *African Image*. His first article in 1969 was "Humanism: Africa's Gift to the World," which attempted to explore "African Socialism" in regard to the healthy balance of traditional socialist and capitalist indigenous roots. Andre Gombako, an Agricultural student at the University of Minnesota, contributed recipes for jollof rice and "African Banana Drink."

I soon found myself feeling at home in Minneapolis. I made new friendships with people such as Timon Bondo, Ben Amoth Owira, George Okayo Obuong, and Isaac Otieno. I reconnected with old friends as well. Martin Nyiendo (my dancing partner from Kisii High School) had arrived in the United States in 1962 and was finishing his engineering studies at nearby Wisconsin State University in Platteville. My friend Laban Otieno from Maseno High School had arrived in the United States in 1964 and was completing undergraduate studies at Wisconsin State University in Eau Clair, Wisconsin. My apartment, located on Erie Street in S.E. Minneapolis, was a frequent location for social events and parties. It was nice to be part of a social circle again.

I continued to send money back home whenever possible, and waited for updates on a special project my father wanted to initiate. Zablon's dream, or vision for the future, was that his children should start a family business in the nearby towns of Yala or Siaya. If such a business was not started, he envisioned a day when the majority of the Odenyo family would be scattered in pursuit of jobs. In his vision he was very forward-thinking, for he was witnessing a trend where the progressive and educated youth in Gem were seeking their fortunes away from their rural villages, with negative consequences on traditional family structure. The new generation of Luos was getting "lost" in the wilderness of the cities. To prevent this from happening in his own home, he wanted to create a family business within commuting distance from Got Regea to serve as a unifying force.

Zablon wrote to me all these ideas and I wanted to support his vision, especially since he requested that Adet and I (his two eldest sons) set an example for the younger generation. It was like he was passing the torch, or the family spear as we may say, over to Adet and me. On

February 18, 1969, my father sent me a letter in Dholuo referring to the business project:

> It is my wish and my desire for you and Adet to pro-
> vide the light and leadership for your younger brothers
> and sisters to follow. Peace and development within our
> family must be accompanied by unity within our family.
> After the construction of the building is done, you can
> all give it one name which reflects the love, unity, and
> determination of our family as one. May the good Lord
> lead you and guide you in your studies and endeavors. I
> am your loving father. Z. Sangoro Odenyo.

The first step was to acquire land for the business. On September 17, 1969, he wrote to tell me that he used my money (as well as part of the 5,000 Kenyan shillings received as death benefits from Lut Ezra Obuong's employer) to buy a plot of land in the town of Siaya. He also gave me estimates for construction materials. His letter included the following message:

> Our beloved son, Amos Otieno. I wish to acknowledge
> the receipt of your letter of September 7, 1969, and
> also the one from the previous month. It is true that I
> have had deep thoughts about the family. I have prayed
> for and wished for the kind of family unity which you
> will all share after I am gone. It would make me very
> happy if you and Adet can bring peace and unity in our
> family. My thoughts and desire for a plot of land is so
> that I can create something which will create peace and
> unity in our family. May the Almighty God guide you,
> lead you and bless you in your studies. I am your loving
> father. Z. S. Odenyo.

I was happy for the update and also glad to know that in less than a year I would be graduating from the University of Minnesota. My plan was to return to Got Regea and discuss how I could further assist in establishing the family venture.

On Wednesday, October 8, 1969, I received a telegram from my brother Robert. It contained only four words: "Father dead burial Sunday." I will not even attempt to describe my emotions. It was too painful. Just one more year…one more year, and I would have been able to return home to see him. His death caught everyone off guard. He had walked on his own into Nyanza Provincial Hospital (the "Russian Hospital") in Kisumu for a relatively minor operation. He never walked out alive. I heard he died from complications with anesthesia.

Attending my father's funeral was not a viable option. Even if I departed the next day, I was in danger of arriving late for the funeral. I also lacked money for airfare and was in a critical phase of research for my doctorate degree. I resigned myself to wait until next year at which time I would spend more time at home.

I was still a keen follower of political events happening in Kenya. I wanted to keep current with major events because my goal was to return to Kenya and play some part in politics or administration. Unfortunately, between 1963 and 1969, I noticed a gradual trend in Kenyan politics. This trend was tribalism, nepotism, and corruption. The Kenya I remembered prior to September 1961 was of a group of different tribes united in a common goal—the end of British colonialism. Tribal identity was recognized, but for the most part it was not adversarial. We all had a common interest—*Uhuru*, or *Uhuru na Sheria* (freedom and law)—as I used to say as a police officer in Mombasa. Even I, a Luo, was proud to mark in my pocket diary the words "Kenyatta released!" on August 14, 1961. After independence, Jomo Kenyatta (a Kikuyu) became prime minister then president. Oginga Odinga (a Luo) became vice-president. Yet by 1966, Kenyatta had cleverly marginalized his vice-president and former supporter to the point that Odinga resigned, formed an opposition party (KPU), and wrote a book titled *Not Yet Uhuru* (1967). Just a year earlier, a critic of Kenyatta, Pio Gama Pinto (of Indian descent), was assassinated. Tensions escalated to the point that in October 1969, Kenyatta publicly berated his former vice-president in a speech in Kisumu, Odinga's stronghold. Kenyatta was reported to have addressed Odinga and his

KPU supporters and said in Kiswahili, "We are going to crush you into flour. Anyone who toys with our progress will be crushed like locusts." Numerous people in the crowd were shot in the chaos that followed. Kenyatta then placed his former vice-president in detention for two years and banned the KPU.

In 1969, Kenyatta also imprisoned Achieng Oneko, the pre-independence freedom fighter from Nyanza Province (Oneko was released in 1975). Oneko used to publish our *Ramogi* newsletter and had been detained with Kenyatta by the colonialists in 1952. In April 1969, Argwings Kodhek died in a mysterious car accident on the streets of Nairobi. Kodhek was Kenya's first African lawyer, a Mau Mau defense attorney, and a cabinet minister from Gem constituency. A pattern seemed to emerge when just three months later, in July 1969, Tom Mboya was assassinated on the streets of Nairobi. Mboya was the minister of economic planning and a personal ally to Kenyatta. However, he was also perceived as the likely heir to the aging president. Just within the last year of his life, Mboya began to speak openly about the corruption of Kenyatta's inner circle, a criticism that could not be tolerated by the Kikuyu elite. When the Kikuyu assassin was apprehended, he kept referring to a "Big Man" that sent him to murder Mboya. Later, when Kenyatta arrived at the Holy Family Cathedral to give a eulogy of Mboya, stones were thrown at his vehicle. The president's eulogy was instead read by my high school teacher, Samuel Onyango Ayodo (Minister for Tourism and Wildlife).

This is just a short overview of the post-independence political climate that I was witnessing from America. In fact, I am sure that every Kenyan in the United States was aware of these events, and watched with horror as our homeland became divided along tribal lines. It affected us so much that in the late 1960s I heard rumors that the East African Students' Association in New York was split along tribal lines (Kikuyu vs. non-Kikuyu). We heard stories of our educated colleagues returning home to assume administrative jobs within the Kenyan government only to be passed over for promotion by uneducated relatives and supporters of the president. Instead of "Africanizing" the civil service, Kenyatta was "Kikuyu-nizing" it. Under the British, we all were calling for *Uhuru*, but when *Uhuru* came, it was something totally different.

I tried to be optimistic about the political situation in Kenya, hoping that the trends I was seeing were just the initial labor pains of a newly independent country, and that over time, with "maturity" (as Professor Hotz at Augustana College was fond of saying), Kenya would evolve into a democracy. While I kept up my hopes, I had bills to pay and a doctorate thesis in sociology to write at the University of Minnesota. My thesis was titled "Africans and Afro-Americans on Campus: A study of some of the relationships between two minority sub-communities." My thesis was approved and in June 1970, I became the first Kenyan to obtain a University of Minnesota doctorate degree.

One week later I landed in Nairobi, where I took the first bus I could find to Kisumu. From there I climbed the roads until I reached the heights of Maseno where I attended school over twenty years ago, and where my father had attended school before me. I continued north, in the direction of Uganda, but paused for a moment when I reached the Dudi market. There were still rows of bananas and *akala* shoes for sale, but there were more buildings, and fewer customers. I made a right turn onto the small dirt road, and soon passed Luanda Primary School. This is where both my father and younger brother held the position of headmaster, and where I once rang the class bell as a student. There were still students playing, but whereas in my day we kicked oranges, these children were kicking a ball made of stuffed plastic bags and string. I crossed over the Dienya River, expecting to hear the sounds of bartering at the Regea market. However, the courtyard was empty, with heaps of dried cow dung and mud where the shops once stood. I walked further, drawing closer to the old magnificent fig tree at the center of Got Regea. I paused beneath it, for its many leaves and twisted branches could still offer me shelter from the hot Nyanza sun. I wished this tree could talk and share with me the details of the community *barazas* held under its branches during the last decade. I last saw this tree at age twenty-six, when I was not yet old enough to join the old men as they debated our village affairs. I was now thirty-five, old enough to listen to their meetings. While standing beneath the fig tree, I marveled over the newly-built Saint Peter's Church, complete with brick walls and an iron roof. It had taken Reverend Simeon Nyende,

Zablon Sangoro Odenyo, Simeon Odera, and others more than a decade to complete the project. According to the inscription near the door, my father's friend, Reverend Festo H. Olang, laid the foundation stone on May 18, 1963. The new brick church stood side by side with the old mud-walled and *olenge* roof church. None of us dared tear down the old church, lest we tear down part of ourselves. It was in that now empty church that as a boy I took Holy Communion, listened to the sermons of my father, and sang along with the magnificent choir of my uncle Simeon Odera.

I continued walking toward the valley between the hills of Otieno and Aruwa. I entered through the *rangach*, the gateway to our home, and recognized my old *simba* to my immediate right, and my mother's house, some forty yards away, directly ahead. I was home.

My mother greeted me and then proceeded into prayer, thanking *Nyasaye* for bringing me home. Over the last nine years I had been to many churches in America, and I had heard many wonderful prayers. Yet none of them could compare to the familiar sound of prayer spoken in one's mother-tongue, and by one's mother. My father used to give these prayers and blessings to each of his children before and after our journeys. When my mother finished her prayer, I greeted my siblings. However, I would talk to each of them later. I first needed to pay my respects and farewells to two people.

I easily located my father's grave, still identified by a round bulge of earth covered with small rocks in the shape of a cross. There were so many things I wanted to tell him, to share with him, to ask him, but now he was gone. Many of my own achievements in life were due to his influence and his values that he had instilled within me. He had always pushed me to do my best, to focus on the goals and not the obstacles. I only wished that he was still alive for me to tell him *erokamano*, meaning "thank you."

I made my way to the gravesite of my brother, Lut Ezra Obuong. His resting place lay near his mud-walled house that he shared with his wife for just one night. His grave had already been cemented in the shape of a cross, with the handwritten words "Third son of Zablon Sangoro" etched into the surface. My dearest brother, my closest age mate, also gone. I stood there in silence, feeling the loss of family, the loss of potential, and the loss of time.

Over the next few days I had time for thought, solitude, and long conversations with the old and the young. Late one afternoon I found myself sitting alone under the shade of the fig tree next to Saint Peter's Church, reflecting on the changes that I discovered in my village. I learned that the *baraza* system of self-governance had virtually collapsed, and the *mlango* (Alfayo Kodhe) had lost all authority. The spiritual leader of the village, Simeon Nyende, had abandoned the Anglican Church in favor of a newly-built *Johera* church.[17] Many young people had never been inspired by the heavenly sounds of Simeon Odera's choir, nor had they heard the wisdom of the *nyatiti* (Luo harp). The only thing bought and sold near the Regea market was *chang'aa* and alcoholism. Luanda Primary School, which my father helped build, was no longer considered part of Nyanza Province. There was gossip and division everywhere.

In my nine years away from home, I had changed too. I had left this place in pursuit of education, of knowledge, and the means to help my family prosper. However, I could not apply the tools and job skills I had acquired in America to any profession within my rural village. I traveled so far, yet now that I was home, I knew I could not permanently stay here.

How would I fare in this new Kenya, this independent Kenya that I so desperately missed for almost a decade? I have always tried to pull myself up by my own merits, never asking for any special favors but only the opportunity to do my best in pursuit of my goals. I left Kenya to acquire education not just for education's sake, but as a way to live to the best of my potential, with the goal of returning home and serving my country. How could I apply this potential in the new Kenya now that *uhuru na sheria* had been replaced by nepotism, tribalism, and corruption? How could I expect to rise by my own merits in any government profession? Those before me such as Tom Mboya, Oginga Odinga, Achieng Oneko, and Argwings Kodhek—all respected leaders and freedom fighters, were either dead or imprisoned. Many of Nyanza's leaders had stood with this nation during our struggle for independence, but now it appeared our nation was turning its back on us, just like the story in which Nyamgondho wuod Ombare turned his back on his wife. Would we learn to work together towards a mature and cooperative nation, or would we assimilate into a culture of frustration and spite, as in the case of the old Luo prison guard in Mombasa?

All these questions weighed heavily on my mind as I sat alone under the fig tree. Ahead of me the sun was slowly setting, casting its last few rays of sunshine from behind Otieno's Hill. I realized there was not enough time to answer all my questions before the sun set, and my village would once again be engulfed in a moonlit darkness. My mother was cooking a very special meal for me tonight—*kuku, sukumawiki,* and *ugali*. This was always my favorite meal, the same meal she cooked for me after I completed *nak*. I knew she preferred to eat before the sun completely set, lest our neighbors assume we are hiding when eating. I resigned to organize these thoughts about my own future tomorrow. If I awoke early enough, I might depart from my *simba*, climb the trail to the top of Otieno's Hill, face east, and greet the rising sun in the manner I had once seen of the old men in our village. Who knows, I might look toward heaven and ask *Nyasaye* for a quick blessing and some guidance for the start of a new day.

As I got up from the fig tree and walked along the path to my mother's house, my immediate concerns turned towards the needs of my family. In 1961 I had left a simple, yet well-maintained home, with signs of life and progress. The home that I found upon my return was a shadow of its former self, with deteriorating buildings and overgrown gardens. The main unifying force in our family, my father, was gone, and many of us still appeared to be in mourning. Only Adet, my elder brother, remained as the family's primary source of income, and he was overwhelmed with the endless burden of maintaining not only his own growing household, but the home of our mother and our younger siblings. Next to my mother, Adet was now the family leader, the one who carried my father's spear—a symbol of courage, leadership and responsibility. I knew that I needed to step in, to give back, and to assist my elder brother in bringing up the family. This was my father's dying wish to me. It was a wish that I started fulfilling immediately, and it has continued until today.

Olivia Adhiambo and Lut Ezra Obuong (siblings)
with their mother Grace Dina, 1964.

(Siblings) Adet Okwata, Olga Achieng, Robert Okwata,
late 1960s.

Parent's day at Alliance High School, 1964. Back row: Lut, Olga, Lucia Odera, Pheadelia Opieche, Jerusha Ohanga, unknown. Front row: Zablon, Simeon Odera, Apeles Odera, Grace Dina, B.A. Ohanga, unknown.

Daniel Dindi Odenyo in Got Regea, 1968.

Funeral for Zablon Sangoro Odenyo under the fig tree,
October 12, 1969. Grace Dina (in chair), Rosalie (holding child),
Olivia (next to Rosalie).

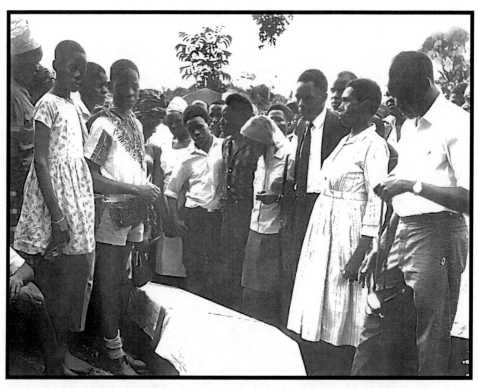

Burial of Zablon Sangoro Odenyo, October 12, 1969.
Grace Dina Adero surrounded by sons and grandchildren.

9

Words from My Father (1970–1983)

My story is a long one and the sun is now quite hot.
Come, let us sit under the fig tree and talk.

—Dr. Amos Otieno Odenyo, 1975 autobiography.

My name is Odera. I am the last born child of Dr. Amos Otieno Odenyo, the author of the first half of this family memoir. I will tell the rest of his story as I have witnessed it, and as I heard it from the lips of Dr. Odenyo himself. I will also share with you how my life has been influenced by my father.

In 1961, while my father was living in Nairobi and preparing for his departure from Kenya to the United States, he was summoned by his father, Zablon Sangoro Odenyo, to Got Regea. According to my father's pocket diary, the date was likely April 1, 1961. When he entered his parents' house, he found his father sitting quietly with his elder brother Timothy Okumu, and cousin Habakuk Wambuya. Timothy and Habakuk explained to Otieno that he needed to marry before going to America. Luo tradition dictated that sons marry in strict sequence of birth. Since Otieno was expected to remain in the United States for at least four years, his younger brothers would not be able to marry until he returned. They also warned him that people who go to America become "lost" and never come back to the village.[18]

Timothy and Habakuk specifically requested that Otieno marry Judith from Ramula. Otieno and Judith had been dating from the time he graduated from Kisii High School in 1958. Judith was greatly admired by the entire Odenyo family, having met the family in Got Regea on several occasions. Zablon was a good friend of Judith's father, Benjamin, whom he met while working in Ramula as a judge in the African Tribunal Courts. Although Zablon was not voicing the request for marriage himself, the fact that he summoned his son home to Got Regea to listen to his brother and cousin meant that it was not only his request, but the expectation of the entire family.

The thought of marrying Judith was in itself not a problem for Otieno. He had a genuine relationship with Judith and it was clear to him that she had all the qualities he would want in a wife. Their relationship may have led to marriage in due course. The problem was timing and logistics in light of his upcoming departure from Kenya.

Otieno solicited the opinion of his high school friend Akich Okola, who had traveled in the 1960 Tom Mboya Airlift to Central State University in Ohio. In a letter received in Nairobi on June 24, 1961, Okola advised against marriage. He gave a precarious description of student life for Africans in America, and confirmed that it would be extremely difficult to survive as a newly-married couple in the United States. Otieno knew he had a big decision to make. However, after careful consultation with Judith, they decided to marry. The plan was that Otieno would return to Kenya in approximately four years to resume their marriage. The families of Otieno and Judith met on the first Saturday in July to finalize dowry payments.

Otieno and Judith married in Saint Peter's Church in Got Regea on Sunday, August 6, 1961. Martin Nyiendo, Otieno's close friend from Kisii High School, performed the role of "best man." The next morning Otieno and Judith left Got Regea for Nairobi to continue preparations for his departure to the United States. The newly-weds were graciously hosted by Nyiendo. Otieno left for America one month later, on September 7, 1961. Otieno's parents and Judith Odenyo stayed overnight with Nyiendo in Nairobi before heading back to Nyanza. Nyiendo remembers that his three guests appeared so solemn and depressed after Otieno's departure that barely a word was spoken that night, and they boarded their bus the next morning without even having breakfast.

Exactly nine months later, in May 1962, Otieno's son was born in

Busia, Kenya. In Luo culture it is common to name children in reference to the position of the sun at the time of childbirth. The boy was born when the sun (*chieng*) was first rising. Therefore, he was named "Omondi" ("born at dawn").

Judith sent a picture of Omondi to his father in South Dakota, and Otieno kept the picture inside his wallet for close to ten years. Unfortunately, the marriage between Otieno and Judith ended in divorce. There was simply too little time prior to Otieno's departure from Kenya to establish a marital foundation strong enough to overcome many years of separation. The divorce was not welcome news to anyone, especially to Zablon and Benjamin. Dowry, in the form of cows, had been paid to the bride's family. Family relationships had already been cemented.

After the divorce, the relationship between Otieno and Judith was based primarily on their son, Omondi. Otieno consistently sent money home for Omondi's welfare. He also sent money home to enable Judith, a community nurse, to continue technical training in furtherance of her career.

In 1967, Otieno married Mayone, who was born of Danish, German, Scottish, and English heritage. Mayone came from a very tight-knit and homogeneous community in rural Minnesota. Needless to say, there were quite a number of people who did not welcome the idea of Mayone marrying an African. Most people in her community had never met an African or even a black American. What they knew of Africa was heavily influenced by childhood stories about Tarzan and the Apes. What they remembered of Kenya were reports of white people fleeing from the Mau Mau. Remember the scene in the 1967 movie *Guess Who's Coming to Dinner*, where Sidney Poitier tries to convince his future white father-in-law that his mixed-race grandchildren could grow up to be "president of the United States" and have a "colorful administration?" My father participated in similar philosophical conversations with his future parents-in-law on a rural Minnesota farm in 1967. Their conversations were not as dry-eyed and diplomatic as they were for Mr. Poitier, and my father did not stay long enough in his future in-laws' house to come up with the idea that a half-Luo, half-white child could grow up to become a United States president!

Mayone had many other suitors. However, when she closed her eyes and pretended color did not matter, it was to Otieno that she was most drawn. He was strong and confident, yet quiet and non-presumptuous. He never pressured her to constantly talk, act witty, or be the life of the party. Despite the overwhelming cultural divide, it seemed like Otieno and Mayone were actually cut from the same cloth. They occasionally went out to dances, but she also felt perfectly comfortable sitting silently beside him for hours while they each read their own books or newspapers. In fact, that is how they met. While students at Augustana College in Sioux Falls, they competed on occasion to be the first to read the *Minneapolis Morning Tribune* in the college library. Otieno was the second black person Mayone had talked to in her entire life. She had trouble pronouncing his name until he taught her by having her quickly say the letters O–T–N–O.

Mayone was impressed that Otieno was such an honest and forthright person. On their second or third date he took out a picture from his wallet, showed it to her, and said, "See, he looks like me." That was his way of breaking the news to her that he had a son and a previous marriage in Kenya. He never tried to hide anything of significance from her. Yet, he was an extremely private person. It was only months after their marriage that she first learned about the Luo adult-initiation rite of *nak* (removal of teeth). While walking through the apartment hallway, she caught a glimpse of him in the reflection of the bathroom mirror inserting his lower dentures into his mouth. Never again did anyone in our family see him without his six lower teeth. I do not believe he was ashamed—he just did not want the attention or misplaced sympathy. My father apparently was not alone in this. The American wife of a friend of my father recently explained to me how she first learned about the existence of *nak* after six years of marriage:

> We were sleeping—I decided to get out of bed. I sat up, put my feet on the floor, and felt a sharp pain. I turned on the light and removed a pair of false teeth with wires sticking out from my foot. This is when my husband first explained to me this thing called *nak*! Something about lockjaw and feeding people…

Words from My Father (1970–1983)

My sister was born in Minnesota in 1970. My sister was born at night, when the sun was hiding. Therefore, my father named her "Atieno." She was also named "Dina" after our paternal grandmother whose name was Grace Dina Adero (Obuong) Odenyo. It was after Atieno was born that my maternal grandparents in Minnesota not only came to terms with their daughter's decision to marry an African, but actually embraced Otieno and our entire family. They showed us nothing but love until their last days, and I certainly loved them as well.

I was born in Minnesota in 1971. My name, Odera, is the masculine version of my grandmother's name Adero. So, my sister and I were both named after our grandmother. My father also named me in honor of Simeon Odera, his uncle (through marriage) and a respected elder near the village of Got Regea. However, when I am in a humorous mood I tell my friends that I was named directly after the great Chief Odera Akang'o of Gem and a little bit of respect is due on their part in addressing me.

All three of Otieno's children were given European names; however, in our home my father generally called us by our Luo names. This reinforced the unique bond I had with my father, and with my Luo identity. Outside of professional circles my father was almost always called by his birth name, Otieno. I cannot recall my mother ever calling my father "Amos" in our home.

In August 2005, I sat down with my elder brother Omondi and our father and asked about the first time they met. I learned that when Dad traveled home to Got Regea in 1970, one of the first things he did was request that Judith bring Omondi to Got Regea for an introduction. Omondi was prepared for the meeting, having always known that his father was in a far-away place called America. When they first met they spent a lot of quiet time together. Dad proceeded gently and did not force any aspect of their first meeting. They walked around Got Regea hand-in-hand while relatives peered over each other's shoulders and discretely observed the interaction between father and son. Dad gave Omondi a pen and paper, and asked him to spell his complete name. He wanted to test his son's writing ability, and confirm that his son knew his last name as Odenyo. In subsequent days, Dad consistently visited Omondi in Kisumu, where he was studying at the Aga Khan

School (1969–1973). From Kisumu, they traveled to Got Regea and surrounding areas. Dad's driving skills learned on the paved and orderly roads of America were apparently of no use to him on the bumpy dirt roads of Nyanza. Passengers whispered to each other: "You see, he went to America but still he cannot drive!"

Omondi accompanied Dad to Nairobi, where they stayed in the New Stanley Hotel. It was a memorable event for Omondi. It was the first time he saw a traffic light, the first time he stayed in a modern hotel, and the first opportunity to bond with his father. He had always bragged to his friends, "My father is in America," but now that his father had returned from America, he appeared for the most part just like other relatives.

Reflecting upon his childhood in 2005, Omondi said his father's early absence never left an emotional void. Omondi described a very happy childhood, saying, "I don't remember lacking anything. I had a sense of security and comfort." Subsequent discussions with Omondi lead me to believe that this is due to the supportive extended-family system that is so common in Africa. Omondi knew his Uncles Adet, Victor, Robert, Booker, and Dan, for they periodically visited him in Kisumu on Dad's behalf. For a time, Omondi lived with his Aunt Olivia, her husband Samson, and their five children. Omondi considered Aunt Olivia almost like a second mother, stating, "I never felt like a stranger in her home. Her children are like my own brothers and sisters. There was always a sense of family." This extended-family support system would eventually include a loving step-mother (my mother), and a caring step-father (Judith's new husband).

While in Nairobi in 1970, my father spent a few weeks staying in Winston Ayoki's new maisonette in Woodley Estate. Winston, Linda, and their two baby girls were in New York City preparing to relocate to Nairobi. On August 14, Dad wrote a postcard, lovingly addressed to his seven-month old daughter in Minnesota.

> Dear Ones, I have been on the road almost every day. In thirty minutes I'll be going to the airport to meet Winston, then back on the road tomorrow. I will fly next Tuesday. Dina Atieno must come to the airport

unless she is in the hospital. All is well. I miss you both so much, but it will only be a few more days. I believe you can persevere. There is quite a bit to tell you when I arrive. Love, Otieno.

Once back in the United States, my father resumed lecturing in sociology at the University of Minnesota, and taught Kiswahili in a new Afro-American Studies program. He was interviewed by the Rockefeller Foundation which offered to send him back to Kenya to lead a Rural Development Program associated with the University of Nairobi. Dad was tempted to accept the offer, but was concerned that the position might only be a temporary one as permanent funding was not guaranteed. He interviewed with York College of the City University of New York (CUNY), and on April 6, 1971, was offered a position as assistant professor of sociology. At that time York College did not have its own campus, and classes were held in various buildings scattered across the Borough of Queens. My father was informed that a permanent campus would eventually be built in Jamaica, New York. Where other job-seekers may have looked askance at the prospects of teaching at a college without a campus, he looked at it as an opportunity and a challenge. At York College he could make a difference, and he could build the sociology program from the ground up. He knew it could be done—he himself had helped design the Afro-American Studies program at the University of Minnesota, and participated in building Ndiru Intermediate School brick-by-brick nearly twenty years earlier. My father accepted the position, and my mother, sister, and I accompanied him to New York City in the fall of 1971.

During his career at York College, Dr. Odenyo taught a variety of courses: Introduction to Sociology, Sociological Analysis, Sociological Theory, Sociology of Work, Comparative Sociology, Occupations and Professions, Collective Behavior, Social Movements, Sociology of Development, Social Change, Deviance and Social Control, Police Behavior and Law Enforcement, Criminology, and Introduction to Africa. My father published several sociological articles, and was the Chairperson of Social Sciences at York College from 1972 to 1976, and 1979 to 1994.[19] Dr. Odenyo was also a consultant to SUNY

College (Sociology Department), New York University (National Endowment for the Humanities), and the New York State Department of Education.

In June 1973, my father accepted a short-term assignment providing cross-cultural training to U.S. Peace Corp volunteers in Nairobi. He acquired the position through the recommendation of his high school friend Winston Ayoki, then the Associate Director of Education for the Peace Corps in Kenya. Mom, Atieno, and I joined him on July 20 in Nairobi, where we stayed with Winston and Linda in Woodley Estate. Atieno and the Ayoki girls played "house" together, and their imitation of mothering skills including strapping toy dolls to their backs with *kangas* and parading themselves around the lawn. Surrounded by four girls, I joined in with the role-playing and tried to breast-feed a plastic toy doll. The four of us departed Nairobi for New York on September 1, in time for my father to teach the fall semester at York College.

On January 28, 1974, my father traveled back to Kenya, where he assumed greater responsibilities in the Peace Corps training program, especially in Nyeri and Embu. Mom took us to visit our grandparents in Minnesota, where I received my first postcard (dated March 12):

> Dear Odera, I hope you are not crying all the time and beating up on your sister. You be good to your grandparents. Daddy.

The three of us flew from Minneapolis to join him in Nairobi, arriving on April 2. This time the four of us stayed in a furnished apartment off of East Church Road in Westlands. After Omondi finished his school semester, he stayed with us in Westlands and joined us in our visits to Got Regea, Kisii, Nanyuki, and Mombasa. My mother fully embraced her environment and anticipated settling in Kenya once my father obtained permanent work in the country. She began learning basic Kiswahili and was able to drive alone around Nairobi conducting various household errands. She describes to me a Nairobi that I have never known—a clean and orderly city, complete with simple but well-maintained roads. Although poverty was evident, crime was rare. During the daytime she could walk around Nairobi with a purse strapped over her shoulder and not gather the immediate attention of purse snatchers or homeless street children tugging on her ankles.

It was difficult for my mother to find a paying job. She was qualified as a Teacher of the Deaf and Hard of Hearing, but there were few professional opportunities for her to earn a salary in her field in Kenya. She was offered work, but was expected to work for minimum wage or for free. Mom, Atieno, and I returned to New York City on August 15. Before Dad departed Kenya on September 3, he enrolled Omondi in Saint Augustine's Preparatory School in Mombasa under Headmaster Lupino De Mello.

Dad thought it important that Omondi know him better, so arrangements were soon made for Omondi to join us in New York. The Ayoki family assisted him in his travel preparations in Nairobi. At Ayoki's house, Omondi met a black American lady who gave him a few tips on life in America, including the recommendation that he try eating pizza. Without knowing what this food was, he assured her that he would eat this food when he arrived in New York.

Omondi, thirteen years old, traveled by himself from Nairobi to Brussels, where he had an eight-hour layover. There, in the airport, he witnessed an event so shocking that he could barely believe his eyes. When he entered the men's room he saw a white man, on his knees, cleaning the toilets. Omondi stood paralyzed near the entrance, his eyes fixated on the incredible sight before him. From his experience in Kenya, white people did not clean their own toilets. They hired poor Africans to do this dirty job.

Omondi arrived in New York City a few days before Christmas 1975, and in January 1976 was enrolled in school. Omondi immediately became part of our family. My mother embraced him as her own son, and showed no favoritism towards any of the three children in the house. One day Omondi asked her for pizza, so my mother took him to a pizza shop on the corner of Hempstead and Springfield Avenue in Queens Village. Omondi was not accustomed to cheese or spaghetti sauce and was thus thoroughly disappointed in this food called pizza. He suspected that the black American woman in Nairobi had played a cruel joke on him by suggesting he eat it. He was confused why it was pronounced "Pete-za" when he clearly observed the sign above the counter refer to it as "pizza."

Omondi had a lot of new experiences. He was given light chores to do, such as walking Atieno and me home from school, and helping clean up around the house. He became Pastor Roth's favorite "altar boy" at Grace Lutheran Church on Springfield Boulevard. Omondi enjoyed riding horses at summer camp, but thoroughly despised skiing due to the cold. He enjoyed using the C.B. radio with my maternal cousins Steve and Mark Bergo in Green Bay, Wisconsin. Steve and Mark had previously told their friends and teachers that they had African relatives, but no one believed them. With Omondi's visit they had sufficient proof such claims were not made-up fairytales.

Unfortunately, my time with Omondi in the 1970s was cut short. Omondi was distracted by his glamorous new American environment and was simply not interested in school. He seemed attracted to entertainment and the fast-life, day-dreaming out loud about becoming a NASCAR driver. Although he was the perfect son at home, he seemed to gravitate toward the trouble-makers in school. Omondi's teachers informed Dr. Odenyo that his son often refused to come to class, and preferred to roam the halls. His English teacher, Ms. Fillmore, summed it up best with her evaluation on April 21, 1978: "Omondi simply does not try, does not do assigned work, and does not seek help." My father felt somewhat duped when he discovered he was paying for Omondi's education twice: an expensive private school, plus expensive private tutoring, and Omondi was not paying attention to either one.

A few classmates were not kind to Omondi, making fun of his Kenyan accent and African roots. Much of this taunting came, ironically, from black American children. This is surprising because there was a strong Black Pride Movement in the 1970s. Alex Haley's *Roots* was published in 1976, and in 1977 almost every black person in America was glued to a television to watch the inspiring miniseries version of the book. Yet, some of these same black children joked that Omondi was "Kunta Kinte." A few cruel students called him "monkey boy," and asked him if he came from the land of the *Planet of the Apes* (a popular science fiction movie series). I think these negative external influences exacerbated his existing adolescent ambivalence towards school. Despite several steps taken by our father to rectify the matter, the situation deteriorated.

I was totally unaware of these events at the time, but I can remember that one day in the summer of 1978 we all jumped into the car and headed towards John F. Kennedy (JFK) International Airport. We posed for pictures. Then my brother boarded the airplane, and was gone.

My father thought Omondi would concentrate in his studies if he was in a familiar and rural Kenyan environment. Unfortunately, despite every possible intervention by his mother, the situation actually became worse. I remember one morning my father driving me to school on the Clearview Expressway, and he was in an exceptionally gloomy and silent mood, bordering on being angry. I asked him what was wrong. He refused to give any details, but slowed the car and said, "I received a letter in the mail regarding Omondi. Omondi, Omondi, Omondi." When Dad said someone's name three times with no explanation, you knew there was a major problem.

I would neither see nor hear from Omondi for another five years, but I never forgot him during that time. I always looked up to him. He was bigger, stronger, and able to take care of me almost as a junior parent. He picked me up from school and performed babysitting duties at home. After he left I was intimidated by some bullies and replied, "I have a big brother and if you don't stop he's going to come and beat you up!" Omondi was always my protector, even when he was not around.

Despite Omondi's adolescent problems, he did manage to continue his high school studies at St. Mary's in Yala (1979), Otieno Oyoo Secondary School (1980–82), and Homa Bay High School (1982–83). Omondi improved along the way, partly due to warnings given by my father. In a letter dated October 29, 1979, he wrote (in part):

> I don't care about all your fun and games as long as you know you are responsible for what you do and its consequences. All these are adolescent sideshows that adolescent stage brings about, but what are you going to do once the side shows are over? My struggle for education is too long and painful to write here. Education for you it is a joke!

Dad went on to warn Omondi that education was the only tangible thing he had to pass along to his children. Otieno informed his son that he would not provide him with future assistance in life (including returning to America) if he was not willing to work hard in school, control his vices, and stop blaming his failures on others. This message clearly caught my brother's attention, and he quickly made a choice to take school seriously. Previously, in July 1979, Headmaster John B.O. Juma described Omondi as "Negligent, insubordinate, and shows a negative attitude towards work. Improve or leave school." In contrast, Headmaster Simon Adongo noted in 1983, "Has desire to learn and works hard for it!"

There were other relatives from Kenya in the United States. Starting around 1970, my father's younger brothers, Victor, Booker, and Dan, each came to the United States for educational purposes. First it was Uncle Victor, who arrived in 1971, received a Master of Arts degree from the University of Minnesota in 1973, and obtained his Ph.D. in Soil Science from Virginia Tech in 1976. Uncle Dan arrived in 1974, and Uncle Booker arrived in 1977. They both obtained Master of Business Administration degrees from Radford University in Virginia. Two of my uncles' wives decided to pursue higher education as well. Aunt Awino (Uncle Dan's fiancée) arrived in the United States in 1976 to study biology, and Aunt Millicent (Uncle Booker's wife) arrived in 1979 to study accounting.

I did not know it at the time, but my father assisted each one of them in various ways, ranging from their immigration paperwork, airfare, logistical support, temporary housing, and first year educational fees. New York City was always the starting point, and my father picked them up from JFK Airport. Our relatives usually stayed in our house before proceeding to various schools, but not before being well-fed with good old-fashioned midwestern cooking and perhaps a few extra dollars in their pockets.

Next came several nieces and nephews. In a way, my father was providing his own Tom Mboya Airlift, or what could be coined the "Otieno Airlift." He never talked about it, never bragged about it, and never complained about it. He just did it.

Three decades into the Otieno Airlift, a middle-aged Kenyan

cousin of mine arrived at JFK Airport unannounced, ready to enroll in school, but without sufficient financial resources for even the first month's rent or tuition. Of course the first phone call this cousin made was to my father, who dropped everything and once again headed back to JFK Airport. By this time my father was approaching retirement and wanting to conserve his financial resources by not committing to yet another series of financial obligations. But relatives in Kenya soon reminded him that he had contributed financially to *only* seven of his eight siblings' households. For the sake of equality, Dad realized he had no choice but to make it a perfect record and help the remaining eighth household via my cousin.

Someone born and raised in America may not fully comprehend the tremendous sense of duty and obligation among extended African households, especially for elders or those more financially capable. Well before the days of free primary education in Kenya, Dad paid school fees for many of my cousins. He financed several of their university degrees in India. Whenever he traveled home to Got Regea, he tackled some family project, such as a new fence, gate, or roof. He even financed the construction of his elder brother Adet's rural home, to thank him for his thirty years of support for the extended family. So far I have only mentioned family. Dad contributed to community development projects, and supplemented the salaries of pastors and teachers. When deaths occurred in Kenya, he sent money for funeral expenses. When deaths occurred within the Kenyan community in America, he sent money for funeral and transportation purposes, even if he did not know the deceased. He did this consistently for nearly forty years.

Not all of this support was charity. Dad had a strategic plan. He knew that only through investing in the educational and professional ambitions of his family would they move forward together. To some extent, it worked. Several of our family members have equaled him in educational and professional accomplishments, enabling them to also be "blessed" with the financial burdens of family leadership.

My father's strong commitment to empowering others was also evident in his professional activities. Between 1975 and 2007 he was a Board of Trustees member for World Education in Boston, an organization founded in 1951 by Welthy Honsinger Fisher. Fisher dedicated much of her long life (1879–1981) to the advanced of education and eradication of poverty, especially for women of the Third World. My father was personally inspired by her life's work, considered it an honor to personally meet her in the late 1970s, and kept more than one copy of her autobiography, *To Light a Candle*. Dr. Odenyo carried out several World Education projects on the African continent, including South Africa and Kenya.[20]

My relationship with my father, especially when I was young, was warm and comforting, but quiet and distant. Although my mother tells many stories about him romping around with us as toddlers, I often have to look at photo albums to convince myself that this was actually a part of my relationship with my father. As I approached the age of five or six I realized that there was an art to interacting with him. When my mother came home from work I could run to her, hug her, and ask her a million questions about her day. When my father came home, my sister and I made ourselves scarce. This might sound terribly wrong, but I have heard the same childhood descriptions from Kenyan friends my age. When Professor Odenyo came home from work, we gave him his space. The last thing he wanted after a hard day's work was little children running around the room asking him about his day. There was only one black and white television in the house, and while just moments ago it was turned to children's shows such as *Sesame Street* or *The Muppet Show*, once we heard his car pull up to the house Atieno and I would dash to the television, turn it off, and go to our rooms or somewhere else out of sight. This enabled my father to enter the house undisturbed, take a few moments to change his clothing, eat supper, and settle down in front of the television where he would watch Walter Cronkite give the evening news. Once the evening news was over, Atieno and I would slowly emerge from the other rooms and observe Professor Odenyo's activities from a respectable distance. If he was reading the newspaper, we waited until he was more than half-way through before we approached him for a few moments of his time and attention. We always gauged the mood carefully. If he put down the newspaper and engaged us in conversation, we knew he was in the mood to talk. If he looked down toward you while still holding the paper in front of him, we knew the timing was not quite right and moved on.

He was the king of his castle, and we knew our place. We were there to be seen and not heard, especially before or after work. Once he finished reading his newspaper, father would descend the steps into the basement where he did scholarly things like reading textbooks and grading papers. The sweet smell of his pipe and the distinct sounds of Luo *nyatiti* music would eventually make their way up the stairs. There, on the first floor, they would clash into the aroma of freshly baked bread and the sound of Lutheran hymns being hummed by my mother in the kitchen.

One of my clearest and earliest memories of my father's personality is when he took me to the circus at Madison Square Garden when I was approximately eight years old. It was not his idea. I had been pestering my mother for weeks to take me to the circus because my mother's friend, Mrs. Lue Tyler, had an extra ticket and took my sister and not me. I was adamant that I too get to go, and my mother must have persuaded my father to take me. I remember we sat high above the crowd in the cheap seats, but I was still excited to see the show even from a distance. The colorfully-dressed entertainers down below encouraged us to cheer and wave green neon lights. I had been looking forward to this moment for weeks, and I eagerly joined along with the crowd by cheering and waving. My father quickly put a stop to my excitement by instructing me to sit still in my seat and respectfully watch the act. This is how I remember my first and last circus performance. In a row all to ourselves, "miles" above the arena floor, the two of us sat perfectly still as if we were listening to a church sermon.

My father was not interested in remembering useless information such as my date of birth. Whenever he enrolled me in school or took me to the doctor, the person behind the counter asked him for my birth date. If I was lucky he would look down at me and say, "Odera, tell her your date of birth," as if he was testing me. If I was unlucky he would reveal he did not know, causing me huge embarrassment. Every other adult I knew placed such a huge emphasis on birthdays by singing songs to me and providing cakes and presents. It was extremely painful at a young age to believe that I was meaningless enough that my own father could never remember when I was born. My mother eventually informed me that in my father's childhood, birthdays were not a cause for celebration, and were in many cases not even known. No one ever celebrated my father's birthday, and perhaps it was only him that remembered it. Around the age of seven I confronted him with the issue, asking him, "Why don't you love me?" He looked very startled and sad when I asked him that question. He then hugged me and explained that he loved me despite not saying "Happy Birthday." He explained to me that his own father did not express his love to him in words, but that he always knew he was loved by his father and I should know this too. While his explanations provided some basic reassurances, they could not completely fill the emotional void that existed due to my misinterpretation of his feelings towards me. It would be almost thirty years before we would verbally express our love for one another again.

Although my father was not approachable on a consistent basis, when he was in the mood to spend time with me he was very affectionate, compassionate, and comforting. It was not the words that he would say, but his calm mannerisms and protective presence. We often sat on the front steps to catch a breeze on a hot summer night. We did not do much talking. For the most part we sat next to each other, or I on his lap, and sometimes we held hands. It was the non-verbal connection that I remember most. His cologne engulfed me; his sideburns tickled me. I would stare at the three-inch scar on his left forearm. I knew he received the scar when he was a policeman in a place he called Mombasa, and the scar bore witness to his strength and power to protect me. I looked at the bottoms of his feet, and wondered why they were as hard as leather and his toenails were either missing or distorted. "It is because when I was your age I played football and walked five miles to school without shoes," he told me.

I grew up hearing about Kenya, but in the 1970s it was still a vague memory to me. Its precise location and distance from New York City was also uncertain. But I knew one thing. Kenya was the home of Daddy's leader, the man who shouted "*Harambee!*" My father told us about the president of his country, Jomo Kenyatta, and when describing him he proudly imitated him by shouting in a deep and drawn-out fashion, "*Haaaaarrraaammmbbbeee!*" "This means pull together," Daddy explained; "Pull together as a nation for one common purpose." It was rare for Daddy to raise his voice or show much emotion, so when he shouted "*Harambee*" I was very impressed and excited. As he shouted "*Harambee*" he would raise one hand up into the air, not in a striking manner, but as if he was trying to touch the sky. On one occasion he repeated this but in his hand he held a stick topped with animal hair that was previously hanging as a decoration on our wall. I was only five or six years old, so I assumed this stick was an African feather duster, such as what we used in America to remove dust from tables and delicate household items. I did not know that this was an honorary fly whisk for elders that President Jomo Kenyatta always carried as a symbol of his wisdom and authority. There was much joy in my father when he admiringly imitated Kenyatta, and on one occasion he actually jogged around the room with me chasing him shouting "*Harambee!*"

In 1978, my father took us to Uppsala, Sweden, to visit his younger brother Victor and his family. On August 22, as we were watching Swedish television, the mood suddenly turned grim. My mother explained to me, "President Kenyatta has just died." I immediately recognized this man as my father's leader, although I did not yet understand the meaning of "president." Kenyatta was the one to pull us all together, the one who rallied us with shouts of "*Harambee!*" I turned towards my father and uncle, who were just sitting watching television, showing no emotion, no expression, no fear, and no sorrow. I waited for some time until I could talk privately to my father. I was confused that Dad's leader died and he was not crying. In fact, he looked like he had just heard the newscaster report that the weather would consist of mild temperatures, sunny skies, with a 50 percent chance of rain. My father took me close to him and calmly stated, "Odera, it is a sad day for Kenya, but with his death the door might be opened for the rest of us now."

I struggled with his words for many years to come. My father was an impossible man to reconcile. He explains that he loves me but never says it. He praises the leader of his country but upon his death shows no emotion. He speaks about this "door." What is this door he is talking about? Where is it? Where does it lead? Now he is no longer talking about *harambee*, but about a new leader who is shouting "*Nyayo!*"

"*Nyayo* means footsteps," he tells me. "This means we need to follow the example of our previous leadership."

This is all too overwhelming for my young mind to handle. Was the previous leadership good or bad? Dad points over to the wall of his basement library, which holds a framed picture of two African men. One is older, with lighter skin and a beard, and wearing a brown leather jacket. The other man is clean shaven, younger, darker, and missing two lower front teeth. "The older man is Kenyatta," Daddy explains. "Moi is the younger man, the new president of Kenya, the one who shouts *Nyayo*."

"Which one is better?" I ask.

"They are both good men, but Moi may do more for the country now that Kenyatta is gone," he explained.

Three years later, in August 1982, we were all sitting in my grandparents' farmhouse in Minnesota, and suddenly the topic turned once again to Kenya and my father. Everyone wanted to talk to Daddy about something called a *coup* happening in his homeland. At first I did not know what a *coup* was, but in short time I realized what it meant. Sections of the Kenyan military were trying to overthrow President Moi. Again, my father did not indicate whether this was a good or bad event. He simply acknowledged his concern over the matter.

It was at that point in my young and unschooled mind that I associated Kenyan politics with instability and bad leadership. It was as if Kenya's leaders were important enough that everyone talked about them, but not worthy enough that they very much mattered. My father was an avid follower of Kenyan politics, subscribing to a Kenyan magazine called *Weekly Review* which arrived at our house by mail. My father always took this red-colored magazine downstairs to read in his library. About once a month my father's friend, Professor Okello Onyango, stopped by our house. My father said Onyango came from an island in Lake Nyanza.[21] Onyango often returned some old *Weekly Review* magazines, and went downstairs to talk to my father. This happened on a reoccurring basis for several years starting in the early 1980s. I held Mr. Onyango, as well as all my father's friends, in high regard for no particular reason other than they were calling on my father, who in my eyes, was the king of our castle. Their calling on the king elevated their image for they now appeared somewhat like ambassadors. They all seemed like such gentlemen, with very dignified personalities and impressive verbal skills that I was otherwise not accustomed to in my encounters with adults in New York City. Each and every one of my father's Luo friends had at least two college degrees. I was never privy to their private conversations, which were conducted in Dholuo, a language I did not understand. Mr. Onyango and my father talked downstairs and my mother would send me to serve them Kenyan tea and biscuits. While I did not look forward to being sent on errands around the house, in such instances I actually appreciated the excuse to go into the basement and catch a glimpse of whatever was occurring in my father's high-court. Of course, nothing but small talk and tea was occurring, but in my youthful eyes I imagined something different. As I served them tea and biscuits I looked over their shoulders at the picture of Kenyatta and Moi. Mr. Onyango was slightly older and lighter than my father and wore a beard resembling that of President Kenyatta's. My father was darker and bore a slight resemblance to President Moi. With the backdrop of the presidents over their heads, I served the two professors tea and biscuits while imagining them as the true presidents of Kenya. I thought to myself that if only these two men could become the real leaders of their country, perhaps many of Kenya's problems could be solved.

We always knew when Dad's Luo friends were calling for him on the phone because they never identified themselves. When we answered the phone, they all said, "Hello, how are you?" Then they entered into a long series of English greetings and questions about how everyone was doing in our house. We always politely answered each one of their questions but often had no clue who was calling unless they happened to indirectly identify themselves in the conversation. Over time we learned to similarly ask how they were doing, just to hear their response and get some sense of who they were. If we dared ask the callers for their names it was taken as a great offense, despite the fact it might have been the first time they had ever called. This was in stark contrast to my mother's relatives who always identified themselves with, "Hi, this is Aunt Dorothy," or, "This is Grandma calling." Not so with Kenyan callers. It was straight into the pleasantries and questions about our family. Eventually, after all the salutations were exhausted, we would hand the phone over to Dad, and it would fall into a familiar pattern:

"*Angima* (I am well)...*ber ahinya* (very good)."

The conversation would last for some time, but we knew when the conversation was coming to a conclusion for they always ended the same way:

"*Onge wach* (no problem)...*aling alinga* (I am fine)."

Aling alinga was our favorite Luo phrase because it sounded very funny to us as children.

After Dad got off the phone we made sure we said to him "*aling alinga*" numerous times for mutual entertainment value.

Dad could walk along the streets of New York City, look at someone, approach him, and start talking in Dholuo. Then the man would respond back in Dholuo. They would shake hands and talk for a few minutes as if they were old friends. This fascinated me. I would ask him afterwards how he knew the person. He usually replied, "I never met him before today."

"So how did you know he was Luo," I would ask.

"I could just tell by looking at him," he always said, and never explained further.

Dad had his own collection of African music. I quickly learned to break them down into two types—old and new. I found it difficult to relate to most of the traditional music, for it leaned heavily on chanting back and forth in a rhythmic pattern, usually between a female leader and a group of women. I could identify the words as Luo, but could not understand what they said. The few instruments in the background sounded like bracelets or fiddles. My father played this type of music in the evenings when he was alone in the basement, or when he was in a reflective mood.

Music has always been a special part of my life. First, I enjoy it. Second, it has served as a conduit for understanding different cultures. I really liked the majority of the contemporary African music that my father played. They were played from albums with covers that had interesting names that frequently referenced the term "Jazz." It seems the word "Jazz" was quite popular in the 1970s and each and every

African band wanted to be affiliated with this phrase. To list a few, there was Jamhuri Jazz Band, Shirati Jazz Band, Mori River Jazz Band, K.Z. Morogoro Jazz Band, Ugunja Jazz Band, Central Siaya Jazz, and of course, T.P. O.K. Jazz, which seemed to be my father's favorite. Other albums had groups with names like Kiwiro Boys, Victoria Kings, Daudi Kabaka, Gem Lucky Boys, Golden Ugenya Boys, and D.O. Misiani. I had no clue what the musicians were singing about, but I grew up listening to all of their songs and enjoying them too. The songs were unique in that most of them started out very slow as if they were love songs, but suddenly—a pause—then a multitude of rhythms in alternating succession which could last another ten minutes. An African album was unique because it might list only four songs, but when played, it felt like there were twelve songs instead.

During a picnic at Cunningham Park in the late 1970s, Uncle Dan asked me to name my favorite African song. I replied immediately and proudly, "Maria Tebbo by Sam Mangwana!" My sister Atieno and I have always considered this our favorite African song for many reasons, starting with the cheerful introduction and laugh of the musician. We could identify a few English words: "I love you Maria Tebbo, Tebbo-la—Give me your love, oh Tebbo-la." Personally, I fell in love with the album cover, which showed a gorgeous lady with long braids. Last, but most important, every time we hear the song up until today it reminds us of our father's laughing and joking among many friends and family in our home. It was a festive and talkative side of him that we seldom used to see. My father was much more talkative when we were visited by his high school friends such as Dr. Shem Olende, a friend of his who lived in Mount Vernon and worked for the United Nations. Dr. Olende was always accompanied to our house with his beautiful wife Rose, their two daughters Achieng and Sharon, and later their son "Junior." My father's high school friend, Akich Okola, and his new wife lived in Flushing, New York, and were frequent guests in our home. We occasionally were visited by Martin Nyiendo from Oregon, who my mother understood was my father's closest friend. I remember my father dancing at the "Ambassador's" house off of Grand Central Parkway and 188th Street in Queens. Michael G. Okeyo was Kenya's Ambassador to the United Nations at the time. It was at the Ambassador's house that his wife served me my first real *uji* (porridge) made of reddish-brown millet instead of the white processed *uji* that we made at home from the box that said "Farina" or "Cream of Wheat."

Amos Otieno Odenyo with wife Mayone in Minneapolis, 1968.

Dr. Amos Otieno Odenyo with wife Mayone and daughter Atieno.
Graduation day, University of Minnesota, 1970.

Amos Otieno Odenyo with wife Mayone in Minneapolis, 1968.

Amos Otieno Odenyo with daughter Atieno. Minneapolis, 1970.

Amos Otieno Odenyo with daughter Atieno. Minneapolis, 1971.

Dr. Odenyo and son Omondi visiting Selesa, daughter
of high school friend Martin Nyiendo. Kenya, 1970.

Amos Otieno Odenyo with youngest son Odera. New York, 1971.

Dr. Victor Odenyo, early 1970s.

Dr. Victor Odenyo, with Atieno Odenyo,
Lake Ripley, Minnesota, 1972.

The two youngest brothers:
Booker Opondo and Daniel Dindi.
Kenya, early 1970s.

Booker Opondo Odenyo pursuing his M.B.A
at Radford University. Virginia, late 1970s.

Adet Okwata Odenyo (eldest son of Zablon Sangoro Odenyo).
Kenya, 1970s.

Atieno and Odera, staring down a calf in
the family home in Got Regea, 1973.

Dr. Amos Otieno Odenyo with his three children,
Omondi, Odera, and Atieno. Nairobi, 1974.

Dr. Amos Otieno Odenyo drinking coconut water with
son Odera and daughter Atieno. Mombasa, 1974.

Omondi experiencing snow for the first time with younger
siblings (on left) and neighbor Dayna Griles (on right).
New York, January 1976.

Elinor Robson (Iowa Boards of Education)
visiting Dr. Odenyo and family in New York, 1977.

Dr. Odenyo with son Odera, and daughter Atieno
in New York, 1977.

Dr. Odenyo's three children (Omondi, Odera, Atieno)
in Blacksburg, Virginia, 1978.

Dr. Odenyo and his children at JFK Airport, 1978.
We would not see Omondi (on right) again for five years.

10
Kenya (1983)

*It is important that my children know where home is. They may
not live here, and I might not live here either, but it is home.*

—Dr. Amos Otieno Odenyo, interview in January 2005
(sitting on the slope of Aruwa's Hill, Kenya).

My first vivid memories of Kenya are from the summer of 1983.
I was almost twelve years old, my sister Atieno was thirteen, and Dad
determined that we were now old enough to visit Kenya. He had visited Kenya numerous times between 1975 and 1983, but ruled out taking Atieno and me with him. He told my mother that we were simply
too young to remember our experiences in Kenya, so there was no
point in paying the expense of our airfare.

My sister and I traveled alone, as my father was already in Kenya.
In fact, this was his second trip home that year. From New York our
plane stopped in Dakar (Senegal), Monrovia (Liberia), Lagos (Nigeria),
and finally arrived at Jomo Kenyatta International Airport on the evening of July 6. We were greeted by Dad and the families of Uncle
Victor and Uncle Booker. We knew everyone except Booker's four
children, the youngest just a few months old and named "Amos" after my father. We piled into Uncle Victor's brown Range Rover and
headed out of the airport into countryside that reminded me of the
rural farmland where my mother grew up in Minnesota.

During the first ten minutes I saw few lights, and virtually no buildings. A strange semi-sweet smell permeated the night, as if some-one was burning wood. I was distracted by the fact that my father was driving Uncle Victor's vehicle. Did my father use his age seniority to commandeer the vehicle from his younger brother? What this some age-old Luo custom? What I did not realize, until the next day, was that it was not my father driving, but Uncle Victor. It had never occurred to me that the steering wheel would be on the right side of the vehicle.

Our father left us to stay with Uncle Victor's family in Hurlingham, Nairobi. His two eldest daughters were similar in age to Atieno and me and we all knew each other from trips between New York and Sweden. Their friends quickly became our friends, and we spent many days playing all sorts of games with a soccer ball (which everyone re-ferred to as a foot ball). I also enjoyed competing in wrestling competi-tions and exploring the dirt trails and roads which meandered through neighboring estates. At that time, Argwings Kodhek road was not the congested and overbuilt thoroughfare that it is today. There were empty lots along the road filled with tall grass, and I remember step-ping over a huge dead snake that someone had killed with a machete. Together with Uncle Victor's children we rode our bicycles up and down the wide dirt sidewalks and open fields until Kilimani Primary School, stopping at the small stores (near present day Yaya Center) to buy candy. We took the back trails leading to Ngong Road, and on a few occasions I walked alone on Mbagathi Way to visit Uncle Booker's family in Ngumo Estate.

I made a few friends of my own and remember visiting them in their apartments and accompanying them to Uhuru Park. Near this park there was a small video arcade which my Kenyan friends referred to only as "the machines." Together we discussed how to solve the problem of having no coins to insert into the machines. There were a lot of empty bottle caps scattered around, and we strategically placed them on the road for cars to run over them and flatten them into coin-sized shapes. We never actually tried to use these "coins." The excitement of squashing bottle caps soon eclipsed our desire to risk punishment for trying to use them as currency. We were all talk and no action.

While in Nairobi there was very little culture shock that I can remember. We ate the same *ugali* and *sukumawiki* (collard greens) that we grew up eating in New York, only now we learned to use our right hand instead of utensils. We heard the same African music and the same Dholuo, but still could not understand what was being said. I learned there was another language called Kiswahili, but had little need for it because most people spoke English. Atieno and I quickly learned that there were two types of our favorite soda. There was Fanta *baridi* (cold) and Fanta *moto* (hot). I also learned to drink *chai* (tea), which annoyed my father because I always tried to put four or five spoonfuls of sugar into the tiny teacups.

Paper currency looked similar to the toy money provided in the Monopoly board game. It was colorful, bigger, and each denomination carried an image of the president, Daniel Arap Moi. His photograph was also prominently displayed in every business. When the evening news began, the first announcements were a thorough review of the president's activities, down to the details of where he went to church, how much money he donated to a local development project, or what local problem he solved that the locals could not. Whenever he returned from his foreign travels, Kenyan flags were posted alongside the road. His presence was omnipotent.

There appeared to exist an informal way of planning. Guests showed up at people's houses unexpectedly, and relatives expected to be given rides in cars that were already full of passengers. I noticed that Kenyans, especially those in the rural areas outside of Nairobi, did not stand in line in the same orderly fashion that I was used to in America. Society seemed to work on the principle of "winner takes all." For example, the person who first enters a doorway is the one who manages to force his way through the crowd. In the rare event that a line exists, the person standing behind you is so close that you can feel his breath on your neck, and he often presses himself upon you as if to remind you of his presence (the reason of course, is to eliminate any physical space for someone to jump ahead in the line). A private conversation in a phone booth was virtually impossible. The person behind you literally stands with one foot inside the booth, and makes it obvious that he is following your conversation, forcing you to be economical with words and time.

Although adult strangers occasionally appeared rude, the young children seemed properly behaved. Compared to Americans, these Kenyan kids were actually likable. They were a little less whiny and a bit more mature than their American counterparts. The Kenyan children seemed to act like little adults in the presence of their parents, to the extent that the children would file out and shake each guest's hand. Then they would quietly entertain themselves, or sit silently until we left the house. By the way, everyone seems to shake hands in Kenya. It is often a long and ceremonious affair.

Prayers were also unjustifiably long. You arrive at someone's house, shake hands for five minutes, then everyone holds hands in a circle, and the host will pray. Before you eat, you pray. Before you are allowed to leave, you must pray. When you get to your next destination, you pray. Praying was not the problem—rather it was the length, frequency, and my inability to understand what was said beyond *erokamano* and *Nyasaye*.

I noticed that with the exception of the city centers, there were no road signs in the country. Roads seemed to meander without any particular planning. Dad often had to stop to ask for directions, and I was always amused to hear the responses:

> You see this road that you are on, you proceed on it over several hills until you see a fallen tree on your right, then you make a left, and go until you see these big *Wahindi* (Indian) houses on your left which are not what you are looking for, but you now know you should be looking for a smaller house with a *mabati* (iron) roof, which is also not what you are looking for, but you should now go slowly and watch out for that big hole in the road as it is now getting dark. You go around this one and make the next right to find your place, unless it has recently rained in that area, then you should first make a left and go a whole separate way...

I quickly learned that pedestrians do not have the right of way. Pedestrians yield to bicycles, bicycles yield to cars, cars yield to bigger cars, and bigger cars yield to trucks. Kenyan roads were very dusty, yet people seemed obsessed with shining their shoes, at least once a day. This obsession with shoe cleanliness seemed like a battle that could never be won, and I wondered why Kenyans, including my father, were still keeping up the fight.

Despite the equatorial climate, Kenyan men tended to dress formally, and had an obsession with business suits. Even in the rural areas I saw old men wearing sandals and old tattered suits. There also seemed to be a national dress code for children under three years of age. It appeared that a child that age was required to wear a heavy wool hat that covered the sides of the face, much like an Eskimo child might wear in the middle of a snow blizzard. It did not matter what the temperature was like outside. More than once I saw a woman walking along the road carrying an umbrella to protect herself from the hot mid-day sun, yet an infant is strapped on her back wearing a wool hat covering all but his tearful eyes. I felt like jumping out of the car and releasing these children from their pain and suffering.

I was not yet concerned about the concept of "tribe." There were simply *Wazungu* (white people), black people, Asian people, and "half-caste." Atieno and I did not like the term "half-caste." The phrase seemed to denote imperfection, like "half" of some scrap metal "cast" away into the recycle bin. We really did not understand the phrase, but everyone, including our cousins, used the term openly with no insult intended.

I met my brother again. Omondi did not like the way I referred to him as my "half-brother," which is the standard American way of referring to our relationship. I thought it was an appropriate term because it would explain to others why we did not look alike. However, he seemed very offended each time I said it. I could understand why. It appeared we shared the same opinion that it does not feel good when anyone refers to you as "half" of something.

Dad did not stay with Atieno and me at Uncle Victor's house in Nairobi, but frequently came by to collect us. On July 14, Dad took us to Treetops, a tree-level lodge built upon stilts in the Aberdares National Park. From the roof we had sweet cakes and tea while observing herds of elephant, wildebeest, and other wild animals drinking from the water hole below. Atieno and I thought we were safe until a rogue baboon scaled the lodge and jumped onto the tables, causing teacups to fly and tourists to run. We slept in the "Queen Elizabeth room," named for the night (February 6, 1952) that Princess Elizabeth stayed in the original "Treetops," a two-room structure built on top of a large fig tree. She went to sleep a Princess, but awoke a Queen, since her father, King George VI, died that night. Dad said that our grandfather was one of many leaders from Nyanza who would have met with Princess Elizabeth if she did not have to abruptly return to England. Before we drove back to Nairobi, Dad took us to Kiganjo Police Training College where he trained to become a police officer in 1959. I remember looking at old photographs on the wall, and being introduced to a police officer whom my father knew from his time at the academy.

Dad took us to local factories where stoves and other items are made from pieces of scrap metal. We also went to the zoo, Nairobi Game Park, and Kenyatta Conference Center. At nine in the morning on July 19, we started the long road trip to Kisumu. It is a trip that we made twice that summer and many more times in years to come. Heading west, we climbed the long hills cutting across the magnificent Rift Valley, East Africa's equivalent of America's Grand Canyon. In the Rift Valley we reached the shores of Lake Naivasha, where we stopped to observe the pink flamingos. In the town of Nakuru we ordered rice, *chapati* (flat bread), mutton stew, and spicy *samosas* (bread patties with potatoes and meat). An hour later, we stopped for tea at the Kericho Tea Hotel. I think my father made it a point to stop at this elegant hotel, for as we slowly sipped our tea in the grand and magnificently manicured veranda he would say, "Now you children know that this hotel in which you are sitting... we would not be sitting here back in the days when I grew up in Kenya. This is a colonial hotel, built exclusively for the British. No Africans were allowed in here unless you were holding a broom or some *Wazungu's* luggage." I think it gave my father a sense of satisfaction to be free to enter any hotel in Kenya, especially a colonial one.

Less than an hour later, as we bounced around the pothole-filled roads leading to Awasi, Dad would mutter, "Ah Ah Ah! These roads...I can't believe it! When I traveled these roads in my youth they were maintained better than this! I am beginning to believe my people cannot maintain anything properly."

We usually arrived in Kisumu around six in the evening. Dad always made it a point to visit his younger sister Olga, who worked at Standard Chartered Bank. Olga has always been the cheerful, smiling, and laughing Auntie—compared to her two older sisters and my father. She has a youthful energy about her. Atieno and I once wanted to take a picture with Aunt Olga near her house. She gasped, "I have to fix my hair," and literally sprinted down the road to her house. I remember that vividly because it was one of the few times that I saw an Odenyo relative run, or do something spontaneously and quickly. In the Odenyo family, everything in life moved slowly, with calmness and much deliberation. Meetings progressed slowly, introductions were drawn-out and elaborate, and time itself often appeared to stand still. Not so with Aunt Olga. She just ran down the dirt road yelling about her hair, leaving us very impressed.

We also stopped to visit Dad's elder brother Adet in Kisumu. Uncle Adet was the oldest brother in the family, and my father had a lot of respect for him. Dad mentioned that Adet paid school fees for him and other siblings. There was a sense of gratitude and appreciation in my father's voice whenever he spoke about Uncle Adet.

The three of us often stayed at Sunset Hotel where we ate tilapia fish and *ugali*. Sunset Hotel occasionally hired traditional Luo musicians, dressed in leopard skins and feathered hats, to play the *nyatiti*. This was a new experience for Atieno and me. We also ate at an Indian restaurant in Hippo Point, named after the occasional hippo seen wading in the waters of Lake Nyanza.

Staying with Dad at the Sunset Hotel was both a blessing and a curse. The issue stems from all three of us sharing one room—me in one bed with my father, and my sister in her own separate bed. In traditional Luo culture a father would never share a room with his two teenage children. Many Luo men of his generation would have booked two hotel rooms. However, Dad was very economical, and he did not want to incur the extra expense. This was the magic of our trips to Africa. In New York City we were not even allowed to enter his bedroom. Here in Kisumu, I was sharing a bed with him. You might think that I would have been overjoyed at the reversal of fortune. Well, I was at first, until his snoring kept Atieno and I awake each and every night, the *entire* night. Dad had the ability to snore so loudly and violently that I think it was possible to hear him perhaps three or four rooms away.

Atieno and I did not get a good night's sleep at the Sunset Hotel as long as we shared a room with Dad. I tried sleeping out on the balcony overlooking Lake Nyanza, but was soon chased inside by the onslaught of mosquitoes. I tried sleeping in the bathtub, but the walls separating my ears from my father's roars may as well have been made of a thin sheet of paper. I remember once requesting that he simply leave me in Got Regea with family so that I could get a good night's sleep.

Dad usually serviced and washed the car while in Kisumu. To clean the car, he simply drove down Oginga Odinga Street, and instead of making a right turn onto Obote Road, he continued straight down a dirt path until all four tires rested on the waters of Lake Nyanza. From there we hopped out and watched him pay some shirtless men to wash the car using only soap, rags, and water from the lake. They did not even have buckets!

The trip from Kisumu to Got Regea was always a long, slow climb, especially when the road was not maintained. They say you can always identify a drunk driver in Kenya because he is driving straight. A sober driver, however, has the sense to dodge and weave around the endless potholes, some so deep they could swallow half a vehicle. Atieno and I marveled over the sight of the low but fast-moving *matatus* (mini-buses). The *matatus* were so overloaded with passengers that some people were riding outside the vehicles with their feet on the rear bumper and hands grasping the roof rack. Dad said that when he was a policeman in Mombasa he tried to enforce a passenger occupancy limit on these buses, but apparently this job was as unenforceable in the 1980s as it was in 1960.

We were amused to read the names of the various "hotels" along the side of the road. In America, the term "hotel" is reserved for large establishments (like the Sunset Hotel) offering places to sleep. However, in Kenya, any commercial structure with four walls qualified as a hotel. Many of these "hotels" offered only a few chairs, a three-legged table, and a "Fanta *moto.*" But that did not stop the aspiring owner from labeling his cow-dung and mud structure "Onyango Hotel," "Hotel Owiti," or my personal favorite, "Hotel Hilton."

The hills of Maseno were always a highlight of our trip, for it signaled that we were crossing from the southern to the northern hemisphere. Atieno and I felt it obligatory on our part to stop on the right side of the road, immediately past the center of Maseno town, and take photographs standing next to the "Lion's Club of Kisumu–Equator" sign. We did not appreciate the significance of the location during our 1983 trip, but we were standing within a two-minute walk from where our father and grandfather once attended school.

Nothing could prepare me for what was to come just up the road in Luanda. This was the busiest market town between Kisumu and Got Regea. Dad decided to pull over and buy a bushel of bananas and *sukumawiki* from the vendors lined up alongside the road. As our car approached the vendors, all of the fifteen women immediately grabbed their fruits and vegetables, raced over to our vehicle, and thrust the produce through our car's open windows while feverishly shouting at my father in Dholuo. It was sheer chaos and I was unprepared for the encounter. I assumed we would simply get out of the car and leisurely make our purchases. Instead, with all the women pressing themselves upon the car, we could not even open the door. The car was completely surrounded by the women, each selling the same produce as the other. Now, from which of the fifteen ladies, each holding the same type of banana, do you make your purchase? Do you purchase your *sukumawiki* from this one lady with the yellow scarf, or do you purchase it from the other fourteen ladies, each wearing a similar scarf and thrusting through the open windows the same *sukumawiki?*

It was evident that my father never enjoyed this situation. His strategy was to get what he wanted quickly and escape the chaos, even if it meant paying a little bit more than he should. I always felt so sorry for the other women on the road who did not manage to make a sale to us. It meant that if their luck did not change, they would end up taking their produce back to their homes, but without money to send their children to school.

Dad bought non-locally made supplies (soda, sugar, rice, kerosene) at the shops in Yala. This town gave an appearance of an old western movie set. Aging storefronts lined each side of the town's short single street, and there appeared to be more wandering goats than customers. Dad explained that Yala was once a bustling and well-maintained business center, with storeowners of Indian descent. His Uncle Timothy Okumu was a part-time beekeeper, and sold honey to the Indians. The Indians had long ago left the rural areas, destined for places like Kisumu, Nairobi, Bombay, or England.

Once we reached Yala we knew that Got Regea was not too far away. Dudi market was the landmark at which we made a right turn and traveled two miles along a bumpy dirt road that at some points looked more like a wide footpath. If it was rainy season, we feared getting stuck, and on more than one occasion I had to help push the car out of the mud. Even when the road was dry, Atieno and I often walked alongside the car while my father tried to navigate above and around half-submerged boulders. There was good reason my father stocked up on supplies. There was no telling how long we might have to stay in rural Got Regea if we got bogged down in mud or experienced mechanical difficulties. This was Kenya before cell phones, and any mishap would result in a very long walk back to the nearest payphone in Yala.

After driving or pushing our way along the Got Regea dirt road for twenty minutes, we eventually reached a clearing between two hills and drove up to the house of our grandmother, Grace Dina Adero Odenyo. She was a slight, elderly lady who always greeted us with a controlled handshake, but never a hug. Like almost everything else that we witnessed with the older generation in Kenya, there was never any sign of affection or emotion.

Grandma did not understand English, and Atieno and I did not understand Dholuo. After a few days in Got Regea I remember my father translating for me that Grandma said I was "spoiling my eyes by wearing glasses." According to Grandma, only old people wear glasses, and by wearing them at such a young age I was weakening my eyes, preventing them from seeing far distances. She theorized that my near-sightedness was actually caused by my glasses, and that I should remove them. "What kind of foolishness is this?" she asked her university-educated son. "Why does Odera want to be an old man?" To my grandmother, wearing glasses at the age of eleven was the same as a healthy child walking around the village using an old person's walking stick. To her, it was simply not right. Upon his mother's insistence, Dr. Odenyo recommended that Atieno and I remove our glasses.

From then on things became a little bit blurry for my sister and me. However, I do remember seeing my father and his mother spend a lot of time talking while sitting outdoors in the middle of the family compound. What they talked about I will never know. I was busy playing games with Uncle Robert's children. Eric, Leo, and I spent our days constructing archery bows with string bought from the Dudi market, and wood stripped from trees alongside Aruwa's Hill. This was actually my idea. I bought the arrows at a look-out point on the Rift Valley road, but I made my bow in Regea by myself. Our grandmother put a quick stop to our target practice, saying we were frightening our neighbors. For fun we instead constructed Olympic-size hurdles out of sticks. We practiced running down the slope between the two hills of Got Regea, leaping over the five or six hurdles in a race for the finish line. When we became tired of that game my sister and I assisted the hired help chase a loose cow, which we then milked together. All these activities were games to us but were also memorable experiences.

I was impressed that my cousins did not need shoes to walk along the rocky trails of Got Regea. The bottoms of their feet were nearly rock-hard and impenetrable like my father's feet. In an effort to toughen up, I tried walking barefoot around the compound. This exercise did not last more than five minutes. My feet were soft and tender, and they did not stand up well to the smallest stick or pebble.

Dad, Atieno, and I stayed in the late Uncle Lut's house, located immediately inside the main gate. It was mud-walled, with a rusted metal roof, and consisted of a living room and a small bedroom. Furniture was scarce and utilitarian. It was always very dark inside because the windows were quite small. In the evening we used a lamp. Once that lamp was extinguished, I could not see my hand if I put it in front of my face. I wondered how I was supposed to get from the house to the pit-latrine in the dark.

I found it odd that the people of Got Regea hung their family photographs so high on the walls. I remember Eddie, Uncle Adet's son, had to climb on top of a table to remove a photograph attached to the ceiling rafter so that I could get a good look at our grandfather Zablon. To this day I find this practice interesting. If I had to guess how the practice started, I would imagine that photographs were once so rare and admired in the rural village that they had to be placed out of reach of "sticky-fingered" guests. I hear that some of our family's missing photos are serving as decoration in the private quarters of neighbors' homes in Got Regea.

There are three specific memories of Got Regea that stand out. One afternoon my cousin Eric was told to help with dinner. For Atieno and me in New York, this assignment might have involved defrosting a chicken and a bag of frozen vegetables. But this is not how it is done in Got Regea. Atieno and I watched Eric as he looked at a group of chickens, selected one, chased it around the yard for ten minutes, scooped it up, and brought it towards us. He then plucked a part of the neck clean of feathers, held it firmly to the ground with his bare feet, took a knife, and chopped off its head. To our amazement, the headless chicken was still thrashing around for a few seconds trying to escape! Atieno and I stayed with the chicken the entire time thereafter. We watched while it was soaked in hot water, stripped of all feathers, washed, dissected, and cooked in a pot on the ground supported by three small stones. At dusk we gathered the kerosene lamps and sat in my grandmother's house where we ate the *kuku* with ugali. The *kuku* did not have an ounce of fat on it. I remember chewing on the *kuku* while at the same time imagining the athletic bird running around the yard trying to escape Eric.

My second clear memory is of the leopard. Uncle Robert had warned Atieno, "Do not go out at night. There is a leopard that is eating our chickens." A few days later, word spread that approximately two miles to the west a leopard had been trapped. Dad walked with us up and down the dirt paths for a long time until we reached a hill where a leopard was trapped inside a steel cage. The cat was surrounded by perhaps twenty children of similar age to us, who were all looking at the leopard through the steel bars. However, when the children saw Atieno and me, their interest in the leopard shifted towards us, and we became the main spectacle, rather than the leopard.

These children were not odd to Atieno and me. As far as we were concerned they were just like us, except we did not share a common language. We had no real interest in them, for we did not know them and had come only to see the leopard. But to these children, it was as if Atieno and I were extraterrestrial beings who just exited a space craft from another galaxy. It is not that we were dressed differently from them. My father had purchased extra *mitumba* (used) clothes for us in one of the open-air markets on the side of the Kisumu-Dudi road. I also remember we wore *pata-pata* (flip-flop) sandals much of the time. He made Atieno wear a sufficiently long and locally-made skirt so she would not give the appearance of being dressed like a boy. However, the children were not interested in how we were dressed. Their stares were all focused on our light skin, my soft hair, and my sister's long hair. My father was a little annoyed at the stares and translated that they were asking each other, "Are these Luo people?" Apparently, none of these rural children had ever seen a "half-caste." So while Atieno and I edged closer to the cat, silently staring into its eyes, observing its teeth, and inspecting its fur, we were circled by over twenty children who did the same to us. For Atieno and me, it was not the children who were odd, but the cat. To the children near Got Regea, we were odder than the cat.

My third memorable incident is precious. One afternoon an older lady entered the gate to our home. She wore a bright smile on her face and a white headdress with a red cross on it. As she walked toward us she clapped her hands together. Everything about her radiated joy and happiness. She stood before my father, greeted him in Dholuo, and continued to clap. Then my father started to clap his hands. Confused, I started clapping my hands. The three of us stood there for a few seconds just smiling at each other and clapping our hands.

They talked for a while, and later when we were alone my father said, "Her name is Hilda. She was once my caretaker—my *japidi*. I lived with her for some time in another village—a place called Yenga. She is also my mother's sister."

At my young age I was more interested in the clapping than family history. Dad explained, "Oh, that was just her way of greeting us.

She is a member of a Roho church—kind of like the 'Born Again' churches in America. Except in a Roho church you clap for joy instead of shaking hands. Her Roho church is no longer Anglican like Saint Peter's." [22]

The summer of 1983 was the first time I recall visiting Saint Peter's Church in Got Regea. During church service Atieno had to sit on the other side of the isle with the women. After the service, Dad introduced us to the pastors. We were told that our grandfather, Zablon Sangoro, used to preach in the church.

On July 22, Dad took us to another compound where I saw a very large concrete gravestone in the form of a cross. It had the following inscription:

> Rapar Mar Japuonj Simeon Odera Ndong'a. Nonyuole 1896. Nonindo dwe 11.7.67. An e chier kendo an e ngima routh owacho: Nga'moyie kuoma kata otho nodok mangima.

Dad pointed to the gravestone and asked me, "Do you recognize any of these words?"

I studied them for a few seconds until my eyes stuck on one word—Odera. "I see my name here," I said, pointing directly at the letters of my name.

"Yes," he replied. "This is your name, and the man who is laying here is the man whom I have named you after. He was one of our greatest elders while I was growing up, and he himself shared this name with one of the greatest chiefs of this village."

I asked my father about the meaning of the name Odera. I thought it might have some connection to the Luo word *dero* (granary). My father in turn consulted with his cousin Paul Obara, son of the late Simeon Odera. Obara told me, "I think Odera has something to do with being born during hunger—somewhat like the name Odenyo."

Aghast, I turned to my father and complained, "So my name is Hunger Hunger?"

Dad took us to visit Aunt Olivia and Aunt Rosalie near Kendu Bay. It was the first time I can remember meeting Aunt Rosalie, and I was surprised to meet a relative who talked even less than Uncle Victor. Aunt Olivia was no stranger, for she had visited us several times in the United States. She even traveled alone in 1982 to rural Minnesota to become more acquainted with my mother's relatives. She viewed her trip as an important extension of dowry customs, where visits solidify family ties. She saw first-hand the rural farmhouse, the barn, the livestock, the crops, and recognized the warmness of family and traditional values. During our visit to Aunt Olivia's home near Kendu Bay, Dad took us to see how soapstone carvings are made by the local craftsmen in Kisii. He brought us to the gate of Kisii High School, and proudly shared a few facts about the school.

In Nairobi, we attended Pentecostal church service on Valley Road. The August 21 service started a little late, and we noticed there were television cameras in the room. The pastor announced that a special guest was coming, and in walked a dignified looking man who took a seat near the front of the church. My father whispered to us, "Do you know that man sitting in the front of the church?" We had no clue, so he discretely explained to us that approximately seven pews ahead of us, on the left side of the church, sat the president of Kenya, Daniel Arap Moi. I was very excited, for I vividly remembered he was the *Nyayo* president, the one who was talking about following in the footsteps of the late President Kenyatta. Just the previous year Dad was concerned over some kind of attempt by Kenyans to overthrow Moi. I was still totally confused about who was right and who was wrong. I remember listening very closely to the pastor as he welcomed President Moi to the church, for I hoped to gauge from the pastor what he really thought about Moi. Despite my attention to the sermon, and to the special prayer made by the pastor asking God to bestow "wisdom" and "guidance" upon the county's leadership, my question about right and wrong, good and bad, was never answered in church that day. It seemed that no one was willing to answer my question.

After perhaps a month in Nairobi, Dad drove us back to see our grandmother in Got Regea. Along the way we stopped to visit with Uncle Dan and his wife Awino in Egerton University, Njoro. When we arrived in Got Regea after eight in the evening, Uncle Robert greeted me with the same confusing phrase that had concerned me for weeks.

With a smile he said, "*Karibu nyumbani* (welcome home), you are lost."

No one had explained to me that "lost" did not mean kidnapped, or lost in the woods. Instead, when used as a greeting, "lost" means "I have not seen you in a while." I was eager to dispel this strange rumor that I had gone missing, so I replied, "No…no I haven't. I've been in Nairobi with Uncle Victor. Daddy knew where I was the whole time."

Uncle Robert simply smiled and asked, "So… how was your *safari*?"

This was another point of confusion. In America the phrase *safari* denotes a week-long trip into the grasslands to hunt wild animals while wearing khaki clothing, helmets, and being followed around by half-dressed Africans carrying supplies on their heads. I had done nothing close to this, and I did not want him to think I was one of those funny-looking tourists I had spotted in the streets of Nairobi. I was eager to quash this rumor before it got off the ground, so I explained that I did not know how to shoot a gun, and was not yet old enough to be out there hunting wild animals. To this, Uncle Robert simply laughed, and changed the subject. It was not until my next trip to Kenya, in 1989, that I realized that *safari* simply meant "trip" in Kiswahili, and that my uncle simply wanted to know about my journey from Nairobi to Got Regea that day.

Giraffe on a road leading to Kisumu (outskirts of Nairobi).

Baboon inspecting the occupants of our car.

Amos Otieno Odenyo with his "japidi,"
Aunt Hilda (Obuong) Awuor. Got Regea, 1996.

Odera and Atieno in a matatu (minibus)
after buying sweet bananas.

Dr. Amos Otieno Odenyo showing his
former high school to son Odera. Kisii, 1983.

Dr. Odenyo showing his son Odera the grave of the
great choirmaster, Simeon Odera. Huluwinu, 1983.

11
New York City (1983–1989)

The Odenyo family has always built bridges between people.
We do not build walls—walls of clanism, tribalism, racism, and religion.

—Dr. Amos Otieno Odenyo, speech on
January 8, 2005, in Westlands, Kenya.

My sister Atieno and I arrived back in New York City on September 4, 1983, and spent the next several days explaining to our mother, in British-influenced accents, our many adventures in Kenya. The trip had a subtle but profound influence on us. Beyond knowing where Kenya is and what it looked like, it helped strengthen our understanding of our unique biracial and bicultural heritage. We always felt comfortable in the presence of white Americans due to our mother's white friends and relatives. This same comfort and familiarity extended to our Kenyan relatives. We were visited by Kenyan family and friends as far back as 1971, when Uncle Victor held me in his arms upon arriving in Minnesota a few weeks after my birth. Our trip to Kenya in 1983 only served to strengthen this bond.

However, Atieno and I did grow up with a weird feeling of being part of everything and nothing at the same time. We never considered ourselves white, for in America a person with even 1 percent African blood is considered black. We could not consider ourselves Kenyan because we were not born and raised there, and could not speak a Kenyan language. The same 1 percent concept seemed to apply in Kenya as well because when we drove through the roads of Got Regea, children would often run alongside the car shouting to us "*Wazungu*! (White people!)" Ironically, it was with these two groups, white Americans and black Africans, that we felt most comfortable.

We did not consider ourselves black Americans in the traditional sense of the term. Black American culture was very foreign to us beyond what we observed in school and television. Any "blackness" that Atieno and I inherited came from our African father, who seemed to have little in common with black Americans. In fact, I never heard Dad describe himself as black. We used to ask him about his sense of identity, and he consistently responded, "First I feel Luo. Then I feel Kenyan. Then I feel African." He never once said, "I feel Black."

One similarity between black Americans and Africans that I can remember from childhood involves music and dancing. This is best understood by first discussing my white heritage. On my mother's side of the family, music appeared to be a sit-down event. A trip to Minnesota always involved my mother sitting in front of the piano harmonizing to hymns with her sisters, Dorothy and Phyllis, and my grandparents, George and Alice. It still brings me great joy to reminisce about the old country farmhouse being filled with such beautiful songs. However, I cannot say with a straight face that these songs included "rhythm." On my grandmother's Danish side, people did not even dance. In fact, eyebrows were raised when in 1936 Alice married George, a man of German ancestry from Cosmos, Minnesota. The Danish community heard rumors that the people of Cosmos were fond of drink, smokes, and late-night barnyard dances—all prohibited activities to the more conservative Danes. However, the dancing by the Germans appears tame by today's standards. From my mother's recollection, when the German relatives really wanted to throw caution to the wind and "party," they would participate in a good-old fashion organized waltz or foxtrot.

These cultural limitations may have had something to do with the look of terror that I witnessed on my mother's face when she was invited in 1977 by Barbara Griles to dance to R & B music at her daughter's birthday party. By my mother's reaction, Barbara might as well have asked her to join a nude sky-diving team or a satanic river-rafting club. My mother seemed to like the music, but wanted no part in the dancing and remained an observer. Barbara's music sounded somewhat foreign to me. We rarely turned on the radio at home and I was thus more familiar with Christian hymns and African music played from records. However, black American music was recognizable to me and African in the one sense that it had rhythm.

Dad was always reserved and dignified when he danced to African music. He flowed with the music, became part of the music—much like he was the source of the music itself. He was simply a key on the piano, a string in the fiddle, or the beat of a drum. In this one way, he was very much like black Americans.

Most black Americans felt we were not sufficiently black. Atieno and I were told numerous times by our black American classmates, some lighter in skin color than us, that we were not black because we sounded and acted "white." This surprised us, for we never considered ourselves white, and neither did white people. We always knew we were different, but by virtue of not having any other viable category to fall into, we simply considered ourselves black. It made sense to us that we should do so. We had African names, ate African food, wore African shirts, and listened to African music. More importantly, we had an African father, an African brother, as well as numerous African uncles, aunts, and cousins. Not only were we able to say from which country in Africa we came, but from which tribe and which village. Dad used to tell us about our great Luo ancestors, especially my favorite story about a warrior whose strength lay in his shadow. He talked about us following the Nile from Sudan into Kenya. I could point to three Africans after whom I had been named—one of them a chief. None of our black American friends could say any of these things. Most of them thought people from Africa spoke "African," and that "Kwanza" was actually a holiday celebrated in Africa. When our black American classmates wanted to reconnect with their heritage, most of them headed down the I-95 freeway towards the "confederate" South. When my family wanted to reconnect with our roots, we boarded a Pan Am flight to Kenya. Yet, black Americans still told us we were not black. Atieno was once told in grade school, "You're not black because you don't know how to fight." I was told I was not really black because

I did not use the same vocabulary or listen to the same songs as black Americans.

In my experience, it was not until the late 1980s that Africa became popular with black Americans my age. At that point they started calling themselves "African-Americans" and inventing African-sounding names for themselves that are never heard of in Africa. However, in the late 1970s and early 1980s I was teased in school and occasionally asked by both white and black classmates if my father knew Tarzan, and whether my family in Kenya wore clothes. Once I was asked if my relatives ate people. These comments were rare, but when they occurred I really did not know how to respond or defend myself against such stereotypes. Even I enjoyed watching the Saturday morning Tarzan cartoon show on television. Whenever Tarzan was ready to fight he intimidated the most ferocious beasts and savage natives by menacingly squinting his eyes. Opponents who did not run away suffered defeat by the white "Lord of the Jungle."

I witnessed many fights in class—mostly between black students. Since I did not know how to fight, for a short time I subconsciously employed the Tarzan squinting technique. It did not work. I was on the receiving end of more than one ass-kicking, which caused one of my elementary school teachers to give a "Blessed are the Meek" lecture to the class. The lecture failed as well, which had a bearing on my transfer to public intermediate school (I.S. 25) in Flushing from 1984 to 1986.

Although the student body at I.S. 25 was larger and more diverse, I was enrolled in honors classes (except math) where there were very few students of color. Surprisingly, my white and Asian classmates either embraced me or were indifferent. I was invited to two Jewish classmates' Bar Mitzvah celebrations, and despite being the only black person in the building, they made me feel at home. My classmates rarely brought up my biracial heritage as an issue. Because of this, my years as I.S. 25 remain the most enjoyable and productive years of education that I can remember as a child. My sister also attended this school and says the exact same thing. However, I.S. 25 still had a large black student population. Almost all of these students were bused into Flushing from predominantly black areas such as Jamaica, New York. Since I did not share many classes with them, and they were not from my neighborhood, there was little opportunity for friendship with black students during intermediate school.

After my 1983 trip to Kenya I was much more comfortable embracing my African heritage despite the negativity that my peers, both black and white, associated with Africa. In 1985, my Social Studies teacher, Mr. Diconstanzo, taught our class about the various Egyptian pharaohs and dynasties. He discussed the importance of the Nile River to Egypt and asked if anyone in the class could identify the source of the river. No one could. So I raised my hand and said, "Lake Victoria" (the Western name for Lake Nyanza). Mr. Diconstanzo was very surprised. He asked me how I knew the answer, and I said, "Because my father was born near that lake." My teacher had doubts that I was telling the truth because I did not look very African to him. He said, "Okay, why don't you come up here and point out where your father was born on the map." I took him up on his challenge and walked to the large map hanging over the chalkboard. Placing my finger on a specific point on the map, I said, "Here, this city called Kisumu is near where my father was born," and walked back to my seat. Mr. Diconstanzo looked closely at the map and verified that indeed there was a place called Kisumu near the source of the Nile River. He smiled and congratulated me in front of the class.

There were four main racial incidents that I can remember in intermediate school. I was used to students asking me if I was the brother to Atieno, who was one year ahead of me in the same school. One day a black American student from another class walked up to me in the hallway and said, "Hey man, are you a brother?" I looked at him and said, "Yes, I have one sister and one brother. But only my sister is in this school." He just looked at me, shook his head, and walked away. Had he said "bro" I think I would have recognized he meant "black." However, by the time I realized the context a few hours later, it was already too late. In my answer to his question I had confirmed to him that I was indeed not black.

In another incident I was changing clothes in the locker room after gym class. I must have not shown enough "respect" to a black American student who was entering the locker room, because he said something like, "you think you're so bad," and wrestled me to the ground, choking me in a headlock. I did not know him or do anything to antagonize him, yet he nearly rendered me unconscious simply because he sensed that he could. It is ironic. To this day I have never been assaulted by a white American, but during my youth, a few black Americans seemed drawn to me much like a boxer is drawn to a punching bag.

The third incident involved a white English teacher. She thought that her black and white students tended to pronounce "Aunt" differently. She asked me, in front of the entire class, to explain the reason for this. She also asked why black people refer to each other using the derogatory word "nigger." I doubt she was being mean, she was just curious. But so was I. Not only did I pronounce "Aunt" like she did, but no one in my family ever used the word nigger. I felt that my teacher was asking me to explain a culture that was not my own.

The fourth example also involves a white teacher. My all-white and Asian honors class made a visit to the school library, and the librarian made an announcement that writing on the desks was prohibited. Apparently there was a graffiti problem in the school. After the class session ended, the librarian noticed that someone had drawn graffiti on the other side of the table from me. As my classmates and I were collecting our belongings to leave the library, the librarian pointed his finger at me and said, "You! You stay right there. You're going to clean up this graffiti that's on this desk." I tried to explain that I had nothing to do with the graffiti, but the librarian accepted none of my excuses. He had concluded that the graffiti problem was caused by black students, and although none of the black students considered me black, the white librarian certainly did. Humiliated, I scrubbed that desk clean while I watched the rest of my class exit the library.

During these early years I did not discuss these confusing racial incidents with my father. Once I reached home, all of the world's color issues seemed to melt away. Dad seemed to have such a strong and quiet confidence in his own identity, and this inspired and sustained me. I was Odera, son of Otieno, and that is all that mattered. Dad also seemed like an impressive man. I knew from my earliest days in elementary school that my father was a professor of sociology, and that he was the chairman of Social Sciences at York College in Queens. I did not know exactly what a chairman did, but it sounded important. I imagined him sitting in a regal-looking chair dispensing words of wisdom all day. I was only at his office a few times. Around the age of six I accompanied him to a commercial building north of the train tracks, near Jamaica Avenue. I remember looking at all the books he had arranged on a shelf. Among them was a book titled *The Black Panthers*. Next to it was another book titled *Encyclopedia of Black American History*. "Wow," I thought, "my Daddy teaches everything—from the color of wild cats in Kenya to the history of black people in America!" A few years later the main campus was built, and we parked south of the train tracks along Guy Brewer Avenue. One day as we were getting out of the car my father witnessed someone snatching a purse from a woman and he ran after the man, caught him, and held him for the police. I was very impressed with my father for doing that. He was like superman, or superchairman. One moment he was dressed in a business suit going to work, the next moment he is speeding down the street apprehending dangerous villains.

I can remember my father constantly reading books and grading papers in his basement office. There was a library of books on an assortment of topics: Africa, sociology, history, women's studies, religions of the world, and economic development. Knowledge and accomplishment permeated every corner. His three advanced degrees were placed on the wall alongside two advanced degrees obtained by my mother. On the shelves were my parents' college yearbooks and an encyclopedia set. A bust of President John F. Kennedy faced my father's desk—a reminder to him of the 1961 Airlift. Subtle signs of Africa were present. There was the Kenya Airways calendar, a soapstone carving from Kisii, little figurines made of banana bark, and a tall wooden giraffe. During the late 1980s he bought a painting of Jomo Kenyatta, hands shackled in front of him, being escorted by several African guards and a white colonial officer. My father explained that the painting captured the moment Kenyatta was being released by the British before he became Kenya's first president. The basement images, combined with my father's distant and firm approach to parenting, reinforced my perception of my father as a man of achievement and mystery. He was a scholarly figure, and we treated him with the respect due to a man of such stature. Much later in life he mentioned to me that he obtained his U.S. residency status through his educational and professional qualifications. He did not lie and cheat his way through the immigration system. It was important that I understand this, he said, for he suspected his American in-laws initially assumed his marriage to Mayone was for immigration purposes. "Everything I have in life I worked hard for," he said. "I was not handed a green-card. I had to earn it."

There was always a special chair in the living room devoted to my father. Although he never forbade us to use it, out of respect for him we never sat in it, even when he was not at home. Atieno and I left the chair at the head of the dinning room table for him as well, and did not touch our *ugali* and *sukumawiki* before Daddy had filled his plate. To do otherwise would have been disrespectful. Personally, it was an acknowledgment that my father, not me, was responsible for the food on the table.

I never heard Dad say a prayer in English. When he prayed, it was always in Dholuo. This happened even in Minnesota at my grandparents' rural home, where there was a decorated Danish plate on the dining room wall inscribed with a Danish prayer (*I Jesu Navn Gar Vi Til Bords...*). There, in that dining room, we held hands with my grandparents, bowed our heads, and listened to my father bless the *lutefisk* and *lefse* (Norwegian food) by giving an *erokamano* (thanks) to the one called *Nyasaye*.

Dad appreciated that we did not adopt many negative habits as young children. He once gave me an example:

> Odera, when you and your sister were little children and entered a room filled with adults, you did not run around wildly or start touching and breaking things like all these neighborhood kids have done in my house for thirty years. Instead, the two of you remained quiet and observed your surroundings. You let the grown-ups talk. If you wanted to say something, you approached me quietly and whispered in my ear so that no one else would be disturbed with what you had to say. You were a good boy Odera.

I believe that to the extent we were "good children," it was less due to personality than to upbringing. Both my parents had a common rural and traditional upbringing that transcended race, language, and culture. Both parents valued responsibility, hard work, and respect for others, especially elders. Traditional gender and age roles could be bent, but they were not broken. Atieno and I did not grow up viewing our parents as our "best friends." This contemporary and fashionable term of calling one's parents "friends" is a concept used in good faith, but I find it slightly insulting as well. Friendship is not a bad word, but it denotes equality and a lack of inhibitions between peers.

My mother was the homemaker. She alone decided what food we ate, what clothes we wore, and our daily regiment within the house. She was someone we could approach to express our feelings, and obtain answers to our childish questions about life. She was our primary caretaker, and we were allowed some leeway to act like children. My father's role was similarly well defined. He was the head of the household, and the primary financial provider, although my mother worked too. While my mother was the "mayor" who made decisions over almost all daily and routine aspects of our lives, my father was the "president" who made the final decision on big matters. They of course consulted with each other, but it was never in front of us children. In public, my mother deferred to my father as the family leader. In both literal and figurative terms, my mother was always a better driver. However, it was my father who always took the wheel.

I remember sitting with my father in the patio lounge in Kisumu Airport when he was approaching seventy years old. We were talking about the qualities of husband and wife that might overcome ethnic and cultural barriers. This led him to reflect on his own marriage, stating that had he married a woman who wanted everything in the household to be equal, his marriage would have ended in divorce shortly after it started. This was not an opinionated statement, it is fact. My mother tells me the same thing, stating, "Your father did not change a dirty diaper even once in his entire life." She told me she had always been a champion of women's equality in education and the workplace. However, when she married Otieno she also married his culture. With regard to domestic affairs and gender roles, there were a lot of

similarities between Luo culture and what she had experienced growing up in rural Minnesota. She had a choice to make in the home—
women's equality, or marriage. She chose marriage.

Recently in Nairobi I talked with childhood friends Achieng and
Sharon Olende. They told me that as a result of their many visits to
our home during the 1970s and 1980s, they grew up viewing "Auntie
Mayone" as very African in the manner in which she interacted with
her husband and guests. I remember their own highly-educated mother, Rose, joining my mother in our kitchen to help make tea while their
husbands sat comfortably in the living room laughing and reminiscing
about their days at Kisii High School. Rose and Mayone (and often
Atieno and I too) would make trips from the kitchen and ensure that
the men were comfortable and not running low on food and drink.
My mother extended this same hospitality to all her guests. I found
out much later in life that a few non-African women "professionals"
(including professors in the social sciences) who visited our home pit-
ied my mother for being so "old-fashioned," and felt my father was
taking advantage of her. I think they wanted her to join the revolu-
tion by throwing away her ankle-length dresses for pants, burning her
bra, and standing up to her man as an equal. I think it irritated them
to see her happy in the role of primary caretaker of the home, which
they could not reconcile with her master's degree in education. The
only guests who had enough courage to bring up the matter directly
with my mother were several of her black American friends. They let
her know that she was too subservient to her husband, and advised,
"Otieno needs to get off his throne, go to the kitchen, and get his own
food, his own sugar, and his own tea."

Few people realized that my father occasionally did his part in domestic work. Dad was always the "ironer," and spent long hours metic-
ulously pressing his suits, shirts, and pants. He even ironed our clothes
too. It appeared he actually enjoyed this task, and did it better than any
one of us could ever attempt to do. He told us that when he was young,
the iron he used was heated with hot timbers or coal instead of electricity. Dad, not Mom, washed and dried our clothes at the laundromat.
I remember joining him at the laundromat on the southeast corner of
Bell Boulevard and 48th Avenue in Bayside. During one visit a washer

machine broke and overflowed with water. There was no staff to clean up the mess, and the patrons, mostly middle-aged and elderly white women, appeared helpless as they waded in inches of water. Somehow my father got hold of a mop and bucket and within minutes had the whole floor cleared of water and the place running smoothly again. One elderly woman complemented him by saying, "Wow, you did that so quickly and professionally, I am really impressed…can I hire you?" My father said, "Well, I used to do this for a living, so it all came back to me." I thought my father was joking. After all, he was a professor, and before that a policeman. In my mind it did not seem possible that my father could have been employed in anything other than a position of authority.

He was forever "clearing the yard." In Kenya a highly-educated man would typically hire someone to clean the yard for him. Not Dad. During my entire childhood he was mowing the lawn himself, pulling tree stumps out of the ground, and planting bushes. My mother was by his side planting tomatoes, carrots, and lettuce. I was out there with them, although I frequently complained and begged my mother, "Let me walk to Francis Lewis Blvd and buy tomatoes for you from the A&P store—they are better!"

While I never noticed any overt differences in the way our father related to us, my sister recalls a relationship with our father that was even more distant than the one I remember between him and me. To listen to my sister's reflections of their relationship, one might even pick up a hint of resentment due to the emotional distance. In his defense, if he did show any emotional bias toward me, he perhaps assumed his wife was devoting extra attention to his daughter. Nevertheless, Dad proved to be equally supportive of us in areas that concerned him. In 1988, when my sister graduated from high school, he summoned her down to his basement office. This in itself was an important statement. To be summoned downstairs by our father was the equivalent of being summoned into the principal's office. They sat for a few minutes in silence as my father collected his thoughts. This was his pattern. You could tell that something of great importance was about to unfold due to the length of time he spent preparing his statements. He told my sister something close to the following:

Atieno, never rely on a man for your financial support.
You must pursue your own educational and professional goals so you will never become reliant on a man.
Always be prepared to walk out the door if you must.
Do this not only for the sake of yourself, but for your
children. If you are self-sufficient, no man will have any
justification to remove your children from you.

My sister always remembered this, and despite the emotional gap
between them, to this day she thanks him for demonstrating his concern over her future. His advice was instrumental in her devotion to
studies in pursuit of a professional career. To me, it demonstrates that
for as much as he was a traditional African man with supposed subconscious biases towards men, he consciously supported educational
and professional equality between the sexes.

My father rarely showed any signs of affection to my mother in
public. This was normal for him because such public acts of affection
are often frowned upon in traditional African culture. I have never
seen my father kiss my mother. He rarely held her hand in public unless it was for a photograph, but he sometimes held her hand while
they watched television at home. On one occasion, my mother and her
friend Mrs. Lue Tyler went to the airport to pick him up upon his return from Kenya. When he exited the airport terminal he extended his
hand to Mrs. Tyler and gave her a professional handshake. He had been
gone several months, but instead of hugging my mother he turned to
her and gave her the same professional handshake, causing Mrs. Tyler's
eyes to widen and jaw to drop. She was convinced that Otieno and
Mayone were soon getting a divorce. My mother had to explain to
her repeatedly that his reserved demeanor was a combination of his
upbringing and personality, and not a true indication of his feelings.
Mrs. Tyler had a hard time believing it, especially when she found out
that Otieno did not give his wife birthday gifts or even remember what
day they were married. Mrs. Tyler explained that if her husband ever
forgot these important dates she would be hurt. My mother, however,
simply learned to accommodate my father's lack of interest in ritual-
izing dates and never let it bother her that she did not receive a gift.

New York City (1983–1989)

Dad could be stern. Our friends were often intimidated by his controlled and serious demeanor. I have heard other people refer to him as stubborn. I have my own stories to tell on this issue. Around age ten, I persistently begged him for a cat, but he refused, stating, "Animals are meant to be outside, not in the house. Cats have only one purpose—they catch mice." My mother was very sympathetic to me because she had grown up with pets and considered them her playmates. She could see the joy in my eyes whenever we visited the farms in Minnesota and I played with kittens as she once did as a child. She wanted to share this part of her childhood with me, so one cold evening in December 1984, she took me to a neighbor's garage and I got to pick out not one, but two little kittens. The black and white one had white feet. I named him "Boots." The other one was calico with two white paws. I named him "Mittens." We purposely chose two same-sex cats so that one would not become pregnant. I brought the kittens home and placed them in my bedroom, hoping to delay the moment my father would encounter them. My fears were unwarranted because my mother had already informed my father of our plans, pitching the idea as an "educational experience for the kids." However, it appeared Dr. Odenyo was not quite convinced of the educational merits of our plans, for after we brought the kittens home he took me to the backyard in an attempt to negotiate terms. It was dark outside, and the yard was filled with ice and snow. He pointed to a large wooden chest about two feet high and four feet long, which held an assortment of garden tools and fertilizer. He pointed to it and said, "Why not keep your cats in that chest, that way you can still have them and they can be outside of the house." I reacted with horror, telling him that they were just precious little infants and would freeze to death. We stood there for half a minute just looking at each other, with the snow falling around us and the wooden chest. Without a word, he just sighed and entered the house. That is when I realized I had won. It is perhaps my greatest childhood victory living with Professor Odenyo.

Within a year things spiraled out of control when one of the supposedly "male" cats became pregnant. Soon we had not two but five cats running around the house. I proudly held up the kittens to my father and said, "Look, Mittens Odenyo and Boots Odenyo have made you a grandfather." My father was clearly not amused by that comment.

We had the kittens adopted as soon as possible. His patience finally reached its limits when Mittens repeatedly failed to obey the golden rule in the Odenyo house, which was: "Thou shalt not go into thy parents' bedroom." My mother had always advised us that our father did not want us to enter his bedroom, although we did not really understand the reason. The only exception to this rule was during the few summer nights when the temperature approached one-hundred degrees. Our parents' room contained the only air conditioner and we were allowed to sleep on mattresses on the floor for humanitarian reasons. Otherwise I might not really know what their bedroom looked like.

Boots learned my father's rule quickly, thus increasing his odds of remaining in the house. At first he used to calmly venture into my parents' room and settle onto the bed, where he was rewarded by affectionate petting by my mother. But whenever my father found the cat on his bed he made a horrified sound of disgust and loudly snapped his fingers to scare the cat out of his bedroom. Boots therefore learned to make his entry very discrete. He would first pause at the top of the steps leading to my father's office. He sat there long enough to confirm the subtle signs that my father was downstairs—the flipping of a textbook page, the repetitive sounds of *nyatiti* music, the steady beats of Lingala music. If Boots was lucky, he would hear a loud snore emanating from the basement office. Once assured that the master of the house was downstairs, he would gently paw at my parents' bedroom door or give a quick "Meow." The door would quickly open and he would disappear into the arms of my mother. Boots often fell asleep next to my mother, but as soon as he heard the door open from the outside he would bolt outside without need for further warning.

Mittens was more bold and affectionate, but generally not that bright. I used to take all the pillows in the house, place them on the bottom of the long stairway, and throw Mittens down the entire flight of steps onto the pillows. She would then run back up the steps while purring, seemingly asking for more. So naturally I threw her down the steps again. This lent itself to a great friendship that I could not establish with Boots, since whenever I threw Boots down the steps, for some reason he never came back. I say Mittens was dumb because when my father would snap his fingers at her and try to chase her from his bed she thought it was a game and eventually came back. Then she started peeing on my parents' bed. This of course went beyond the bounds of both Luo and midwestern culture. Mittens had to go.

Boots and my father learned to accommodate each other over the next fourteen years. Boots' food was placed downstairs and it was inevitable that they would run into each other from time to time. Their relationship is a testimony to my father's character. He was stubborn, but sometimes willing to bend. He was stern, yet could be very compassionate. I never will forget the few times that I returned home as a young adult, and I ventured downstairs, late at night, to catch a few moments of conversation with my father. There my father was, sitting on his leather reclining chair, reading glasses on his face, textbook in hand, and cat snuggled up against him on his lap. He would look slightly embarrassed, and explain that he did not have the heart to refuse the cat, who realized that among the four of us in the house, my father was the most calm, patient, and compassionate. I would check back on the two of them several hours later, and many times they would both be sleeping in the same position—my father not wanting to get up after finishing his book for fear of disturbing the cat.

I never saw Dad lose his temper or raise a hand to anyone. However, he could impose discipline through his mere presence. It was enough that I knew he was disappointed in me for me to correct my own actions. He could instill discipline from across the room by just giving me a silent look. I understood the look; it said, "Odera, I taught you better than that—stop it." If I did something very wrong he put his disappointment into words, telling me that I was letting him down, and that I knew better. It would be a one-way discussion. I looked down, felt ashamed, and if I could muster enough courage, I told him I was sorry. I would avoid him for some time afterwards, not out of anger at him, but of embarrassment. Perhaps some evening later in the week we could sit side-by-side on the house steps, holding each other's hands in silence. If Boots could find redemption in my father's presence, there was room for me as well.

Dad was not a push-over. He was willing to sacrifice to help others, but he did not want to suffer for their mistakes. My father demonstrated this principle to me very early in life, in the spring of 1983. I was attending fifth grade in a private school near Kissena Park in Flushing. Every day I was picked up by a school bus near our home in Bayside, and driven approximately five miles to school. The bus service was not free—my parents paid for it through school tuition. The bus arrived at the same time and place each day. All I had to do was wake up on time and walk five blocks to the bus stop on the corner of Francis Lewis Boulevard and Northern Boulevard. Occasionally I woke up late or procrastinated at home, in which case I missed the school bus. My father drove me to school when this happened, since Mom left the house before him. One day I was lazy and failed to wake up in time to meet the bus, which I again missed. I walked home from the bus stop and asked my father to take me to school. "Odera," he said, with a look of impatience, "the reason you missed the bus is because you did not leave the house in time. Today you will find your own way to school." He then walked out of the house and drove to work. I stood there for a few moments, contemplating on what just occurred. I wanted to blame my father but knew that the situation was truly my fault. I tried to figure out how I was to reach the school in time for class, which would start in about forty-five minutes. I quickly realized I had no options. I had to run to school. That is what I did, with a heavy book-bag. I arrived at school exhausted, sweaty, and slightly late, but as opposed to the lessons that were taught that day in school, I do remember the lesson my father taught me that morning.

I was not yet a teenager when I first learned the term "deferred gratification." I did not know what either of these words meant, so when my father used the phrase I was mystified about it.

"Odera," he said, "there are two types of people. There are people who constantly spend money satisfying their immediate desires, and they never save for their future. This is called immediate gratification. Many of them die poor people. On the other hand, there are people who do not spend money to fulfill their immediate desires because they are saving their money for bigger, better, and more important desires down the road. This is called deferred gratification."

I listened carefully to what he said, understood it, and was impressed. Impressed not only that he was teaching me the concept, but that he used such big words to explain it. "Certainly my father is very smart," I remember thinking to myself.

My father never strayed too far from his modest roots. He provided us basic necessities, a few simple luxury items, but it was never excessive. He did not lavish us with gifts. We eventually learned during birthdays and Christmas that whenever Dad handed us a wrapped present, he did not know what was inside. It was my mother who bought the gifts and created the illusion that they were from both our parents. Yet, when I was around six years old, I asked him to buy me a bicycle and he did. Around 1984, Atieno and I pleaded with him to buy us a video game system, and eventually he caved in and took us to the Toys "R" Us store to buy us a Coleco-Vision. You could tell he thought this toy was unnecessary. We knew not to ask him for much more because of the example he set. He bought not luxury vehicles, but economical cars with no air conditioning. We used to drive around the sweltering city with the windows cranked down and an old portable cassette player thrown in between the seats. I did not even know FM radio existed until I was around ten years old.

My father took me to the movies in New York City on only two occasions. I was really excited in 1981 because the title of the movie, *Chariots of Fire,* sounded exciting. I anticipated medieval knights on horse-drawn chariots battling fire-breathing dragons. When the movie started however, there were no chariots, and no fire. There were only skinny men in white underwear running barefoot in slow motion to classical music on the beach, training for something called the Olympics. Perhaps I was a bit too young to appreciate the fact that running was a theme of interest to my Kenyan father. I liked the second and last movie, *Out of Africa* (1985), a bit more.

My sister and I were reluctant to ask for name-brand clothes, despite being teased by children at school (some on welfare by the way) for wearing what they considered "old-fashioned" or "cheap clothing." Around 1983, Atieno asked Dad for new clothes, but she chose to do so in an indirect way. We must have been snooping around in his basement office while he was teaching evening classes at York College, because my sister decided to leave him a silly note on his desk—a note she still holds onto today:

> Hello! What's up? Dina Atieno was here! Yes, I ruined your clean sheet of paper. Anyway, why are you reading this? Why? There is no point! You should be doing your work! You're a college professor! You went to college to get your education! You have plenty of work to do. Think of your students, their waiting for you to make up their tests! Now, go back to work. You have to get paid, so you can buy me some new clothes! From, Dina Atieno.

To show my "support" to my sister's cause, I waited until she had left the basement, took a pen, crossed out the name "Dina" on her letter, and replaced it with "Dino," the fictional purple dinosaur (but with the personality and role of a pet dog) in the animated television show the *Flintstones*. When my father came home from work he read the letter and responded:

> Dear Dina Atieno, how come you still can't write 'they are' waiting for you. It is not 'their' waiting for you. But I know you will keep learning. Wow, if I get paid I don't think I should buy you clothes. You already have too many of them! Why do you want to look like a model? Models get their clothes free! Anyway, you are a fine young lady. You do not need a wardrobe to be a lady. Dina Atieno Odenyo is one young lady who always thinks something is wrong with her. She wants a big wardrobe of new clothes to make her feel right. But she does not know she is fine the way she is! So what are we going to do about this young lady? I think

this young lady should know that what you are 'inside' is far more important than what you are 'outside.' The Odenyos have a certain metal inside them. That is, doing the right thing even if others do not approve. So dear Dina, do not let people judge you by the clothes you wear; they should judge you by the inside character which is your true self!

Dad must have shown the note to Mom, because she concluded it with "Amen to that!"

Through our parents' example we adopted an early sense of self-reliance and a work ethic. I vividly remember the day in 1980 when my sister Atieno (age ten) and I (age eight), came up with a solution to our lack of money. We made a list of snacks we liked to eat and drink (brownies, rice-krispie bars, cookies, Cool-Aid, etc.). Together with my mother's help, we set up a food stand on the sidewalk immediately in front of the 7-Eleven store on Northern Boulevard and 203rd Street. Our plan was to compete with the 7-Eleven, draw away its most loyal customers, and eventually replace the convenience store. We were joined by our young friends Amrita and Anuradha Patel (two first-generation Americans of Indian descent) who sensed a good opportunity when they saw one (their father operated his own convenience store in the city). Unfortunately, Atieno, Amrita, Anuradha and I sold perhaps just one brownie that day, and we never did take over the 7-Eleven franchise in New York City.

Following this was my failed attempt to sell greeting cards door to door around St. Kevins Church in Flushing at the age of twelve. I took this job because I wanted a new bicycle, but was embarrassed to ask my parents because they had already bought one for me when I was around six years old and it was still working. While marketing these greeting cards I had every single door slammed in my face. Instead of giving up, at age thirteen I took a part-time summer job as a janitor at Resurrection Lutheran Church in Flushing. Around the age of fourteen I took over two neighborhood children's newspaper delivery routes, delivering papers before dawn to perhaps forty homes in a two-mile route between Thirty-ninth Avenue and the Long Island

Expressway in Bayside. When collection time came and I knocked on my customers' doors for payment, several of them thanked me with, "We knew there was someone else on the job since we now get our paper before we leave for work, rather than after we get home, or not at all!" I quit this job because with the heavy weight of all the newspapers my bicycle was constantly getting flat tires and wheel alignment damage, which soaked up all my profit. Being chased by a loose Doberman Pinscher guard dog did not help either. Around age sixteen I helped sell Christmas trees on Francis Lewis Boulevard, and at age seventeen I worked as a stock boy and a cashier at a King Kullen grocery store on Northern Boulevard.

Although our parents were very frugal with us, they spent money on us in more discrete and important ways. How many New York City children can say that most of their birthdays occurred in Minnesota, Africa, or Sweden? Due to our life experiences, Atieno and I were studying sociology and international affairs since birth! After our births, our parents automatically deducted money from their monthly paychecks to invest in our college savings fund. Although my mother preferred to have more children, my father refused on financial grounds. It was more important to provide for the children he had, rather than to have children for whom he could not provide. My mother was in harmony with his principles. Yet my father was willing to provide money to non-relatives if it was a good cause. In the mid-1980s I mentioned to my father that my Jamaican-American friend Sheldon Styles could not spend the summer with his father in Canada due to lack of travel funds. I was surprised when my father took an immediate interest in the situation. He instructed me to inform Sheldon that if travel money was all he needed to see his father, he would provide Sheldon with all the necessary funds. My father did not have to explain it to me. I knew he felt it was important that Sheldon know his father, just like he wanted my brother Omondi to know his father.

Dad brought Omondi back to the United States in 1985. I had seen him only one time since he left, and that was in Kenya in 1983. That same year, in Omondi's final school transcripts from Homa Bay High School, Headmaster Adongo noted: "A competent games captain; good basketball player; chairman in Drama; has good conduct."

Omondi had grown up a lot, and my father was in constant communication with him the entire time he was away from us. My father's secretary at York College for almost fifteen years, Ruth Papa, recently remarked to me, "It seemed that every several weeks your father placed a stamped envelope in the out-going mail box in the office. After I inquired, he explained that he was providing support for his son to continue in school. I always admired this about him—he was such a principled and dedicated father."

Although my father welcomed the opportunity to spend more time with his son, in 1984 he wrote to Omondi and established the conditions of his return to America. Essentially, Dad stated that he would bring Omondi back only if the purpose was to obtain a college degree. Omondi responded via letter:

> Dad, Uncle Victor was here last night, and thank you for the letter and the clothes. I went through your letter and it occurs to me that I am indeed lucky. I want to bring to your attention that I do understand your conditions you set down, and what you are ready to do for me is already much more than what other boys manage to get and I really do appreciate your efforts.

After Omondi returned to the United States, he continued receiving letters and educational funding from our father. Dad was very optimistic about Omondi's future, especially when compared with the manner of his own arrival in the United States in 1961. Omondi was only twenty-three years old and already familiar with American culture. When he returned to the United States in 1985 he was handed a residency card which immediately opened the door to job opportunities. Omondi had a family support system on two continents. He bought a car, then enrolled in a university in Virginia, and pursued a degree in business. By the late 1980s, Omondi was moving up the ladder of a large telecommunication company that provided college-tuition reimbursement.

Omondi Odenyo (eldest son of Dr. Odenyo)
in Virginia, 1988.

New York City (1983–1989)

While Omondi was excelling in the late 1980s, I was not. School was no longer a priority—it became something I had to endure. My father used to talk about his time in high school as some of the best years of his life. Mine were the worst. They say that the most racially segregated place in America is church on Sunday. They should add to this list the high school cafeteria from Monday through Friday. On my very first day in high school in September 1986, I sat at a lunch table with Robert, a white friend whom I had known since intermediate school. We must have looked very odd— black and white getting along amicably. About ten minutes into our lunch, a six-foot tall black American "super-senior" (twenty-year old student who cannot seem to graduate) gathered a group of his friends and surrounded us at our table. They proceeded to harass us, referring to our "uncool" clothes, studious appearance, and racial combination. The super-senior then demanded that I get on top of the table and demonstrate, for the entire school, how to do the "Wop." The Wop was a popular hip-hop dance that was perhaps known to every black American student in New York. I, however, had absolutely no clue what the Wop was. This saved me from getting on top of the table, but once again confirmed that I was indeed not black.

That evening I sat in my bedroom and made a conscious choice. For the sake of my own survival and sense of identity, I would do everything in my power to become what was considered by my peers as "black." That became my priority from the second day of high school until the day I graduated. To become black I needed to act "black." I had to completely change my cultural behavior and knowledge. Literally overnight, my role-models were no longer my father and his highly-educated friends, but rap artists such as Run-DMC, LL Kool J, and Biz Markie. Instead of borrowing books from the library, my afterschool activities included riding the bus down to Jamaica Avenue and immersing myself in whatever culture I found being sold on the streets. This included buying a fake gold chain to occasionally wear around my neck, a baseball cap to wear backwards on my head in class, and the latest Nike shoes to wear on my feet. I purposely learned to speak Ebonics. I minimized my interactions with white people. I never again spoke to my friend Robert, a decision for which I still feel guilt over today. In an effort to look "cool" and "tough," I sat in the back of class, at times acted like the class clown, and was occasionally rude to my teachers.

I cut school just for the thrill of it in December 1986. Once out on the streets I realized I had nowhere to go, so I wandered around my neighborhood. My father observed me loafing on Francis Lewis Blvd in the late morning while he was driving to work at York College. Our eyes locked for a brief moment, and I saw in him a flash of anger and surprise. Terrified, I dashed east, running all the way through side streets until Bell Boulevard. I found refuge in a movie theatre where I watched Clint Eastwood's *Heartbreak Ridge* five consecutive times, until I realized I could not escape going home. I found my father waiting for me in my bedroom. Dad did not lift a finger or even raise his voice. He simply explained how disappointed he was that I did not value education.

On June 25, 1987, my American history teacher noted: "A distractive influence in class."

On May 5, 1989, my English teacher noted: "Poor/Missing Homework. Has ability to do better."

On June 23, 1989, my music teacher commented: "Lack of Class Participation."

My report card now included a few grades of F. I was not an exceptionally bad kid. I just fit in, which was my only goal.

I am not saying that every black American student in the United States fits this profile that I was adopting. I know a few black students who were the complete opposite, and managed to balance culture, peer pressure, and academics. However, it was not the black American bookworms who were putting me in headlocks and questioning my blackness. It was the bullies. To survive against the bullies, I had to take a crash course not in the behavior of the bookworms, but in the art of what these inner-city bullies considered "black." Unfortunately, this consisted of a lot of unproductive behavior. The famous black American comedian, Bill Cosby, spoke out against this behavior in the early 2000s, and received both praise and anger from the black community. In 2000, a black American linguist, John McWhorter, wrote a book titled *Losing the Race: Self-Sabotage in Black America*. The author was also heavily criticized. However, his book seemed to perfectly describe my own experiences, observations, and bad choices during high school. My sister Atieno recalls similar experiences. Instead of being accepted by black Americans in high school, her friends were mostly "misfits." This included academic-oriented Asian immigrants, unpopular white students, or students of any race who could not fit into a homogeneous social group. Unlike me however, Atieno had the internal fortitude to prevent her social anguish from turning into social deviancy. In the end, it is a personal choice.

For the majority of my three years in high school (1986–1989), my African heritage appeared entirely irrelevant to my identity. However, my reconnection to my heritage began a few months prior to my high school graduation. Although I wish I could say this conversion was a result of my father's influence, it was not. My conversion started late one night while I was recording rap songs from the radio. Understanding the culture of rap music enabled me to better relate to my peers in high school. It was my habit to record rap music after midnight, when certain radio stations were allowed to play unedited versions of vulgar songs such as Slick Rick's "Treat her like a Prostitute." I must have fallen asleep and forgotten to end the recording, so by mistake I recorded the first song of the next radio program. The next night I played back the cassette, and at the end it included the most beautiful, melodic, and charismatic song I have ever before or since heard. Unlike what I had been listening to for almost three years, this song embraced me with feelings of compassion and purpose. I listened to the song repeatedly throughout the week, falling more in love with it each time I heard it. It seemed to connect with a humanitarian side of me that I had been suppressing for some time. That song was the live version of Bob Marley's "No Woman No Cry." Over the course of the next year I immersed myself in his music, which talked about social inequality in "Them Belly Full (But we Hungry)," African unity in "Africa Unite," and faith in God in "Forever Loving Jah (Jehovah)." I also listened to Peter Tosh, who sang about cultural mental slavery in "400 years," and racial segregation in "Fight Apartheid." Through their music and others, I learned about the self-determination of Marcus Garvey, and the spirit of Pan-Africanism.

I have talked to some older adult relatives in Africa, including my father, who draw little personal inspiration from Bob Marley and I can understand why. They were raised in African culture, can understand the lyrics to their Dholuo records talking about "Ramogi," and never had their ethnic identity questioned. This applies as well to my brother Omondi, who dealt with cultural teasing as a new immigrant to America in the 1970s. While people may have asked Omondi what African country he came from, he never was asked, "What are you?" Omondi had a cultural and ethnic stability that was forever out of my reach.

When my African relatives see someone with dreadlocks they immediately think of counter-culture hippies. Many of them are. However, it was not the "One Love," "We're Jammin," or "Kaya" theme that most appealed to me. It was the "Get Up Stand Up," "Zion Train" and "Blackman Redemption" message of social justice, cultural identity, and faith in God. Marley was my personal "Moses." He was 100 percent responsible for my reconnection to my African heritage, and gave me, a "half-caste," a confidence in my bi-racial identity. I have never come across anyone, either in New York or Africa, who has ever asked if Bob Marley was black. Yet, he was a "half-caste" just like me.

Marley and Tosh opened the door to a love of Africa, African history, as well as Black American history. I learned more about the American civil rights struggle, and read a lot about its leaders, especially Malcolm X. However, I became greatly troubled by America's racist past. As in Marley's song "Concrete Jungle," although there were no chains around my feet, I often felt like I was living in captivity. I was young, idealistic, and thought I could change the world through protest. By summer 1989, hardly a day went by without me wearing some display of "the cause," which ranged from African clothes, Reggae T-shirts, to Black Power symbols of clenched fists. Through my youthful exuberance, I often felt like I could single-handedly tackle 400 years of oppression.

12
Africa (1989–2001)

There are good people and bad people all over the world.
The challenge is to find the good people and build bridges with them.

—Dr. Amos Otieno Odenyo, speech on
January 8, 2005, in Westlands, Kenya.

The next time my sister Atieno and I traveled together to Kenya was in the summer of 1989. I was almost turning eighteen. Although I was no longer a child, I still had a lot to learn about myself and the world.

I was not yet ready to accept the fact that I was, in most Kenyans' eyes, just another tourist. I had whole-heartedly embraced the lyrics to Peter Tosh's song "African," which told me not to mind my complexion, and that there was no rejection, for I was an African. I felt that my visit to Africa was returning home. I still feel this today, but in a more realistic way. Kenyans in the United States often ask me, "So, when was the last time you went home?" I know they are not referring to New York City. When I arrive at Jomo Kenyatta Airport, the immigration officer reads my Luo name in my American passport and often says, "Welcome home." In 1989, my problem was that when Kenyans told me I was home, I believed they meant it.

I was now exposed to the economics of being a "half-caste" in Kenya. With the pocket money that I had acquired from my part-time jobs, I ventured into Nairobi city market to buy Kenyan souvenirs. I was accompanied by two cousins, Christine and Dorothy. After I identified the types of items I wished to purchase, I allowed them to take over. I knew that my cousins would have a better understanding of the quality and prices of the items. After my cousins made the purchases for me, I asked them the price. They told me they purchased the items for 300 Kenyan shillings. However, my cousins let me know the vendor asked if they were purchasing the items for me. If so, the price would be 1000 shillings. My cousins also advised that had I not been seen with them at all, perhaps they could have purchased the items at a price of 200 shillings.

I was naively surprised that the seller would so openly reveal the price distinction. Obviously he was basing it entirely on my appearance and accent. In America, such price discrimination, if proven, would be grounds for a lawsuit. Lawyers and civil rights leaders would descend from the heavens, hold press conferences on national television, and organize boycotts of the perpetrators of the crime, who would pay a hefty fine. Yet, here in Africa, this discrimination seemed normal. It was even expected.

This same year my father took my sister and me to Mombasa where we visited Fort Jesus, built by the Portuguese in 1593 (and declared a historical monument in 1958). We also took walks through Mombasa's business district. On one occasion I walked ahead of Atieno and my father, and suddenly two girls walking in the opposite direction bumped into me. I was startled, but also pleased because these girls were quite attractive. The girls invited me to a club that night where I could meet them. I assured them that I would try to meet them that night, and walked back to my father and sister with an inflated ego. After this same scenario repeated itself several times over the next several days, I realized the girls were not interested in me. They were actually prostitutes, and to them, I was just another *Wazungu* that they could bump into on the street and make a quick profit.

While in Kenya, my sister and I used to occasionally joke around with our father by calling him "Driver" instead of "Dad." The reason for this is that whenever we approached a gate, parked the car, or stopped on the side of the road to purchase some sugar cane, every Kenyan assumed Professor Odenyo was a hired driver for either two rich Nairobi kids or children of some foreign embassy official. While driving we used to say to him things like, "Driver, if you can get us from Got Regea to Kisumu before dark, we'll give you a few extra shillings tip!" Dad took it in good stride and always grinned when we said things like that.

Looking back, it is ironic that the Africans were treating us differently, but I only focused on whites as capable of discrimination. To be fair, the African "discrimination" was economic-based and not oppressive. Still, my world-view at the time, which was based on Pan-Africanism, refused to address these inequalities. I was looking at Africa as a Utopia—a place where I could reconnect to my African roots. I was happy in the knowledge that for the next two months I would be free from the influence and distraction of Western culture.

Imagine my utter horror when we arrived in our home village of Got Regea one evening and found my grandmother and a few relatives eating *nyoyo* (boiled maize and beans) with a white couple from Scandinavia. The husband and wife explained to us through their thick accents that our family had allowed them into our home for a few weeks. They were there to study rural African society, share development ideas, and would be staying with us for one more week.

Now, I would have been perfectly happy eating and talking to them anywhere in the world except Got Regea. Had they visited New York City I would have offered them my own bed. However, their presence in Got Regea bothered me. I was now viewing the world through the single lens of black versus white, oppressed versus oppressor. The presence of white people in Got Regea somehow diluted the authenticity of my African experience. After all, if these blond-haired, blue-eyed people could be sitting in my mecca of African heritage, eating food with their hands just like me, how African could I be? So, while my father amicably discussed sociological theory with our Scandinavian guests via candlelight, I sat there in silence, protesting their presence by giving them the evil eye.

My evil eye must have worked, because the next morning we found them on the road near Luanda Primary School. They told us that they had decided to move elsewhere. I made sure that I did not say goodbye, and continued giving them silent stares. That evening I spent several hours trying to indoctrinate my cousin "Sylvia" into my interpretation of black liberation and empowerment. Sylvia seemed to be enamored by the presence of these Scandinavians, and I was hell-bent on reversing this.

"Don't be fooled by these white people," I lectured her. "Outside of Africa most of them won't even allow you into their homes, yet when they come to Africa they pretend to feel at ease with you." This may often be true, but I failed to explain to Sylvia that in my eighteen years I had experienced more discrimination by blacks than whites. I continued, "White people will write reports about you as if you are some animal in a zoo!" I spent another two or three hours lecturing Sylvia on the history of white oppression against Native Americans and Africans. I finished by advising her not to admire Western culture, and used Michael Jackson (who was becoming whiter by the minute) as an example of the end-product for such misplaced admiration.

In that same week I took an interest in the smaller and run-down *Johera* church near Saint Peter's. We always ignored the mud-walled church as if it did not exist. "That is the splinter church that broke off from the Anglican Church," Dad said. "The splinter church allows traditional Luo customs such as polygamy, traditional songs, and certain Luo burial rites. These are all things the Anglican Church prohibits."

I always felt a little sorry for, and a little curious about, the little splinter church, not so much because it was the "right" church, but because it always represented to me that elusive part of African culture to which I was never exposed. I desired to learn more about my traditional Luo heritage, but it appeared that within our home in Got Regea, all aspects of Luo spirituality were erased. This bothered me a great deal. Why should the white Anglican missionaries be so inflexible about African beliefs when many of their own teachings were influenced by pagan customs? In an effort to defend Luo culture, I often debated my father with counter-arguments:

"Daddy, why is it that polygamy is so discouraged by the Anglican Church, but so many people in the Old Testament, like Abraham, Isaac, David, and Solomon, had multiple wives?"

"Well Odera, I suppose the emphasis by the Anglican Church is on the New Testament, rather than the Old Testament."

"But Daddy, if the emphasis is on the New Testament, why is it that you and most of your family have Old Testament names like Zablon, Amos, Ezra, and Adet? I've also read that the Anglican Church used to refuse baptism to children who had only Luo names. Does God require that we de-Africanize ourselves in order to enter the gates of Heaven?"

"Well, you have a good point, but I guess we were following the new customs," Dad replied.

I countered with, "But are the new customs entirely Biblical? For example, Luos no longer pray before the sun but instead worship in Church on *Sun*-day, named after the Roman Sun God. I am not sure this meets the standards of the Fourth Commandment. Also, we celebrate Christmas on December 25, a day the pagan world associated with the rebirth of the sun."

I could tell I was wearing my father down as I hit him from all angles with historical facts, but I would not stop until I managed to draw out a strong response from him.

Why can't we sing some traditional Luo songs in Saint Peter's? Does God only allow European songs? And why do all portraits of Jesus depict him like a *Mzungu* from Germany? If the Anglican Church can change Jesus into a European, why can't we change him into a Luo, or at least depict him as the Middle Eastern man that he was? And he ate food with his hands Daddy, just like us. Look at the picture of the last supper. He is probably eating *ugali*!"

I never managed to draw out a satisfactory response on all these cultural and religious issues from my father. He just gave me the "that's how it is—get over it" response that I so desperately did not want to hear. I did not realize it at the time, but in the early 1960s my father struggled with some of the same philosophical questions.

He often repeated the same stories from his childhood, but Atieno and I were always thankful to hear them again. Inevitably, a memory would surface, and some suppressed emotion would be unveiled. We enjoyed walking with him around the village, impressed that he remembered so many people.

"Who was that?" we would ask him.

"A cousin," he often said.

He took us to the south-west side of Otieno's Hill, where we sat in a small house with a very old and quiet man. "This is my father's brother Gilbert Owuor," Dad explained with reverence. "He used to be a prison guard in Nairobi," pointing to a photograph of a younger

Uncle Gilbert in uniform.

Dad took us to the top of Aruwa's Hill, and pointed in the direction of far-off places and said, "There is where your grandmother comes from (Ugenya), there is where Zablon Sangoro's mother comes from (Alego), there is where I learned to read and write (in Yenga)." With each trip, we learned a little bit more about our father, and in this process, a little bit more about ourselves.

He told me that at my age he had already built his own little house called *simba*. My ears perked up. I said, "Oh...like a bachelor pad?" Dad paused for a brief second as if he was unfamiliar with the term. But eventually he grinned and said, "Yes, very much like a bachelor pad!"

Dad always had a sense of dedication to his mother. When she began having trouble walking he installed plumbing facilities in her house, which is virtually unheard of in Got Regea even today. He mentioned to us that he wanted to install a new roof on her house, for she told him she did not want her guests to someday mourn her death while sitting under a leaking roof.

I fondly remember the many times he took us to see Beryl Oludhe. Beryl was perhaps twenty years older than Dad, and she was once married to my grandfather's uncle, the late Musa Oludhe. We frequently sat inside her mud-walled house where she referred to me as "Simeon" (as in Simeon Odera). She jokingly chastised me in Dholuo for not being able to speak the language of my people when I had been named after such a famous elder. My father used to walk hand-in-hand with her to steady her on the bumpy trails of Got Regea. I do not know what they discussed, but my father really seemed to enjoy their brief moments together. I asked him about his fondness for her one day. He replied that they have always been kind to each other, even when he was a small boy in the village. He explained that since he came back to Kenya in 1970, she never once asked him for money, or implied that he owed anything to her. I knew Dad appreciated this in her, because often times when he stopped on the village road to talk to someone, his casual mood suddenly changed after an open palm was thrust in front of him. Despite being home, it was difficult for him to navigate the seemingly endless financial needs of people who always referred to him as "brother" or "son." He knew he could lend a helping hand today, but as a result, tomorrow there might be five more hands to help.

We visited a lot of family in Got Regea, Kisumu, Kendu Bay, and other locations in Nyanza. What I remember from all of these visits was my father would often talk to a brother, sister, niece, or nephew, alone. I was never invited, and my father would never tell me the details of what was discussed. However, whenever I had the courage to ask, my father would say one or two things: "So and so wants money," or, "so and so wants to come to America." On a few occasions he offered extra bits of information out of frustration. Dad would say, "She wants to go to America but she has no clue what she wants to do when she gets there—all she wants is America, America, America. If she gets to America, all her problems will be magically solved."

It was in 1989 that I became aware of the tremendous burdens placed upon Dad every time we went to Kenya. Going home was not a vacation. When we went to visit my cousins, it was not always to say hello, but for my father to pay tuition. I recall that in 1983 he had taken us to visit the boarding schools of my cousins "Sylvia" and "Janet." Now I realize that the purpose of the visit was not just to take pictures.

I vividly remember one meeting my father had with his sister Olivia in Got Regea around 2001. They sat alone, at a distance, and I noticed my father was doing more listening than talking. His head was cast downward, his lips were pressed together, and he was staring at the ground in deep frustration. Later that day, as we were driving on the Kisumu-Busia road, I dared to ask him what he discussed with Aunt Olivia. Once again he did not share the details, but I already knew the answer. There was another financial need. Who knows, it could be one more airline ticket out of Kenya, one more round of school fees, or one more medical bill to pay. Whatever it was, Dad did not share it with me, but said, "I told her I am tired of having to assist once more! I am over sixty-five years old, and ready for retirement."

"What are you going to do?" I asked him.

After a long pause, he replied, but without revealing the answer. He said something like, "She tells me I am the tree from which people eat—the tree from which people get their strength. But I told Olivia I did not ask to become this tree—I am tired of being this tree." [23]

I do not know the result of their conversation, but I can assure you, if there was one sibling who could convince him to do something, it was Aunt Olivia. She was his closest and dearest sibling.

Although Dad kept the pressure of family obligations to himself, he would more easily let slip his frustration over what I consider "misappropriation" of his generosity. There are numerous examples, but I will share only a few. While walking around our home in Got Regea he once said out loud, "Gosh, how many times do I have to send money to have a fence built around our compound. I have given money twice to have this project done, yet, there is no fence here!" These situations frustrated him to no end, and he was very angry about it. He would say, "Whenever there is a need here at home, I wire enough money to cover the project, but why is it that I never get a refund, even if the project is never started? My money just disappears!"

This reminds me of an interesting story. In August 2001, I was videotaping my Dad, sister Atieno, and cousin Eddie walking down the small trail between the two hills (Got ka Otieno and Got ka Aruwa). Unannounced, a young child we had met for the first time sneaked up behind us and reached out in a loving manner to hold my sister's hand. It was a cute moment. He was about four years old, dressed immaculately, with polished shoes, suspenders, and a collared shirt. He really stood out from the other young boys in the village who at that age often ran around barefoot wearing second-hand clothes. Atieno and the boy walked hand-in-hand for a while, with Atieno repeatedly gushing over how "cute" he was. As we were walking through the *rangach* (main gate) of someone's home, our new young friend rushed up to Dad to grasp his hand. Dad took it for a second, stopped, tossed the boy's hand away, looked down at him in a very serious manner, and sternly said, "I am not your Daddy." I was videotaping all of this and was shocked at Dad's atypical behavior. He noticed our reaction, and realizing that he was caught on camera, replied, "You know why he was sent out here to us, don't you," then kept on walking. After analyzing the situation further, I recalled that the young boy had over seven older siblings, each with their own children. Half of the young boy's siblings had been educated by my father, either at the high school or college level. Although no one was employed, their family kept growing, and so did their economic needs. In all likelihood, that young boy's parents purposely dressed their son in his Sunday best and instructed him to run down the village path to join us and establish a close connection that hopefully could be exploited later. But instead of referring to my father with the now commonly-used term of "Uncle," the boy must have called him "Daddy." This in itself is not bad. My father told me he used to regard his elders in the same way when he was a boy. However, my father was tired of being the "financial Daddy" to everyone else's children, and he wanted people to know it.

Dad was always surprised to come across some niece or nephew back home in Kenya, on holiday from foreign studies. "Wow, how does this young man manage to come back to Kenya for holidays every other year? Back when I was going to school I did not come home for nine years and this person has been back to Kenya twice in four years! If he has enough money to come home this often, why am I paying his tuition?" He was frustrated to see that while he was making financial sacrifices in New York, such as taking a crowded bus to York College, not upgrading his worn-out carpet, or not patching the leaking basement walls, a young person he was putting through school was living a life of "immediate gratification."

Our many road trips in Kenya were always learning opportunities for us because of the rare opportunity for conversation. We must have been discussing poverty or economic development issues when Dad used a phrase I remember very clearly. He said, "Socialism is the let's all be poor together philosophy." I was immediately intrigued with what he was saying, but a bit confused. I was confused because he recently urged me to consider a study-abroad program in the Soviet Union. He had explained that it was a good opportunity to "widen your horizons," "expose yourself to a new environment," and "see things that few people get to see." I, on the other hand, envisioned a cold, snowy place, with KGB officers chasing after me like in the movie *Rocky IV*. I wanted no part of his plan, and I told him so. Yet, here he was telling me that socialism is bad. I paid close attention to his statements because he often came up with simple and practical explanations for an otherwise boring and complicated textbook subject. I forget his exact words, but his explanation was simple: Africa is a place with more poverty than opportunity. This mathematically limits the number of people who will have access to the tools necessary to pull themselves out of poverty. If each wealthy person distributes his or her own money with the intent of eliminating poverty, the result will be no wealthy people, but almost the same numbers of poor people. The ratios between the two groups are simply too skewed for this policy to work, and if it did work, it would soon become unsustainable because no one would have an incentive to work when they are getting a free check. So, instead of only distributing your wealth, enjoy the wealth that you have worked hard to create, but also try to create more opportunities so that people can similarly obtain wealth. He also explained that whenever socialists come to Africa and try to implement a European-style socialist development policy in a rural village, they fail completely, and create conditions worse than what they original found.

Throughout my father's four decades of providing assistance to various development causes, he emphasized that the recipients and donors should have a joint stake in the outcome of the project. He theorized that if either donor or recipient participated without mutual effort or interest, the project would be prone to mismanagement, neglect, or outright abuse. He drafted his own children into his development plans. As soon as my sister and I graduated from high school, Dad asked us to contribute money to development projects in Got Regea, such as renovations of Saint Peter's Church, electrification, and the extensions of underground water lines. At first it was financially and psychologically difficult to contribute because we did not have a lot of our own money and knew that he could afford to donate for all of us. Later, we noticed he would conclude his emails to his brothers with "make sure everyone participates, even if it is a little amount. That way they will have a vested interest in the success of the project. Some people think that money grows on trees." My father was very wise in involving us at an early age in development projects within Got Regea. Whenever I visit, I look around and try to see the results of my $50 donation that I provided five or ten years ago. If I do not see any noticeable improvement in the project, I ask questions.

It was around 1992 when I first noticed Dad did not automatically stay overnight with relatives. While in Nyanza, he preferred to visit Got Regea during the day but drive forty-five minutes to sleep at a hotel in Kisumu. I suspect that by not staying with relatives, he was removing an opportunity for a relative to say to others: "Look at Otieno, he always stays at my house and eats my food while in Kenya. Yet, he refuses to take my two sons and daughter with him to America. Can you believe it? Now that he has a Ph.D. and all that money, he does not want to share any of it with us. What a stingy relative that Otieno is—we treat him like family and he does not do the same."

In Nairobi, my father often stayed at the home of his childhood friend Mr. "Abuto." Their fathers were also good friends, so the bond between our two families was exceptionally strong. Mr. Abuto was highly educated, with more than one advanced degree from two foreign countries. He worked for the Kenyan government, married a non-Kenyan of mixed ancestry, and together with their three children, lived an elite lifestyle in an exclusive neighborhood in Nairobi. Their house was extremely big and luxurious even by American standards. My father used to describe it as a mansion. The two-level mansion had at least six bedrooms, three dens, four bathrooms, and an upstairs private balcony supported by massive Greco-Roman columns. The construction was top-notch, with hand-carved ceiling ornaments, luxurious chandeliers, and rare imported wood floors. The estate had separate servants' quarters to house the nanny, cooks, and gardeners. The Abuto guard dogs lived well too. Their dog-house had two separate entrances, with a red brick tile roof to keep them cool during the day. When Mrs. Abuto wanted meals prepared, all she had to do was give instructions and a short time later the servants would bring the meals to the table. The Abuto children never had to walk to school, for they were assigned a special driver. I remember being shocked when one of the teenage Abuto girls told me she had never even traveled in a *matatu* (shared minibus).

Atieno and I marveled at the luxury that we found in the Abuto mansion, and teased Dad that he should have permanently returned to Kenya so that we could live in a huge house with servants:

"Why are we living in poverty in the United States when we could live like princes and princesses in Kenya!"

"Yeah," mom chimed in. "Why do I have to go to work and still do all the cooking and cleaning! If we lived in Kenya I could stay home like Mrs. Abuto and be waited on by an army of servants!"

We were teasing Dad, but there was a basis for truth in what we were telling him. We were living a middle-class life in America, but the Abuto family seemed able to maintain an upper-class lifestyle in Kenya.

Beyond the long-standing friendship that existed between our two families, I believe it was Mr. Abuto's perceived wealth that enabled my father, as years went by, to actually prefer to stay with Mr. Abuto in Nairobi as opposed to relatives. First of all, Mr. Abuto never lacked a spare room, or even two. My father never felt obligated to compensate for Mr. Abuto's hospitality. It was a reciprocal, rewarding, and trusting relationship. Mr. Abuto made annual trips to New York where he always stayed with our family. Atieno and I called Mr. Abuto "Uncle," and Mrs. Abuto "Auntie." However, when we stayed at the Abuto mansion in Nairobi, Dad always thanked them by contributing food or paying a month's salary for their house help. In 1998 we took the entire Abuto family on a multi-day excursion to see the animals at Masaii Mara gamepark. I cannot count the number of times my father took the Abuto family to Carnivore restaurant where we would sample exotic foods like giraffe, elephant, zebra, and wildebeest.

My father liked to eat in small restaurants located on the banks of Lake Nyanza. He often admired his plate of *ugali, sukumawiki,* and tilapia, and told us, "Now this is how you eat fish. It is not a real fish unless it comes to you intact, with all the bones. Do not ask me to share the head with you, for this is the best part."

"We won't ask you for it Daddy," we replied in quick unison, as the tilapia's eyes seemingly stared at us.

Then he delved into stories of Chief Odera Akang'o, or the political and geographical boundaries of Gem. He told us how he traversed the lake to attend his sister's wedding in Kendu Bay, and how he was terrified as he could not swim. Although Dad was always afraid of water, he liked being close to Lake Nyanza. At Sunset Hotel, he often stood at the balcony and admired the tranquility and beauty of the lake.

It was at Dunga Refreshments (renamed Kiboko Bay Beach Resort), an Indian restaurant near Hippo Point, that I saw him complete the dowry process for my brother Omondi in 1992. My father and brother had previously sent money from the United States to Uncle Booker.

This was so that Booker could negotiate and buy the right number of cows to bring to the Oromo family, and receive permission for Omondi to marry Florence Oromo from Karachuonyo. I had already met Florence in the United States, but now that Dad and I were in Kenya we finalized the dowry process in a series of long speeches on both sides of the family. I remember taking many family photos with my back turned to the lake, wondering just when that submerged hippo would rise out from the waters and snatch up either me or one of our guests. It was a memorable event. The Oromo family jested that perhaps I should choose another one of their daughters as a wife, now that the Odenyo and Oromo families were already connected. There was a humor behind it, but I really do think that they were serious!

In 1989, President Moi's photograph was still hanging on the wall of every business. Dad reminded us that Moi is a Kalenjin and a Nilotic cousin to the Luo. "We share common traditions —that's why Moi is missing two lower teeth, while the Luo remove six teeth. Although Moi is not a Bantu, to stay in power he aligns himself more with the Kikuyu than the Luo. The Kalenjin and Kikuyu fear the day a Luo might become president. They fear we will do to them what they have done to us," he explained. "It's all a game over power and wealth."

We were curious to learn more, so he explained the historical rivalries between the Luo and the Kikuyu going back to the murder of Tom Mboya and detention of former Vice-President Oginga Odinga.

I had recently skimmed through Odinga's autobiography, *Not Yet Uhuru*, which I found in my father's basement library. I was attracted to the book simply by the name of the author. The name Oginga Odinga seemed powerful, and like my own name, very Luo. However, I was more impressed with the man himself. He refused to call the largest lake in Africa "Lake Victoria," a name attributed to a white queen who never once saw the lake herself. Instead, he referred to it by a local name—Lake Nyanza. I was proud of Odinga for standing up to Missionary E. Carey Francis at Maseno School, and refusing to be called "Adonijah" (his assigned baptismal name). I admired Odinga's struggle for economic independence through the creation of the Luo Thrift and Trading Corporation (LUTATCO). Although Odinga wrote that LUTATCO "did not bring impressive returns," and that some business endeavors "suffered losses by pilfering," I was proud of his efforts. I also sympathized with him for being detained by each of Kenya's two presidents (in 1969 and 1982).

The revelation that tribalism existed threatened to stain my image of Africa as a black man's paradise. I knew I was powerless to solve Africa's tribal problems by myself, but that did not stop me from dreaming about it. I remember my father driving us through the cloud-covered Rift Valley, and I was staring out into the magnificent landscape. I had my headphones on, immersed in the lyrics of Bob Marley's song "So Jah Seh (So God Says)." I let my mind wander into an idealistic place and suddenly I was no longer traveling through the Rift Valley, but singing on stage in Nyayo Stadium before thousands of Kenyans. With the moon right over my head, I sang out to Odinga and Moi, asking why if "Puss and Dog" can learn to live together, they could not.

In the summer of 1989, Dad took Atieno and me to visit Uncle Victor, who was working as the chief technical advisor for a United Nations project in Zimbabwe. I was very excited for I knew Zimbabwe (formerly Rhodesia) played a significant part in the resistance against colonialism and apartheid in Southern Africa. It was in the capital city of Harare that Bob Marley in April 1980 sang his song "Zimbabwe" as the flag of Britain was lowered, and the Zimbabwe flag was raised.

It was in this spirit that I religiously wore my "Africa Unite" T-shirt while my father drove Atieno and me around Harare and Victoria Falls. During our travels I subjected my father to endless rounds of Marley and Peter Tosh music played from the car's cassette player, sweet revenge for hours of his playing "We Are the World" in 1985 (that was the only American song we ever heard him play by the way). At the time I had the audacity to believe that by bombarding my father with my music, I was actually educating him on matters such as African pride, history, and equality. I remember him making a general acknowledgment of his interest in the lyrics to two Tosh songs: "Equal Rights" and "African." As usual, he did not share his opinions about them, which frustrated me to no end. However, the songs provided a gateway for us to probe him about his experiences with discrimination and interracial marriage.

We asked him, half-jokingly, "So…Daddy, what nationality or race would you not want us to marry?"

"No one,'" he replied. "Marry any race you want, just make sure they are good people."

We were not surprised by his answer, but were not done testing him.

"A Chinese person?"

"Absolutely," he replied.

"How about a Samoan?"

"Fine, go ahead."

"An Eskimo?" I suggested.

"That's fine by me," he said.

We gave up, because an Eskimo was the most remote person we had to offer him. He continued driving, just staring ahead at the road. Moments later he told my sister, "Atieno, just do not marry a Nigerian."

This was the last thing we expected him to say. What I knew of Nigerians was that I admired their traditional African clothes that Kenyans do not wear, they ate *ugali* like we did (they call it *fufu*), they like fish, and some of them had Luo sounding names—even the name Odera! They are almost more Luo than we are, so why not marry them?

Dad was at first hesitant to explain, but he stated, "Nigerians will easily con you out of your money—especially the men. You would be wise not to trust them. It's best if you do not bring home a Nigerian to me."

This was a remarkable and surprising response from him. I had expected him to say, "Don't marry Kikuyu people" (due to political reasons in Kenya), or "Don't marry an Eskimo," (because of cultural differences). But not to marry a Nigerian? Now, my father was half-way joking, but half-way serious when he said this. Of course he would have entertained the notion of one of his children marrying a Nigerian, and held no personal animosity towards any nationality. But as the lyrics to Peter Tosh's "African" blared at him from the car speakers for perhaps the fifth time, the point he was trying to make was that we should not be overly blinded by race or nationality. Instead, we should look at the quality and character of the person.

My father valued honesty. If you were not an honest person he would rather not deal with you, despite your race, your family connection, or your position. He was aware of Nigeria's corruption problem well before the days of the 419 emails scams. They are referred to as "419" after the section of Nigerian penal code the scam violates. Today, oil-rich Nigeria is so corrupt that conning people out of their money is not only a perfected skill, it is a respected part of the culture. Nigerian artist Osofia even produced a much-celebrated song, "I Go Chop Your Money," that brags about stealing money from greedy white people.

Kenya did not seem to be associated with these big scams, at least back in the 1980s. We were frustrated however, over simple things, such as receiving birthday cards and packages in the mail in Nairobi from my grandmother in Minnesota, only to find out that the contents had already been removed by the Kenyan Postal Service. My grandmother mailed me a birthday card every year with a ten dollar bill inside. Imagine my surprise to receive the birthday envelope, but not the ten dollar bill, and not even the card itself! I thought to myself, "Gosh, if you are going to steal my money at the post office, at least have some dignity and give me the card!" When I opened the empty envelope from my grandmother it felt like a punch in the face by the Kenyan Postal Service. I imagined them saying, "Ha ha ha—we have your money and there is nothing you can do about it!"

One year Aunt Rosalie's son Kennedy requested that my sister send him a walkman (music player). It was a big order to fill as Atieno was a poor high school student, but my sister saved her money, bought the walkman, and mailed it to Kennedy. She no doubt properly declared the export as a "walkman" on the U.S. shipping labels affixed to the package, which by doing so sealed that walkman's fate the moment it reached Kenyan Customs. Atieno might as well have filled out the paperwork with a red pen saying "*Steal Me!*" This is the dilemma. You can be honest on the U.S. side, but that same honesty will bite you in your rear in Kenya. In Kenya the system works *against*, not *for* the person who does the right thing. Kennedy never did get that walkman.

Mrs. "Abuto," the wife of my father's friend, would always chuckle when she heard our stories. "You cannot trust the system in this country," she said. "I still don't have my driver's license, because even after having paid all the fees and passing the driving test, the examiner refused to stamp my paperwork until I handed him his *chai* (tea). I refused to bribe him, and he refused to give me my driver's license. What am I to do?"

Mrs. Abuto put matters in perspective by humorously narrating the following story. Her husband used to order *Ebony* magazines from the United States, which would arrive on a monthly basis at the family's post office box in Nairobi. But over time they arrived with less frequency. This frustrated Mr. Abuto to no end since he looked forward to reading the magazine, and in particular, an upcoming issue of special interest to him. One day after he failed to locate his monthly issue at the post office, he drove home in frustration, only to stop at a red light and encounter street boys walking up and down the rows of cars, selling to the drivers a variety of cheap electronics, fruits, newspapers, and magazines. Mr. Abuto noticed one street vendor holding up the latest issue of *Ebony*, the very issue that he had been eagerly anticipating, but which had not yet arrived at his post office box. Mr. Abuto bought it from the street vendor and took it home. After supper he sat down to read it, and on the front page, left hand side, was a shipping label: Mr. Abuto, P.O. Box 123456, Nairobi, Kenya. Mr. Abuto finally received his *Ebony* magazine, but he had to pay for it twice.

I returned to Kenya many times in the 1990s, both with my father and alone. During this period I spent a cumulative two years on the continent. Prior to coming to Kenya in 1992, I spent two months in a rural village in Western Uganda (near Ibanda) where I assisted in the building of a boarding school and a church. When not socializing with my neighbors, my time was spent breaking rocks by hand, mixing the soil, mud, and concrete mix, and hauling water from the well. I remember eating a lot of *matoke* (mashed bananas), drinking traditional beer out of a long thin straw, and greeting people with "*Agandi*," to which was replied "*Nimarungi*." After time spent with relatives in Kenya I took a series of buses to visit Dar es Salaam, the capitol of Tanzania, and continued by ferry to the island of Zanzibar. I felt I learned a lot from these two side trips from Kenya.

Between 1993 and 2005, I returned on several occasions to Tanzania, once spending a ten-month period at the University of Dar es Salaam (1993–94). To get around the country I used the *dala-dala*, the equivalent of the Kenyan *matatu*. I formally and informally studied African history, culture, politics, and Kiswahili. I learned to understand the lyrics of songs I had heard since childhood. By day I read an endless series of books, including *How Europe Underdeveloped Africa*, by Walter Rodney. By night I recorded and listened to analysis of local and world events on Radio Tanzania's *Mazungumzo Baada ya Habari*. Twice a week I practiced and became very proficient in using a traditional washing machine, which consisted of a bucket, bar of soap, and my hands.

I danced to Tarab and Lingala music, and ate *nyama choma* (roasted meat) until the wee hours of the morning in clubs such as Bilicanas. I explored the ruins at Kaole, swam off the shore of Bagamoyo, crawled through the Amboni caves in Tanga, walked the streets of Arusha, and took a photograph with the famous singer Remmy Ongala during one of my many trips to Zanzibar.

I traveled throughout eastern Africa by rail, bus, and foot. I spent Christmas day, alone, in Mombasa, and New Year's Eve with relatives in Nairobi. When a bus broke down in southern Kenya, I hitched a ride on the back of a flat-bed truck filled with gravel and three Masaii women. I slept overnight on the aisle of a stalled and crowded bus heading from the Kenyan border town of Namanga to Dar es Salaam. When I woke up, I was partially soaked in some baby's urine which had trickled down to me from a few rows ahead. I took the TAZARA train to Zambia, where I spent my first night awake in Lusaka, waiting with everyone else on the tarmac for the morning buses to arrive.

In Zimbabwe, I traveled once again to Victoria Falls and Harare, but also to new places such as Bulawayo and Masavingo. I walked with awe throughout the stone-walled city of "Great Zimbabwe." [24] I provided "voice-over" services for the Swahili version of the 1992 movie *Neria*, produced by Media for Development Trust in Zimbabwe, and distributed by Development through Self-Reliance in the United States. If you can find this movie, listen to the European judge, who is speaking in western-accented Swahili. You are listening to my voice.

I walked across the remote border of Mozambique with my passport in hand, unable to distinguish between border guard and thief due to the lack of uniforms or protocol. I again spent the entire night in a bus stop, this time somewhere north of Lilongwe, Malawi. There I witnessed drunk policemen with machine guns harassing female travelers around three o'clock in the morning.

I returned to Kenya where I rode the overnight Akamba bus from Nairobi to Nyanza to visit my grandmother. However, when I arrived, we still could not communicate directly. I continued by *matatu* to Kampala, where I once again climbed the hill to visit the Kasubi Tombs, resting place of the last four *Kabakas* (Kings) of the Buganda Kingdom. It was to this location that Chief Odera Akang'o of Gem, a "king" in his own right, may have traveled nearly a century before me. Although we were both named Odera, are both from Gem, and traveled from Gem to Kampala, I did not live like a king while I visited Uganda. For the cost of one U.S. dollar a night I was allowed to sleep in the safety of a local day school in Kampala. I showered in the bathroom sink and slept on top of the students' desks. The occasional sound of mice running around the legs of the desks eventually lulled me to sleep.

After a time spent back in the United States, I again returned to Africa, this time staying in Ethiopia for three months. I visited the Organization of African Unity (OAU) building, drank Ethiopian coffee on Bole road, volunteered to distribute free *injera* bread to the homeless, talked to the Somali people living in the desolate town of Gode, rode a donkey-taxi outside of the walled city of Harar, prayed in the subterranean rock-hewn churches of Lalibela, and peered up at the ancient obelisks in Axum. Within the grounds near St. Mary's Church of Zion, I caught a glimpse of the High Priest of Axum, said to live his entire life in one chapel, guarding the original ark of the covenant of the Old Testament. While in Ethiopia, I visited my aunt Awino, who was working with International Livestock Research Institute as a microbial ecologist based in Debre Zeyit. I watched as she unplugged a round plastic seal on the side of cow, and inserted her whole arm inside the cow to verify the contents of the stomach. With one arm seemingly missing, Aunt Awino explained to me her preliminary findings. Throughout the entire process the cow merrily chewed on grass. I, however, almost passed out.

The historical experiences in Ethiopia were so valuable that several years later I encouraged my sister to return with me to revisit these same holy sites, as well as the ancient palaces of Gondar, the remote island monasteries in Lake Tana, and the house where my maternal second cousin Dana and her husband Tom (both Peace Corp workers from Minnesota) were living in Bahir Dar. My sister and I visited all the major historical sites in Egypt from Abu Simbel in the south to Alexandria in the north.

Now you have a taste of my experiences in Africa without my father. These moments were a mixture of academia, development work, and tourism, combined with a lot of uneventful daily living. When my sister, father, and I returned to Got Regea in 2001, Uncle Robert greeted me with the now familiar *"Karibu nyumbani."* He then grinned and said, "Odera, *umepotea*! (Odera, you have become lost!)" I grinned back and hugged him. This time, I knew exactly what he meant.

Odera Odenyo in Uganda, 1992.

Odera Odenyo in Kenya, 1992.

Gilbert Owuor (younger brother to Zablon Sangoro Odenyo).
Got Regea, 1996.

The two eldest brothers, Adet Odenyo and Amos Otieno Odenyo, discussing family matters in Kenya, 1994.

Robert Okwata Odenyo, on the slope of
Aruwa's hill in Got Regea, 1998.

(Siblings) Booker, Rosalie, Olivia, Amos Otieno,
Olga, Robert, and Victor in Got Regea, 1998.

13
Maendeleo (1989–2001)

Wich liech turo mana wuongo
(The elephant's head is its owner's burden)

—Luo proverb, emphasizing self-reliance.

Although I traveled to Africa numerous times between 1989 and 2001, during these years I spent the majority of my time in the United States pursuing my educational and professional goals. When I graduated from high school in 1989 with poor grades, I felt that I not only disappointed myself but my parents. I remember sitting in my room in New York City, the Run-DMC posters recently replaced by Marley and Tosh, and purposely thinking into the future. I asked myself a very simple question: "What type of life would I be living at age thirty?" What I envisioned, if I did not obtain some type of higher education, was that at age thirty I would be sitting there looking at the same childhood posters and earning the same minimum wage.

I had little self-direction, but I did one thing right. I enrolled in Queensborough Community College (of the City University of New York), became reacquainted with the library, came to class prepared every day, sat in the front row, and treated education like a precious opportunity rather than a burden. In my first semester, my psychology instructor congratulated me in front of the class for being prepared and engaged. After two years, my good grades enabled me to join my sister at the Queens College campus in Flushing. Atieno was also studying

hard, and I still remember the two years that we rode our bicycles together to school, rain or shine.

I maintained my good work ethic. While pursuing my undergraduate degree I worked at least two or three part-time jobs per day. After
class I worked alternate afternoons on campus. Then I took a series of
buses and trains to Manhattan where I loaded boxes for United Parcel
Service from six to ten in the evening. After reversing the commute
home to Queens, several nights a week I jumped on my bicycle and
pedaled to an outdoor golf range in Douglaston. There I picked up
golf balls (often by hand) and cleaned toilets from midnight until eight
in the morning. During the summers I was attacked by mosquitoes,
and during the winters my hands nearly froze. My schedule worked out
so that some days I slept only three hours in the morning, or not at all,
before repeating the same school-work cycle. I studied between classes,
on the train, and on weekends, and managed to graduate with honors
and a double major (sociology and African studies) in 1993. That year
my sister also graduated from Queens College with a Bachelor of Arts
degree in Sociology, and in 1995 she received a Master of Arts degree
in Special Education from Hunter College.

During my undergraduate years I still struggled with issues related
to racial justice and equality. I heeded the call of the black Baptist
reverends in Bayside who urged us to support liberation and healing by voting for black mayoral candidate David Dinkins over white
Republican candidate Rudy Giuliani. I wore my African themed shirts
to college on a daily basis and protested against racism at any opportunity. During the week of Thanksgiving in 1990, I hung on the campus
bulletin boards old pictures of whipped black American slaves with
the caption: "Is this what we have to be thankful for?" I volunteered
to donate my blood during a charity event on campus, but was refused
(the theory was that my travels to Africa exposed me to the AIDS virus). I exited the hall angry about racism, but was secretly proud that
for once in my life I was considered "too African." I recalled for my
classmates the story about my father being forced by a teacher to stare
at the sun in colonial Kenya. This was proof, I told them, of the cruel
nature of white people. It never crossed my mind that the teacher was
not a British colonialist, but a Luo.

Maendeleo (1989–2001)

I was aware of my rich pioneer heritage in Meeker County, Minnesota, but no longer embraced it. After all, was it not true that the Native Americans were removed from their lands through the government's "Doctrine of Discovery" and the white man's "Manifest Destiny?" Did not the U.S. Supreme Court rule in 1823 (*Johnson v. McIntosh*) that Native Americans did not own any land? Were they not maneuvered to the bargaining table through hunger, false promises, fear, and free alcohol? Was it not true that hungry Dakota Indians in Minnesota had a right to retaliate against repeated treaty violations, and that this was the cause behind the 1862 Dakota War, which was sparked by the tragic "Acton Massacre" in Meeker County?

In 1990, in a crowded movie theater near predominantly white Bell Boulevard, my Guyanese-American girlfriend and I watched the movie *Dances with Wolves*. We both stood up and hollered a war cry of approval at the scene where Sioux warriors overpowered the invading American soldiers. When CUNY raised its tuition, I joined the protesters marching around Queens College claiming it was a way to prevent minorities from affording higher education. In my sociology of racism class, I stood before the class wearing my favorite Bob Marley shirt and explained how Europe's version of Christianity was inaccurate and racist. I hung a picture of a black Jesus in my parents' home, and when it was taken down in anticipation of my white grandmother's visit to New York City, I took it as solid evidence that my parents were not committed to black equality. When my father advised me not to wear my goatee too long because we are a Christian family and people might mistake me for a Muslim, I replied, "So, what's the difference? If the colonialists in Kenya had been Arabs instead of British, your father would have been brainwashed into Islam instead of being brainwashed into Christianity!" I really hurt my father when I said that, using the word "brainwashed." It is not that my opinions had no merit. It was that I was obsessed with justice and equality to the point that it threatened to overshadow any other ambitions I had in life.

I was searching to correct any sign of racial injustice, real or unreal, at every corner, stoplight, and intersection of life. New York City also seemed to be suffering from the same racial confusion. White police officers were vindicated against charges by a black girl (Tawana

Brawley) that they assaulted, raped, and smeared her with feces. Her civil rights advocate, Al Sharpton, was being assaulted on national television by civil rights advocate Roy Innis at the Apollo Theater in Harlem. In Bensonhurst, Brooklyn, Italian-Americans with baseball bats and guns were beating black men, killing Yusuf Hawkins. Black supremacist Khalid Mohammed of the Nation of Islam was calling for a race war against the white "devils." Crown Heights erupted in riots over the killing of a Guyanese-American (Gavin Cato) by a Jewish driver. Al Sharpton was again assaulted, this time with a knife by an Italian man in Bensonhurst.

There was racial chaos everywhere. This contributed to me viewing academics as a mechanism for comprehending racial issues rather than a means for finding a meaningful career. Although my school performance never suffered, I was not taking advantage of all the opportunities at hand. For example, I did not network or apply for professional internships that might have enabled me to find a decent job with my bachelor's degree. When in my last semester I finally walked through the door of the college career counseling office at Queens College, I was told, "You know, you really are supposed to have applied for these positions in your sophomore year, not three weeks prior to graduation. You are ineligible for these internships now."

I felt like a complete idiot. While I was busy tracking every perceived racial injustice in New York City, I had let valuable professional opportunities slip through my fingers. I had a college degree, but in the four years it took me to acquire it, I never once figured out what I would actually do with it. I was a college-educated man picking up golf balls and cleaning dirty toilets. This taught me a valuable lesson. Do not let ideology blind you to the opportunity at hand. In my case, instead of just protesting CUNY's raised tuition (which my father was paying), I should have taken better advantage of what my tuition offered—career counseling.

It was at that time that I left New York City to study for one year at the University of Dar es Salaam in Tanzania. I found the Tanzanian people very welcoming, and I generally had positive experiences—too many to list here. If I had to live again in Africa, Tanzania would be at the top of my list, even over Kenya. Overall, the students' knowledge, maturity, and exposure to world events far exceeded my own. For example, they could name the capitals of countries I never knew existed. However, I encountered a fair share of students and teachers who seemed to think the source of Africa's problems were external (mostly from America and Europe), and I heard comparatively little about domestic solutions. The sources of problems were the standard themes: the American slave trade, colonialism, American imperialism, and bad International Monetary Fund (IMF) and World Bank policies. It was not that the Africans' positions were entirely wrong, for I sympathized with them on a certain level. However, I was now in a position to scrutinize these ideologies more thoroughly, and they all seemed so one-sided. Also, I was surprised at the extent to which a few Muslim students (with origins in Oman, Yemen and Zanzibar) actually vilified the United States. In our classroom discussions they seemed happy that the U.S. humanitarian and security operations in Somalia failed. One graduate student was overjoyed that President George Bush recently embarrassed himself by fainting and vomiting on Japanese Prime Minister Miyazawa. Outside class, one otherwise peaceful Muslim student commented favorably on the February 1993 bombing of the World Trade Center in Manhattan, but in the same breath expressed admiration for America's new president, Bill Clinton. I found such comments illogical and appalling.

Since I represented America, Tanzanians occasionally made statements holding me accountable for U.S. foreign policy. I countered this through the game of devil's advocate: "Why do you keep on saying Americans are trying to divide Africa when Zanzibar would like to secede from Tanzania, and Rwandans are slaughtering each other like chickens? You keep on talking about Americans killing Lumumba. Are we also responsible for shooting down the airplane carrying the presidents of Burundi and Rwanda (in April 1994)? It seems like debt relief is the thrust of your plan for *maendeleo* (development). If I defaulted on my debt to you, would you loan me another shilling?"

I had reached a point in life where I was more interested in "results" than "ideology." I was more focused on the future than the past, the practical instead of the theoretical. I found that it was popular overseas for people to blame the world's problems on Western racism and imperialism while not paying equal attention to their domestic sources of problems. I realized that I had been making the same mistake, and I wanted to chart a new course for my future.

Outside every American embassy in Africa is a long line of men and women desperate to obtain a visa to reach the shores of America. Few who make it plan to go back. Many who return to Africa make sure they have first given birth on U.S. soil. Their American children are raised in Africa, but return to the United States as young-adults to attend school or petition for their parents to join them.

In contrast, when is the last time you heard of poor and disadvantaged black Americans begging to trade their U.S. citizenship with that of even the most prosperous African country? How many would want to live in diamond-rich West Africa, where children walk around with their limbs chopped off by their countrymen? How about becoming a citizen of liberated Zimbabwe under President Mugabe? Once the bread-basket of Africa, Zimbabwe's politicians now sit on barren farms while their nation literally starves to death. Tired of working for greedy white capitalists in corporate America? How about becoming a swashbuckling Somali pirate intercepting American-aid shipments and commercial cargo off the coast of the motherland? Would *you* throw away your U.S. passport to live in modern South Africa?

During one of my many trips to Zanzibar in 1993–1994, I had dinner in Stone Town with a family who requested that I take their infant child to America, presumably, for a better life. On another occasion I was told by a black American student in Dar es Salaam that his Tanzanian friend confided in him: "You are so lucky, I almost wish my ancestors had been taken to America." In Tanzania I fully realized the extent to which I was blessed to be an American. I realized that before I attempt to solve each and every injustice, I should first solve the injustice of not living up to my full potential. Uncle Dan also shared this opinion with me in a letter sent to Tanzania, dated November 14, 1993:

> Dear Odera, I was extremely happy for you, when your Dad told me that you would be pursuing further studies at the University of Dar es Salaam in Tanzania. It

will not be easy for you as I believe you will go through different race, colour, national, and all the world's bigotry, but I'm sure you have survived this before in one type or another. The last time I was in Dar es Salaam and Zanzibar was June 1990, and it was just beginning to ideologically and commercially reorient itself to economics of free enterprise. You will find them different in style to Kenya. I hope that you survive the "Everyday is a holiday and idle talk do nothing" philosophy and culture that is trendy in East African coastal towns, and more pronounced in Dar Es Salaam! I mean, I would be happier if your enterprising spirit remains intact. Otherwise, keep in touch and when you can, visit Awino in Egerton. Love, Uncle Dan.

My experience in Tanzania was a defining moment in my life. To me, it represents my transition from childhood to adulthood. During this time I was able to balance "idealism" with "realism." It marks the return to the point in my life that I could listen to, embrace, and find great joy in both Peter Tosh's "Mama Africa," and Lee Greenwood's "God Bless the U.S.A." However, I sing only one anthem, say only one pledge of allegiance, and salute only one flag—and that flag has the colors red, white, and blue.

In Dar es Salaam in 1994, I realized that all my African pride T-shirts and necklaces were utterly useless to myself and others if I did not acquire skills and a career. With this in my thoughts, I sat down in front of a typewriter and applied for admission to several universities in the United States (much like my father did in Mombasa in 1960). Several respected universities in New York City accepted me, but I decided to attend American University in Washington D.C. I knew it would be more of a challenge to attend a school away from the comforts of home, but it was precisely that challenge of being independent that excited me. Returning to my bedroom in New York City seemed like a step backward in my quest to become independent. Washington D.C. also seemed to offer more professional opportunities in the field of international relations, which is what I wanted to study.

Staring at the Nyanza Sun

I arrived in Washington D.C. in September of 1994. I had precious little money, so during my first semester I lived in a dilapidated group house on the intersection of New Jersey Avenue and New York Avenue, considered a ghetto at the time. I slept on blankets on the floor of my room for several months. I eventually managed to trade up to a mattress I purchased for exactly one dollar from a neighbor's attic sale. It had urine stains on one side, so I turned it over and used the other side.

I bought a conservative-looking suit and tie and made immediate use of American University's career counseling office before I had even attended my first class. I was lucky to be employed by the second week of class in a business where I could network with professionals. My typical schedule was to wake up at four o'clock in the morning, ride my bicycle to work (arriving at five o'clock), and attend class in the afternoons or evenings. My grandmother gave me her relatively new car since her advanced age prevented her from driving. I hugged her, took the car, and immediately gave it to my parents back in New York. Although I was often bicycling up to twenty miles a day between home, work, and school, at least it was free. I was also getting in shape without having to pay for a private gym. I had calculated the cost of car insurance, registration fees, fuel, and maintenance, and I simply did not want to take on another financial burden. It was logistically tough. There was snow, rain, invisible ice, as well as late-night study sessions in the school library. On one occasion I simply showered in the university's locker room and camped out overnight in a secluded classroom. This was actually preferable during the first winter because my landlord had turned off the hot water and heat, all in an attempt to evict my roommate whom he did not like. I was constantly short of money and struggled to juggle rent, utilities, food, and school expenses, plus I worried about maintaining good grades.

In December 1994, my brother Omondi passed through Washington D.C. on an important business trip and called to tell me he was coming over to see me. Realizing my refrigerator was virtually bare, I dashed across the icy street to the convenience store. I pushed all my loose change under the bullet-proof glass separating me and the Korean clerk, and returned home with a bag of potato chips and the best two cans of soda a dollar-fifty could buy. For the next hour we sat at the kitchen table and I briefed him about my recent adventures in Africa. It was great to see Omondi again, but I remember feeling a bit embarrassed that my successful brother (who was now a father) would see me living in such squalor. We kept our coats on due to the lack of heat, and not too far from where we sat, a chair was laid flat across the floor, protecting us from falling into a three-foot round hole that led straight through to the basement.

There were many times I felt like giving up and returning to New York City where I would not have so much stress. What prevented me from doing so was the inspiration of my father. When I had to get up at four in the morning, I thought of him at age four planting crops with his mother in the morning moonlight. When I used a bicycle instead of a car to get to school, I remembered that my father had to walk barefoot to Luanda Primary School. When my nearly frozen fingers could barely grasp the handlebars of my bicycle, I remembered my father survived not only the adult-initiation process of *nak*, but being forced to stare at the Nyanza sun. While I slept on my pee-stained mattress and showered with cold water, I thought of my father sleeping on a thin mat on the floor in Ndiru Intermediate School, and collecting water from a spring two miles away. By experiencing an infinitesimal drop of the pain my father had to endure in his early life, I finally felt that I understood my father. My father had overcome many of life's inequalities through self-determination, rather than protest. He became a success through action, rather than words. I knew that I must do the same. I had to make use of the opportunities at hand before I could complain about the opportunities I did not have.

On October 16, 1995, it seemed like every black American male in the Washington D.C. area was attending the "Million Man March." This event was celebrated as a day of black male unity for the cause of unity, atonement, and brotherhood—all causes I support. Had the event occurred in 1993 I most likely would have attended. This time around, I spent the day studying in the library. The March was organized by Minister Louis Farrakhan of the Nation of Islam (NOI), and I already had my fill of NOI speeches on the street corners of Jamaica Avenue in Queens, and 125th Street in Harlem. I knew the Million Man March would also be filled with the "reverends." I did not see how marching alongside Reverend Al Sharpton would inspire me not to drop out of college. I did not see how listening to Reverend Jeremiah Wright would lead me to a career protecting my country against those abroad who would like America to be damned. I did not see how Reverend Jesse Jackson could serve as any better a role model for self-determination than my father's friends from Kisii High School.

I was also not convinced that the black American community was ready to embrace change. After all, one of the main speakers during the "Atonement and Responsibility" hour was none other than Mayor Marion Barry. The majority-black population of Washington D.C. had only a year earlier re-elected Marion Barry (over a white Republican opponent) for a fourth term, despite the fact that in 1990 the Federal Bureau of Investigation caught Barry smoking crack-cocaine in a Washington D.C. hotel room.

Mid-way through my university studies, my father mailed an envelope to me which contained a printout of a three-page email titled "The Myth of Foreign Aid." The email was written by an unnamed former International Aid (I.A.) worker, and it was apparently intended as a wake-up call to students pursuing degrees related to international relations. In his email this I.A. worker described his career in Africa, which consisted of jumping from relief project to relief project, administering architectural, environmental, agricultural, and other assistance as dictated by his various contracts. The problem was, he was not trained in any of these fields, and no one seemed to care. According to the I.A. worker, after many years on the job he was totally disillusioned by his mission, for it appeared to be driven solely on the basis of how much financial and other forms of assistance was distributed, rather than on what assistance was needed. The goal was to give assistance, not solve problems, for if problems were solved it would put the I.A. workers out of a job. The benchmark for success each fiscal year was an increase in the international relief organization's annual budget over the previous year, not how many problems were solved on the continent. In several instances, the aid caused more harm than good. The email closed with a warning for the idealist who thinks he will change the international aid business from within. Such idealism will soon succumb to the reality of the bureaucracy, which he will find he is unable to leave. The I.A. worker will have grown accustomed to a plush lifestyle, will have new family obligations, and will lack any skill useful outside the Third World.[25]

It appeared that my father had received this article from my brother Omondi. There was a handwritten note from Omondi dated September 12, 1995:

> Dad, enjoy this. There are moments I wish I had the opportunity to see/enjoy the world using other people's money. Omondi.

On top of this my father stapled his own note, dated September 18, 1995:

> This article is interesting except the speaker should have known these things before going overseas. It is common knowledge that one does these things because it is a job. One who takes them with the fervor of changing the world is bound to be disappointed. It is not the world of idealists. Dad.

What I took from that article, and the comments of my father and brother, is fairly obvious. Money and good intentions alone rarely solve development problems. By him sending that article to me, I believe my father was warning me to not get caught up in a career, like the author of the article, where I would profit from other people's misery by being paid to administer ill-conceived development projects.

Many years later I came across an academic paper that my father wrote in 1994, titled *Alternative Development Strategies for Africa*. According to the abstract for the paper, he wrote it in connection with the United Nation's Development Fund for Women (UNIFEM). Far from disparaging development projects, he was reviewing the need to set a new course in development, incorporating a "ground-up" approach. In his paper, he referenced case studies of Onoka Ginnery (Siaya, Kenya), and Bomani Bakery Association (Mombasa, Kenya). He cited specific examples of micro-development projects that fostered "capacity build-ing, human development, confidence, job creation," and other ben-efits. Dr. Odenyo concluded that the key ingredients of an alternative development model in Africa are:

> ...that the origin of the development activity be bot-tom up and not top down; the process be participatory; the resources to be used in the activity be mostly avail-able locally; and that the activity be one that that fills a clearly visible need in the eyes of the participants.

At American University I had the choice of selecting several "con-centrations" within International Relations, ranging from "Foreign Policy," "International Development," "International Peace and Conflict Resolution," to "International Economic Policy (IEP)." For reasons that should be clear by now, I wanted absolutely nothing to do with International Development *coursework*. However, third world development, and in particular African development, was still one of my primary interests. Courses such as Micro and Macro Economics, International Economics, and International Trade and Investment all seemed practical from a historical and contemporary standpoint. "NAFTA" (North American Free Trade Agreement) was one of the biggest international topics of the day, and President Clinton had just been elected on the basis of his slogan, "It's the economy, stupid!"

I graduated from American University with a Master of Arts de-gree in 1996, at the age of twenty-four. My graduate thesis was titled "Japan's Foreign Direct Investment in East Asia." I received a grade of A- for my paper, which explored the dynamics of Japanese for-eign direct investment (FDI) into the Association of Southeast Asian Nations (ASEAN). While my paper made no mention of Africa, the purpose of my research was to learn what the ASEAN region did right to become economic tigers. I knew that when Kenya became indepen-dent in 1963 it had an economy on par with many ASEAN nations, yet forty years later several ASEAN countries had modernized to the point they were no longer "Third World" economies. Why was Kenya not following the same path of *maendeleo*?

Maendeleo (1989–2001)

After graduation I moved to Arlington, Virginia, and worked at one full-time job and two part-time jobs. I made decent money, but I had decided to pay off my student loans ahead of schedule and needed to remain frugal. For example, walking home from work one day in 1997, I saw a large Zenith television set out with the trash near Washington Lee High School. Rather than pass by it, I balanced it on top of my head with my hands and kept walking home. I had to use a wire hanger as an antenna, and a screwdriver to change the channel, but the television served me well for another three years. Similarly, I could have easily bought my own computer and printer, but I chose to ride my bicycle from Virginia to the free computer lab at American University in Washington D.C. When I found a better full-time job in Germantown, Maryland (approximately thirty miles away), I used intermodal transportation (bicycle, train, bus, and foot) to commute from Virginia to Maryland, but I never once considered buying a car. I wanted to instead accumulate enough money for a down-payment on a decent car to avoid paying for expensive repairs on a piece of junk. My sister bought her first car at age twenty-five, and I at age twenty-seven. More than ten years later, I still drive that same car.

In 1998, I found a career in International Trade, and was sent on business meetings to South America, Central America, Asia, and Europe. To increase my skills, I took additional business-related courses at local community colleges. When not traveling for business, I worked twenty hours a week at a part-time job, and applied the extra money toward an individual retirement account. At age thirty I purchased my first home.

This personal review is not for the sake of self-adoration. I was rarely the top performing student, did not get a degree in nuclear physics, and I still hold onto a stack of rejection letters in order to keep my feet firmly planted on the ground. All I am trying to explain are my personal stages of development (*maendeleo*)—which include both my failures and successes. *Maendeleo* is primarily a result of opportunity, hard work, sacrifice, and making the right decisions. You cannot fault someone who does not progress in life if never given the opportunity. But some people never progress because they never take advantage of opportunity.

In the late 1990s, a newly-arrived Kenyan cousin of mine, "Alfred," asked me to co-sign a loan to pay for one semester of his college tuition. Alfred repeatedly assured me that within one month the loan would be repaid from his employer's college reimbursement plan. I was very cautious in my approach. I asked all the necessary questions, and he had all the right answers. I made him articulate to me once again that this was a short-term "loan" and not a gift. Two years later, interest payments were piling up on the unpaid loan, and bills from the bank were arriving at my door. I forwarded all the bills to Alfred, but still, there was no response. My confusion over the issue soon turned to silent anger. I was furious because I knew that if the tables were turned I would have at least called Alfred and explained why I was having trouble paying off the loan. I decided to express my disappointment by writing him a letter in September 2001.

Alfred apologized on October 25, 2001. In his letter he described his dire financial situation, stating his car needed $4,500 in repairs, so he instead purchased a newer car for $5,500. He used his employer's college tuition reimbursement money to pay off that car loan, which carried a 23 percent interest rate. To further justify matters, Alfred explained that he had to support his two unemployed sisters, and accommodate his brother who was visiting on vacation.

I was appreciative of Alfred's response, but yet stunned. Why did Alfred not ask my permission before deviating from our pre-arranged repayment agreement? Why did he continue to buy cars when he could not afford them, and he lived in a city with good public transportation? Why did he think it acceptable to make his siblings my financial responsibility?

In 1989, my father called "socialism" the "let's all be poor together philosophy." I think my experience with Alfred may have been exactly what my father was describing. I understand there are many definitions and interpretations of the word socialism, which is a discussion beyond the scope of this book. However, my father used the term in reference to his experience within Africa, and primarily in the context of family and community relationships. Thus, one may interpret that my father was using the Western term for the African concept of *ujamaa*. *Ujamaa* is the Kiswahili word for "familyhood." The word is stronger than its literal translation. It represents the African tradition of a strong extended family network in which the individual is often expected to share his or her efforts and resources for the benefit of relatives and community. In criticizing "socialism," my father was explaining the limitations, abuses, and inefficiency of a development policy built principally on *socialism/ujamaa*. He was not attacking the humanitarian spirit of *socialism/ujamaa*. Some of the most principled and well-intentioned individuals on earth have described themselves as "socialists." [26]

In 1966, my father explained to University of Wyoming students:

> African Socialism is actually just a way of describing a political or an economic system that is typically African. The whole philosophy is that the future should utilize the best African tradition. Incorporate them so they can be used in modern ways. [27]

In the January 1969 edition of the *African Image* magazine, my father's friend, Joachim M. Banda, equated African Socialism with Humanism. Banda wrote that to understand this Humanism, we must analyze the background and way of life enjoyed by our forefathers.

Let us do exactly that. In former Vice-President Oginga Odinga's 1967 autobiography (*Not Yet Uhuru*), he described his early life in his village in Bondo, Nyanza. He described a system of communalism where even animals were community property, and the concept of land ownership was not entrenched. Land was distributed equally to families, and Odinga referred to traditional Luo farming methods as "halfway to socialism." It all sounds very fair, but Odinga pointed out that the system worked only under strict discipline. For example, the midday meals were brought to the fields so that only those who labored were fed. As a child, Odinga and his mother were banished from their village for three full days because his mother had given him food after he neglected his animals.[28]

Odinga described a system of communalism that only functioned well on the basis of transparency and discipline—where there were clear rewards (food) for hard work, and punishment (hunger) for laziness. *Ujamaa* (mutual assistance) and *kujitegemea* (self-reliance) were intricately entwined. [29]

Odinga's description of communalism sounds very utopian, but how does it apply to my long-distance and urban relationship with my cousin in America? Alfred was more than willing to seek refuge in the African tradition of communalism, but what was missing was the African tradition of transparency and discipline. I did not live in the same "village" as Alfred or his sisters, and I had no ability to verify that Alfred and his sisters awoke at the same early time I did to go to the "fields." If I discovered Alfred was sleeping all day instead of working, how could I "banish" or "punish" him?

In 1966, my father provided his anthropology instructor, Professor Hodge, with his own observations of African communalism (which parallels what he explained to me in 1989):

> When relatives come to ask you for money, it's not really asking; it's a demand. They feel that it is a right that they have. The whole culture emphasizes helping one another and that's what they used to do in the village. They used to help one another at harvesting periods, so they think that if one of their relatives is successful with money…well, they feel that they have the right to share it. And the [successful] man also feels obligated. If he refuses to help it will be said he is not part of African culture. As soon as he begins doing that [i.e. distributing his wealth], he's really not going to be making a success out of his life because he is sharing his salary too much. On the other hand, there are those that do it objectively in the sense that they will help their young relatives go to school so that they too become independent, but to those who simply want a good shirt or a bicycle they will say no.

My father is stating "they *used to* help each other in the fields," using the *past* tense. However, the expectation of sharing wealth is still in the *present* tense.

Maendeleo (1989-2001)

In August 2001, I visited Kenya, and Mrs. "Abuto" mentioned that she was aware of what had happened between Alfred and me. "Make sure he pays you back what you loaned him," she said. "Don't let him take advantage of you. If you let this slide they will not respect you." I had not informed Mrs. Abuto of what had transpired with Alfred, so by process of elimination it could only have been my father that had mentioned it to her. It was Mrs. Abuto that gave me the moral courage to press Alfred to repay his loan to the bank, and to his credit, he did.

I was not surprised that Mrs. Abuto supported this strict approach to family loans. Mrs. Abuto was married into a large Luo family and shared many stories about the expectation that one successful person literally feed the entire extended family. She usually talked about it in negative terms. Moreover, like my father and now me, Mrs. Abuto had a problem with "misappropriation." I remember Mrs. Abuto telling me that for several years they had paid for their nieces' and nephews' school fees, only to find out years later they had never even attended school. Mrs. Abuto knew too well the pain of giving money to a worthy cause, only to have that person divert the money to entirely separate purposes.

It would be a disservice if I failed to compare my Kenyan and American experiences with financial relationships within the extended family. Both my parents came from fairly large and tight-knit families. However, in rural Meeker County, Minnesota, it was not unusual for extended families and close friends to live side-by-side on separate farms with great disparities in wealth. Some family members were quite prosperous, yielding successful harvests that enabled them to own a car, install indoor plumbing, buy clothes from stores, or provide funds for their children's college education. However, a few miles away, a brother or cousin might live in a very rudimentary house with no plumbing. Their children may have slept on straw-filled mattresses and worn clothes sewn out of the remains of empty feed sacks from the barn. Yet there was rarely any expectation that the rich relative simply give money to the poor relative, even for a benevolent purpose like school, transportation, or clothes. According to my mother, she grew up in a totally different culture from what she later experienced in the Odenyo family. In Minnesota, people simply "made do" and "lived within their means." If loans were asked for, loans were repaid, even if it meant that the borrower's children might not be able to attend school beyond fifth grade (as in the case of my maternal grandfather). To ask for a loan and treat it like a gift would be to demonstrate the greatest dishonor and disrespect. To a Jenson, Olson, Johnson, or Peterson in her community, charity was given when necessary, but it was never expected. The focus was on what the individual could do for himself, rather than what the family could do for the individual. One can make the argument that in her culture there is a presumption of *kujitegemea* (self-reliance) over *ujamaa* (communalism). With that outlook in mind, my mother says, a person struggled to the best of his ability, made do with the results, and with the exception of the Great Depression, there was almost never a need for an extended-family "social net."

An African may perhaps look at these Euro-American values as indicative of a "selfish" or "non-humanitarian" culture. However, the Euro-American emphasis on "individuality" and "self-reliance" did not mean my mother's ancestors did not come together in the spirit of cooperation. The church provided humanitarian assistance to widows and orphans, and farmers joined forces to plow the fields of neighbors who had broken machinery or suddenly fell sick. My Minnesotan ancestors even institutionalized the concept of *harambee*. For example, one of the first successful cooperative creameries in the state of Minnesota (in Clarks Grove) was started by my great-great grandmother's brother, Hans Peter Jensen, in January 1890. It was the success of this community creamery that spurred my great-great grandfather, Soren Nelson (born in Denmark in 1834), to consult with his brother-in-law and help organize, build, and operate what some consider the second cooperative creamery in the state, in Rosendale (Danielson Township). The Rosendale creamery would have been unsuccessful if it were not for the collective efforts of extended family members united behind a common economic cause. Such collective efforts were so productive that by 1918 there were 630 cooperative creameries in Minnesota. In 1921, approximately 320 of these creameries formed the basis of the Minnesota Cooperative Creameries Association (MCCA). This organization marketed cream but also grew to create jobs, including a secretarial job for my grandmother's sister, Florence Nelson (who in 1924 made $95 per month).[30]

In 1926, the MCCA changed its name to Land O'Lakes, Inc., which has grown from selling butter and cream to also providing agricultural products and services. The company became so profitable that in 1981, Land O'Lakes created an International Development Division which has been instrumental in establishing sustainable development projects in Third World countries. For example, Land O'Lakes assisted the creation of the first cooperative (Riwoto Livestock Cooperative Society, or RILICOS) in Southern Sudan and is a donor to the non-profit organization Prosperity Worldwide.[31]

This is a wonderful illustration of how Euro-American individualism, capitalism, and self-determination can be compatible with the spirit of communalism, and even promote local and international economic development. The Minnesota cooperatives grew out of the belief that "if they can do it we can do it too," rather than "they did it, so now they have to share it too." And it all started with what? Cows. You cannot get any more basic than cows.

Now, I know that Kenya may have successful cooperatives and businesses as well, and Kenya's history is different from that of Minnesota. There are also valid arguments against excessive capitalism, and perhaps against other points I will make in this book. However, this book is written primarily for Dr. Odenyo's descendents, and I want to rely as much as I can on family history for important socio-economic lessons that are never taught in liberal arts classrooms. So save all your side arguments, such as what type of cows exist in Africa (the Zebu variety) for another discussion. If the Danish can teach our Nilotic brothers in the pastoralist communities of Sudan about cows, there is no reason why we cannot create a Lake Nyanza International Development Organization to teach the Danish people in Minnesota how to fish.

For sake of rough comparison, let us compare the Minnesota "cooperative creamery" experience with two specific businesses in Kenya that my father wrote about in the early 1970s (discussed in Chapter 2). First, there is the case of Gideon Obuolo, who was the principal partner of the butcher shop at the Regea market (1940s until early 1960s). His customers (all relatives and kinsmen) labeled him "stingy" (*jaguondo*) because Obuolo ran a tight ship and did not bend to his customers' unrealistic expectations that he provide handouts. Obuolo's approach was primarily a *kujitegemea* approach, for he required each customer to (*ku*) rely on (*tegemea*) himself (*ji*) to get the money to purchase the equivalent value of meat that Obuolo himself acquired through *kujitegemea*. He made no price allowances for customers. However, the concept of *kujitegemea* did not prevent Obuolo from joining in collective efforts with a common purpose (*harambee*), for he shared his business and overhead expenses with four other partners. By comparison, Obuolo's four partners could not withstand the obligatory requests by their customers for *ujamaa*, and thus converted their successful operation into a quasi-charitable organization with insufficient funds. Of the five partners of the business, it was only Obuolo that flourished—a miserable 20 percent success rate! Yet, it demonstrates that business is possible in rural Africa, when it is allowed to flourish. It was *kujitegemea* and not *ujamaa* that ultimately made Obuolo succeed, and it was *ujamaa* that ultimately made the other four partners unsuccessful.

The second company is the "Karadha" company that was started by Reverend Simeon Nyende and other leaders in Gem. There may have been a multitude of reasons for its failure in the 1940s, but the fact remains that in my father's casual recollections (1965–66) he attributed it only to one, which is this same distorted version of *ujamaa*. Customers simply felt the business was an extension of family resources which they were not required to pay back. They felt they could take a service or loan from the company under strict re-payment terms but later change their minds because the lender (a relative) would not take the borrower to court. It was an imbalance of *ujamaa* over *kujitegemea*, and the business failed completely. Regarding the failed transportation venture, my father once wrote:

> One wonders whether Simeon [Nyende] himself paid
> for the driver's time and the gas that went towards haul-
> ing him to meetings.[32]

I remember my father in 1989 explaining to me that whenever socialists come to Africa and try to implement a European-style socialist development policy in a rural village, they fail completely, and create conditions worse than what they originally found. One may look to Sweden for an example of European Socialism. Beginning in 1932, Sweden started laying the foundation for a "cradle-to-grave" welfare state, in which income-distribution (through personal income taxes of up to 87 percent) ensured that even the most unproductive citizens were near-equal partners at the table of prosperity. Entrepreneurs were often portrayed as exploitive pariahs, and many simply left the country (such as Ingvar Kamprad of "Ikea"). Starting in the 1970s, Sweden's economy and standard of living deteriorated to the point that in 1991 the government was forced to reverse many of its economic policies (with positive results). However, Sweden's pro-equality development themes are not limited to economics. They include gender-based proposals such as gender-neutral names for babies, mandatory parental leave for fathers of infants (proposed by the Feminist Initiative Party), gender quotas for businesses, and a tax on all men to pay for violence against women by the male gender (proposed by Equality Minister Margareta Winberg). Starting in the 1970s, many elementary schools abolished grades on the theory that grades fostered unhealthy competition and developmental inequality among children.

There is at least one instance when European Socialism intersected with African Socialism in my father's village of Got Regea in Gem. Remember the male and female researchers who received my evil eye in 1989? This couple was just one of several good-hearted European Socialists who visited Got Regea in the 1970s and 1980s. They must have found rural Got Regea a very curious place. Many Kenyans who spend their entire lives in "poor" villages are often the very young, the old, the uneducated, and any other person employed outside the spheres of the modern economy. In other words, a rural goat-herder does not work himself up to a Ph.D. in Engineering, Philosophy, or Medicine, simply to return to his village and herd more goats. Due to the influence of Chief Odera Akang'o, Gem has always produced a large number of persons with highly-skilled degrees, and many of them work in Kisumu, Nairobi, or Mombasa, rather than their villages. During holidays they leave their modern houses behind in the cities, drive back to the rural villages, and park their cars next to family members' mud "huts." The women take charge of the kitchen, children, and hospitality affairs, while the men socialize with their relatives and friends who have started arriving in the compound after hearing the rare sound of a car. During church service, seating is often segregated by gender. Children are supposed to be "seen and not heard," and if they are disrespectful to their elders they are given a swift smack on their rear. Students' grades are ranked and stapled to a public bulletin board (often a tree), or read out loud from the newspaper. Elders publically praise students who bring honor to the village through good grades, and admonish those who do not make an effort.

When the "European Socialist Feminist (ESF) Group" visited Got Regea for the first time in the 1970s, this scene must have looked intolerable. Within weeks, the ESF Group had dissected the village into two broad socio-economic classes: rich versus poor, and male versus female. The ESF Group wasted no time in establishing strong relationships with the poor as opposed to what they frequently referred to as the "upperclass" or the "elites." In one particular extended-family, they identified the young household of "Mariam and Samuel Okiro." To the extent Got Regea may have "looked down" upon Mariam and Samuel, it was not because the couple was uneducated, poor, and living in a mud hut. Rather, it was because they often lived reckless lives. In contrast to their more responsible and employable relatives in the extended Okiro family, Mariam and Samuel rarely took the initiative to become stable and support their growing number of children.

From what I can deconstruct, the ESF Group spent a lot of time sharing their liberation theories with the "oppressed" women of Got Regea, which included Mariam Okiro. Literally overnight, a few village women disposed of their African head wraps and starting wearing donated T-shirts embossed with the words "Woman Power." The T-shirts were blue, and the two "O" letters had been changed to the feminist power symbol which looks similar to a circle connected to an inverted cross. Mariam increasingly became involved in activities of the *Maendeleo ya Wanawake* (Women's Development) groups throughout Got Regea. Until this day, people refer to Mariam as the "Empowerment Lady," and the members of the ESF Group have nothing but good things to say about their special relationship with her.

To some extent, Mariam and her immediate family benefitted

from their relationship with the ESF Group, at least indirectly. Samuel Okiro's educated brothers, for reasons I do not know, decided they would demolish his mud-house and replace it with the largest and most modern brick house in miles. With Mariam (who dropped out of secondary school) out and about preaching women's empowerment, and Samuel at home most of the day enjoying his new home built with *ujamaa* money, it appeared to all on-lookers that the European Socialist Feminist philosophy was a very superior development model.

Mariam and her ESF friends were frequent visitors to the Odenyo compound. This may have been due to my own grandmother's support and participation in *Maendeleo ya Wanawake* group meetings within Got Regea. Additionally, Aunt Olivia worked as a community development officer until her retirement in 1985, at which time she devoted herself to women's development projects in conjunction with the Diocese of South Maseno. Aunt Olivia was so respected in her employment that she was selected to represent Kenyan women during development conferences in Israel and the United Nations.

In 1988, my father and sister traveled alone to Kenya and saw first-hand the "fruits" of Mariam's ESF lifestyle. As usual, they brought clothing and shoes from New York to distribute in Got Regea. My sister carried the clothes in a suitcase to Grandmother Grace Dina Adero's house, where she was sitting with Mariam, my aunt Olivia, and two other ladies. Together, all five ladies sorted through the clothing, dividing them amongst themselves in an orderly and equitable fashion. That soon changed when Mariam decided she wanted all the clothes for herself. Mariam began to speak angrily in Dholuo, then grabbed all the clothing from her fellow women and started throwing them back into my sister's suitcase. She did it with such haste that she even gave a modest shove to my frail seventy-seven year old grandmother, who was caught off-balance. Once Mariam stuffed all of the clothes into my sister's suitcase, she walked out with it, heading back to her modern *ujamaa* house. The other ladies were left with no clothes, my sister with no suitcase, and all my grandmother could do was sit and shake her head in pure disgust. My sister Atieno, just eighteen years old at the time, found herself racing out of our grandmother's house in a panic, trying to locate my father so that he could interpret what had just happened.

Well, it is quite clear what had happened. Mariam, once the quiet underachiever, was now "empowered." She was liberated and knew her rights. She had a large family, and more on the way. She was no longer used to taking care of her children with her own resources. Why should she and her husband be solely responsible for their immediate family? After all, the educated men of the Odenyo family represented the "elites," and the suitcase represented "wealth." Why should a family with so many elites have more wealth than Mariam?

Essentially, this is how Mariam Okiro and her husband raised their family in Got Regea for nearly thirty years. Mariam preached the ESF message of "empowerment" and "equality," but never seemed to empower herself or her own household. In her quest to be equal, she full-heartedly embraced almost every self-destructive habit usually attributed to the male gender. This trend extends to many of the children of Mariam and Samuel. The large and modern *ujamaa* house that the Okiro children long ago inherited sits empty like a mausoleum. From high up on the walls, photographs of the Okiro brothers and the ESF group, smiles frozen in time, peer down with pride upon a dusty and barren living room. I am not saying that it was African Socialism, or the ESF Group, that created this lingering problem (although it is a plausible theory). What I am saying is that these ideologies did not make a bad situation better.

However, there is one success story. From my father's photographs from the mid-1970s, I see another young Luo woman who came into contact with the blue women's power T-shirts. However, it appears that over time this young Luo lady traded these protest T-shirts for other items—a cap, a gown, and a college degree. This woman, my aunt Awino Odenyo, worked her way up from humble beginnings in Ugenya to acquire a Ph.D. in Animal Science (Rumen Microbial Ecology), and unlike the ESF Group, actually acquired practical skills useful for the development of rural areas. Dr. Awino's career options are not limited to the international relief jobs described in the 1995 article, "The Myth of Foreign Aid," or the non-income producing activism of the ESF idealists. For some years, Dr. Awino Odenyo has actively promoted development in Got Regea and other rural areas through her scientific research, promotion of education, and involvement in entrepreneurial activities. In Got Regea she has remodeled old unused houses and turned them into livable homes. She has created jobs for others, including idle men. Dr. Awino Odenyo has inspired not only me, but a new generation of young women. Dr. Awino Odenyo made the personal choice to combine "opportunity" with *kujitegemea*, and thus represents the true meaning of "woman power" and development.

**Dr. Agnes Awino Odenyo and husband
Daniel Dindi Odenyo in Virginia, late 1970s.**

14

Broken Dreams

I don't know how it would have worked had I gone back to Kenya. Other Kenyans who returned home became district officers and millionaires through corruption. I don't know if it would have been possible for me to have returned and survived on my own merits.

—Dr. Amos Otieno Odenyo, interview on August 26, 2005.

Dr. Odenyo witnessed many sad developments in Kenya since he first returned in 1970. In 1975, a minister of parliament, Josiah Mwangi Kariuki, was found dead in Ngong Forest—his fingers cut off and eyes gouged out. Kariuki was the former personal secretary of President Jomo Kenyatta, and was emerging as a critic of the corruption that existed in the Kenyatta government. Kariuki was reportedly last seen alive in the company of Kenyatta's personal bodyguard. In 1990, the body of Kenya's foreign minister, Robert Ouko, was found with his eyes gouged out, his torso burned, and bones broken. The Kenyan police immediately ruled the death a suicide, leaving the Kenyan people wondering how someone could kill himself and then burn his own body. Ouko was one of Kenya's most respected statesmen, and it is widely rumored that before his death he was compiling a report on political corruption involving the Kisumu Molasses project. Within one or two years after Ouko's death, many high-ranking persons associated with the murder investigation died of mysterious causes.

I know my father closely followed these events in Kenya. During my trip with him to Kenya in 1998, I saw him reading a book that he had neatly jacketed with brown paper. I never saw him do this before, so when he finished reading the book, I borrowed it. It was a book written by Jonah Anguka, titled *Absolute Power*, which detailed the plots surrounding the murder of Robert Ouko. My father was never involved in politics; he was simply an observer. In the United States he would have been able to read any book without fear. He could not do this in his home country.

Dad did not hesitate to comment on the deteriorating conditions in Kenya. In July 1992, he wrote a letter to my sister, which detailed his observations:

> Generally, Kisumu and the country as a whole is experiencing more hunger, poverty and sheer desperation. There are beggars everywhere. Children with babies strapped on their backs begging at car stops. It is not just begging but aggressive begging—so if you do not give, they curse you New York style! I do not know what Odera is experiencing in Uganda since he does not write, but I surely hope it is better there. Kenya is experiencing difficult times. People are hungry, angry, and desperate.

With observations like these it must have been difficult for him to continue teaching subjects at York College such as course number 366: "Sociology of Development." Several of Dr. Odenyo's essay questions from the mid-1990s were as follows:

1) Hunger and famine are caused by multifactors. Discuss the main factors.
2) The World Bank uses G.N.P. to measure economies of countries. When this is done, countries in the South consistently show growth in their annual G.N.P., yet at the same time, exhibit extreme poverty. Why?
3) Discuss some of the effects of merchant capitalism, especially

the triangular trade, on African society.

In my personal opinion, the above test should have included the following essay question: "Describe the effects of political corruption on Africa's development." I am not sure if my father lectured on the political aspects of Africa's underdevelopment, but I can assure you, he was an active researcher on the issue. He followed the events surrounding the infamous "Goldenberg" scandal, even to the point of attending the public meetings of the commission of inquiry known as the "Bosire Commission." [33]

The essence of the Goldenberg scandal is allegedly as follows. In the early 1990s, high-ranking members of the Kenyan government conspired to subsidize exports of diamonds and gold from Kenya. However, none (or minimal amounts) of these items were actually exported from Kenya, and its land is not known to posses measurable quantities of these deposits. Goldenberg International, operated by a Kenyan businessman, was the conduit for the "exports," as well as the recipient of taxpayer funds associated with the fictious subsidies. The scandal was reported to have cost the Kenyan taxpayers as much as US $850 million—a fifth of the gross domestic product. It involved the highest members of the government of President Daniel Arap Moi, many who returned to power within the next administration.

It is sad to note that the whistleblower of the Goldenberg scandal, David Munyakei, was fired from the Central Bank of Kenya and spent the next decade of his life poor and unemployed. He was reportedly handed an "integrity award" by the government, but never a letter of recommendation. This prevented him from finding another suitable job. He died in 2006, leaving behind a wife and three children. This is what corruption does to the honest man in Kenya. If the system does not corrupt the man, it takes food away from his table, and ultimately destroys him and his family.

Corruption in Kenya did not start in the 1980s during the Moi government, but almost immediately after independence in 1963. Uncle Victor once briefed me on the "Gatundu Hospital" scandal. For years, President Jomo Kenyatta used the call of *harambee* to rally

Kenyans, corporations, embassies, and visiting dignitaries into donating money toward the building of a hospital in his home village of Gatundu (in Kiambu). Kenyatta personally involved himself in the collection of funds to build the nation's most modern and accessible medical facility. Senior government officials and businessmen were expected to give donations toward the project whenever they visited Kenyatta or his home constituency. The political joke of the era was that this was truly a "*self*-help" project, for the amount of funds collected should have easily covered the cost of not one but *two* modern hospitals.

The culture of corruption by Kenyan officials has trickled down and permeated the very fabric of Kenyan society. I listen to stories about Kenya from Kenyan friends in the United States. Many of these stories follow the same script. It is not the script I used to hear from my father's generation, which emphasized self-determination, self-reliance, deferred gratification, integrity, and compassion. The script now involves a get-rich-quick scheme that manipulates the African traditions of *ujamaa* and *harambee*.[34] It used to be in the 1980s that well-to-do Nairobi relatives would send money to the village to pay for relatives' school fees, but find out years later that the relatives never enrolled in school and squandered the money. Today, you might hear the same basic story, but the relatives have conspired with the school bursar's office to obtain fake school invoices. I have personally witnessed Kenyans holding fund-raising events where the proceeds are kept for personal use instead of given to bereaved families to cover burial costs. I am not talking just about incidents in the Luo community. A Kikuyu-American recently narrated to me a story of his friend in the United States sending money to his brother in Nyeri (Central Province). The brother in Nyeri had agreed to build a house for his sibling, and sent construction updates to America. Upon hearing that his house was near completion, the brother returned home to prepare for his retirement. Upon arrival in Nyeri, he found only a barren plot of land, with no house. He was so disgusted he left Kenya and has no intention of returning.

Our family is not immune to this trend. In the 1960s, my grandfather, Zablon Sangoro Odenyo, had a vision of a family-owned business that would provide jobs and stability for his children near the village of Got Regea. My father responded to his vision and in the 1960s sent money from America in support of the project. After my uncle Victor acquired his doctorate degree he similarly pursued Zablon's vision. By the 1990s, Victor organized the actual construction and operation of a family business in Siaya, creating several jobs for previously unemployed family members. I remember helping my father and uncles stock the store shelves, sweep the floor, and take pride that our family (through Uncle Victor's efforts) had finally accomplished Zablon's dream.

Within perhaps a year or two, all that was left of Zablon's dream were empty shelves, unpaid bills, and missing sales revenue. Just as fast as the money went into the business, the money left the business into the personal accounts and daily luxuries of soon-to-be unemployed relatives. The business went bankrupt, and most of the employees have since been jobless. Just like the failed Karadha business of the 1940s, our family business failed too, and for similar reasons. A minority of family members simply felt entitled to the proceeds and inventory of any family business. Emboldened by their interpretation of *ujamaa*, they pilfered every moveable asset.

The building still stands in Siaya. For many years it looked very much like a gravestone marking the death of a still-born child. People walk by the empty store every day, but have no knowledge or interest in the history behind the building. Family members do not discuss it, for fear of talking negatively about relatives. In time history might repeat itself. New generations of family grow to adulthood, set out to accomplish their own dreams, but through the grim-reaper of historical ignorance and *ujamaa*, more and more gravestones are added to the cemetery of family dreams.

My father opened up to me about these issues in later years. With much sadness in his voice, he wondered why relatives in rural Got Regea would disrespect the gift of managing a fully-functioning business. Instead of nurturing the opportunity, they feasted on it until the opportunity collapsed. In my father's own words he described the situation as "theft," and "bringing the family down." He said, "When I found out what was happening, I walked away from the situation, and advised others to do so as well. I wish they would have listened to me sooner, but they felt obligated to help out family and continued throwing money into that business until they too had nothing left."

I add to this my own observations. There was no external source to the demise of Zablon's dream. All the textbook excuses for Africa's problems were not applicable. There were no British colonialists suppressing the indigenous population. There was no foreign "manipulation of nation-state boundaries." There were no "greedy capitalist Americans" or "Asians" manipulating terms of trade. There was no "Kiambu mafia" (Kikuyu crime syndicate) suppressing Luo business. There was no recession where supply exceeded demand. There was no lack of investment resources. There was no lack of rain. There were no floods. No drought. No grasshoppers. No brimstone. There were simply us. The reason for the demise of Zablon's dream was us, Zablon's descendents.

In January 1995, Uncle Dan thanked his elder brother Victor for his efforts, lamented the loss of the family business, and urged that we evaluate the problem. Uncle Dan did this in a letter addressed to Uncle Victor, but also sent to my father:

> You, Otieno, and Adet helped all of us keep our hope up in Got Regea. You inspired me when I thought the world and circumstances were forcing me to under-achieve. You sacrificed with me in Blacksburg, Virginia, while you were going through your own difficult academic situation. You supported me and my wife [Awino] and gave us a head start even though your own family situation could not afford it. Besides me, you have tried your best to completely transform all of our lives, whilst yours continued to be filled with the demands of your own family. I was really hoping that the Siaya project would have been successful so that I could have merged my own efforts into one family business. The deteriorating situation we have at home will provide us with a family challenge for the next two decades. Of all

of the grandchildren of *Baba* [Father], there seems to be none rising above the water that can help the future generation fifteen years from now. It is beyond doubt that one of the secrets to our success lies in Baba's deep Christian faith that made him rise above everyone in the Got Regea environment.

Dad kept abreast of current events and went home to Kenya frequently. He traveled to Kenya on average once every two years. In 1999 he decided to buy an apartment in Nairobi. This was a signal to us that he was preparing for retirement in Kenya. If he could not work in Kenya, at least he could retire in Kenya. He went so far as to select the actual apartment he would purchase. However, before he could finalize the paperwork, he was introduced to the reality of every day living in Kenya. He was robbed. He was caught up in the incident quite randomly, and the robbers were not targeting him directly. It was just his turn. As he drove up to the gate of a friend's house in Nairobi, the following events unfolded (names in his letter have been changed):

> Yesterday, Friday evening at 8:15 p.m.—it was my turn to experience the Nairobi crime wave. As I pulled into Akoth's gate, I honked as usual for someone to open the gate. I had spotted three men casually walking on this street, but all of a sudden, while the gate was being opened, one of them came to the window of the car and pulled a pistol on my face and said, "Give me your money or I shoot!" The other two men surrounded the car. My reaction was to raise my arms and say, "No problem—*Hakuna matata.*" The next order—"Get out of the car!" He opens the door to the back of the car. The next order —"Get in and sit down!" I obeyed. The next thing I knew, the new security gate man we just hired three days ago is ordered at gunpoint to sit next to me. In a few seconds, a third worker who actually had the key to the gate is ordered to sit with us

at the back seat. The gunman then drives the car into the compound. We are then marched to the house at gunpoint. The men walk into the house and find everyone eating dinner. "Lie down—Lie down!" Everyone lies on their bellies below the dinner table, me included. Next, my hands and legs are tied up with a rope. Everyone is tied up. My watch is removed. My wallet is removed. At this point the robbers begin a systematic inquiry. Jane is marched upstairs, holding the baby. "Give us money!" they shout. Jane gives whatever is in the house. She is asked to identify everyone lying on the floor. "Who is the Master of the house?" She identifies Wilfred—then Wilfred is marched upstairs. "Give us the money!" Wilfred gives whatever he has, including Francs that Mary was going to use tomorrow on her visit to France. Next, Rachel is marched upstairs. "Give us the money!" Rachel tells them she is a student and has no money. "Any jewelry?" Rachel gives them all her jewelry. Next, the gunmen start shouting in Swahili at some of the house guests who are actually visitors to Kenya and do not speak Swahili. Their handbags and wallets are snatched once this is explained to the gunman. The gunmen locate all the keys to the cars parked outside and deactivate their alarms. They start filling the cars with the stolen items. They have by this time gone through my wallet and found my credit cards and New York driver's license. They have already taken USD $200 and KSH 5,000 from my wallet, but they think I have more money. So they come for me. They search me thoroughly a second time, yelling at me in Swahili, "Where is your money?" They insist on taking me with them until I give them more money. They turn me over for a third time and search me. Wilfred finally convinces them that I am staying with them because I left New York homeless, penniless and sickly. They leave me alone. Well, it is 2 a.m. by the time they leave.

Everyone is exhausted. We rise from the floor and find a knife to cut ourselves loose. It is 4 a.m. by the time the police arrive. Police are supposed to ask certain basic investigative questions and collect evidence like finger-prints. They do none of that. They are quite useless. Luckily for me, the robbers only took my money and left the other items in my wallet. I sure hope the robbers do not return. This is unreal. Two robberies at the house in just two weeks. Last week it was the watchman that betrayed the family.

As a result of this experience my father decided not to retire in Kenya. It was simply too dangerous. Nairobi was now being referred to in Kenyan circles as "Nai-robbery." My father chose to continue teaching at York College and shorten the lengths of his trips to Kenya. He often awoke from his dreams in a cold sweat, his mind filled with images of his countrymen binding him with rope, beating him, and threatening his life in Kiswahili. We all felt sorry for him. Thirty-eight years living in America, and it took a trip back home to Kenya to experience his first robbery.

I think my father internalized a great sadness and depression over Kenya's deteriorating direction. After all, the sole purpose he traveled to the United States on the Tom Mboya Airlift was to become educated, return to Kenya, and work as a public servant. By the 1970s my father recognized he made the right choice in remaining in the United States. He would have had to compromise too many of his ideals by joining the Kenyatta and Moi governments. Although he was at times depressed, he never fully discussed his deepest thoughts. I think his childhood upbringing contributed to his personality. He was taught from the earliest age in Nyanza that the measure of a man is his ability to overcome pain, work through emotions, and serve as the symbol of strength and stability for the family. All emotional pain was suppressed to serve this one goal. Even his Luo adult initiation rite (*nak*) was designed to instill this discipline in him. If he were to cry out or show emotion during the process of yanking his six lower teeth from his mouth, he would be forever labeled a child. Similarly, if he confided in his wife and children his disappointments, he would be giving up his core inner strength, lowering himself to an inferior position. Whenever my mother asked him to share with her his problems, he would say, "You *could* never understand." Dr. Odenyo did not seek assistance from anyone. Instead, at night he quieted his invisible tears by playing old *nyatiti* music, and dulled the pain with a few shots of gin. He always woke up early in the morning to clear his head with a five-mile run, and silently face the burdens of the day.

The combination of broken dreams and never-ending family obligations created a situation where he both loved and loathed Kenya. It was a place that he could not do without, for it formed the essence of his being. But it was also a place from which he had to keep a respectable distance. I can use the analogy of the sun as an example. For the Luo, the sun (*chieng*) represents the center of the universe, and the manifestation of strength. The sun represents all things good on earth. The sun is something that must rise in the morning, for its absence would signal the end of all life as we know it. Even Luo names, such as Otieno, Omondi, and Achieng, are references to the position of the sun during the time of birth. To my father, his village of Got Regea was that sun. He needed to be assured it was there. He had to visit it regularly to be blessed by its glorious rays, to be reminded that the universe was indeed in balance, and to confirm his place in it. But to stay for too long was impossible, for it was like staring at the sun. The longer he remained in Kenya, the longer he was staring at the sun, and the sun when stared at is no longer the source of strength, but of pain.

There were many instances at night when my sister and mother found my father sitting in his chair, deep in thought. He would interrupt his silence to say, "I do not have a home. I am a man without a home." This is a deeply Kenyan, and in particular, a Luo concept. What he was saying is that although he had spent the majority of his life in the United States, home was Kenya. This was a cultural expression, not a political statement. His house in the United States was simply a temporary shelter, but it was not, and could never be, a home. Home could not be a house in Nairobi, or even Kisumu. Home could only be in Got Regea. It could be a mud-walled, tin roof shack, but due to that structure's location in Got Regea, in his Luo heart he would always recognize it as home. Yet, since he left his *simba* in 1961, he had not rebuilt such a home. His academic training and personal dedication to the concept of being "practical" made such an act impossible. Unless he was permanently moving back to Kenya he could not rationalize building a house there. Therein lay the conflict between his traditional upbringing and modern training. Returning home was forever just out of reach.

Perhaps sensing my father's depression over the state of affairs in Kenya, on December 21, 2002, his sister Olivia sent him a message of optimism:

> Otieno,
>
> I wish to express my sincere, heartfelt appreciation for the new generation you have created. America can be a place of utter loneliness. The attitude you have instilled in our people of being caring and loving is one to be recognized and highly encouraged. You and Mayone have brought friends and relatives together creating altogether a new sense of family and community values. Thank you very much. It is my wish that you continue with this spirit. At the same time, please try to identify a person who can take the mantle from you in future, the way Moses handed over to Joshua the task of leading the Israelites into Canaan. Let us put this in prayer. Olivia.

These later years continued to bring a mixture of joy and pain. My father officiated at his mother's funeral in February 1996, and also at his brother Adet's funeral in September 1996. With their passing, my father assumed the traditional role of family elder. I sat with disbelief next to my father during the August 1997 memorial of his friend Okello Onyango. When one of my cousins was tragically killed in a car accident in 2002, my father officiated at her funeral. Uncle Robert died in October 2001. His son Eric died in 2004.

Uncle Dan unexpectedly died in 2004. For more than ten years he worked an exhausting two full-time jobs in order to support his family. He wrote letters to my father explaining his support for his wife (Awino) while she was studying for her Ph.D. and looking for work. He said that he was tired, but wanted to keep working extra hours so that his children could obtain the best education and not have to work while going to school. He said he would give up his night-shift job once his daughter Adhiambo received her master's degree in accounting. Uncle Dan had a chance to witness his daughter receive that degree. Two or three days later, Uncle Dan collapsed from a heart attack. Education was Uncle Dan's final gift to his daughter.

His death had profound cultural implications. Dan was the youngest uncle. He was the child of Zablon Sangoro and Grace Dina Adero who was supposed to outlive all the other siblings. Dad said that under Luo tradition, the youngest son (*chogo*) had the right and obligation to inherit his parents' house. Uncle Dan was the symbol of our family's future, and with his passing, our future looked a little less certain.

The years between 1996 and 2004 brought great sorrow to the Odenyo family due to the loss of so many loved ones. I remember well the day in 2005 that my father and I visited Got Regea and silently stood in our family cemetery. Tears literally rolled down our faces as we looked around and realized just how many headstones had been recently added. That was the first and last time I saw my father shed a tear.

However, births and deaths go hand in hand, and in 2004 my parents were blessed with their first grandson, born to my sister Atieno in New York. My sister knew in advance that she would name her son "(Jean-Luc) Otieno" in honor of our father, and the name Otieno, which means "born at night" was fitting because her son was indeed born at night. Before she made an announcement regarding the birth name, Dad made note of the time his grandson was born, and said to Atieno, "You know, he really is an Otieno."

During the next several years, my sister witnessed an emotional side to my father that none of us had ever seen. My father developed an inseparable bond with Jean-Luc Otieno that seemingly eclipsed the relationship that he had with his own children. For the first time in his life, Dr. Odenyo appeared to actively look forward to spending quality time with a rambunctious child. When the professor came home from work, he asked my sister, "Is Jean-Luc coming over today? When can I see Jean-Luc?" It was an amazing sight. My father took J.L.Otieno for walks, fed him, and held him on his lap for hours until the two of them drifted off to sleep. My father verbally expressed his feelings toward J.L.Otieno, to the complete astonishment of my sister and mother. It was a complete reversal of our own experiences with him in the 1970s and 1980s. No one knows for certain what accounts for this change, but perhaps due to nearing retirement age he was now able to balance the professional side of himself with his emotional side. It was as if he was seeing the light at the end of the tunnel. He was no longer the sole provider to his immediate family. He could take on a less managerial and more intimate approach to family relationships, perhaps reminiscent of what he observed the "grandparents" of his village doing for him sixty years earlier.

Atieno's distant emotional relationship with Dad found healing and redemption through the bond she witnessed between her father and son. Her father was now the doting parent she never had. He was the source of warmth and affection that she had missed throughout her entire youth. For the first time in her life, she felt unrestrained feelings of emotion emanating from Professor Odenyo through the medium of J.L.Otieno. Her son therefore became more than her father's grandson. He became an affirmation of her father's love.

In 2005, I witnessed my father make on my behalf the first payment of dowry to my new father-in-law in Kenya. My father took it as his ceremonial role to represent our family and seal the deal. We provided to my in-laws what seemed like an endless list of household gifts. For logistical reasons we could not give cows, but my father stood up, handed over a sealed envelope, and explained, "Please view this envelope as cows without legs." I was relieved when our gifts were accepted. At that moment, under African tradition, I had a wife. That trip to Kenya was particularly joyous. One of my cherished memories is of my father dancing to music played by Tony Nyadundo (the "King of Ohangla" music) at the Sunset Hotel in Kisumu.

Kisii High School Friends: Shem Arungu Olende, Fred Ouka, and Amos Otieno Odenyo in New York, late 1990s.

Kisii High School Friends: Winston Ochoro Ayoki
and Amos Otieno Odenyo in Nairobi, 1998.

Atieno with her father Amos Otieno Odenyo in New York, 1995.

(Siblings) Daniel Dindi, Olivia Adhiambo, and Amos Otieno Odenyo
in New York, 2003.

Rosalie and Amos Otieno Odenyo (siblings) in Got Regea, 2005.

Amos Otieno Odenyo and wife Mayone Odenyo
in California, 2007.

Atieno Odenyo with Persis Omolo (youngest sister
of Grandmother Grace Dina Adero Odenyo).
Got Regea, August 2007.

Broken Dreams

In the summer of 2005, Dad was diagnosed with cancer. An intensely private man, he was upset to discover my mother told us about his condition. I traveled to New York to visit him. Even though we all knew about his condition, I did not ask him about it. That was the way it had always been between us. If he was not willing to talk, you knew better than to ask questions. What I did gather the strength to do was to ask him detailed questions about his life, and those of his ancestors. I wanted to record, on video-tape, all history that I had previously overlooked or had been reluctant to ask. I asked him about Luo history, culture, and tradition. I asked him to tell me traditional stories just as he heard them as a boy. I asked him to again tell me the story of Luanda Magere, which always reminded me of the story of Samson and Delilah in the Bible. I asked him about his life in Got Regea village, what he ate, how he slept, and how he brushed his teeth. I wanted to listen to his story of being forced by his grade-school teacher to stare at the sun. I asked about his hopes, his dreams, and his disappointments. For the first time in my life, I gathered the courage to ask him the specifics about *nak*, the Luo initiation rite. In hushed tones, he mentioned by name the officers in Mombasa who tortured prisoners in 1960. Over the course of a week, whenever he felt like talking, I asked him just a little bit more about his life. When I had finished, I had approximately twenty hours of video-taped interviews, spanning the history between the nineteenth century and 1976. During this week-long interview, the only time that he asked me to stop recording, to give him a little time to compose himself, to perhaps force back a tear, was when he was talking about his childhood feelings of leaving his home in Got Regea.

Christmas 2006 was the last holiday we spent together as a family, and it was spent in my home. I proudly watched as my father tenderly embraced my newborn son in his arms. I was so happy when my wife gave birth at night so that I too could name my son Otieno, in honor of my father. The first gift my wife and I gave our son was a college investment account (as my parents did for me in the 1970s). My mother sent my brother Omondi an airplane ticket so that he could join us (his wife and children were in Kenya visiting relatives). Christmas was just like old times again, only better. Within the last two years my relationship with Omondi had strengthened considerably. Now that I was older and had my own family, we could talk for hours about topics of mutual interest. During Christmas he discussed the increasing responsibilities he was receiving as a paratransit manager. Life was getting better each day, he said. Omondi told me that he felt refreshed and reinvigorated, and was ready to embrace the challenges of 2007.

It was a complete shock to the entire family when a few months later we received the news that my brother Omondi had quietly passed away. It fell upon me to inform Dad. It anguished me to even say the words, least they become true. How exactly does one tell a father that he has lost a son? To make matters worse, my father was in the advanced stage of cancer and would soon be confined to a wheelchair. When I first saw my father in this state my heart sank. In just a few weeks he had lost almost fifty pounds, could not walk two steps without assistance, and he looked like he had aged thirty years. Dad's doctors may have suspected his condition was irreversible, for they granted him permission to travel to Kenya for Omondi's funeral.

Our entire family gathered at Dulles airport in Virginia, and my father and I prepared to take Omondi home. Dad told Omondi's two children, "I am taking your father to a special place in Kenya called Got Regea. This is a special place for the whole family. You will find me there someday." My sister reflected upon his last sentence and wondered if Dad thought he might die during the two week trip in Kenya. She thought it might be the last time she saw him alive. Almost as if he read her thoughts, Dad drew her close to him. In a weak but determined voice he looked up at her and said, "Atieno, I know you are worried about me, but I'll be back. You will see." With that said, I pushed my father in his wheelchair past the various security check-points and onto the plane. The flights to Kenya were exhausting for both of us. He did not eat during the entire trip. Whenever a wheelchair was not available I literally had to carry him to and from his seat. He constantly shivered under the plane's air-conditioning, despite me giving him my own sweaters and blankets. But he never complained once. When we cleared Kenyan customs I handed him over to the care of Uncle Booker. Dad and I were both physically and emotionally drained.

The entire extended family was very supportive and provided

harambee funds and logistical support. I could not have managed the events without the assistance of family, which demonstrated the positive side of *ujamaa*. Unfortunately, my father, who had always taken an active role as a family spokesperson during ceremonies, was only able to participate in Omondi's funeral from his wheelchair. It fell upon me to walk to the family cemetery in Got Regea and choose the burial place for my brother. What a horrible decision to make. I walked alongside the rows of gravestones until I found an available plot. I turned toward my father for his approval. He studied the graves from a distance and whispered, "It is a good place —you may go ahead." With his approval, prayers in Dholuo were conducted, the mark of the cross was etched from the earth with a *jembe* (hoe), and the grave was prepared.

The funeral service was conducted the next day in Saint Peter's Church. My father sat at the rear of the church, and I eulogized my brother on his behalf. During the service Dad became uncomfortable sitting on the wooden church bench, and asked that two of his nephews help him out of the church so he could rest under the shade of the fig tree. As the funeral ceremony was proceeding, a well-dressed middle-aged member of the congregation approached my ailing and grieving father, greeted him as "uncle," and asked him for money. My father had been conserving his strength by remaining silent the whole day, but was forced to respond that he did not have any money to give that day. The man did not seem happy with my father's response and lingered for some time before gradually walking away. This is the bad side of *ujamaa*.

The following day there was a church fundraising event. My father seemed stronger, and with the funeral completed we both felt a sense of relief and accomplishment. We reflected on Omondi's funeral, affirming that we had given him a respectable send-off. I sat alongside my father in the back of Saint Peter's Church as we watched members of the congregation donate or purchase small items. Uncle Booker helped officiate near the altar, holding up for sale some good clothing that I had donated to the church. Under the donation table sat a live chicken provided by Aunt Awino. In the spirit of *ujamaa*, she later purchased back her own chicken for three times the going-price in the

Dudi market.

My father handed me a respectable sum of money sealed in an envelope and requested that I walk to the altar and donate it to the church "in the name of the Odenyo family." I noted that he did not instruct me to say it was from him. Once again, he was helping the community without requesting any personal recognition. However, when I stood in front of Saint Peter's Church, I could only focus on my father sitting in the last pew. I feared that it might be his last church service in Got Regea, and I wanted to ensure that this service be a memorable one for him. He had discreetly supported this church for nearly forty years, often paying the pastors' annual salary from his own pocket. In fact, for more than half of his life he helped feed, clothe, and educate numerous members of Got Regea. I did not want anyone to be mistaken that I was the source of the donation, so I stated it was coming directly from the hands of my father, Amos Otieno Odenyo. With that said, the congregation turned and gave him a respectable and loving applause. This was my father's last service at Saint Peter's Church.

Once the church events were over we had time for family discussion and reflection. I worried if my father would have the strength to make it back to the United States. He went for days without eating, but seemed to regain his energy when least expected. Almost all of his strong moments occurred when he was surrounded by his friends and family and we discussed old times. With my video camera in hand I recorded him sharing more details about his life. There were still new stories for us, more history to share. I learned about his birth nickname, "Akoko," given to him based upon fighting that was occurring in the village at the time. He talked once again about our clan history, the failed "Karadha" company, and elders who had preceded us in life. The teacher in him was still very much alive.

Each night before he went to sleep I made sure that he was comfortable. In Kisumu, he allowed me to rub mosquito repellant over his face, arms, and feet. Before I left him for the night I hugged him, and for the first time in my adult life I told him I loved him. He responded that he loved me too, was proud of me, and hugged me back. I will cherish this moment for as long as I live. I checked on him periodically throughout the night, to confirm he was still breathing. When we all awoke the next morning, it was as if God was blessing us with one more miracle.

Numerous friends from Kisii High School came to see him. Shem Olende and his family came to visit, and reminisced about their shared academic and sports activities of their youth. Akich Okola and his family did the same. While Shem and Akich were briefed in advance about my father's rapid deterioration, his friend Winston Ayoki may not have been. Their meeting was bittersweet. Ayoki gave Dad many words of encouragement. However, when Ayoki first saw my father he had to steady his emotions over seeing his friend in such a poor state. I could tell Ayoki was desperately trying to prevent the tears from falling, and my father sensed this too. For the first five minutes of their meeting they sat opposite each other, motionless, speechless and tearless, like two aging Luo warriors made of stone. Through the silence they were communicating their deep feelings and respect for one another. They were doing it in the old Luo way—the way they were taught as teenagers—where leadership meant suffering through pain with silence and dignity.

When Dad and I returned to the United States we hugged for what would be the last time, and I left him in the care of my mother and sister in New York. He spent most of his time lying in bed at the hospital, where my sister and mother visited him daily. Our father showed no outward sign of weakness, telling them that he would soon recover and return home. However, he made certain statements to my sister that made her wonder if he was reflecting on his life. He interrupted his silence to say, "I think I am going to sleep for a long time," but would not clarify what he meant by it. He inquired if any of us were jealous of the special bond he had developed with his grandson J.L. Otieno. Atieno assured him that his unique bond with her son was cherished and not envied. My sister thanked him for repeatedly taking us to Kenya as children, and specifically mentioned the time when our cousin Eric ran barefoot after a chicken, which we ate for dinner. My father smiled and whispered, "Well, at least you know where chickens come from—they do not come from the grocery store." Atieno promised him she would take J.L. Otieno to Got Regea so that he grows up knowing where he comes from. Always the practical man, Dad instructed my sister to take J.L. Otieno to Got Regea not only now, but later as a teenager when he is old enough to remember what he sees and hears.

My father hated being in the hospital, and managed to get permission to return home where he was treated by a nurse. News spread of my father's deteriorating condition. His good friend from Kisii High School, Martin Nyiendo, arrived with his wife Joanne from Oregon to spend a final moment with my father. My father always considered Mr. Nyiendo his closest friend and confidant. Their relationship was based on more than shared experiences. They seemed perfectly comfortable in each other's presence. They could talk for hours on end, or simply enjoy each other's presence while silently reading or enjoying *nyatiti* music. Laban Otieno, who competed against my father in high school hockey, arrived from Minnesota. For days Laban and Martin sat on each side of their dear friend, their arms draped around my father's shoulders, talking with him in Dholuo, and reminiscing about their half-century long friendship.

On the morning of July 28, 2007, my father started whispering to my mother at his bedside. He expressed joy at seeing the renovations done to his mother's house in Got Regea, and marveled over the renewed signs of life that were emerging in the Odenyo family compound. He specifically praised his sister-in-law, Awino Odenyo, for her development initiatives not only in our home, but within the village school. He requested that my mother not forget Got Regea, and asked that she lend a helping hand whenever possible to those in the family who were working hard to make Got Regea a better place. With this last request, his breathing became irregular. His friends and family gathered around his bedside, and each fought back tears as they tried to comfort him with their presence. J.L.Otieno said, "Grandpa— I love you!" Grandpa smiled at his grandson and reached out to hold his hand. Then my father quietly passed away.

Words cannot describe the loss that I felt when I heard the news of my father's death. Seeing his body at the funeral home was even more emotional. Though I had anticipated this day for several weeks, nothing could prepare me for this moment. I requested that only my sister and mother join me as I opened the door to the room which held his casket. As I walked forward, my eyes caught hold of him, my knees suddenly grew weak, my body slumped, and the tears and moaning started before I took my third step. I was now limping closer and closer to him, half walking and half crawling. By the time I reached him I could not fully stand. I knelt before him with each of my hands grasping the side of his coffin. Every time I glanced up at his face my moans grew loader and loader, to the point of near convulsion and despair. I was seeing the impossible. My greatest mentor, inspiration, and strength—my father, was dead. It was like seeing the mighty World Trade Center Towers fall to the earth. The shock and pain were indescribable. He was more than a father. He was my professor, my president, my king, and my emperor. He was the center of my universe. He was to me like Got Regea was to him.

I continued kneeling and weeping for perhaps fifteen minutes, until I could moan and cry no more. I remember thinking of how exceptionally tragic our family's loss was, coming just months after the death of Omondi. With that thought in my head I eventually stood up, wiped my tears, and put one arm around my mother on my left, the other around my sister on my right, and said, "It's just the three of us now. We have to be strong."

Two days later we provided Dr. Amos Otieno Odenyo with a beautiful memorial service attended by many friends and family. We played Lillian Odera's *"Duto Mag Yesu* (All to Jesus)" in the background. Dad heard this music the previous year during the funeral of his high school friend Fred Ouka, and commented that he liked it. Reverend Peter Osano and his wife Dr. Ann Osano (also a reverend) stood with others in front of my father's casket and sang the Luo song *"E Polo."* Shem Olende eulogized my father, drawing upon their shared experiences since high school. Professional colleagues from York College and World Education described my father just as I knew him—a kind, just, and compassionate man. Dr. Bill Divale, a colleague from York College who had worked with Dr. Odenyo for over thirty years, described him as a chairman of social sciences who was fair and accommodative of everyone's viewpoints, but willing to take a contrary position if he felt doing so was right. My father was described as a non-vindictive man. When the professorship was divided on an issue,

Chairman Odenyo refused to retaliate against the losing side, stating, "I'm the chairman of the whole department, not just of my friends." Mr. Tom Keehn of World Education in Boston described him as "a gentle soul, with a strong social conscience."

My eldest cousin Kenneth read from his prepared speech:

> Uncle Amos was a man filled with immeasurable drive, a deep moral fiber, steadfast beliefs, and undying love for family. He was a man whose greatest pleasures in life came not from just using the well-traveled road, but going where no one had been, and creating a trail for others to follow. He left Kenya when I was just five years old. He was everyone's inspiration. All the extended family talked about him and his accomplishments. In our culture, accomplishments are worn on the sleeve. Success is measured by where you live, how you dress, and what you drive. Yet, for Uncle Amos, his success lays in the many he helped uplift, inspire, and show the way. As we bid you farewell, be content, that you accomplished your purpose. In us, your purpose and dreams lives, and we are forever grateful to the Lord, for giving us you.

From the moment my father died, my mother, sister, and I knew there was something we had to do. It would be our gift to our father. We would bring him home. We intimately knew the man, and understood that our house in New York was just a dwelling, and its location just a convenience. Despite staying forty-six years in America, not a day went by that he did not think about, wonder about, pray about, going home. Home for him was not just Kenya. It was Got Regea. We, his family, would fulfill his lifelong dream—the only dream left unaccomplished, the dream to go home.

We planned the funeral for Saturday, August 11, 2007. His body was to be transported from Nairobi to Kisumu on Friday morning, and taken to Got Regea village to lay overnight in his section of the family compound. This did not happen as planned. Friday morning when the airport workers in Nairobi transferred his casket to the local plane destined for Kisumu, they realized that the American-made metal casket would not fit inside the cargo hold. The plane departed without my father, disappointing over thirty friends and family who took time off work to wait for him at the Kisumu airport. I personally wondered how such a mistake could happen. Certainly this was not the first American casket ever loaded onto a domestic flight in Kenya. My father's casket had arrived at Jomo Kenyatta Airport on Wednesday, and the transfer itinerary was known in advance by airport staff. Was there not one airline employee who thought to use a measuring stick? We were later told by family friends that this was not an isolated incident at Nairobi Airport. To make sure things go right, you have to *toa kitu kidogo* (pay extra money).

My father's friend Akich Okola replaced the large metal American casket with a smaller and locally-made casket, constructed of wood. Family and friends waited in Kisumu and wondered if the Nairobi airport "mistake" was my father's way of dictating the course of his own funeral. My father always opposed what he called the unnecessary "partying" or "feasting" which occurs at Luo funerals. Although he was a big proponent of Luo identity, he stressed that the culture should rid itself of habits that do not have social benefits. He did not see how it benefited the deceased's family to lay out the deceased for days of public viewing while crowds of guests descend on the family with expectations of food, drink, and entertainment. He called it an unnecessary financial inconvenience at the worst possible time. Instead, he advocated simple funerals, with the entire event occurring in a single morning or afternoon, with no partying. This is the funeral my father received.

Once his casket arrived in Kisumu on Saturday morning, Pastor Zebedee Odenyo said a prayer of thanks. Then our funeral caravan proceeded to Got Regea. We headed north, climbing the roads until we reached the heights of Maseno where our father had attended school nearly sixty years ago. We continued in the direction of Uganda. I glanced out of the window to observe the Dudi market. This is where my father once came to buy sugar and flour for his aunt Patroba, the one who told him all the stories of our ancestors. We made our way past Luanda Dudi School (formerly Luanda Primary School) where Grandfather Zablon Sangoro and Uncle Lut Ezra Obuong were once headmasters, and where my father used to ring the class bell as a student. As we drove, we intentionally set off our car alarms to inform the community that an important event was about to occur. We reached Saint Peter's Church where my father had taken us during each visit home to Kenya, and where I had stood just a few weeks earlier during my brother's funeral. Numerous cars had already arrived and were parked under the old fig tree, its many leaves and twisted branches offering shelter from the hot Nyanza sun.

We proceeded to my father's section of the family compound, through a recently-cut section of the perimeter fence. The space was still cleared of banana trees that had been cut down for my brother's burial. It is here that my father ventured during his trips home. During his life he often lost himself among the trees, silently inspecting them, touching them, and smelling them. He could have built himself a large house—a lasting legacy to his professional success, but he chose to leave his land barren for crops to be grown and sold for the benefit of the family. The crops were cleared in preparation for his arrival, thus his land now looked larger, and the uprooted soil was still not firm beneath our feet. Dad's casket was placed under a tent, which served as his symbolic house. My sister Atieno stood on one side of his casket, holding her son J.L. Otieno, who occasionally glanced down to get a final glimpse of his grandfather's face through the glass-top coffin. Even at the young age of three, J.L. Otieno took the events very seriously. He even requested that he get "one more look at Grandpa" before the coffin was taken away. J.L. Otieno's father, Jeanlou, was also present, and provided a measure of support that was much welcome during the emotional events of the day. My mother stood at the head of the casket, and I stood on the opposite side of my sister. Together we greeted each and every person who had lined up to pay him their final respects. We were all suffering inside. While I always knew this day would come, it did not lessen the pain within my heart. I tried my best to compose myself and remain strong for the benefit of the family. But deep down inside I felt powerless.

Once the viewing was over we proceeded to Saint Peter's Church.

My father's casket was placed in the center of the aisle, before the pulpit. For the second time that year I sat in the first row, this time joined by my mother, sister, sister-in-law, niece, and five nephews. Several close friends and family members stood before the congregation and talked about my father. It was hard for me to pay attention, for I had not yet come to terms with what was happening. Just eight months ago we were having Christmas dinner with my father and brother; now they were both dead. I knew that in minutes I would stand before the church and do something I never thought I would have to do, which is to eulogize my father. I always thought this role would befall my brother Omondi, who had many advantages over me. He was the eldest, and therefore the wisest. He was the one who was born in this land, looked like he belonged to this land, and sounded like he came from this land. Omondi was to be our living connection to Kenya. He was the one to eulogize our father in Dholuo—the one to accept my father's role as head of the immediate family. He was the articulate one—the one who knew the right words to say at the right time. How was I to stand in front of this congregation and speak to them, connect to them, and honor my father's memory?

By the time I stood in front of the congregation, I had decided what I had to say. I would speak about the things in my father's life that contributed to him becoming such a successful and respected person. I would share it with the congregation, but in order to find my strength I would subconsciously speak to only my late brother's four children in the audience. Questions about their future were constantly in my mind, which provided me with the only sense of focus during months of emotional chaos. How could I inspire them to live up to their best potential? Have they created hopes and dreams for their own future, or do they consider their future buried with their father and grandfather? I knew that no assistance from me could ever substitute for their own dreams, initiative, and perseverance. So what I would try to provide them was Professor Odenyo's final lesson—the story of his life. I spoke from the heart without notes. I talked about self-reliance, diligence, hard-work, compassion, never giving up hope, and never forgetting about one's family. I talked about my father saying no to brutality while a police officer, and about his love for education. I talked about the struggles he overcame in life, including working as a domestic servant as a boy, and cleaning toilets in America. I implored Dr. Odenyo's grandchildren to incorporate into their own lives the positive traits of their grandfather, and use them to fulfill their own dreams and ambitions. I had planned to speak for only ten minutes. I was told I spoke for more than twenty. I wished I had an hour; there was still more about my father that I wanted to say.

I ended my speech by saying that should we all be so fortunate, someday we will meet Dr. Odenyo again in heaven, and that we should expect him to ask each one of us, including me, two questions: "*Umefanya nini na maisha yako? Umefanya nini, kusaidia familia yako?* (What have you done with your life? How have you helped your family?)" What I was emphasizing was the importance of balancing two themes—*kujitegemea* and *ujamaa*.

After the speeches we slowly proceeded down the familiar path to our family cemetery. As we marched, my sister Atieno and I were grateful to hear the church choir drumming and singing traditional Luo songs. We had requested it for a specific reason. During our entire childhood we grew up hearing our father playing traditional Luo music— not Christian hymns (although he seemed to know all the words of the hymns and could sing along to them in three languages). Now that he was making his way to his final resting place we wanted him to "listen" to the Luo drums and know that he was returning home to Got Regea, and not to some Anglican church in London. We watched as his casket was slowly lowered into the ground, just to the right of Omondi's grave. Various prayers were said in Dholuo. Once completed, the entire immediate family took turns covering his casket with earth, in order of seniority. As the last few shovels of earth were placed on him, gentle rain started falling from the sky, and the crowd dispersed. Many guests went home, fearing they would be trapped by the muddy trail leading out of the village. Was the rain a Luo blessing, or was it again my father, dictating the length of his funeral from the heavens?"

The next day my sister and I returned to Got Regea with my niece and nephews. We wanted them to be exposed to the same history once explained to us by our father. We stopped in Maseno, Luanda Dudi School, and Got Regea Primary School. With Aunt Awino's help, I encouraged my American-born nephews to stand in front of the students in this mud-walled school and answer questions about America. My own father had done this with us in 1983. I wanted my nephews to take a good look around this barren room, which contained no glass panes in the windows, no computers, no light bulbs, and virtually no books. I wanted them to see the reality for themselves, that had it not been for their grandfather following a dream in 1961, they would be sitting among these barefoot students, asking questions about America instead of answering them.

I sat down with the students and showed them how my laptop computer worked. Aunt Awino told me that most of these students had never seen a computer. My laptop lesson was perfect timing because written on the chalkboard were vocabulary lessons for the day, which included terms like facsimile, telephone, modem, and computer.

My sister and I explained to Omondi's four children the history of each gravestone in the family cemetery, but I could not locate Uncle Lut Ezra Obuong's grave. Prior to 1969 our family followed the Luo custom of burying the dead directly in front of the deceased's house. But Uncle Lut's mud-walled house had long ago returned to the earth. I tried to locate the cross-shaped gravestone with his name handwritten on it as well as the message: "Third son of Zablon Sangoro." I knew it existed, because my father had taken a picture of it in 1970. I walked around in frustration, wondering how a concrete grave could simply disappear. As I meandered, I observed a large tree relatively close to the spot where my uncle's house previously stood. There were broken pieces of concrete around its base. The mystery had been solved. A tree had taken root below the concrete slab and over the course of four decades completely shattered my uncle's grave. Although I was relieved to solve the mystery, I was a bit dismayed. Would this same fate befall my father? Will the memory of him, which is so fresh in all of our minds, someday be lost among a crumbling heap of rock? Is this to be my father's legacy—a lost gravesite? Is this what will happen to all of Zablon Sangoro's descendants? Will my own grandchildren someday visit Got Regea and wander around picking up shattered pieces of rock, hoping to piece together the story of their past?

15
Ujamaa

*Whilst our family tragedies appear normal in life for most people,
there now appears to be a deteriorating pattern, and we must analyze
more deeply the cause. We must guard against Disease, Alcohol,
Lust, Procreation and Financial Waste.*

—Daniel Dindi Odenyo, letter on January 27, 1995,
to brothers Otieno and Victor.

I have always had a fear of flying, and a fear of death. But as I sat
in my seat on the flight from Kenya to the United States, I was focused instead on the loss of my father and brother. As the plane glided
through the heavens, I stared out at the rays of the sun through the
clouds. I realized that for as long as I live, this was as close as I could
get to two people I loved. It had all happened too quickly, and life
now lost much of its meaning for me. Death suddenly posed no fear
for me, and I found myself wishing I could float on these glimmering
clouds forever.

From my portable music player I selected a playlist from Bob
Marley and Peter Tosh. Through their lyrics, these two men have always provided me extra joy through the good times, and the strength
to endure through the bad times. It was Bob Marley's song "She's
Gone" that I listened to, over and over again, immediately after my
relationship ended with my girlfriend in college. This time it would be
Peter Tosh's "Lessons in My Life" that would speak to me, captivate

me, and console me on my long journey from Kenya to America. The lyrics seemed to perfectly capture my feelings about myself, society, and in particular, the events that follow in this chapter. Sitting silently in my airline seat I played Tosh's "Lessons in My Life" in a repetitious cycle. Each time I gained more strength to believe that right was still right, wrong was still wrong, and that I had not yet lost my mind. What I had witnessed this year, and what I would witness in months to come, would forever haunt me.

My first lesson involves the death of my brother Omondi. It was an unexpected death to everyone around him, but in hindsight it was predictable. For more than a decade leading to his death, Omondi battled a variety of "health-related" issues that were self-induced, but correctable though proper decision making. He decided not to correct his problems, and they multiplied and negatively affected every aspect of his professional, financial, marital, and parental life. All these issues fed off each other in an endless loop until it became difficult to identify the true nature of the problem.

Omondi had every resource to assist him to correct his problems, but he either turned them down or did not commit to any of them. His parents, wife, and siblings were supportive of him from the beginning. We tried "tough love," and allowed him to hit rock-bottom. At other times we tried "unconditional love." He was given things in life that generally do not come free. These things included free medical insurance, gym and pool membership (to improve his health), free computer and Internet access (for job searching), a free car (to get to work), subsidized housing (so he could repay debts), and free cross-country trips to see family (for emotional support). By many standards, Omondi lived better than the rest of us.

I remember all the private talks my father, Aunt Olivia, and other relatives had with Omondi over the course of ten years. I did not feel excluded, for I knew my place. Omondi was the elder brother, and I had no right to question his decisions in life. Due to my junior status I could not disrespect him by acting like a parent. I also kept my assistance to Omondi a secret. I feared that if the extended family realized I was being so helpful to him, Omondi would resent me for reversing our traditional roles. So, I worked discretely behind the scenes.

My efforts were devoted toward providing him with stability and the means to increase the time spent with his two young sons. They were his greatest joy and I knew he loved them dearly.

Throughout this entire time my brother repeatedly assured me that he was on the right track in life and taking full advantage of all the assistance provided to him. I vividly remember the conversations we had at my home in December 2006, in which he described with glowing detail all the steady progress he had made over the past two years. He told me about the added responsibilities he was receiving at work, and how they relied on him to solve critical managerial problems. He thanked me for all my assistance, saying he was now able to take care of his financial debts and spend more time with his children. My father later told me that he had an identical conversation with Omondi at my home in December 2006, and was provided with the same assurances. During the same week in December, my sister Atieno also had a private conservation with Omondi on the same issues, and Omondi provided the same assurances.

I held my last long-distance telephone conversation with Omondi two weeks before he died in early 2007. According to my telephone records we talked for forty-one minutes. I was actually the most aggressive I had ever been by raising the issues I thought most often derailed his life. He immediately shot them all down, saying, "No, none of those things are an issue. All I need is more time. Just give me some time so that I can work matters out."

"Omondi, I'll give you some time, but please review these things for only you can take the steps forward. I cannot do that for you." These were the last words I spoke to him.

After my brother's sudden death, it was difficult for our family to accept the overwhelming evidence that almost everything Omondi told us, until the last day of his life, was completely false. Omondi, once the chairman of the drama club in high school, could have been an accomplished actor in Hollywood had he developed the interest. He was apparently that talented. Just like he did in the late 1970s, Omondi told us only what he thought we would like to hear, even if the truth was the complete opposite. This type of deflection extended across the ocean. Many relatives in Kenya appeared willing to perpetuate the story that Omondi's American relatives purposely withheld all forms of assistance to him.

After Omondi's death, I helped my father and Omondi's mother Judith sort through his personal effects in his two-bedroom condominium that I had provided him for the last two years of his life. I helped them search for a checking account, investment account, life insurance account, or college-savings account left by Omondi for his children. We looked for anything tangible that we could present his children as financial support. My father searched for Omondi's college diploma, hoping to confirm that all the tuition money Omondi received was not in vain. I wish I could say we found something positive, but we did not. We found only unpaid bills stacked in unopened envelopes and twenty-two years of deception. Recent letters from his employer included stern advisements to Omondi which paralleled the warnings made to him in 1979 by Headmaster John B.O. Juma. While these revelations were painful for everyone, it was especially painful for my father. My sister Atieno remembers Dad sitting in his house, staring at the wall, and wondering out loud why Omondi's life ended the way it did. She recalls a tone of anger and hurt in my father's voice. From 1962 until 2007, my father gave Omondi all the opportunities in life that Zablon Sangoro Odenyo could have only dreamed about giving his own children. It angered and disappointed Dad that although he sacrificed to give Omondi all the opportunities he never had, Omondi's life had the opposite result.

Atieno remembers Dad saying, "When I brought Omondi to the United States, he literally had a permanent residency card waiting for him. He could have done anything he wanted in this country—not like his peers, who had to work in the shadows. But I can't find even one thing that he accomplished once he got here. He took all my weaknesses, but none of my strengths."

When summarized in this perspective, it seems like Omondi's main goal in life, or at least his greatest accomplishment, was simply coming to America.

It pains me to say these things, but it does not diminish my love for Omondi. My brother had a conflicting mixture of good and bad traits. Omondi was a very loyal brother, a likeable friend, and a faithful father to his two youngest children. He exemplified the "carefree, out-going, and bubbly" father that I longed for as a child. Omondi easily sat down on the floor and played games with his children as if he was one of them. He shopped for Christmas and birthday gifts and took his children to the mall and arcades, even if it required borrowing the money. I remember Omondi buying an expensive Sega video game system for his children before the youngest one had even learned to talk. He took his children to the movies and splurged for candy and popcorn. Omondi participated in most duties of childcare, and for several years was actually the primary parent while his wife finished college. He knew the value of education. When he realized he lived in a bad school zone he moved into a more expensive neighborhood so that his children could have access to better teachers. Omondi was everybody's friend. He had a deep and joyous laugh that engulfed the entire room and drew strangers close to him. Due to his cheery and outgoing personality, people naturally gravitated toward Omondi, rath-er than to me. Omondi was the life of the party, and the party was part of him. I was often the shy, uncertain brother, while Omondi radiated confidence everywhere he went. He was naturally intelligent, with or-ganizational and speaking skills that enabled him to have several suc-cessful careers without a college degree. These same skills made him a valuable and popular community organizer within the Kenyan com-munity in America.

In terms of personality and character, Omondi was everything our father was not. I can see how a child of any age would prefer Omondi as a father rather than the silent and cerebral Dr. Odenyo who could not remember his own children's birthdates. Unfortunately, when it comes to life's major decisions, none of these positive attributes of Omondi very much mattered. The lack of discipline and focus in his life reversed each and every positive action and ultimately left a permanent scar on his family. Omondi's positive attributes did not mean much to Opiyo and Adongo, his two oldest children living in Kenya. They had only seen their father twice in twenty-two years, and barely knew the sound of his voice. With their father's death they became orphans—their mother hav-ing already met a similar fate. Omondi did not do for Opiyo and Adongo what his own father, Otieno, had done for him. From the month my father received his Ph.D., he saw Omondi in Kenya almost every year. Dad brought Omondi to America not once, but twice. Omondi knew Otieno more than Otieno knew his own father. Omondi never slept hungry on the floor of a stranger's house. He was not forced to stare at the sun, nor was he initiated into manhood through the removal of his six lower teeth. In 1961, Otieno's first Christmas in the United States was spent alone in a dormitory room. Omondi's first and last Christmas in the United States was spent surrounded by loving family. By the age of forty-four, my father was supporting the educational and professional ambitions of what appeared at times to be an entire village. Because Omondi never learned to control his vices, nor invested in the future during the good-times, at age forty-four he could not even support himself. This created feelings of disappointment and unhappiness that he blamed on others. Omondi's life-long habit was to pursue short-term satisfaction. He did not learn to overcome short-term unhappiness to achieve long-term gain. My father alluded to this in a letter on July 18, 1978:

> I too am concerned about my children being happy. However, there is a limit. In no way will I let my child dictate his/her own terms of happiness to me. If they cannot be happy in the normal conditions of the home I create for them—too bad, but I cannot go out of my way to make a child happy. Children have to learn to live with unhappiness simply because they are going to go through some unhappiness in life too. The theory that if a child is made to be happy he/she will pay attention to school and work is simply not convincing.

Amos Otieno Odenyo was often an "aloof" and "managerial" parent. He led a "deferred gratification" lifestyle. Otieno set a leadership example, made wise choices that benefited his children and extended family, and left a legacy that can be passed down to future generations. Otieno adopted the parenting style of his father, Zablon Sangoro Odenyo, while Omondi's approach had no resemblance to that of his forefathers.

Ujamaa

For years I have been hearing my fellow Americans proudly reciting the phrase, "It takes a village to raise a child." This is supposedly an African proverb that reflects the tradition of extended family and *ujamaa*. Omondi had that *ujamaa*. He had an entire village of elders, parents, and role models who raised him, inspired him, guided him, and corrected him. However, having a village is not always enough. It takes personal responsibility and correct choices.

After Omondi's death I joined my father and sister in Maryland to prepare for his memorial. Many guests were expected, and Omondi's wife, my sister Atieno, and I spent the better part of a day trying to find a suitable hall for post-church gatherings. Most halls are reserved months in advance, so when we found one still available in Gaithersburg, we booked it immediately. It was perfect. It was close to the church in Rockville, had ample parking, and would be available from five in the afternoon to eleven at night. We brought my father to the location for his review and approval. This is how our family normally operates. Whenever there is a decision impacting the extended family, we always bring it up the chain to the chief commander, Dr. Odenyo, to give his blessing.

We were aware however, that Omondi's friends and casual acquaintances were organizing a "funeral committee." It is said that the "committee" is the Luo way of lending emotional, financial, and logistical support to a grieving family. According to professional anthropologists, this is an extension of African tradition, where community ties are reaffirmed during moments of crises. However, in reality we knew that some committee members might have ideas leaning toward a party. So, at the start of the funeral committee meeting, Dad and Omondi's mother Judith made a joint statement explaining that the official memorial event would begin at five in the afternoon, end at eleven at night, and would not include any liquor. My father and Judith explained that this was not only their wish, but that of Omondi's wife, his siblings, and children. Dad politely explained that if Omondi's friends wanted to host another event with different rules, they were free to do so after eleven at night.

Once my father and Judith had spoken, my sister and I assumed the matter was closed. After all, not only was my father representing the grieving family, but he was the most senior elder in the entire house. Second in seniority was Judith. In every aspect, both traditional and modern, African and American, their wishes for their son's memorial event should be unquestioned.

Immediately after Omondi's parents had provided the parameters for their son's memorial, the crowd started mumbling amongst themselves: "Eeh, what kind of send-off is this? Eleven o'clock at night? *Omera* (brother), this is unreasonable! No alcohol?"

The rumblings throughout the funeral committee, including from those who barely knew Omondi, lasted for quite some time. At first I assumed they allowed me to overhear because I was mistaken for a non-relative. However, the rumblings grew to the point that they came out in the open and were directed squarely at my father. To the committee chairman they asked, "*Apenji* (I'm asking you), what kind of rules are these? How are we expected to move from one function to another at that late time of night? Surely you must say these arrangements are unreasonable!"

Some of the funeral committee leaders privately told our family that our wishes would cause a revolt among the persons in attendance. According to them, our existing memorial plans were too "restrictive" and "inconvenient" for the Luo community. A middle-aged funeral committee leader, "Nehemiah Aduor," pulled me aside. He began to counsel me like a pastor would counsel a wayward sinner: "Look, Odera, you cannot restrict alcohol at a funeral." To bolster his argument, Aduor confidently explained, "I come from Gem too, and it was at my grandfather's funeral that I tasted my first alcohol. I was only fourteen years old!"

Please do not mistake me for a hypocrite. I think that an icy cold beer on a Saturday afternoon is one of life's finest pleasures. Make it a "Tusker" and I will gladly have two. Play the song "Sina Makosa" and I might have three. But through trial and error I have come to realize that too much of a good thing is a bad thing. I also do not demand beer at other people's funerals. There is a difference, you see.

Our family tried to reassure the committee by repeating, "No one is telling you not to have your own function for Omondi at whatever hour or location you want. Simply allow us to have ours."

Still, the pressure from the committee, most of whom I had never met in my life, was overwhelming. A man adjacent to me balanced his Heineken beer on one knee, and using his other hand, gestured in the air while demanding the specific details of transport and burial in Kenya. Emboldened, the funeral committee leadership stood up and addressed the tense crowd, craftfully stating, "Perhaps the family of Omondi would take our requests, reconsider them, and come back to us with some sort of compromise. Perhaps they will listen to the community and incorporate some of our ideas."

Compromise? What was there to compromise? The wishes of the entire Odenyo family versus Omondi's friends? I was dumbstruck by the premise.

Around twelve-thirty in the morning, after hours of debating, my father finally succumbed to the endless pressure of the Luo community. He simply gave up. He put the entire memorial arrangements in the hands of the committee, which meant Omondi's memorial would essentially be a party. Throughout the last twenty years my father consistently stated to me and all who would listen that he could not tolerate endless partying at funerals. Much of it was his personality. He was a calm, measured, and practical man. He simply did not see how partying to the wee hours of the morning (usually at the expense of the family) was beneficial to the bereaved. He expressed this time and time again, both in Kenya and in America. He wanted his own funeral to be limited to an afternoon affair. "Get in, and get out!" he used to instruct me, with his finger pointed in the direction of the nearest dirt road leading out of Got Regea. Now, as the representative of the Odenyo family, he was going to be attending such a party for his very own son. Once again he was sacrificing his own needs and wants for the sake of the Luo community.

I was stunned. It meant that the entire day I had spent with Atieno and my sister-in-law going over the details of the memorial events was wasted. I had to forfeit a down-payment on a hall reservation and accommodate another that would probably sit empty until almost midnight. No respectable African party ever begins before that magic hour. You can repeatedly tell people that your party is from eight until midnight, but at three o'clock in the morning when you are fast asleep,

Owuor, Ogweno, Apuda, and Akinyi are knocking on your door. The four of them having grown bored of the last two party locations are now telling you in *Sheng* (Kenyan version of Ebonics): *Sasa? Osiepna, wapi hang? Leta pombe jamani, tufanye hii party right!* (Whassup? My friend, where's your party? Bring out some beers my countryman, and let's make this party happen!)

After the funeral committee took over the planning for Omondi's memorial, our family simply faded into the background as if we never existed. I privately stated to Nehemiah Aduor and the other funeral committee leaders that like my father, I would attend and symbolically support whatever arrangements they made. However, I refused to be tasked with any logistical planning. I had already tried and it was all in vain.

After I had voiced my position, I sat down with my sister in a semi-private room, and slowly but surely, felt like I was going to cry. So did Atieno. We were not as skilled as our father in holding back our emotions, but we did not want to cry in public. We quickly left before our tears had been noticed, and headed outside to sit in our car. Together on that dark and lonely street in Severn, Maryland, we started to weep. Up until that moment, both of us had managed to control the pain over our brother's death in order to concentrate on arranging the memorial events ahead of us. We had been internally weeping, but had masked the external signs of pain for the sake of making key family decisions. Now that the entire memorial event was swept out from under our feet, there was no need to hold back our emotions. The tears, however, were now combined with frustration over a funeral committee that seemed to think they knew better than we did how to mourn the loss of our brother.

I will never, and I repeat NEVER, be able to shake the memory of that night from my mind. It will linger with me until my dying day, for it was the last time I would ever see my father in the position of protector and comforter. It was approximately one o'clock in the morning, and Atieno and I were weeping uncontrollably in the front seats of our vehicle. Through our tears we saw our father emerge from the house, walk slowly toward us with an unsteady and weary limp, and take a seat behind us in the back seat of the car. He held out his left hand to me, his right hand to my sister, and instructed us, "Odera, take my hand. Atieno, take my hand."

We each managed to grasp a hand, but continued our sobbing, through which we asked him, "Who are these people to tell us how to arrange the memorial events for Omondi? What nerve they have, asking us to *negotiate* on *their* terms. We don't even know most of these people!"

My father, holding tightly onto both our hands, did not know how to answer our questions. The only thing he could manage to say was, "This is the only way they know how to remember Omondi. He was one of them. They want to say good-bye to him the way they knew him, and how they related to him. Sorry. I'm so sorry."

To our credit, the next week we put aside all of our differences and fully participated in the memorial events for Omondi. In the afternoon we held a very nice memorial service officiated by Reverend Peter Osano. Omondi's wife Florence arranged a beautiful memorial brochure picturing her husband standing with his mother in a Kisumu photo studio in the mid-1960s. Omondi's twelve year old son (also named Otieno) read a letter telling his father how much he loved him and would miss him. I played a fifteen minute video tribute of my brother that left people in tears.

As I predicted, the committee's post-church event in Tacoma Park, Maryland, did not start until around midnight. My father was too worn out to give a thank-you speech, so I did so in his place. I meant every word of it too. "If you can't beat 'em, join 'em," was my philosophy that evening. I was going to have a positive attitude and join my Luo sisters and brothers in commemorating a fallen son. Behind me sat my father and Judith. I felt a bit sorry for them at their age. If they adhered to custom, they would have to wait until the last person left the function at sunrise.

The mood quickly became festive, encouraged by the availability of food and drink. Fundraising occurred, for which our family is extremely grateful. As was done that night, and again immediately following the event, I say, "*erokamano ahinya* (thank you very much)" to everyone who supported my family.

Around one-thirty in the morning, my cousin "Calvin" approached me at the party and expressed condolences over Omondi's death. But in the same breath he wondered how I, Omondi's brother, could simply "allow" Omondi to die. According to Calvin, since Omondi was dead, whatever we did to support him was not enough, and we were responsible.

Now, this was the second time in a week that I had heard this sentiment from a relative. I was torn between a desire to punch Calvin in the face or take him aside and explain to him all the steps we had taken, until the very last day, to support and counsel Omondi, and how Omondi, to the very last day, had blocked, distorted, or misdirected all of our efforts. I resorted to neither approach, for neither would bring my point across to Calvin. You see, for many Luos, a premature death is not the responsibility of the deceased. Death is often attributed to an external factor, such as a jealous neighbor, a political enemy, or a revengeful spirit. If it is an identifiable source, such as the AIDs virus, it is turned into a more socially acceptable and random cause such as "malaria," or a "sudden illness." If he was a drunk speeding the wrong way down a road on a Saturday night with a prostitute, he was killed "driving to church on Sunday." If the hearse had a mechanical breakdown en route to the cemetery, it is because the deceased was wronged in life by a family member, and his spirit was retaliating in death.

In this instance, in Calvin's mind, the cause of death was us, the immediate family. I am certain that many in attendance that night, while joyously celebrating Omondi's life, were talking amongst themselves, sipping their brew, and wondering exactly which one of us caused or failed to prevent Omondi's death. Which one of us orchestrated the chain of events that cast a spell over Omondi's life? Which one of us "*kingo-ed*" (bewitched) Omondi? [35]

The evening ended as follows. My cousin Adhiambo was leaning over to my sister, translating the master of ceremony's comments which were being shouted into a microphone and came out blaring from two huge speakers. She refrained from translating word for word because some of the jokes were sexual in nature and designed to rile up the crowd into dancing, partying, and donating more *harambee* money. Around two o'clock in the morning, a lone Montgomery Park policewoman entered the hall (which was actually the basement of a church).

She warned us that the neighbors were complaining we were making too much noise. I was going along with everything up until this point, smiling, shaking hands, and thanking everyone for attending.

I next checked on my father. He was sitting silently, observing the party. He told me he was feeling extremely tired and would soon leave the function despite the expectation that he stay until the end. Some fifteen minutes later, funeral committee leader Nehemiah Aduor approached me and said, "Odera, there is a problem." I expected him to tell me that we had all been ordered out of the premises by the policewoman, or that someone's car had been towed. Instead, he told me, "We are running out of beer. Can you make a trip to the liquor store and buy a few cases of Heineken and Budweiser?"

I am not making up any of this. I was surprised and angry, but did not express it since I did not want to be labeled as "un-Luo." But inside my head, I knew that if leaving my brother's memorial event to buy beer for the party made me more Luo, then from that moment until the sun rose again I would simply not be Luo. I made an excuse how I could not buy the beer, and I left the function.

Up until that moment I had played along with every request made by the funeral committee, even to the point that I was being acculturated into their way of doing things. I wanted to feel and demonstrate that I was part of the Luo community. I was adapting, just like I adapted to the black American community in high school. But I had learned my lesson, and this time I had my limits. Specifically, it was the last request concerning beer. I could not imagine myself, the deceased's grieving brother, making "beer runs" back and forth between the liquor store and house of God so that the crowd could maintain its beer buzz. What was the priority of the evening? Was it liquor, or was it support for the grieving family? If it was the latter, why was I chosen, out of everyone present at the function, to make that drive to get more beer? Not only had my family not wanted alcohol to be present, but I had specifically informed Nehemiah Aduor that I would no longer take part in any logistical planning.

Although Dad's pre-existing diagnosis of cancer prevents me from making a direct correlation, I think it was more than a coincidence that after Omondi's death my father's health rapidly deteriorated. Within a week or two of Omondi's memorial service, Dad lost all interest in food. In just a few short weeks he dropped fifty pounds in weight, and soon after that, he was dead.

With my father's death, of the seven sons of Zablon Sangoro Odenyo, only two, Victor and Booker, remained alive. To me, it was a sobering realization that a new era in our family history was approaching. In time shorter than what we might expect, the responsibility of family leadership would rest entirely upon the shoulders of my own generation. However, many of us were suffering from the same afflictions as my brother Omondi. In Kenya, such situations are worsened by the lack of jobs for the growing population. The streets of Nairobi are congested by the educated but unemployed. This situation breeds despair, corruption, violent crime, and in many instances, death. I feared the day I would return to Got Regea and find a ghost-town, except for a few cousins who might beg from me in the same manner that the well-dressed man begged from my father at my brother's funeral. This scene wreaked havoc on my mind. If begging at a funeral was not out of bounds today, what tactics would be employed tomorrow?

On the evening of August 11, 2007, after my father's funeral in Got Regea, I was successful in calling for a small meeting which included several key family members. The meeting included the new patriarch of our family, Uncle Victor Odenyo, as well as Uncle Booker and Aunt Awino. Between them they held two doctorate degrees, and one M.B.A. They were all very accomplished researchers, teachers, and managers.

I specifically requested that several of my cousins, both male and female, attend the meeting. The basis for selection was simple. First, they were the cousins who were physically available because they had decided to sleep overnight in Got Regea. Second, they were the cousins who were most likely to live in Got Regea or, as in my case, inherit responsibilities connected to Got Regea. Beyond that, their individual backgrounds varied. There were a few cousins with little education, few marketable skills, unreliable work histories, and bleak prospects for the future. On the other hand, there were cousins with prestigious university degrees. There was "Emmanuel," a trustworthy and reliable cousin who after ten years was still trying to find his first professional job in business. There was "Veronica," who had a very successful career within the international aid and development community.

It is interesting how each one of us in the room, due to our own experiences and ideology, addressed the issue of "development." I started the meeting by stating, "I think our family can progress a lot more. Personally, I believe a key ingredient to our future is to have at least one family business or self-sustaining goal that we can rally behind. For example, during these last two funerals I have paid thousands of shillings to coffin makers, transport companies, tent suppliers, cooks, and photographers. These are just a few examples of the businesses in which our family could be engaged. Why should we pay money to these companies when we can be providing this same service to others? I know one of our relatives from Kanjira has started a very successful business in Kisumu—why can't we do the same? I have recently visited my in-law's village where I see them holding family business meetings, growing coffee, and now they have started constructing a dairy farm. We have cows too! I know we have had our difficulties with 'business management' before, but perhaps we have learned from our mistakes and can take a new approach. I would like to hear if anyone in this room has similar goals which I could help support. I don't want to simply give something away. I want to invest in our future and actually see profits. How can I invest in this family?"

Aunt Awino replied, "That is a very good idea Odera. Why don't we provide your cousins with a pair of goats. If this works well we can expand to other things."

I thought this answer was simple, yet brilliant. It was a development plan that relied on internal, not external solutions. It was specific and tangible. If we all agreed upon this course of action, we could pass by the Dudi market the very next morning and purchase our very first pair of goats. If this worked out, we might in time have a whole herd of goats, and a practical dairy or *nyama choma* business. I was feeling very optimistic.

Uncle Booker spoke next, and addressed several of us with, "I think any steps we take are futile until the lying, cheating, and drinking stops. I have had enough of these self-destructive actions. It's time to grow up and act responsible. Coming home at four in the morning reeking like *chang'aa* (moonshine) when there is work to do at dawn is not a recipe for progress! Four o'clock in the morning is when we used to get up and go to the fields, not go to sleep!"

Uncle Victor was silent throughout the entire meeting, as has always been his style. He finally leaned forward from the dark corner, made his face visible in the candlelight, and said, "Odera, here in Got Regea there are endless ideas." Pointing his finger directly at several of my cousins, but looking straight at me, he continued, "The problem is not lack of ideas, but lack of responsibility. If we get a pair of goats, will they get out of bed in time to milk and feed the goats? And how do we know that they will nurture a family business instead of simply milking it dry until it dies! We have all seen this happen too many times before."

I was impressed that Uncle Booker and Uncle Victor addressed these character issues. My uncles were sounding very much like my own father. They were talking about important values such as honesty, hard work, and responsibility. They were analyzing the problems in the family and pointing out solutions. All their suggestions were specific, tangible, and immediately implementable.

Individually, each one of my cousins responded to my question with regard to their goals. I was relieved to hear they understood our generation was not reaching the same high standards as the older generation (I fault myself as well, for none in my generation has a Ph.D.). They all admitted there was a need to be more proactive. However, they were all unanimous in not articulating any identifiable mechanism through which our family could progress. The closest thing to a goal was when Veronica recommended, "We need to have a healthy balance of development policies using internal and external approaches for sustainable results."

Now, this suggestion sounded impressive, except for one problem. The problem was how to implement this development strategy the very next morning. I envisioned all of us waking up the next morning, scratching our heads, and wondering what our development tasks were for the day, because there simply were no tasks. We would have a "politically-correct" ideology and a very nice set of developmental talking points, but no goals, delineation of responsibilities, and no plan.

Next, my cousin Veronica started arguing that the meeting was invalid because there were not enough women in the meeting. I was taken aback by this concept. Here, deep inside rural Africa, while discussing family matters over candlelight, the concept of "affirmative action" was a priority rather than "real action."

It got worse. Veronica started talking back to Uncle Victor and Uncle Booker, questioning their qualifications for dispensing parental advice. Veronica did not seem to care whether their advice was justified or not. She was so driven by the concept of equality that she felt free to rebuke her elders and put everyone in the room on the same level.

Next, Veronica turned her attention to me. With a wag of a finger I was reprimanded with, "Odera, don't forget they are your agemates!" I could not believe my eyes and ears. Veronica apparently thought I was disrespectful for engaging in dialogue with my peers regarding their own goals. Yet, just thirty seconds earlier Veronica was being disrespectful by rebuking the two most senior elders in the room!

It was immediately after this point that our family meeting disintegrated and we all went our separate ways into the moonless night, never again to talk about the issues that were raised. I felt demoralized and confused. I was taking the hands-on approach that Calvin had accused me of not taking with my brother, but still I was being criticized. Damned if you do, and damned if you don't!

Through the pitch-black darkness I heard the voice of Uncle Victor requesting that I come back inside his house for a private conversation. I sat down in front of him, and to be honest I was apprehensive as to what he might say. I looked at Uncle Victor like my own father, and was ready for some admonishment. During the meeting my head was spinning so much that I started to question the difference between right and wrong. My agemates created in me a lot of self-doubt regarding my fundamental beliefs.

I was relieved to hear him say, "Odera, I like your ideas."

We proceeded to have a brief and very private conversation, which led me to conclude two things. First, Zablon's dream for the family was not completely dead. Older members of the family still believed in a family enterprise and were actively engaged in projects similar to what I had proposed in the meeting. However, it was only a partial dream, for the older generation did not trust many in the younger generation to involve them in any business. (There were several trustworthy relatives, but they were too consumed with the immediate financial obligations of their own families to have time for entrepreneurship.) The construction of Zablon's dream was currently unattainable, for a successful family business would lead to more irresponsibility on the part of the younger family members. The same "let's all be poor together philosophy" that my father had talked about was still lurking around every corner.[36]

Later that night one of the cousins from that failed meeting approached me and privately thanked me for my efforts, saying he knew exactly what I was trying to do. I appreciated "Okombo's" comments and told him how valuable he was to the future of our family. But there was no action. Within two years of our failed family discussion, three male cousins, and one female cousin, were dead. The exact circumstances of their deaths remain a mystery to me, but I see parallels with Omondi. No one dares ask, and no one dares tell. We just organize more *harambees* to cover the cost of burying our dead in Nyanza.

I found it odd that in some people's definition of *ujamaa* it is considered rude to ask a family member how you can help him achieve his goals. Yet, at the same time, friends, relatives, and strangers use the platform of *ujamaa* to demand something for free, even if the goals are not defined.

Take the case of Mr. "Okoth," a man I first met after my father's funeral. He learned my cell phone number and relentlessly called me requesting financial support for a project he referred to as "Elimination of Poverty in Got Regea." Each time he called he reminded me that he was my "grandfather" and I was his "grandson." His description of our relationship made me chuckle at first, but after the fourth telephone call I felt like asking him why, if he was my grandfather, he was absent from the funerals of his "son" (Otieno Odenyo) and "grandson" (Omondi Odenyo).

"Hannah Odhiambo" was not at my father's funeral as well. Although not a relative, she was the niece of my father's close friend, Mr. "Abuto." Our affection for the Abuto family also spilled over to her. She had emailed me in America during my father's last days, requesting I help her, her son, and her son's father travel to America for a visit. She said she missed "Uncle Otieno" and "Auntie Mayone," and felt bad that she did not have the opportunity to see us during our recent trip to Kenya for Omondi's funeral. I sent a reply a week later, giving her information about my father's upcoming funeral so that she could pay her last respects to him and spend time with us in Nyanza. Even though her home is nearby (in Sirembe), I never heard from Hannah again.

Consider "Thomas Owiti," a distant cousin of mine who told me he was finishing his first semester at Kenyatta University. Thomas forwarded to me a note requesting that I buy him a computer to "make schoolwork more efficient." I was torn by his request because there are many students who spend more time playing games on their computers than learning. Instead of refusing his request I asked him to further justify it. I also asked to see his college transcripts. I felt like asking Thomas why he felt entitled to a free computer at age twenty-two when I bought my first computer in 2005 at the age of thirty-four. My sister Atieno bought her first computer in 2006. I never did receive Thomas' transcripts.

Consider "Lucy," a young relative who asked to meet with me. Over the course of an hour, she told me a sad story about how her parents were not supportive of her educational goals, and had refused to pay for her school fees. Lucy then asked if I could give her money for school fees. Unbeknownst to Lucy, the very next day I met with her father, "Mzee," in his downtown Nairobi office. I asked him about Lucy's situation.

"I am very concerned about Lucy." he said. "My wife and I keep trying to encourage her to get some education but she does not commit to anything. I send her to secretarial school, she drops out. I send her to business school, she drops out."

Sensing my confusion, Mzee pulled out from his desk a stack of papers, receipts, and bills.

"Look at all these! These are all payments I have made for Lucy's various schools, including the school that she should be enrolled in this week, but which she has not bothered attending. I've wasted a lot of money on her. If she does not want to go to school, fine, but at least she should find a job. Instead, she prefers to stay out late at night and sleep in all day. When I find her a job, she thinks she's too good to get her hands dirty."

Under similar circumstances I sat down with "Oscar," a relative who was a year or two younger than Lucy. I asked him about his future plans.

"I'd like to go to America," he said, without any further clarification.

Our conversation continued, but in the back of my mind I could not help but notice the irony of this historical situation. I had simply replaced my father. Every time Dr. Odenyo came to Kenya he sat down with some young person whose biggest goal in life was "I want to go to America." Now it was my turn.

I looked at Oscar, and said, "I can understand why you want to come to America, and some day that might be possible. But you don't even have a high school diploma. You have no marketable skills, and have no employment history. Do you know that if you came to America today, with your foreign accent and no skills, you will be cleaning toilets for a living?"

I know my response was not what Oscar was expecting, especially the part about cleaning toilets. I think he considered it beneath him, especially when he had such "wealthy" relatives in America. The silence in the room was deafening, so I hit home my point by asking him, "So, what do you want to do for a *living* in America, and how do you expect to do it? What is your plan?"

I sat down for over an hour with Oscar, and tried to break down all the misconceptions that I suspected he had about life. I tried to instill some responsibility, hope, and focus into him. I told him that his request to go to America was a bit premature, but that I was willing to sacrifice my time and money so he could first pursue worthy goals in Kenya. I left the goals to him, but was clear that to the extent I could afford it I would even pay for technical training or a university degree in Kenya. Once that was accomplished we could reevaluate America. I was being firm, but extremely generous. Oscar said he understood my position, and I left our meeting with an optimistic attitude, hoping that in a few days Oscar would clarify his goals and I could further assist as we had discussed.

Imagine my surprise when a few days later I was pulled aside by a relative who had a look of concern on her face. She said, "Odera, what is this I am hearing you told Oscar? Oscar told me he asked you for help and you refused!"

This was not the *maendeleo* from Oscar that I had envisioned. Oscar was now spreading malicious rumors that I am *ok en jawat* (one who does not value family), and *jaguondo* (a selfish person). There is almost nothing more despicable in Luo culture than a wealthy man hoarding food and refusing to share it with a hungry and hard-working relative, which is how Oscar was portraying our encounter. He was distorting our conversation to misdirect all of his future failings directly at my feet, and make me ultimately responsible for them. It was a defeatist attitude. He was emphasizing the traditional African concept of *ujamaa*, but ignoring the African concept of *kujitegemea*. He was distorting *ujamaa* in such a way that if he became a street bum or thief, relatives would hopefully say, "You know, Oscar was such a promising young boy, if only Odera would have helped."

To tell you the truth, with Oscar's attitude I could have walked away from his life completely, but I did not. Oscar's behavior was juvenile, and young people often misinterpret advice of older people. I too misinterpreted my own father for nearly a decade, thinking his lack of gifts or remembrance of my birthday indicated he did not love me. My father did not throw me away simply because I was too immature to understand his true love for me, and I would not throw away Oscar either. I knew that Oscar's thinking was indicative of the "money grows on trees" attitude. In Kenya, the wealthy are often those who work the least, which is made possible through corruption and nepotism. Oscar fully expected that I would be nepotistic with him and "spread the wealth." Since I refused to play this game he found me arrogant. When I offered Oscar the chance to work hard and rise through life on his own merits, he envisioned a life of working hard and living in a mud hut in Kenya. He did not want to join the ranks of the Odenyo relatives who had college degrees but no job. Oscar simply could not draw the connection between "hard work" and "success."

There is a tentative happy ending with Oscar. Instead of walking away from him, I systematically removed any excuse Oscar had at his disposal to perpetuate his lies about me. I reluctantly made sure that people understood the opportunities I was willing to provide for him, thus placing the prime responsibility on him, rather than me. Confronted with this new dilemma, Oscar wisely chose to accept my assistance.

The next issue that depressed me even further involved my cousin "Beverly." She was using my father's death to generate money from the community that she kept in her own pockets. To be fair, one may say that she was very entrepreneurial and capitalistic. However, the platform that she used to generate profits was *ujamaa*. In a figurative sense, she was weeping over my father's casket while pick-pocketing her fellow mourners. Her actions made me sick to my stomach. While it would have been easier for me to ignore the situation for the sake of family relations, I could not allow my father's name to be used to steal money from the community. I chose to speak up.

I was mildly irritated by the behavior of "Mr. Okoth," "Hannah," and "Thomas." However, I was thoroughly disappointed in the behavior of "Nehemiah Aduor," "Calvin," "Veronica," "Lucy," "Oscar," and now "Beverly." Their behavior shared one common trait—a distorted view of the concept of *ujamaa*.

I had faith that our good friend Mrs. "Abuto" would understand exactly what I was going through. She had often sympathized with me on such issues during the past fifteen years, so I already knew what she would say about the situation: "Don't let your family walk all over you! Be helpful, but firm! Make sure you know where your money is going! People are looking for handouts!"

After my father's funeral, Mrs. Abuto told me she was aware that I had tried to give assistance to youths and orphans in my family. She cautioned me with, "Be very careful! They will expect you to help not only them but their extended families."

What Mrs. Abuto was telling me was of course not new to me. She was once again warning me of the dangers of *ujamaa*. However, she was saying it with such urgency that it made me feel that I was being too naïve and compassionate to my relatives. In other words, Mrs. Abuto was advising me that I was extending myself financially in a way that she would not do herself. I took special note of her advice for two reasons. First, although Mrs. Abuto was very strict about finances and family, she was very compassionate to orphans. I remember a few years back she took me to an orphanage in Nairobi and tearfully explained how important it was to give these children a second chance in life. Secondly, it was the Abuto family that recently approached my parents for a financial loan.

Several historical facts are necessary here. Some time ago, Mr. "Abuto" took an emergency loan from my parents for the stated purpose of saving his mansion from foreclosure. The funds represented part of my parents' retirement savings which they had accumulated from many years of financial sacrifice. The loan my parents provided to Mr. Abuto represented more than ten times the medium gross annual salary for a middle-class Kenyan. It was forty-three times the amount I provided in the 1990s for my cousin Alfred to attend one semester of college in the United States. My parents provided the interest-free loan to Mr. Abuto with the understanding (per the words of Mr. Abuto) that the loan would be paid back with assets that Mr. Abuto was in the process of liquidating. Mr. Abuto would save his mansion from foreclosure and refund my parents' money.

In 2007, during my brother's funeral in Kenya, my father was very saddened to learn that the Abutos had been evicted from their mansion. However, Mrs. Abuto told my father that his money was still safe with the bank in furtherance of an on-going legal petition to reverse the foreclosure of the Abuto mansion. She told me and my father that due to the corrupt legal system in Kenya the process could take up to ten years.

My father was quite distraught about the sudden change of events and urged the Abutos to repay him from their remaining assets as quickly as possible. Mrs. Abuto acknowledged the debt and assured us that she and her husband would repay the debt with all due haste. My father even summoned an attorney and me to a meeting to discuss the details of the loan repayment.

These financial matters took a back seat to the issue of my father's deteriorating health, but they were raised unexpectedly by him during our last conversation on Friday, July 27, 2007. He could barely talk, and he must have known he was dying. Dad struggled to force out his last words with a strained and distressed whisper. Each of his statements to me concerned the outstanding loan to the Abuto family. In particular, he asked about the status of the court proceedings between the Abutos and the bank, as well as the status of his money the Abutos had placed in escrow. He wanted to know when his money was going to be returned.

I told him, "Dad, you just rest. You have explained everything that needs to be done, and I will handle the rest for you. I promise you that your loan will be repaid. Auntie Abuto has assured me of this." I repeated this promise once more for him, to which he struggled to reply "Okay." Eager to let him rest, I told him, "Dad, I love you. You know that right? I love you." He faintly whispered "Yes." These were the last words we exchanged to each other, for he died the next afternoon.

For more than a year the Abutos had repeatedly explained to us that they were losing their house due to corruption involving the bank. Knowing that corruption permeates every sector of Kenyan society, my parents and I were very sympathetic to the Abutos. For their court case to take ten years seemed like an awfully long time, and I wanted to provide any assistance I could. I considered inviting them to temporarily live in the United States in my home. I also considered buying a house in Nairobi that we could share with them. However, to afford this we had to settle the issue of the outstanding loan.

After my father's funeral I proceeded with hashing out a repayment plan for the Abutos that was even more generous than the one proposed by my father. I felt somewhat uncomfortable pressuring Mr. Abuto to be immediately accountable for the loan. After all, he was my elder, and a respected member of the Luo community. Mr. Abuto was one of the few Kenyans who worked for the government but was still considered trustworthy. I remember Mr. Abuto playing games with me as a child in a way that I once craved from my own father. Mr. Abuto was always bursting with smiles and emotion, just like my brother Omondi. It was rumored Mr. Abuto never drank alcohol in his life—a rare accomplishment in many Kenyan families, including my own. I admired him so much that I was planning on naming my next child "Abuto" in honor of our two families' friendship.

I could never have anticipated what occurred next. While the re-payment agreement was being drafted for our signatures, Mrs. Abuto expressed her distress with my mother: "I can't believe how Odera could chase his father's money before the body is even cold. Our own son! We have no money—not even enough to buy groceries. We want-ed our two youngest children to have as many opportunities as our first three children." Mr. Abuto sat nearby—listening but not intervening.

When I next met with Mr. and Mrs. Abuto, they told me, "Your father promised us half of this money so we can pay for our children's education." I was speechless, as was my mother. Not only had my fa-ther not mentioned this to us, but on numerous occasions prior to his death he demonstrated only concern about being *repaid* his money, not *giving* more money.

The sudden change in behavior by Mr. and Mrs. Abuto was unset-tling. However, I declined to defend my actions. I finalized the written agreement and waited for them to fulfill it. However, I continued to treat them like family, and carried on traditions set in place by my fa-ther. For example, I gave to Mr. Abuto a surprise gift of new computer software that I purchased in America (he bought an expensive Sony laptop that year). Before we left Kenya my sister and I went to the Abuto's apartment and thanked them for their hospitality by paying a month's salary for their three servants. Mrs. Abuto could not even look me directly in the eye when I handed her the envelope filled with Kenyan shillings. That night at Carnivore restaurant, the seats I had reserved for the Abuto family were noticeably empty.

During the next full year, Mr. Abuto missed every single deadline that he had agreed to in Kenya. He also ignored my attorney's request for an explanation. I was so concerned over the behavior of the Abutos that I conducted a little investigative research. What I found further de-pressed me. I found documentary evidence that the Abutos had *perma-nently* lost their home *before* they received the full loan from my father, and that Mr. Abuto had not even attended a previously-scheduled court hearing to save his own home. The foreclosure was final, and even as they borrowed money from my father they must have known it would not go toward the purpose it was intended. I also deduced, from the sworn testimony of the Abutos, that their financial difficultly was many years in the making. It was not as sudden and unexpected as they had portrayed to my family. The Abutos were granted ample time to satisfy a debt. They had simply defaulted on their obligations to the bank. Now they were defaulting on their obligations to us.

By any account, this activity falls under the definition of misappropriation, and that is exactly the word I used when I confronted the Abutos with the facts. Mrs. Abuto immediately accused me of being "disrespectful to my elders," and being on a "diatribe." She said my use of the word misappropriation likened them to "thieves" and that she was "raised in a culture where we do not fight about the property of the deceased" (implying that it was not my mother's money). She quoted the Bible (Proverbs 15:1), and implied that I was unsympathetic to those in need. She said she could not remember my father specifying how the money was to be used, and that it was not a loan (contradicting her recent discussion with my father and me). She insinuated that he did not necessarily want all the money back because of all the times he had stayed in their house.

This is the same Mrs. Abuto who in August 2001 told me to be strict with enforcing my loan with my cousin Alfred. This is the same Mrs. Abuto who once advised: "Don't let them stay in your house or you will never get them out." This was the same woman who raised her eyebrows when I wanted to lend a helping hand to orphans in my family. In other words, Mrs. Abuto, for thirty years my family's most staunch supporter of a strict interpretation of *ujamaa*, was now its most ardent distorter and manipulator.

I simply responded to the Abutos:

> I will not let age stand between right and wrong. My father asked me on his deathbed where his money was. He would ask you this today if he were alive. Please give me the answer.

I ended my letter with:

> Despite anything you may or may not believe, I am actually wishing the best for you and your entire family.

While the Abutos have never explained to me where my parents' money actually went, what I did hear were false rumors about me (from Mrs. Abuto) that are too undignified to be included in this book. Also, Mrs. Abuto told my mother that the money (that she previously stated was in escrow with the bank) was "gone," once again due to Kenyan corruption.[37]

The Abutos originally requested a loan from my parents so they could stay in their mansion in Kenya. Yet, only several months after my father's funeral, the majority of the Abuto family departed Kenya for Toronto, Canada. The two youngest children were enrolled in new primary schools, and the three older children continued in college. Only Mr. Abuto remained in Kenya, where he liquidated assets promised as collateral to my father. To date, not one penny from these assets has been turned over to my family. The money is only one issue. Mr. Abuto still promises that the money will be repaid. However, even if the loan is repaid, how can he restore lost trust? How can he erase the memory of my father's last words to me?

I remember so vividly the day in August 1998 when my father and I sat in the veranda of the Abuto mansion in Nairobi. My father was reading the newspaper and drinking tea served by one of the servants when he turned to me and said, "I am so worried for my friend." He explained in short sentences that Mr. Abuto was past retirement age in Kenya, had three college-age children, but was considering having more children. My father waved his hand at the Abuto mansion and said, "I don't know how he is going to pay for all of this on top of more children. I see a disaster happening here." Perhaps thinking he had said too much, he kept quiet and resumed reading his newspaper.

Even as far back as the early 1980s my father described to me what would happen if a person did not live according to the principles of "deferred gratification." Essentially, the Abutos had lived beyond their means and lost everything as a result. However, why should the Odenyo family suffer for the mistakes of the Abuto family? After all, was it not the Abutos who tore down their modest home to build themselves a mansion, while my parents instead downsized and remodeled their home into a two-unit rental property? Was it not my parents who lived for decades with worn-out carpets, while the Abutos imported their hardwood floors? As my father said to me a month before his death, why did Mrs. Abuto choose not to work for the majority of her three decades in Kenya, yet employ three servants? Was it not true that what happened to the Abutos was actually caused by corruption of priorities, rather than just corruption of the banking and legal industry? Was it not true that Mrs. Abuto's hostile response to me almost perfectly mimicked the response in 1960 by the old prison guard to my father when he stood up to her and made her be accountable?

Mr. Abuto's misappropriation of my parents' money disturbed me so much that I decided to further investigate his background. I wanted to determine if there was room in my heart for forgiveness, just like I have been forgiven for my sins in life. Perhaps Mr. Abuto had a momentary lapse in judgment, brought on by the financial burdens of parenthood. However, what I uncovered disturbed me even more. I unearthed an official legal document from the 1970s which began with the following abstract:

> Particulars of Complaint (professional misconduct): misappropriation (3); execution and registration of 2 spurious documents; indication he had taken the affidavits of persons executing two different mortgages when such was not the case; failure to deposit trust money in trust account; failure to maintain necessary books and records.

MISAPPROPRIATION! The same word I used to describe Mr. Abuto's handling of my parents' money thirty years later! I looked through the names of the five plaintiffs, and even recognized several of them as close friends to both Mr. and Mrs. Abuto— again, fitting a pattern. The testimony from the 1970s included charges Mr. Abuto misdirected people's money into his personal checking accounts and businesses. Several of Mr. Abuto's clients testified that their signatures had been forged on mortgage documents. I read further to see if Mr. Abuto rebutted these allegations. What I found was that Mr. Abuto did not even attend his own hearing in the 1970s (fitting another pattern). His legal defense counsel informed the courtroom that Mr. Abuto was missing. Instead of rebutting the allegations, Mr. Abuto skipped town (with his wife), headed to New York. My father welcomed them, but never knew the true details behind their arrival.

The incident with the Abuto family was the final nail in the coffin for my own dreams of Kenya. In fact, just like my father before me, I began to have my own nightmares of Kenya. I recorded one in an email, sent to my mother and sister on the 28th of September:

> I had the most vivid dream this morning. In my dream I was at Uncle Booker's house, and Dad appeared. He was very sickly—like he was in July 2007. I was excited to see him and told him, "We had a funeral for you—they thought you were dead, but I can see we were wrong."
>
> He looked puzzled and said, "How did your mother react to the funeral?"
>
> I replied, "Don't worry about that now. Please let's go into the bedroom. I must tell you something quickly." I eased him into bed, just like I did every night at Booker's, and my mind was racing to tell him, "Your friend is going to take advantage of you and misuse your money—how do you want me to handle this?" But before those words left my mouth, he vanished from under the sheets. I raced out crying to Atieno, saying, "I saw him! I saw him! But I could not tell him in time!" In my dream I knelt down on the floor and wept, just like I did at the funeral home in Queens. When I awoke my entire face was wet from tears.

Within three short weeks of my father's death there were too many incidents of mistrust and abuse of the concept of *ujamaa*. The incidents all involved family and close friends. I experienced, in weeks, the same pain that my father must have suppressed for decades in the United States. It was the pain of people not doing the right thing, and people not being accountable for their own actions. What I saw demoralized me and my immediate family so much that we wondered why we would ever return to Kenya. What was there to go back to? It used to be that when people asked me what I thought about Kenya, I would say, "The politics are bad, but the people are good." How could I ever say this again with a straight face?

I do not wish to lump everyone in the same basket, for that would destroy the good that I witnessed and the support that I received from a multitude of still-cherished relationships. My experience in 2007 was similar to the phrase "a few bad apples spoil the bunch." In other words, the majority of my experiences were positive, however, they were overshadowed with the disappointments caused by a few people. It was not simply a problem of the Luo, for Mrs. Abuto was not Luo, not born in Africa, and not raised by African parents. It was simply a human problem—a problem of moral corruption best described in the lyrics to Peter Tosh's song "That's What They Will Do."

After I arrived back in the United States following my father's funeral, my thoughts remained centered on my brother's four children, especially the eldest two that remained in Kenya. Opiyo and Adongo lived in a country where so many things were headed in the wrong direction. I knew that a high school graduate in Kenya had fewer opportunities (per capita) than my father had when he graduated from Kisii High School in 1958. One recent hope for the nation was the liberalization of the political process, which included multi-party politics, the call for electoral reforms, and increased freedom of the press. In December 2002, Kenyans voted for the "anti-corruption" candidate, Mwai Kibaki (from Nyeri). His presidential campaign was assisted by Raila Odinga, the son of the late Oginga Odinga (from Nyanza Province). Incoming President Kibaki appointed one of his own, John Githongo, to be the nation's chief investigator on corruption. Githongo took his job seriously, exposing corruption at the highest levels. Apparently he did his job too well. Githongo was soon forced to flee the country after receiving death-threats.

In 2005, the non-governmental organization Transparency International ranked Kenya 144 out of 159 countries on the Corruption Perception Index (CPI) (a higher ranking indicates more corruption).

The data also demonstrated a strong correlation between corruption and poverty.

On December 27, 2007, Kenyans peacefully voiced their frustration through the ballot box in the presidential contest, mainly between incumbent President Kibaki, and opposition leader Raila Odinga. By election-day, almost all domestic and international polls gave Odinga a comfortable lead over Kibaki. Foreign newspapers had headlines such as "Odinga moves ahead in polls," "Odinga stays ahead of Kibaki in Kenya," and "Odinga could defeat incumbent in Kenya." I followed the hourly updates of the election results, which forecasted that Kenya would elect its first Luo president.

However, when the official 2007 election results were released, it showed Kibaki as the presidential winner with 46 percent of votes compared to 44 percent of votes won by Odinga. This was in stark contrast to the parliamentary results showing Odinga's party winning 48 percent of seats and Kibaki's party winning only 21 percent. This was a glaring discrepancy that could not be rationally explained. There was more. In certain instances, voter turnout in Kibaki strongholds such as Maragua were tallied at an impossible 115 percent, yet, the results were not invalidated. There were voting discrepancies in Nyanza too.

As Kibaki hurriedly took the oath of office for a second term, I watched as Kenya was engulfed in the flames of ethnic hatred. Odinga supporters of various ethnic tribes actively searched for and killed Kikuyus, including innocent women and children, in retribution for what they considered a stolen election. Kikuyus violently retaliated against the various groups united against them. By February 2008, more than 1,500 people were killed, and 300,000 others homeless. The economic situation was equally dire, with almost all sectors of the economy at a standstill. The violence between Kibaki and Odinga supporters continued until the two leaders agreed, at the end of February 2008, to a coalition government with Kibaki as president and Odinga as prime minister. One of the first moves by Kenya's new coalition government was to call upon international donors to provide funds to help clean up Kenya's self-made mess.

Although the root problems of the violence were never rectified, the creation of a coalition government allowed Kenya to superficially return to normalcy. Meanwhile, I focused more and more on organizing my father's personal and professional documents. Among them were documents he kept in his office at York College. The documents spanned the course of fifty years. There were personal and professional letters, books, and pictures. I was surprised when I located a short autobiography, written around 1975. Consisting of seventy-nine typed pages, it covered many of the same stories that he had already shared with me. However, there were more details. His autobiography provided precise dates and names. It provided a chronological order to events. There were also new stories, such as picking up tennis balls for Europeans in Maseno Junior School. While he had previously mentioned attending Ndiru Intermediate School, now I read that he actually helped build the school, and he was one of only two Ndiru students who continued to high school. I learned the precise details of his employment with the Education Suppliers Association after Kisii High School, and training with the Kenyan Police. For the first time I learned about his encounters with KADU officers in Mombasa. He added more detail to his early impressions of Augustana College in South Dakota.

There was more. I found written transcripts of a series of interviews he provided between November 1965 and May 1966 to Anthropology Professor William H. Hodge (University of Wyoming). My father provided Professor Hodge with a vivid description of Got Regea with regard to traditional religion, marriage, life-cycles, medicine, agriculture, family lineage (back to Nyamwanga), and various other topics of anthropological interest. These were unresearched personal reflections by my father. When I read his autobiography and interview transcripts, I realized that I had an obligation to share his history with my children, nieces, and nephews. I was motivated by the hope that through telling my father's life story, I could present his descendants with lessons that might inspire them to similarly walk a path to greatness—defined by compassion, self-determination, and education.

I learned a lot by reviewing my father's memoirs. My father's reflections of traditional Luo culture provided additional clues to certain death and funeral behavior. As a child, my father watched Got Regea villagers "chasing after the witch," rather than trying to identify the immediate cause of illness and death. This seemed strikingly similar to the Luo community's behavior in trying to chase after an external cause to Omondi's death in 2007. This is one reason I have revealed not only some of my own shortcomings, but also a comparatively smaller sample of shortcomings from the life of my brother Omondi. To solve a problem we must do less chasing after non-existent witches. As Uncle Dan wrote in 1995, we must "analyze more deeply the cause." [38]

I was intrigued with the way the Got Regea community in the 1940s and 1950s tried to appease a troubled spirit by sharing food and beer with the deceased. Is this why the Luo community in Maryland was so insistent upon remembering Omondi through endless music, food, and beer? Were they partying for Omondi, or for themselves? Did they even know the reason?

My father recalled traditional funerals in the 1940s and 1950s where the Luo community brought additional cows to a funeral in order to provide the image to the community that the deceased was successful and died a "Big Man." Although no cows were brought to Omondi's funeral, there was never a lack of people willing to memorialize Omondi with such adoration that a guest might think there was no difference between the character of my brother and father. The Luo-American mourners called Omondi *Ratego* ("the strong one"), although it was actually my father who was the strong one. I agree that to expose such differences at a funeral would be insensitive. I admire and find value in the boisterous processional march of the *tero buru*. However, once the "bad luck" is thrown across the river and into someone else's backyard, must all the dead be praised the same? Are we afraid our loved ones are forever listening to us, ready to turn into *jochiende* (ghosts) and cause mischief if people discuss and learn from their faults? Must the boastfulness of *pakruok* be applied equally to the departed, regardless of merit? Have we forgotten our Luo proverbs, such as *Ng'at ma miel mamit ema iting 'o bade* (It's the good dancer whose arms are raised), reflecting that praise is due to those who work hard and succeed?

My father attributed the increase in social deviance to an abandonment of Luo moral customs (*kweche*) and erosion of authority figures.

In 1975, Dr. Odenyo wrote:

> The current disunity in Got Regea tends to promote self-interest at the expense of community welfare, thus diminishing the sense of collective responsibility, solidarity, and pride that the village once had. Deviance is not viewed as a collective concern, as it would have been in earlier times. There exists an ambivalence on the part of everyone toward traditional and national authority.

Where have all our *nyatiti* players gone? My father told of Luo harpists who narrated important stories filled with moral and comparative themes.

Do we no longer remember our evening meals at the footstool of our elders? The old wise men and women were once allowed to lavish praise on young people who were following in the footsteps of their ancestors, and young people who had lost their way were reprimanded. Today, it is the young who reprimand the old.[39]

16
Inheritance

Peace and development within our family must be accompanied by unity within our family. Also, the older members of the family must be willing to forgive the younger members of the family.

—Zablon Sangoro Odenyo, letter to son Otieno, on February 18, 1969, Translated from Dholuo.

There is a song by the East African musician, Remmy Ongala, that so captivated me during my travels throughout Africa in the 1990s, that till this day it remains my second favorite African song. It is called *"Narudi Nyumbani"* (I am returning home). It was one of the first songs in Kiswahili that I was able to fully understand. I still cherish its lyrics, which carries the message that despite the problems that may exist in your village, it is still home and should not be abandoned. Your home is where your father comes from, and you should go back home to unite with the elders of the village. I identified with the song from the moment I understood the lyrics, for it perfectly articulated my father's deep dedication to his village, and in a small way, of mine.

The spirit of this song was expressed in my father's dying wish that his family never forget Got Regea. It was his last wish that enabled me to overcome my disappointments with Kenya and return to Nyanza Province in December 2008. First I checked on the status of my late brother's two eldest children, Opiyo and Adongo. For the third time since their father's death I shared whatever guidance I could give so that they could become self-reliant people. I reminded them that I was willing to sacrifice for their future now, but I could not sacrifice forever.

I had only two other goals. I wanted to engage my father's siblings in serious conversation regarding the direction of the extended Zablon Sangoro Odenyo family. At every opportunity, I asked complex questions to better understand the past, comprehend the present, and plan for the future. I also wanted to properly cement and tile the graves of my brother and father. It was important that steps be taken to prevent their gravesites from disintegrating to dust, like that of Uncle Lut Ezra Obuong.

I visited Siaya town again. I last traveled there in 1994 to see my grandmother, who at the time lived in the quarters behind our new family business. Grace Dina Adero lived another two years—long enough to see the rise and fall of Zablon Sangoro's dream for a family business. Now, fifteen years later, her son Victor was trying to resurrect that dream. Uncle Victor had repainted the building and prepared it to reopen as an "Agro-Vet" store (incorporating both an animal feed processing mill and a veterinary dispensary). In tribute to his mother and late daughter, Uncle Victor had written their names on the front of the building. From there I visited his tilapia fish farm, also in Siaya. He took me to see two other business projects, one in the transportation sector, and the other in tourism and hospitality. Uncle Victor was a very busy man, supervising four businesses in addition to his professional responsibilities at Moi University in Eldoret.

On the way back to Kisumu from Siaya, Uncle Victor took me to the Anglican Church in Ng'iya where my grandparents married in 1925. We stood silently inside the remodeled church and looked around for clues to the original structure and the wedding between Zablon Sangoro Odenyo and Grace Dina Adero Obuong.

Uncle Victor broke the silence with, "You know, it makes me feel sort of good, just standing here where *mama* and *baba* started their lives together."

I was having similar nostalgic sentiments, and replied, "It makes me feel good too Uncle. I never thought that I would get to see this place." That was the extent of our conversation at Ng'iya, and I was not expecting much more. Uncle Victor has always been a very re-served man.

Among the sons of Zablon Sangoro, Uncle Victor reminds me the most of my father. I remember in the streets of Uppsala, Sweden, in 1978, and later in Nairobi, Kenya, in 1983, I occasionally walked up to Uncle Victor and mistakenly called him "Daddy." They not only share a family resemblance, but the same silent demeanor, the same walk, and the same intellectual talk. They share the same thoughtful pauses to gather their thoughts before answering a question, and they rarely give an explanation longer than necessary to drive home a point. You often do not know what they are thinking, but you never doubt they are among the most thoughtful people on Earth. My father wrote that he grew up referring to his uncles as his "fathers." Now more than ever, I was viewing Uncle Victor in the same way, and I was embracing every moment.

In Got Regea, Uncle Victor took me to the home of the late B.A. Ohanga (the first African government minister), located behind Saint Peter's Church. We visited the home of the late Gilbert Owuor (my grandfather's brother), located on the south-west slope of my great-great grandfather's hill (Got ka Otieno). We also went to the home of Bishop Daniel Omolo on the north side of Got ka Aruwa. There I discussed with Francis Omolo, an engineer, how his father and my grandfather (headmasters of Luanda Primary School) set high educa-tional and moral standards for their children. I cherished every mo-ment I spent with his mother Persis Omolo, the only living sister of my grandmother. I told Persis that in keeping with Luo tradition I would now call her grandmother (rather than "Auntie"). Over a meal of *ugali* and liver, I asked her questions about her upbringing in Ugenya and introduction to Got Regea. Grandma Persis confirmed that she and her sisters were first exposed to education through the influence of Zablon Sangoro Odenyo. She stated that for as long as she has known the Odenyo home, it has always provided equal opportunity for women.

After lunch I viewed photographs of her late husband Bishop Omolo, and brothers-in-law Ibrahim Owuor Mango and Agande. I studied each of their faces, recalling the stories my father had told of them. I also saw a photograph of one of the first white men Grandma Persis ever met, E. Carey Francis (a missionary and teacher at C.M.S. Maseno from 1928 to 1940). Grandma Persis' sons made sure that Uncle Victor and I did not leave their home empty-handed, giving us a huge bushel of sweet bananas to carry home. I was beginning to find faith once again in the true meaning of *ujamaa*.

Uncle Victor also took me to the home of his uncle Simeon Odera, the great choirmaster. Simeon Odera's granddaughter, Beryl Ouma, gave me an updated tour of her family's compound. I entered the still-standing mud-walled *siwindhe* of her grandmother Apeles (sister to my grandmother), and peered up at the six-story high eucalyptus tree that served as a landmark and beacon for early converts to the Christian faith. Ouma, an accomplished attorney, discussed the numerous similarities between our two families, such as the positive influence our pioneering grandfathers had on their children's lives. We discussed a lot of family history, and I truly felt a sense of belonging.

The next day I asked Uncle Booker to show me the two rivers that my father described in his 1975 autobiography. When we reached the Dienya River, which looked more like a stream, Uncle Booker explained, "Across this river is Huluwinu, where you were yesterday. You can just get a glimpse of Simeon Odera's home, near the tall tree. That whole village is perhaps more than 90 percent Luo and used to be part of Siaya District. But one day around independence enough of them registered as Luhyas in order to leave Nyanza Province and join Western Province, which is largely Luhya. They may have assumed that as residents of a non-Luo Province they would receive more financial assistance from the government. It is difficult for some people to remember where the boundaries are. You can wake up from your bed in Nyanza Province, walk over to your kitchen and find that you are in Western Province, then walk behind your house and milk your cows in Nyanza Province. We are always trying to realign ourselves for political and economic reasons, but I don't think the price of bread is any cheaper in Huluwinu than in Got Regea, which is still in Nyanza Province, at least for the moment. By the way Odera, as children we used to bring our father's cattle here to drink from this river. While they were drinking, we took banana leaves, sat on them, and slid down the slopes of the hill from Huluwinu into the river. That was as far as we got to an amusement ride in those days!"

On our return from the Dienya River, we shared the path with barefoot young girls balancing large bundles of firewood on their heads. It was an image I have encountered numerous times before. However, each time I see it I am reminded that as an American, I had a privileged childhood.

Uncle Booker and I passed a young boy and girl crouching by a pool of water fed by an underground spring. "This spring, which we call Kulo, is where we used to collect our drinking water," Uncle explained. "The children have accidently disturbed the water, so they are waiting until the dirt settles, then they will scoop up the clear water on top."

As I walked past the barefoot children, I could not help but imagine my own father and his sister Olivia collecting water from this spring over sixty years ago. Perhaps it was here where the two of them discussed their hopes and aspirations for the future, while patiently waiting for the water to clear. Maybe it was at this very location where they dreamed of education, where they dreamed of a profession, and where they dreamed of reaching new heights of self-empowerment for themselves and their families. Six decades later, hopefully these two young children, now sitting in this same spot, might similarly work hard for their own dreams. With effort and opportunity, maybe one of them could become the first Kenyan astronaut to land on the Moon, or even Mars, for that matter.

As we made our way back up the hill, we stopped at the grounds of B.A. Ohanga Secondary School, located in the same grounds as Regea Primary School. Workers were busy repairing the rudimentary structures. Some buildings were constructed with mud, others with concrete, but all with the same leaky *mabati* roofs. I asked to speak with the headmistress of the secondary school, to learn what challenges she faced in improving the quality of education for the children of the village. She named a few: "salaries to bring qualified teachers, a science laboratory, a kitchen and dining hall, textbooks, a library, and more pit-latrines." I could see with my own eyes that the list was potentially endless. There was virtually nothing in some classrooms except four walls, a broken chalkboard, and a few chairs—some with three legs. The headmistress pointed at a single drawer, and told me this is where they kept the science equipment for the entire school.

The Siga River is on the northern side of Got Regea, much further away than I expected. Ten minutes into our drive I observed that there were virtually no brick houses. Instead, there were many round, mud-walled houses with *olenge* grass roofs.

"Yes, you see this difference too," Uncle Booker said. "The further away you drive from our home near Saint Peter's Church, the more traditional your surroundings become—like Ugenya where your grandmother was raised. It is here on the outskirts of Got Regea where we used to see traditional Luo activity such as the beating of drums and dancing. Many of these homes profess to be Christian, but their lives actually incorporate a mixture of Luo and Christian beliefs—beliefs that are not always compatible. *Baba* did not want us to spend too much time in these parts adopting their ideas. Many of the people here had no time for school or church and frequently consulted with the local witchdoctors."

We continued driving north until the dirt path ended. To avoid drawing unwanted attention to the vehicle we parked it off the road inside a stranger's home, fenced by euphorbia trees. As we drove through the *rangach* (main gate), two ladies peered out at us from the open door of their small house, not sure what to make of us.

Uncle Booker commented, "You see these women? This is probably the first time a vehicle has ever entered their home. If you see them start to run away, it is because they think we are police cracking down on breweries of *chang'aa* (illicit alcohol)."

"What makes you think they are making *chang'aa*?" I asked.

As the car came to a stop, Uncle Booker replied, "I am just guessing. But we are virtually in the middle of nowhere. There are only two mud houses. I see no livestock, no granaries, no children, no men—and these two women are out here surviving! How do they eat?"

I slowly exited the vehicle and with a big smile greeted them using the few Dholuo words that I knew. "*Amosi* (I greet you)." "*Ingima*? (Are you fine?)" After they replied, I threw in a "*ber ahinya* (very good)" for extra effect.

With my friendly approach, *Mwarabu* (Arab) features, two cameras, and poor Dholuo, I appeared less of a threat and more of an oddity. If these women had thoughts of fleeing, curiosity got the better of them. After Uncle Booker explained the purpose of our visit, I asked for their permission to take their picture with my digital camera, and then showed it to them on the small LCD screen. They both looked at their images in the camera, then at their clothes, and back at the camera, trying to verify they were actually looking at themselves. Even after Uncle Booker and I had already made our way out of the gate and toward the river, I could still hear them yelling and hollering over the great magic that had visited them that afternoon.

To reach the Siga River we followed a well-worn cattle path. The path had been used a lot over the decades, and sections of it had sunk down to seven feet below ground level. At times it seemed like we were walking through a deep army trench. I hoped not to meet any long-horn cows being herded from opposite directions, for I doubted there would have been any means of escape for the two of us. Uncle Booker stopped to show me the deep holes that are still mined of *atoya*—the whitewash used to paint the walls of traditional homes.

"As children we used to dig here every November, and paint our home in time for Christmas. We had to be careful," he warned, "sometimes the sides of the cliffs would become so unstable they would collapse and suffocate the miners."

I could now hear the sounds of the Siga River. As we approached, I had my video camera recording the moment of discovery. I have always felt funny walking around Got Regea with a camera in hand. It makes me look too much like a tourist in my own village. This time I felt extra silly, for I was looking very much like the British explorer John Hanning Speke trying to locate the source of the Nile, with Uncle Booker as my trusted native guide. Although I must have looked very comical, for the sake of history I swallowed my pride and filmed the moment. There was a section of the river filled with rocks, which people were using to beat and wash clothes, and another section that several people were using to bathe, forcing me to turn off my recording equipment. The Siga was much more powerful than the Dienya, and it had two wooden planks forming a bridge between Got Regea and the neighboring village leading to Butere.

Further west along the Siga River, we found the spot where the water-powered mill used to operate. The mill was deserted a half-century ago, so we found the site only through the assistance of a local elder. We stumbled across the gate of the elder's home by chance, and we were soon sitting on his living room sofa, shaking hands with people we did not know, and being offered tea. "Booker, *wuod* (son of) Sangoro…." my uncle began to introduce himself. No more explanation was needed. By our hosts' reaction they instantaneously knew who we were. Even at the edge of Nyanza Province, and after the passing of nearly four decades, the name Sangoro was still remembered.

When we returned to the center of Got Regea, Uncle Booker and I climbed to the top of Got ka Aruwa, the highest hill in the area. From the hilltop we could look down upon Bunyore Hills, Butere, Ugenya, Malanga, Kodiaga, as well as the tiny cars traveling like ants on the Kisumu-Busia road. Uncle pointed out the various sections of land, both on the top of the hill and below, where as a child he planted maize, beans, and millet alongside his mother and siblings. He explained that the top of the hill was owned by his brother Victor, and that all of Zablon's sons inherited parcels of land around the hill. Uncle put his hand on my shoulder and advised, "So Odera, with your father gone, you now have a stake in this land. But you cannot sell it, for that would be like selling away part of yourself, and a part of me."

Uncle showed me the indentation mark on a large boulder once used as a base for the *boya* (surveyor mark), installed by the colonial surveyors. "From what I recall," Uncle said, "that *boya* was a white metal structure that reflected light. Supposedly, at least two other hills in this area, one of them being in Maseno, had a similar *boya* that could triangulate with this one using an instrument called a theodoite. The *boya* was placed here by the colonialists when I was around eleven years old. I vividly recall the day the surveyors came to install it. A man living on the slope of this hill attacked the surveyors and the *boya*, thinking the metal structure was some type of instrument the *Wazungu* were going to use to steal the land. The British had to come back from Kisumu with armed reinforcements to arrest the man and install the *boya*. It was an important technical instrument, but over time it fell into disuse. I saw it up here as late as the 1980s, but I suppose some child may have removed it to use as a toy, or perhaps an adult used it as construction material in his home. We are very resourceful here in Got Regea, but sometimes a little bit too resourceful!"

I cherished every minute with my two Uncles. I learned a lot more about our village and of the childhood of my father. My experiences were overwhelming positive, and I saw a lot of hard-working people. However, there are a few select incidents in Got Regea that I will mention for educational purposes. One day Uncle Victor and I were walking in the valley between the hills of Aruwa and Otieno. He was showing me the borders of our ancestral land, and the section where he hoped to start a guava farm. While walking along the narrow paths, my uncle stopped to have a friendly chat with a man walking in the opposite direction. They acted very cordially, even shaking hands, making small talk, and laughing. When we parted ways, I inquired about our relationship with him, and uncle confirmed we were all descendents of Okwata (my great-grandfather).

"You know," Uncle Victor said with a slight grin, "a few years back, I parked my car behind your grandmother's house, and the next morning when I walked to my car I found my headlights had been removed. I conducted an investigation and found my headlights being sold at a market in Butere by that cousin you just met. Everyone else was selling bananas, *sukumawiki, unga,* and things, but our cousin was out there selling my headlights!"

I found Uncle's story amusing but depressing. It made me wonder what sense it made to start a guava plantation in the middle of Got Regea if during the night a relative might harvest the crops and sell them on the other side of the river Siga. I asked, "What did you do, I mean, how did you resolve the issue with the headlights?"

Uncle Victor stopped walking. He put his hands on his hips, and gazed out at the hills while carefully thinking of his answer.

He eventually replied in a low voice, "Well… I got my headlights back, and he apologized, but what am I to do then? I put him in jail, now I've just alienated a whole wing of our family. If he dies in jail, I am blamed for his death. If he survives, he'll return to find his children are starving, and next time he'll steal my car. If he hears me crying out for help at night, maybe he won't come to my aid. So, when it comes to family, there is not a whole lot that you can do except to be careful with your relationships and possessions."

The conversation allowed me an opening to ask my very private uncle about his various business ventures. Through his investments, Uncle Victor was the embodiment of the Zablon Sangoro Odenyo dream of developing a family enterprise. Victor was the one keeping the dream alive, and with a fury and passion not seen in entrepreneurs half his age. However, it was telling that in most of his businesses his employees were non-relatives.

"I still can't trust many of my own nieces and nephews to look after my businesses while I am teaching in Eldoret," he explained. "I want to employ them all, but I find that a simple task such as depositing money in my bank account is often too much for them to handle. There are always stories, stories, and more stories. One week the story is that the money was left by mistake on the *matatu*. The next week robbers have taken the money. The third week all the money went for repairs. The next week only half the week's proceeds are accounted for. Then the cycle repeats itself. That is why you now see so many strange faces managing my businesses for me. I have to go outside our family, and sometimes outside Got Regea, just to find an employee who will be accountable."

Then he said with a look of desperation, "Odera, sometimes I get so angry I want to take a *kiboko* and start beating them with it. Do you know what a *kiboko* is?"

"Yes, a whip," I replied.

Uncle raised his arm and mimicked whipping somebody, "Yes, I feel like taking a whip and whipping some sense into these young people. I don't know what it will take for them to change."

I did not know how to reply to Uncle Victor, for I was as stumped as he was. Also, it was the first time in my life I ever saw Uncle so animated, and frustrated. I felt he did not deserve this frustration, especially after being so generous with his efforts to create opportunities for our extended family. That is when an idea struck me. Just that morning, Uncle Victor told me his nickname has always been "Okong'o," (a variation of Akang'o) and while we were walking along the village trails, I noticed a few men his age greeted him under that name. So, when "Uncle Okong'o" raised his arms and grasped his imaginary whip, I recalled how Chief Odera Akang'o in the old days used caning to enforce his development policy, with positive results still bragged about today. "Perhaps that's what we need in Gem—another Chief Akang'o," I thought to myself. We are always invoking the name of Chief Odera Akang'o, even lending his name to the new campus of Moi University in Yala. Since we are always singing the praises of our last great chief, perhaps we should bring back a little bit of his discipline too.

This visit to Got Regea allowed me to become familiar with some new storylines for begging. There is an unappreciated art to begging, for the tactic is to appear to be asking for something you deserve. The first incident occurred while I stood next to Uncle Victor. He was explaining the layout of his childhood home, as well as adjacent compounds where suspected families of *jojouk* (night-runners) once lived. Out of nowhere, a man approached us and said he was curious because he did not recognize our vehicle. We politely engaged him in conversation for perhaps three minutes. He then stretched out his right hand, palm up, and said, "*Mimi sijakuwa na Merry Christmas. Nataka Merry Christmas* (I have not had a Merry Christmas. I want a Merry Christmas)."

I refrained from telling him what I was thinking: "*Unafikiri mimi ni nani, Santa Claus?* (Who do you think I am, Santa Claus?)"

The good thing about Christmas is that everybody knows the holiday comes around only once a year. Imagine the opportunities that will open up for this man if the tradition of birthday presents is introduced to Gem. He could beg for a "Happy Birthday" every day!

The second incident occurred on a Sunday morning, under the shade of the old fig tree next to Saint Peter's Church. Uncle Victor walked toward me with "Hezekiah," an elder of the village. I was honored to be introduced to this man. He was around eighty years old and a potential wealth of knowledge about Got Regea history. I wanted to question him on his claim that my great-grandfather Okwata was buried between the houses of Uncle Adet and Uncle Booker, at the base of Got ka Aruwa. I had already performed some basic age and date calculations, and it was impossible for him to have witnessed my great-grandfather's funeral. He must have heard this information from someone else, and I wanted to trace the source. Hezekiah walked up to me and I engaged him in casual conversation. During this time, Uncle Victor's attention shifted to Uncle Booker, who was busy trying to scare monkeys away from our crops. With both Uncles' attention diverted, Hezekiah sensed an opening.

Shoving his open palm toward me, he said, "*Mimi sipendi ndevu. Nataka kunyoa ndevu* (I don't like this beard. I want to shave this beard)."

He repeated this again, palm thrust toward me, his other hand caressing his face. I knew he was demanding a handout but disguising it as a need to buy a razor. I was worried that I might not handle the situation with sufficient diplomacy, and feared jeopardizing a future interview with him. I reached to tap Uncle on his shoulder.

Old Hezekiah was quicker than I was. Before my hand could reach Uncle's shoulder, Hezekiah grabbed my outstretched arm and warned, "*Achana na Victor! Achana naye!* (Leave him alone!)"

When Uncle Victor noticed the commotion and turned around, Hezekiah simply walked away as if nothing had happened.

"Did you see that?!" I asked incredulously. I then explained what had happened.

Uncle Victor just shook his head and sighed, "You know, just five minutes ago he asked me for money to shave, and I gave it to him. For once I wish he would actually use it to shave!"

I spent a lot of time thinking about the subject of begging, for when able-bodied people blatantly engage in this behavior it is a symptom of something broken in society. It is a strain of the "entitlement disease," an offshoot of the "let's all be poor together disease." Much like the common cold, it is infectious, and almost impossible to eradicate once it takes hold. I tried to figure out at what point in Got Regea history this behavior started. I could not imagine my "strong and enterprising" great-grandfather, Okwata, walking up to a stranger a hundred years ago and demanding money, cows, or chickens, for free.

I asked Uncle Booker his opinion, and he replied, "I don't remember much of this begging when I was a child. But things began to change in the 1960s. I remember just three weeks after your grandfather died at the Russian hospital in Kisumu, Kenyatta came to that same hospital and gave a speech. On the one hand he talked about bringing development, but on the other hand he threatened to crush us like bugs if we questioned him. A lot of us feel that since that time Nyanza has been crushed like a bug, both politically and economically."

"However, there is a cycle of poverty that people perpetuate. Even if people have a piece of land to farm, cows to milk, and chickens to raise, this is no longer their sole frame of reference for wealth. They are comparing their rural lifestyles to your city lifestyle. The fact that you live in a house with plumbing, visit the countryside in a car, and carry a cell phone makes you seem like a filthy-rich person. The problem is, the more money you hand out, the more it confirms for them that money is free, or grows on trees, as your father used to say. You cease to become a regular person to them. You are now just a bank account with legs. That's why I long ago stopped giving money, because I could see it was going nowhere, and it actually had the potential to damage most of my relationships with people in this village."

Uncle Booker continued, "I know your father must have shared with you what happened with your cousin 'Sylvia.' One year she won big money playing the lottery. It was probably an amount equivalent to what a school teacher in Regea Primary School would earn over the course of ten years. Well, she came back with it to Got Regea and it was one big party for months! Her home was flooded with clothes, dishes, radios, furniture—even a baby stroller that was useless on the rocky trails of this village. And when Sylvia brought that money here, I think everyone in her home got a piece, because the next thing you know her parents and siblings are scattering to places like Yala, Dudi, and Malanga, getting lost in the bars and shops. You couldn't even find them in the fields anymore. It was like they had to spend the money right away, and they stayed out of Got Regea until the money ran out. Till this day, Sylvia is barely surviving, and the only time I see her is when she comes to me with some financial need. But if you keep on giving more money, it is you who are going to sink down to the same poverty level as them. While they were praising you before, now they are laughing at you behind your back, snickering at you because you thought you were the "Big Man," and now you are as poor as they are.

They may even try to hasten your downfall! This happens in Kenya all the time. We have a proverb in Dholuo—*Wang' mithiedho ema gawi*, warning us that the person receiving your help might turn against you. So instead of money, I devote my time to counseling people, or I try to create whatever small jobs I can for them, such as fixing my shed, milking my cow, or cutting the napier grass. Sometimes I pay for a young person's school fees in exchange for house help. I tithe to the church, I donate to the school, and I participate in *harambees*, but that's about it. Never free money."

"Uncle Booker," I asked, "what did you think of our family meeting the night of my father's funeral, and was this meeting typical?"

He replied, "There are a few focused and ambitious young people in our family, but you would not know it based on that particular meeting. That night they seemed to care only about feelings, empty slogans, and other petty issues. There was no sense of accountability or vision. I don't know if you are aware Odera, but whenever your father visited Kenya he held meetings to assess the family situation. It was often your father, alone, who was unafraid to speak up and ask the hard questions. This offended some people, but the people it offended were doing nothing for the family. The observations and conclusions you and I are making today—he was discussing them way back in 1970. Perhaps it was because he was professionally trained in the social sciences. Whatever it was, he picked up on our family dynamics very quickly every time he came home. You could tell he cared a great deal about what was happening here because he was always prompting us to discuss what we needed to do to improve."

I asked Uncle Booker about my cousin "Osewe," who participated in our family meeting the night of my father's funeral the previous year. Osewe emailed me in November 2007, and thanked me for my efforts to help the family. He then asked for a cell phone and airtime. He explained that Uncle Booker and Uncle Victor had paid for his truck driving lessons, and since he now had a driving certificate he was looking for work. However, he explained, in the trucking business it is essential that drivers have cell phones in order to properly liaison with employers and vendors. I verified Osewe's request through my uncles, and wired two hundred dollars to cover the cost of the phone plus six months of airtime.

"Odera," Uncle Booker replied, shaking his head, "It's up to Osewe and God now. I've tried my best for over ten years. I'm sorry to say it, but your investment, as well as mine, was short-lived. Perhaps just two weeks after Osewe received his driving permit, and your cell phone, he went back to drinking *chang'aa*. This *chang'aa* is a curse to this country, just like crack and heroin is a curse to America. Osewe's addiction is so bad that he probably exchanged your cell phone for *chang'aa* the moment he got it. Since then he has continued drinking so much that I fear he has lost his mind. One day he decided he wanted to eat *nyama choma*. The problem is that he had nothing to sell in order to buy the meat. So, he simply walked over to his sister's *shamba*, picked up a *jembe* (hoe), and slammed it down with all his might on the head of his sister's cow, which fell down dead. Then he butchered that cow in his sister's yard, roasted the meat, and invited all his drunken friends to the feast! The next day Osewe decided to sell his sister's remaining cow, but the chief was alerted and put a stop to it. Not only were they not Osewe's cows, but they were the same cows that Osewe's sister allowed him to milk in order to feed his two young children. Looking at this situation, I have no doubt that someday Osewe's two young children will walk up to my door and tell me they are hungry and parentless. They'll call me grandfather, just like Opiyo and Adongo are thinking of you as their father now. And I tell you Odera, it won't be just Osewe's children looking for me. In a decade there will be perhaps twenty Odenyo orphans coming looking for Grandpa Booker…but I can assure you, Grandpa Booker doesn't have the funds to run that orphanage!"

Now, I had come to Kenya thinking I had heard and seen it all, but the story of Osewe still shocks me. It is a true story that shocks me in its brutality and in its insanity. But, on an analytical level, it is a metaphor for Kenyan society as a whole. For me, the cow represents opportunity. For close to four decades of independence, Kenyan society, on the top and now on the bottom, has taken part in a drunken orgy of killing cows of opportunity. When politicians kill the cow they give it names like "Goldenberg" and "Anglo-leasing," then set up exploratory committees to distract the public until they can identify the next cow to slaughter. In the meantime these "big men" build huge houses and businesses, and talk about how clever and hard-working they are as opposed to their neighbors and other tribes. When the common man kills the cow, they simply call him a drunk.

My father talked to me about coming back to Kenya in 1970 and finding his home in a state of disarray. At that time, he wondered whether his community and nation would implode under the weight of frustration and spite. Well, the answer, nearly four decades later, was never clearer than in the case of Osewe. It is obvious that what is needed across Nyanza, and Kenya as a whole, is change.

In November 2008, change came to both Kenya and America in the form of a man named Barack Obama, the first African-American elected to the Office of the President of the United States. During my three weeks in Kenya, Obama's name and likeness was depicted from almost every billboard, T-shirt, and *matatu* in Nyanza. In fact, when Uncle Victor and his son Baraka Odenyo picked me up from the Kisumu Airport, Uncle Victor welcomed me with, "Welcome to the future Barack Obama International Airport."

In short summary, Barack Obama is a son of Nyanza just like I am a son of Nyanza. Our fathers were born in the mid-1930s in rural Luo villages near Lake Nyanza. They were raised approximately twenty miles apart from each other in Siaya District. Obama's home village of Kogelo is in Alego, where my great-grandmother Muhula was born. Ng'iya, where my grandparents married, is also in Alego. Both our fathers studied in Maseno, valued education, and received scholarships to study in the United States. Our fathers were previously married to Luo women. Both fathers remarried white American women from midwestern states, and fathered half-white and half-Luo children.

While eating *mandazis* and drinking tea at Uncle Booker's house, his cousin, Professor Lucia Omondi (Apeles Odera's daughter) and her husband, Professor Washington Omondi,[40] quizzed me about my interest and connection to President-elect Obama. "What can I say?" I responded. "I share the same excitement as everyone else about the election. I perhaps have even more of a connection to him than anyone in this room. Obama and I are both Americans, both Luos, perhaps with similar struggles and appreciation about the issue of race. I never thought a person that so perfectly represented my unique background would ever become president of the United States. He is an inspiration to me. He makes me even more proud to be an American. He is the affirmation of the American dream."

Professor Washington Omondi pressed me a bit further with, "Well, don't you want to meet him? Do you think it is possible that you can go see him in the White House—you know, with your similar background and interest in family connections?"

"Of course I'd like to meet him," I replied. "I've known about him since my father brought home his book for us to read in 1996. My father and Obama Sr. knew of each other while they attended college in the United States. Dad told me their paths eventually crossed one evening following a Kenyan student conference in New York City around 1964 or 1965. Dad described Obama Sr. as brilliant and reckless, and several other people who knew him tell me the same thing."

Returning to Professor Omondi's question, I said, "I'd like to meet Obama, but not because he is going to be our new president. I know it sounds funny for me to say that. It's just that I'm afraid if I meet him I'd be too casual around him—you know, giving him a hug instead of shaking his hand. I'm afraid I might act too much like a long-lost brother, calling him Barack instead of Mr. President. Maybe it would be better that he come to my home so my wife can make us some *ugali* and *sukumawiki*. I'd like to share with him some stories. I want him to know about my Dad, because he never got to know his own father."

I had no fewer than ten conversations along these same lines during my stay in Kenya in 2008. Even the two suspected *"chang'aa la-dies"* near the Siga River joked that they thought I was Obama coming to save them. The entire nation, including non-Luos, was obsessed with everything Obama. "Change We Can Believe In," seemed to have replaced *"Harambee"* and *"Nyayo"* as the new slogan of Kenya. And change it did. Just twelve months ago Luos and Kikuyus were slaughtering each other like sheep in tribal-based election violence. Now, just a year later, everyone, even the Kikuyu, Meru, and Embu (most would never dream about voting for a Kenyan-Luo), were singing the praises of "their son Obama." I did not want to bring up the irony of it, for it was irony in the right direction, but let us analyze the situation a bit further.

Kenyans have embraced the slogan of "change," but do Kenyans really know how to "change?" Historically, it seems like every person in post-colonial Kenya who has stood up for change has been killed, driven underground, or corrupted by the very forces he or she was trying to change. Compare Barack Obama with Tom Mboya. Both were of Luo heritage, transcended their tribal and racial backgrounds, were community leaders with captivating oratory powers, and had broad international support. Both called for "change" in their national policies. When a Kenyan has this background he ends up with a bullet in his head from another tribe. Yet, when an American of Kenyan descent has this background, he is every Kenyan's son, even down to the villages of the opposing tribes. It seems like every Kenyan welcomes change when it is foreign-based, but many do not want change when it is home-grown.

Do black Americans know the meaning of change? On Father's Day, June 15, 2008, presidential candidate Obama gave a speech to a black American church in Chicago. Obama's theme was "personal responsibility," and in particular the need for both parents to take an active role in the upbringing of their children. He talked about the need for parents to set high expectations for their children and exchange the television remote control for more books. Obama talked about "choices," saying we must make it easier for fathers to make responsible choices and harder for them to avoid them. It was a speech well received by many in the congregation and in much of the black American community.

Interestingly, this theme of change and personal responsibility was not well received by the self-appointed leader of the black American community, the Reverend Jesse Jackson. In July 2008, just weeks after Obama's uplifting speech, Rev. Jackson was caught on videotape expressing his desire to castrate Obama for "talking down to black people." Several news outlets reported that in the unreleased second half of the video, Rev. Jackson referred to black people as "niggers." Rev. Jackson was not aware that he was being recorded, and his statements came as a surprise to many people, including Jackson Jr., who repudiated his father most earnestly. However, Rev. Jackson's opinions were of no surprise to me. Rev. Jackson represents that person who is so fixated on protesting against social injustice that protest becomes the sole message, often at the exclusion of internal reflection, responsibility, and accountability.[41]

The afternoon of my arrival in Kenya in December 2008, I stood at a check-in counter at Jomo Kenyatta International Airport and presented my Nairobi-Kisumu ticket. The two airline representatives behind the counter commented on my Luo last name. This happens all the time. They first ask if I am Luo. I usually say yes. Then they insist that I cannot be Luo. However, had I responded that I am not Luo, they ask why I do not think of myself as Luo.

This time I was asked by the Luo airline representative, "Where did you get your last name."

"From my father, in Gem," I replied cooly.

Now even his Kamba partner behind the desk was interested, and quizzed me about my sub-clan, as if to test that I was truly Luo.

"JoKagola," I replied, as I placed my baggage on the weighing machine.

Both of them became increasingly excited and made a lot of small talk about President-elect Obama and the need for "change," while a third employee weighed my luggage (why three people were doing one person's job is a topic for another day).

I was now told by this third employee that my luggage was six kilograms overweight. I inquired about the fee for excess luggage, for I was considering either paying for it, or getting rid of some of the weight. I handed the "excess luggage fee" to the third employee, in plain view of all of them, expecting him to fill out a receipt, hand over the money to a cashier, bring me my change, and perhaps behind the scenes inform the captain of the total excess weight of all passengers' luggage. The first two employees kept on beaming back at me, talking about "change" and my duty as a Kenyan-American to go back and run for some political office in order to bring more "change" to Kenya.

"We need more of you," the Luo man told me.

It was all pleasant and uplifting talk about "change," but it was becoming apparent they had forgotten to return some of my change to my wallet. I was running late for my flight and tried to prompt the third employee to return my receipt and change by asking him, "Tumemaliza (are we finished)?"

He looked at the large shilling note in his hand, slipped it into his breast pocket, and said very disappointedly, "no…we haven't finished! But go ahead."

It was the kind of sarcastic and disgruntled response a waiter gives to a patron who has left a measly ten cent tip after being served a two-hundred dollar lobster dinner. This is when I realized that I had just bribed my way onto the plane with my excess luggage. I guess I was a little more Kenyan than I thought. Not wanting to make an incident or miss my flight, I raced to board the plane. However, as I sat in my airline seat listening to the plane start its engines, I wondered just how many passengers had bribed their excess baggage onboard in similar fashion, and whether our plane would actually lift off the ground due to all the unanticipated weight.

One morning after Christmas, I found myself on Oginga Odinga Street in Kisumu waiting for my cousin "Janet" to arrive from Sakwa. Janet had requested I meet her at eleven o'clock in front of Al-Imran Plaza. My cousin arrived around noon, giving me ample time to observe the crowds of unemployed youths standing idly on the sidewalks. Across the street I could see the blackened shell of the Ukwala supermarket, burned down to its foundation by angry Luo youths following the 2007 presidential election. Ukwala supermarket was one of the largest businesses in Kisumu, once employing an estimated one hundred and fifty employees in its two stores.

While I was watching the street activity, "Penelope," a cousin I had not been expecting, walked up to me with a big smile, saying, "Odera, you're back! Welcome home." We talked for perhaps two minutes, and then Penelope interrupted me.

"We are so proud about Obama. When he won the election we were all saying to ourselves, gosh…we wish Odera could have won that election instead of Obama. I mean, that way we can get some new roads and electricity in Got Regea like in Kogelo."

I just smiled and gave her some kind of neutral response that apparently did not satisfy her.

"Odera…do you have any plans to run for president? I mean,

seriously, I wish you would consider it. We really need to have some development at home too, and you can bring that to us. Have you ever considered joining politics?"

"I have never considered it, nor do I have any interest in politics. In fact, I want nothing to do with it—it's a dirty game."

By the disappointed look that appeared on Penelope's face, it was obvious my response was not the one she had hoped for, and I was not surprised. Kenyans have all but given up hope on a Kenyan leader bringing about change in their lives, unless that leader is from their village. Instead, they look outside Kenya for hope, betting on some kind of foreign connection—an NGO (non-governmental organization), a sister parish, the Peace Corp—anything that would bring about change that is not forthcoming from their own leaders.

In a warped sense, Penelope's view was very reasonable. Just that week, Uncle Booker and I visited the Obama home in Kogelo, hoping to meet with Mama Sarah. We arrived too late, for Obama's grandmother was picked up a few hours earlier by no less than the Kenyan prime minster, Raila Odinga. Since she was not home we paid our respects to the gravesites of the president-elect's father and grandfather. We concluded our visit by taking a zillion photographs of ourselves embracing a life-sized cardboard picture of our "cousin," Barack Obama. The entire time I was there, signs of development were everywhere. Once a sleepy little village like Got Regea, government workers were out in force paving the road, installing utilities, and renovating buildings. As we drove away, I said to Uncle Booker, "Gosh, nine years ago we all contributed a lot of money for the electrification of Got Regea, but even today we still have to travel the three miles to Dudi to charge our cell phones. Here in Kogelo they have leapfrogged over us in just one month!"

After Penelope left me standing on the Kisumu street, I had time to ponder the nature of my upcoming meeting with my cousin Janet. Due to my stressful encounters with *ujamaa* last year, I had decided to ask questions from the elders of my family about Janet's situation prior to our meeting. I confirmed that she was still married, lived far from Got Regea in her marital home, had an advanced educational certificate financed by another relative, and was living a relatively comfortable but modest life with her husband who had a successful job. "Don't worry," I was told, "out of all of your cousins, Janet has no reason to ask you for money." This assurance made me feel a little bit guilty for investigating her background. I looked forward to exchanging updates with Janet and showing her some family pictures on my digital camera.

After she arrived, we entered a restaurant down the street. Before we even sat down Janet blurted out, "Odera, it is so nice that you have agreed to meet with me. You know, it's only Uncle Victor, Uncle Booker and you who are left for us to rely on. We are looking to the three of you now!"

I noticed that Janet's premise excluded all the women in our extended family. There was no mention of my aunts Rosalie, Olivia, Olga, Millicent, Tabitha, and Awino. There was no reference to my cousins Pamela, Linda, Dorothy, Maureen, Christine, Adhiambo, Atieno, Adero, and Achieng—all very responsible and capable women (to name just a few). It was a blatant reversal of attitude from what I had witnessed from my peers during the meeting that night of my father's funeral, when the theme was "equality," including that of "gender equality." Janet was setting me up for some favor, and she was now more than willing to ditch all signs of feminism or equality. "European Socialist Feminism (ESF)" was suddenly thrown out of the kitchen window like a piece of stale *ugali*. The theme of the hour was now a mixture of "African Socialism" and the "Big-Man" philosophy. Essentially, Janet was emphasizing my extra responsibilities as a man to help her out in some way.

We stood at the counter where we ordered our meals. I noticed that Janet let me pay for her food, although she was the one who had requested to see me. Before her Tangawizi soda and my Fanta *baridi* could even be brought to the table, Janet got down to business. She requested that I finance her four-year college degree due to her family's poor financial condition.

While Janet elaborated on her financial problems, I started to analyze the situation in what is often described as traditional African "male chauvinistic" terms, since she herself had approached me in such a traditional manner. My money was extremely tight, so why of all people should I help her? She was my age, married, and dowry had already been paid. She had moved away to a distant village that I would never visit, to a clan I did not know, and all rewards of her schooling would primarily benefit her own children in her new home. Even after death, as a married woman she would not be permitted to be buried in our family cemetery in Got Regea, nor would her husband allow it if it was possible. So if Janet wanted to approach me on traditional African terms, why would I invest in her rather than a male cousin who shares my same last name? Of course I did not explain this to her. If I did, Janet might switch to an ESF agenda and start lecturing me on gender equality. I am no genius, but I had enough sense to keep my mouth shut on that subject.

How I resolved my dilemma was simple. Once again, I simply told the truth. I could not afford to take on yet another long-term financial project. I had already paid for Oscar to attend technical training school. Just that morning, at nine o'clock, I had provided funds for my nephew Opiyo's second semester in college. I knew that I would pay for my niece Adongo's entire first year in college as well.

It was a tough moment. After all, Janet was doing the right thing by trying to acquire more education. Unfortunately, I had to prioritize my resources. I call this the "lifeboat" decision. I am in the middle of Lake Nyanza, making the long and arduous journey back to the Kisumu shore, and along the way picking up relatives who are out in the lake treading water and pleading "*Ujamaa!*" I want to pick up everyone, but I can only fit a certain number in my lifeboat before it becomes unstable and sinks. I have already picked up Oscar, Opiyo and Adongo. There are still one or two spaces left, but I have to leave most of my distant relatives behind in the water because I know that just a few miles ahead, my son and daughter are treading water without a life preserver. I see my mother wearily pleading to Mr. Abuto to give back her life preserver, while Mrs. Abuto is floating on it, pretending it does not exist.

Not touching her food, Janet looked at me with quiet disbelief, while slowly digesting my response. The silence continued for so long that I began to feel the fish's eyes on her plate seemingly stare at me too. Janet said she understood, but I am not sure she did. From her perspective I can see why. All of her education in life had always been paid by relatives other than her immediate family, and perhaps I was the first person who ever declined her request for assistance. Here I was in Kenya, having taken my third expensive international plane trip in two years, and I was carrying around my now familiar cameras that I used for conducting family research. For her, my mere presence and possessions were conclusive evidence of the contradiction in my words. Essentially, I was a liar. She saw no valid reason why I could not sell my equipment and "spread the wealth" in the spirit of *ujamaa*.

It was then that Janet's cell phone rang. I was soon put on the phone with our cousin Sylvia. "Hello Odera!" Sylvia shouted into the phone. "*Karibu nyumbani!* I say, are you planning to stop by Naivasha? I really want to visit me...you know, to catch up on old times. Just like we used to do when we were young. We really need to talk..."

To this I replied, "Well, I've been at home (Got Regea) for almost a week, I'd love to see you there."

Sylvia made some excuse why she could not travel to the village of her birth, and then half-jokingly lectured me, "Odera, I hear last year you had a meeting and refused to invite the women. I hope next time you'll invite me to one of your meetings!"

I was annoyed to hear this from her, not only because I knew it was inaccurate, but because it symbolized years of misplaced priorities. I had come all the way from America to our home village during Christmas, but I did not see Sylvia there even once. Sylvia had wasted practically every opportunity that had come her way in life, and the only things she had left to cling to were equality slogans that she had learned from her teenage years. However, neither her ESF slogans, nor my black liberation speeches that I gave her in 1989, would help feed her children's bellies now.

I noticed that Uncle Victor and Uncle Booker were similarly swamped with requests for meetings with extended family. It seemed like half their days were spent putting out "fires" in the form of dispensing financial assistance, advice, or simply engaging in ceremonial roles as respected leaders in the village. With only days left till my departure, I discussed with them the existence of the draft of this book, and shared thoughts on the future of the Odenyo family. We were in agreement with the main themes of importance. Zablon Sangoro

Odenyo, Simeon Odera, B.A. Ohanga, Daniel Omolo, as well as many others in their generation, lived in that crucial period of time in Kenya's history that witnessed the most change. Some change was good, some was bad, but these men were able to prosper because they were able to embrace new values, such as education, without abandoning certain old ones, such as responsibility.

Take my grandfather for example. He was given the name Odenyo at birth, which in Dholuo literally means "no food" or "hungry." To most people that last name may be a curse, for it symbolizes the famine or hunger that existed at the time Odenyo was born. However, Odenyo turned the negative into something positive. He did it by turning his "hunger" into self-determination. He set high standards not only for himself, but for his own household and community. He was compassionate, however, he allowed his children to struggle for their own goals, never giving them a ride on his bicycle to school. Similarly, remember Chief Odera Akang'o of Gem. Odera was hungry to bring development and education to Gem, and through his strict influence and guidance we acquired much of it before other places in Kenya. But that hunger always included, and never excluded, hard work, personal responsibility, and forward thinking. Let us not forget my own father, who was given the nickname "Akoko," signifying noise or trouble. He went through many trials and tribulations, yet, through his own initiative, he rose above them and led a very successful and inspiring life.

These characteristics were not exclusively theirs. Before the sun rose, Grace Dina Adero Odenyo was out in the fields, planting maize, potatoes, and millet, even on the steep slopes of Got ka Otieno and Got ka Aruwa. She did not plant alone. Each one of her children worked alongside her, and learned about personal responsibility and the value of hard work. Grace and Zablon never had much money, but they were rich in the values of honesty and self-determination. They set aside vices that brought down many of their peers, such as drunkenness, dishonesty, and idleness. Zablon shared the empowerment of education not only with his wife, but with almost all of her sisters, who learned to read and write in the Odenyo home in Got Regea. The Odenyo home has always been a place where both men and women can find empowerment, should they choose it.

The positive values of Zablon and Grace filtered down to their children, but it was up to each one of them to choose to embrace these values. The same is true for their grandchildren and great-grand-children. Our family, and our tribe, has always been one of pioneers, having migrated from as far north as Sudan, down to Kenya, and now to the four corners of the earth, including the United States' Executive Office. In future generations we may no longer refer to Got Regea or Nyanza as home, but our home can be in the solidarity of purpose, and understanding of our rich history.

The key to our success is about personal choices. It is the choice between honesty and dishonesty, sobriety and addiction, hard work and idleness, deferred gratification and immediate gratification, education and ignorance. Choice is so important that in 2008 I named my new-born daughter "Ayiera," reflecting the Luo word *yiero*, which means to make a careful and wise choice. The Luo tradition is to name children after time and events surrounding their birth. My daughter was born as I wrote the final chapters of this book—a time when I reflected heavily on the personal choices of family members both past, present, and future. I hope that my beautiful daughter Ayiera grows up to be a very empowered and successful woman, not based on what she says, or what she protests against, but instead on what she chooses to achieve.

In late December 2008, I spoke on some of these same themes during a small ceremony for my brother and father at Saint Peter's Church in Got Regea. I stood near the altar, where my grandfa-ther once gave sermons, and my father was baptized, married, and eulogized. It was the third time in two years that I gave a major speech in the church. Once again, I turned to speak directly to my nephew Opiyo and niece Adongo, who that day represented all of Amos Otieno Odenyo's grandchildren. Through them, I spoke to their generation about some of the choices of their grandfather that made him such a respected person. I talked about the incident during his youth when he refused to join the other children in hid-ing the tennis balls from the *Wazungu* players at Maseno. Even at that young age, Amos Otieno Odenyo was setting an example of personal character, which his agemates, some who may have gone on to various careers in Kenyan business and government, chose not to follow. I talked about his drive to work hard at Kisii High School by choosing to wake up at four o'clock in the morning to study. I talked about his personal choice, in 1960, to stand up to the old Luo prison guard who was abusive of her prisoners. My father was not a perfect man. However, he was a better man than most. Truth and justice was my father's moral compass, and it guided him wherever he went in life, and in everything he did.

Still facing the audience, I asked Opiyo and Adongo to stand up from their pews. I explained to them the significance of the four words that my sister, mother, and I jointly decided to engrave on their grandfather's headstone. These four words, I told them, are COMPASSION, SELF-DETERMINATON, EDUCATION, and INSPIRATION. These were the four basic qualities that made their grandfather such a decent man, I explained. In addition, this was the only inheritance from Zablon Sangoro Odenyo that Amos Otieno Odenyo ever received, other than a piece of land that he could not sell, even if he wanted to. This same inheritance, I explained, is the only inheritance that I have received to date. It is the only inheritance I may ever receive, the only inheritance I have prepared for them, and the only inheritance they should ever expect to receive from me. But, I emphasized, it is a rich inheritance, not one I would trade for all the diamonds or gold in the world. As I concluded my speech, I told them that it did not so much matter that I was passing this inheritance to their generation. What matters more, I said, is that they embrace it.

In the evening, after everyone had departed for their homes, I walked to the family cemetery behind my grandmother's house to stand before the grave of my father. It was a sober moment, with no tears. I reflected on what now seemed like our brief time together, and once again felt torn between a desire to be with him and my loved-ones on earth. Although I was speechless, my heart was telling him— thank you. *Erokamano ahinya baba*, for your guidance, your inspiration, and your love. Thank you for showing us the way forward through your life's example.

While standing near him, I also thought of my children, and wondered how they would fare when the sun finally sets on my own life. There might be tears, and grief. But what I hope they would know is that through their tears, they should rejoice. When I hear my creator calling—when I see for the last time the sun set behind Otieno's Hill—my children should sing Hallelujah for me. For I have walked through the *rangach* of my real home, and am once again in the loving presence of my father.

The next morning I attended Sunday services. It was an otherwise uneventful service, with the exception that a teenage girl, wearing a second-hand dress, volunteered to stand up in front of Saint Peter's Church to sing a song that she had learned in school. She sang beautifully, with a rich and seemingly professionally trained voice. All that I could understand of the Dholuo was that she was glorifying *Nyasaye*, our creator. It was not the lyrics that impressed me, but the manner in which she was singing. She was singing with love, praise, and a pure spirit. She was singing about the joy in her heart, and the love and redemption *Nyasaye* has for all of his children. It did not matter in what language she sang, or whether I comprehended every lyric, for I felt every word in my soul. Her song brought to my face the first tears of joy that I had felt in a long time. Although her message was universal, for reasons I cannot explain, it also filled me with a burst of pride for being Luo. Her angelic song gave me hope. Perhaps it was part of a higher spiritual plan that she sang the song this day, and in that way. For me, the rest of the service was a blur. I could only focus on that song.

After the service ended I walked over to her and asked if she could wait until the church cleared so that she could sing the song for me and my uncles once again. She graciously obliged. While standing outside of Saint Peter's Church, under the shade of the aging fig tree, she sang for us not only the first song, but another. Then, without expecting anything in return, she turned and prepared to walk away.

I stopped her.

"*Dada— jina lako nani?* (Sister, what is your name?) Are you in school?"

She replied that her name was Mercy, and that she was in "Form One," indicating she was about fourteen years old.

"What is it that you want to be when you grow older?" I asked.

She replied that she was interested in taking sewing lessons to learn how to become a seamstress.

I told her that if she could learn to sew as beautifully as she could sing, she would have no difficulty finding customers for her trade.

She replied that she had received a bit of mentoring, but did not know if she would continue.

I did not fully understand if she was referring to her sewing or her singing, but I did not want to pry further. "Study hard," I begged her, "please study hard, and *practice*! Whatever you do, please do not stop singing!"

Contrary to my self-imposed rules about money, I reached into my wallet and pulled out a few shillings. It was not an extremely large amount of money, perhaps twenty U.S. dollars. But in a rural village like Got Regea, it was probably more than what her parents earn in a month. It was also enough to show her that there was real value in her voice. If she was wise enough, hopefully she would remain motivated and keep training for a little while longer, and turn her voice, her sewing, or something else, into a profession. Squeezing the notes into her hand I said, "Take this, spend a little for yourself and your family if you must, but not before you have used some of it pursuing your schooling and your dreams!"

"*Asante* (Thank you)," she replied, and looked up at me and my uncles with a smile. Then she picked up her small bag from the base of the fig tree, and without once looking back behind her, ran full speed down the dirt road, and out of my sight—hopefully, in pursuit of her future.

SOURCES and NOTES

1   In colonial times, Nyanza Province extended north until Mount
    Elgon (Gem was in Central Nyanza). Currently, sections of
    Nyanza Province have been reclassified as Western Province,
    home to the Luhya people of Bantu origin. Nyanza means "large
    mass of water" to the Sukuma people, who live on the shores of
    Lake Nyanza in Tanzania.

2   B.A. Ohanga (born in 1913) served on the Legislative Council
    for over ten years, and as a minister for community develop-
    ment and rehabilitation from April 20, 1954 to March 25, 1957.
    Wellington Aruwa (born in 1920) is said to be the first Kenyan
    African to independently publish a medical article ("A case
    about relapsing fever in a child of nine years old," *East African
    Medical Journal*, April 1950).

3   Amos Otieno Odenyo learned about the history of his parents'
    first meeting and wedding when he was in his fifties. Under the
    Luo tradition in which he was raised, it was considered impolite
    to ask parents such intimate questions.

4   Literally: people of (*Jo*) the place (*Ka*) of Agola. Tradition states
    that Nyamwanga is a descendent of a woman named Agola.
    Agola may be a wife of Ramogi Ajwang', although this is based
    upon popular belief and is unverified by the authors. *Dhoot*
    (clan) literally means "the door," a metaphor for sharing the
    same house.

5   Alfayo Kodhe is a descendent of Nyamwanga, through the line of Aruwa. Alfayo Kodhe is the father to Dr. Wellington Aruwa, and grandfather to Dr. Julyan Otieno Aruwa.

6   Amos Otieno Odenyo narrated the story of Zakayo Were from memory in August 2005. When he came to the part of shooting the monkeys from the trees, he laughed almost uncontrollably, which was very unusual for him to do.

7   This funeral demonstration, which Amos Otieno Odenyo is describing from memory in 1965, is likely the *Tero Buru* ceremony. In 1978 he provided a more detailed description of this ceremony in a jointly-published article, "The Luo Way of Death: Rendezvous with Rebellion."

8   Amos Otieno Odenyo told these two Luo stories (and their morals) from memory in August 2005. There are different versions. For example, many versions state Magere was fighting against the Nandi (or Masaii), and that it was Luanda Magere's wife, not a doctor, who administered the medicine to his shadow. The site of the Luanda Magere rock is in Nyando District, near Awasi. *Luanda* (or *Lwanda*) means "rock" in Dholuo.

9   Ibrahim Owuor Mango would become the future bishop of the Musanda Holy Ghost ("*Roho*") Church of East Africa. He was the son of the founder of the Roho Movement (Alfayo Odongo Mango), who was burnt alive for his faith in 1934.

10   Amos Otieno Odenyo in August 2005: "I now realize that out of all of Zablon Sangoro Odenyo's seven sons, I was the only one who undertook *nak*. My older brother Adet for some reason did not do it, and neither did my five younger brothers. *Nak* has been an important Luo ritual for centuries. One might say that within the Odenyo family I symbolize the end of that traditional era."

11 Classmate Martin Miruka Nyiendo recalls that one night an African instructor caught Amos Otieno Odenyo and two other students studying after hours. The three were each sitting in their own bed with a lamp, concealing the light by covering themselves with blankets. The next day the instructor caned all three students in front of the entire school. Otieno endured the pain without making a sound. Otieno's quest for education was so strong that he continued to study illegally. (Interview, September 2009).

12 My friend Laban Otieno was a student at Maseno High School, and his school competed against mine during athletic competitions. As I remember it, Kisii High School usually won, although Laban still insists Maseno usually won. It is interesting to note that I first met Laban in 1953 when I was introduced to him by his uncle, Eli Uyoma, who was a classmate of mine at Ndiru Intermediate School.

13 To the best of the authors' knowledge, there are no fictionalized persons or events in this memoir. Names introduced in "quotations" are surrogate names. Mr. "Cambrian," a European police inspector in Mombasa, left Kenya in 1964 and joined the British Army.

14 Amos Otieno Odenyo's 1964 application to the University of Wyoming, and interview in 1965 by Professor William H. Hodge.

15 I shared the 1965–66 academic year at the University of Wyoming with a future vice-president of the United States, Dick Cheney. I gave lectures in African Studies, primarily on the topics of "the Luo homestead," "nation-building," and "African Socialism."

16 The levirate system is mandated in the Bible, book of Deuteronomy, Chapter 25, versus 5-10.

17 Johera in Dholuo means "people of love." Inspired by the teachings of Martin Luther, in the early 1950s Reverend Abednego Matthew Ajuoga wrote a series of reformist letters (the most famous called "The Light") addressing the perceived marginalization of rural Anglican churches in Nyanza. Ajuoga was demoted, and then exiled from the Anglican Church (in 1957). His congregation expanded and officially became known as the Church of Christ in Africa.

18 In August 2005, Dad told me he was the second person from Got Regea to travel to America. A prominent (living) friend of his was the first to travel to America in the 1950s, and his family in Got Regea still inquires of his whereabouts.

19 Dr. Odenyo's publications include: "Conquest, Clientage and Land Law among the Luo of Kenya," *Law & Society Review,* (1973); "The Luo Way of Death," *Studia Africana* (1978); "Professionalization Amidst Change: The Case of the Emerging Legal Profession in Kenya," *The African Studies Review* (1979); "An Assessment of the African Brain Drain," *A Quarterly Journal of Africanist Opinion* (1979); "Professionalization and Change: The Emergent Kenyan Lawyer," *Scandinavian Institute of African Studies Press* (1981).

20 Dr. Odenyo's participation in World Education projects include the October 1977 joint World Education-National Christian Council of Kenya seminar in Mombasa, which culminated in him writing a detailed evaluation report for the Carnegie Corporation in New York. The seminar included an assessment of Tototo Home Industries, a self-help and income-generating program for Kenyan women.

21 Samuel Okello Onyango was from Kakiimba, Mfangano Island, home to the Suba people of Bantu origin. Onyango participated in the 1960 Mboya Airlift, studied at Morgan State and Brooklyn College, and acquired a Bachelor of Arts degree in Economics and Master of Arts degree in mathematics.

22　The "Roho" (Spirit) movement began among the Luo in the early 20th century. It emphasizes the Holy Ghost, prophecy, speaking in tongues, spiritual healing, and singing of hymns. The movement has evolved into many independent sub-denominations. Roho churches generally permit Old Testament traditions (polygamy and cleansing rites), and African traditions (drumming and dancing). Hilda Anyango Mango and her husband Ibrahim Owuor Mango are featured in *Women of Fire and Spirit: History, Faith, and Gender in Roho religion*, by Cynthia Hoehler-Fatton, Oxford University Press (1996).

23　According to Aunt Olivia's children, she describes her brother as "a tree on which all birds chose to perch, despite the many trees in the forest."

24　Similar stone structures, built without mortar, exist in Nyanza Province, Kenya. The historical site, named "Thim Lich Ohinga," is located in North East Kadem in Migori District.

25　The contents of the article appear almost identical to experiences described by Michael Maren in his 1996 book, *"The Road to Hell: The Ravaging Effects of Foreign Aid and International Charity."*

26　The first president of Tanzania, Julius Nyerere, implemented a national development policy of *ujamaa*. The policy included the concept of self-reliance (*kujitegemea*), but in the context of collective groups, strong social safety nets, and shared resources and wealth. *Mwalimu* (Teacher) Nyerere's contribution to Tanzania's unity and national identity is well-documented. Unfortunately, *Mwalimu's ujamaa* policies were economically unsuccessful, described by East Africa's leading academic, Professor Ali Mazrui, as a "Heroic Failure."

27　Lecture recorded and transcribed by Professor William H. Hodge.

28 Odinga, Oginga. 1967. *Not Yet Uhuru*. Hill and Wang, pages 13-14.

29 Even Oginga Odinga, who was labeled a "Socialist," recognized the importance of self-reliance and capitalism. In his 1967 autobiography, he references the fact that the Luo people [in the 1940s] had grown accustomed to "petitioning [the government]," and that as a result they grew accustomed "not to do anything for themselves" (pg. 77). This prompted Odinga to organize various business ventures through the Luo Thrift and Trading Corporation (LUTATCO). Although LUTATCO may be considered a political success, it was described by Odinga as an economic failure (pg. 87). There were colonial obstacles, however, Luo business ventures also suffered losses by pilfering (pg. 83), misappropriation of funds (pg. 85), and high default rates on loans (pg. 77). In many ways, Odinga's 1967 reflections of failed Luo businesses parallel Amos Otieno Odenyo's reflections recorded in Wyoming in 1965.

30 Video-taped interview by Odenyo family of Alice Nelson, granddaughter of Soren Nelson (October 8, 2000); June D. Holmquist, "They Chose Minnesota," page 281 (1981); Everett E. Edwards, "T.L. Haecker, the Father of Dairying in Minnesota," in Minnesota History, 19:152, 155-157 (June, 1938); Meeker County Historical Society, internet on November 27, 2008; Florence (Nelson) Hillman 60th Wedding Anniversary family document (1984).

31 Prosperity Worldwide(.org) press release, internet on November 27, 2008.

32 Amos Otieno Odenyo, "The Rise and Fall of Simeon: The Conflicting Modes of Authority," This unpublished manuscript appears to have been written around 1974, and is partially based upon interviews of elders in Got Regea between 1970 and 1974.

33 Dr. Odenyo's photograph was included in the *East African Standard* on January 9, 2004, under the article, "Bank staffers burnt forms," and the January 22, 2004 edition, under the headline, "Cheserem was impatient: Team felt under pressure, gave incomplete report."

34 For example: Emily Wax, "Corruption Saps a Rich Tradition in Kenya; Culture of Dishonesty Leads Government to Consider Ban on Community Fundraisers," *The Washington Post*, October 24, 2003.

35 It is common knowledge that in the Luo community, there is always someone spreading rumors (which are widely accepted) that the cause of death is witchcraft. For example: Odhalo, Joash. "A Report on the Luo Culture and Health," *The East African Medical Journal*, Vol. 39, No. 12, December 1962, page 701.

36 During the August 2007 family meeting it was my hope that we could resurrect "Zablon's dream" for Odenyo family economic prosperity, the "enterprising spirit" of Uncle Dan and my great-grandfather Okwata, implement my father's 1994 "bottom-up development strategy," the "Foreign Direct Investment" strategy that I wrote about in 1996, and build a powerbase as suggested by Professor Alfred J. Hotz. Instead, the foundation consisted of only "tantrums and emotions" and "European Socialist Feminism."

37 It is also a tragedy that the Odenyo family is no longer contacted by the Abuto children, due to misinformation fed to them by their parents. They do not know that whatever funds their father has provided to them since 2006 for college tuition, birthday presents, wedding presents, etc., is not necessarily the result of their parents' sacrifice, but of thirty years of sacrifice from my own parents. Despite the sudden silence, our love and good wishes for them have never ceased.

38 By traditional Luo standards, chapters nine through sixteen of this memoir reveal too much personal and family information. Based upon my observations, the generally accepted code of conduct is to publicly embellish positive family information, and conceal negative information. However, by Western/American standards, I have been overly restrained. I have purposely excluded many interesting facts and details to the detriment of the historical record. It was extremely difficult to balance the expectations of two opposite cultures, knowing I would be criticized by both.

39 The dire socio-economic condition in Kenya is best described by its residents: Peter Ngare, "Two Decades When State Failed the People," *The Nation*, October 31, 2007; Mangoa Mosota, "Slaves of handout culture," *The Standard*, June 10, 2008; Dennis Onyango, "Poverty leaves Nyanza relying on handouts," *The Standard*, June 29, 2008; Bernard Omung'a, "Nyanza can grow if culture does not interfere with enterprise," *Daily Nation*, August 7, 2008; Rasna Warah, "Is Corrupt Kenya finally in the throes of moral bankruptcy?" *Daily Nation*, January 29, 2009; Allan Kisia and Joel Okwayo, "Raila tells residents to look beyond handouts," *The Standard*, October 10, 2009; Lucianne Limo, "Parents 'helping children' to be corrupt," *The Standard*, March 25, 2010.

40 Washington Omondi, from Gem, is a co-composer of the Kenyan national anthem.

41 For example: Timmerman, Kenneth R. 2002. "*Shakedown: Exposing the real Jesse Jackson*," Regnery Publishing, Inc.; Peterson, Reverend Jesse Lee. 2005. "*Scam: How the Black Leadership exploits Black America*," Thomas Nelson; Elder, Larry. 2008. "*Stupid Black Men: How to play the race card and lose*," St. Martin's Press.

Your heart has not abandoned my thoughts and ideas.

—Zablon Sangoro Odenyo, letter to son Otieno, September 17, 1969.
Translated from Dholuo.

Breinigsville, PA USA
30 November 2010
250358BV00004B/28/P